ᵀᴴᴱ BARBOUR COLLECTION
ᴼᶠ CONNECTICUT TOWN
VITAL RECORDS

THE BARBOUR COLLECTION
OF CONNECTICUT TOWN
VITAL RECORDS

BRISTOL 1785–1854
BROOKFIELD 1788–1852
BROOKLYN 1786–1850
BURLINGTON 1806–1852

Compiled by

Lorraine Cook White

INTRODUCTION

As early as 1640 the Connecticut Court of Election ordered all magistrates to keep a record of the marriages they performed. In 1644 the registration of births and marriages became the official responsibility of town clerks and registrars, with deaths added to their duties in 1650. From 1660 until the close of the Revolutionary War these vital records of birth, marriage, and death were generally well kept, but then for a period of about two generations until the mid-nineteenth century, the faithful recording of vital records declined in some towns.

General Lucius Barnes Barbour was the Connecticut Examiner of Public Records from 1911 to 1934 and in that capacity directed a project in which the vital records kept by the towns up to about 1850 were copied and abstracted. Barbour previously had directed the publication of the Bolton and Vernon vital records for the Connecticut Historical Society. For this new project he hired several individuals who were experienced in copying old records and familiar with the old script.

Barbour presented the completed transcriptions of town vital records to the Connecticut State Library where the information was typed onto printed forms. The form sheets were then cut, producing twelve small slips from each sheet. The slips for most towns were then alphabetized and the information was then typed a second time on large sheets of rag paper, which were subsequently bound into separate volumes for each town. The slips for all towns were then interfiled, forming a statewide alphabetized slip index for most surviving town vital records.

The dates of coverage vary from town to town, and of course the records of some towns are more complete than others. There are many cases in which an entry may appear two or three times, apparently because that entry was entered by one or more persons. Altogether the entire Barbour Collection--one of the great genealogical manuscript collections and one of the last to be published--covers 137 towns and comprises 14,333 typed pages.

TABLE OF CONTENTS

ABBREVIATIONS

ae.------------age
b. ------------born, both
bd.------------buried
B. G.---------Burying Ground
d. ------------died, day, or daughter
decd.---------deceased
f.---------------father
h.---------------hour
J. P.-----------Justice of Peace
m.-------------married or month
res.------------resident
s.---------------son
st.--------------stillborn
w. -----------wife
wid.----------widow
wk.-----------week
y. ------------year

THE BARBOUR

COLLECTION

OF CONNECTICUT TOWN

VITAL RECORDS

BRISTOL VITAL RECORDS
1785 - 1854

	Vol.	Page
ADAMS, ADAMES, Elizabeth, d. Samuell, b. Jan. 24, 1791	TR1	488
George A., of Waterbury, m. Candace E. **CARRINGTON**, of Plymouth, July 16, 1848, by Rev. Samuel I. Evans	3	39
James, Jr., s. Luke, b. Aug. 18, 1789	TR1	488
Joseph, s. Luke, b. July 15, 1792	TR1	488
Leve Rende, m. Stephan **ROW**, Feb. 5, 1783	TR1	494
Lucy N., of Bristol, m. Nathaniel C. **LEWIS**, of Wolcott, Apr. 18, 1823, by Rev. Jonathan Cone	1	20
Lucy Nancy, d. Luke, b. Jan. 25, 1795	TR1	488
Luther, of Waterbury, m. Cornelia **NORTON**, of Bristol, Nov. 20, 1851, by Rev. W. H. Goodrich	3	59
Marially, d. Luke, b. Jan. 7, 1798	TR1	488
Sally, d. Joseph, m. Tracy **PECK**, Feb. 3, 1812, at Litchfield, by Rev. Lyman Beecher	TR1	521
Samuel, or his w. Elezebeth, owned Rosesatte **HARKABUS**, who was b. Sept. 1, 1782	TR1	1
Susannah, of Bristol, m. Moses **BYINGTON**, of Wolcott, Apr. 12, 1826, by Jonathan Cone, V. D. M.	1	31
ALDERMAN, Carlina, [twin with Chryslina], d. Eli, b. Apr. 28, 1802	TR1	488
Chryslina, [twin with Carlina], d. Eli, b. Apr. 28, 1802	TR1	488
Manna, s. Eli, b. July 6, 1796	TR1	488
Tanlly, d. Eli, b. Jan. 22, 1799	TR1	488
ALFRED, Albro, of Harwinton, m. Jane **BOTSFORD**, of Bristol, Apr. 22, 1833, by Rev. Grant Powers, of Goshen. Int. Pub.	1	84
ALLEN, Abigail, of Plymouth, m. Joel N. **CHURCHILL**, of Bristol, [Nov. 12, 1827], by Rev. Noah Porter, of Farmington	1	45
Alvira, m. Samuel **CURTISS**, b. of Bristol, Apr. 18, 1843, by Rev. Joseph S. Covell	3	11
Burton, m. Mary **BROWN**, of Plymouth, May 30, 1847, by Rev. Lester Lewis	3	35
Elizabeth, of Leedgoam, England, m. Henry **HORE**, of England, Nov. 15, 1849, by Rev. S. J. Evans	3	54
Emily, m. Daniel E. **NORTON**, b. of Bristol, Aug. 19, 1832, by Rev. Henry Stanwood	1	75
Garry, of Bristol, m. Cordelia **JOHNSON**, of Wolcott, Nov. 25, 1832, by Rev. Henry Stanwood	1	82
Garry, m. Sarah A. **HORTON**, b. of Bristol, Oct. 16, 1853,	3	67

	Vol.	Page
ALLEN, (cont.)		
by Rev. Lester Lewis	3	67
Henry, of Bristol, m. Angeline E. **WRIGHT**, of Waterbury, June 1, 1852, by Rev. Henry Fitch	3	60
Jared, of Plymouth, m. Nancy **SUTLIFF**, of Wolcott, Nov. 28, 1821, by Rev. Orra Martin	1	11
Jason, of Davenport, N. Y., m. Elizabeth **BATES**, of Bristol, Dec. 21, 1851, by Irenus Atkins	3	56
Mary E., of Hartford, m. Lucius G. **ROSSITER**, of Bristol, Oct. 31, 1849, by Rev. Lester Lewis	3	46
Miles F., m. Wealthy **JOHNSON**, b. of Bristol, Dec. 25, 1836, by Rev. Orsamus Allen	1	112
Norman, m. Rebeckah **PRITCHARD**, b. of Waterbury, Aug. 4, 1833, by Rev. Augustus Bolles	1	88
Norman, of Bristol, m. Charlottee E. **BUNNELL**, of Burlington, May 13, 1844, by Rev. Joseph S. Covill	3	17
Orsemus, Rev. m. Adaline Julia **HUMPHREY**, b. of Bristol, July 12, 1835, by Rev. George Phippit, of Canton	1	101
Salmon, of Bristol, m. Melenda **BRADLEY**, of Wolcott, Dec. 14, 1820, by Rev. Caleb Read	1	2
Samuel W., m. Candace **JEROME**, Oct. 5, 1840, by Rev. David L. Parmelee	1	140
Sarah, of Bristol, m. John **CURTISS**, of Wolcott, Nov. 30, 1826, by Jonathan Cone, V. D. M.	1	36
Susanna, of Plymouth, m. Levi **BROWN**, May 26, 1845, by Rev. Edward Savage	3	23
ALPRESS, Alvin F., m. Pautince *BARTHOLOMEW, Sept. 12, 1832, by Rev. David L. Parmelee *(Should be **PAULINA**", corrected by G. W. Bartholomew)	1	75
ANDREWS, ANDRUS, ANDRUSS, Almira, m. Alphonzo **BARNS**, b. of Bristol, Oct. 13, 1825, by Rev. Daniel Wildman	1	30
Jennell, of Farmington, m. Leander G. **HUNGERFORD**, of Bristol, Feb. 25, 1849, by Rev. Charles Chittenden	3	42
Laura, of Southington, m. Ira **LEWIS**, of Bristol, Jan. 10, 1822, by Rev. Jonathan Cone	1	13
Levia, m. Roswell B. **WHEATON**, Sept. 29, 1838, by Rev. David L. Parmelee	1	124
Orrilla, of Bristol, m. John **WIGHTMAN**, of Southington, Oct. 9, 1821, by Rev. Orra Martin	1	11
Sarah, m. Daniel B. **HINMAN**, b. of Bristol, Oct. 13, 1825, by Rev. Daniel Wildman	1	30
APPLETON, Morgan, m. Almira **BENJAMIN**, of Springfield, Mass., Aug. 4, 1839, by F. B. Woodward	3	5
ATKINS, Alden A., of Bristol, m. Adeline C. **BIDWELL**, of Middletown, Sept. 20, 1832, by Rev. Henry Stanwood	1	76
Andrew Fuller, [s. Rev. Irenus & Eunice], b. Oct. 19, 1828	2	30
Andrew Fuller, m. Helen Maria **WELCH**, b. of Bristol, May 6, 1849, by Rev. Lester Lewis	3	47

	Vol.	Page
ATKINS, (con.)		
Columbus Irenus, [s. Rev. Irenus & Eunice], b. Mar. 14, 1817	2	30
Columbus Irenus, [s. Rev. Irenus & Eunice], d. Mar. 6, 1818	2	30
Eleanor Eunice, [d. Rev. Irenus & Eunice], b. June 26, 1815	2	30
Eleanor Eunice, [d. Rev. Irenus & Eunice], d. Mar. 3, 1818	2	30
Ellen A., of Bristol, m. Volney G. **BARBER,** of Canton, July 30, 1837, by Rev. Orsamus Allen	1	117
Eunice, of Bristol, m. Roswell A. **NEAL,** of Springfield, N. Y., Apr. 14, 1846, by Edward Savage	3	28
Eunice Eleanor, [d. Rev. Irenus & Eunice], b. Dec. 16, 1821	2	30
Eunice Eleana, [d. Irenus & Eunice], d. Mar. 8, 1826	2	30
Evelina Josephine, [d. Rev. Irenus & Eunice], b. Apr. 7, 1825	2	30
George S., m. Frances **FOSTER,** Dec. 5, 1850, by Rev. William H. Goodrich	3	52
Harriet B., m. Charles S. **GRANT,** July 24, 1844, by Edward Savage	3	18
Irenus Columbus, [s. Rev. Irenus & Eunice], b. July 4, 1819	2	30
Irenus Columbus, [s. Rev. Irenus & Eunice], d. Dec. 13, 1834	2	30
Levia, of Bristol, m. David H. **FROST,** Jr., of Wolcott, Jan. 1, 1822, by Rev. Isaac Merriam	1	13
Mary Ann, of Bristol, m. Junius **OAKLY,** of Winsted, Sept. 19, 1852, by Rev. Lester Lewis	3	63
Merit W., of Bristol, m. Mary **HORTON,** of Bristol, May 4, 1825, by Rev. Isaac Merriman	1	27
Nancy, m. John **HENDRICKS,** b. of Bristol, Sept. 23, 1830, by Rev. Henry Stanwood	1	62
Roswell, m. Sarah A. **BARNUM,** b. of Bristol, Sept. 25, 1853, by Rev. Henry Fitch	3	67
ATWATER, Almira C., m. Everett **HORTON,** b. of Bristol, July 2, 1854, by Rev. Josiah T. Smith	3	70
George D., m. Adaline **NORTON,** Aug. 15, 1832, by Rev. David L. Parmelee	1	74
Harriet E., of Bristol, m. Jesse H. **FARNSWORTH,** of Burlington, July 19, 1843, by Edward Savage	3	13
Julia, of Bristol, m. John **CRANDALL,** of Burlington, Aug. 21, 1844, by Edward Savage	3	18
Lucius, Jr., m. Angelina **NORTON,** b. of Bristol, Oct. 11, 1820, by Rev. Jonathan Coe	1	2
Mary, m. Sheldon W. **TWITCHEL,** Mar. 22, 1826, by Rev. Daniel Wildman	1	32
Mary A., m. Orrin R. **TREAT,** b. of Bristol, July 22, 1839, by Rev. Orsamus Allen	1	130
Olive, of Bristol, m. Willys **HINMAN,** of Plymouth, Apr. 9, 1823, by Rev. Rodney Rossiter, of Plymouth	1	20
Rhoda, m. Allen **BUNNELL,** Feb. 8, 1826, by Rev. Daniel Wildman	1	32
Sophronia, m. Hiram J. **WELCH,** b. of Bristol, May 3, 1837, by Rev. Orsamus Allen	1	112

	Vol.	Page
ATWATER, (cont.)		
Stephen, of Plymouth, m. Jane E. **TUTTLE**, of Bristol, Oct. 27, 1851, by Rev. Lewis Gunn	3	58
ATWOOD, Abiram S., of Woodbury, m. Cornelia N. **NORTH**, of Bristol, Jan. 1, 1846, by Rev. A. S. Francis	3	27
Anson L., m. Eliza Ann M. **HOOKER**, Nov. 18, 1840, by Rev. David L. Parmelee	1	141
George, of Milford, m. Roxanna **HART**, of Bristol, July 5, 1846, by Rev. A. S. Francis	3	32
Sarah A., m. Charles W. **BLAKESLEE**, Dec. 15, 1844, by Rev. Andrew L. Stone	3	21
AUSTIN, Leveret C., of Waterbury, m. Jane J. **NORTON**, of Bristol, Oct. 23, 1835, by Rev. Orsamus Allen	1	103
AVEREST, Charles L., m. Sarah E. **BARNES**, b. of Bristol, Apr. 21, 1853, by Rev. Lester Lewis	3	64
AVERY, AVERRY, Frances J., m. John W. **STILLMAN**, b. of Bristol, Nov. 22, 1848, by Rev. R. H. Seeley	3	45
Jane E., m. John C. **MACK**, Nov. 21, 1849, by Rev. Lester Lewis	3	46
BABCOCK, Emily M., of New Haven, m. Oliver B. **BANNON**, of Springfield, Mass., Apr. 29, 1844, by Rev. Merrill Richardson, Int. Pub.	3	17
BACON, Charles H., [s. John & Lucinda], b. Mar. 10, 1832	2	31
Ellbridge H., [s. John & Lucinda], b. Mar. 2, 1837	2	31
John T., [s. John & Lucinda], b. July 9, 1842	2	31
Mary, of Waterbury, m. Timothy **GLADDING**, of Wethersfield, July 1, 1850, by William H. Goodrich	3	49
BAILEY, Anna M., of Wolcott, m. Eneas **BLAKESLEE**, of Bristol, Nov. 24, 1830, by Rev. Henry Stanwood	1	64
Emily A., of Harwinton, m. C. **PARKHURST**, of Springfield, Mass., Oct. 11, 1846, by Rev. Edward Savage	3	29
BALDWIN, Betsey, of Bristol, m. Eli **JOHNSON**, of Lyons, N. Y., Sept. 17, 1827, by Jonathan Cone, V. D. M.	1	42
Charlotte, m. Justus P. **HARD**, May 16, 1826, by Jonathan Cone, V. D. M.	1	33
Ezra, m. Mary H. **RICHARDS**, Apr. 10, 1834, by Rev. David L. Parmelee	1	95
George W., of Litchfield, m. Bridget **RUSSELL**, of Bristol, Oct. 9, 1853, by Rev. N. C. Lewis	3	68
Julia A., of New Hartford, m. Alonso **WEST**, of Stafford, Aug. 8, 1849, by Rev. Lester Lewis	3	44
Merritt, of Westville, m. Harriet **SHEPARD**, of Portland, Nov. 20, 1842, by Rev. Joseph S. Covell	3	10
Sylvanus, s. Joseph & Rosetta, d. Dec. 17, 1811	TR1	536
Synderilla, d. Joseph C. & Rosetta, b. July 6, 1811	TR1	517
BALL, Elmina, of Bristol, m. Edward **PRITCHARD**, of Waterbury, Nov. 25, 1847, by Rev. Joseph H. Nichols	3	37
Hiram, of Bristol, m. Lucy E. **HAWLEY**, of Sandisfield,		

	Vol.	Page

BALL, (cont.)

Mass., Dec. 3, 1851, by Rev. Henry Fitch — 3 — 56

Mary Ann, m. Nathan E. **HAWLEY**, b. of Bristol, June 11, 1851, by Rev. Henry Fitch — 3 — 53

BANCROFT, Maria, m. Lewis A. **BLAKESLEY**, July 5, 1837, by Rev. David L. Parmelee — 1 — 115

BANNON, Oliver B., of Springfield, Mass., m. Emily M. **BABCOCK**, of New Haven, Apr. 29, 1844, by Rev. Merrill Richardson, Int. Pub. — 3 — 17

BARBER, Volney G., of Canton, m. Ellen A. **ATKINS**, of Bristol, July 30, 1837, by Rev. Orsamus Allen — 1 — 117

BARD, Mabel Mary, d. Ephraim, b. Aug. 18, 1795 — TR1 — 489

BARKER, Burritt E., of Plymouth, m. Lorena S. **YALE**, of Bristol, Apr. 8, 1845, by Rev. Edward Savage — 3 — 22

Esther J., of Bristol, m. Marshall **UPSON**, of Wolcott, Sept. 28, 1848, by Rev. R. H. Seeley — 3 — 45

Mary J., of Bristol, m. Elam A. **FENN**, of Plymouth, Oct. 15, 1842, by Rev. Merritt Richardson, Int. Pub. Oct. 9, 1842, Plymouth — 3 — 9

BARNARD, Ellen S., m. Josiah T. **PECK**, b. of Bristol, Nov. 23, 1847, by Rev. R. H. Seeley — 3 — 36

Theodore, of Hartford, m. Amy **LEWIS**, of Bristol, Feb. 6, 1823, by Rev. Jonathan Cone — 1 — 19

BARNES, BARNS, Abigael, m. Benjamin **CHURCHILL**, Apr. 19, 1753 — TR1 — 494

Alphonzo, m. Almira **ANDRUSS**, b. of Bristol, Oct. 13, 1825, by Rev. Daniel Wildman — 1 — 30

Alphonso, of Bristol, m. Mary **ELY**, of Harwinton, Jan. 26, 1841, by Rev. Parmelee Chamberlin — 3 — 1

Alphonso, m. Mary **HINMAN**, Jan. 20, 1845, by R. H. Seely — 3 — 21

Ambrose, of Plymouth, m. wid. Rhoda **WILMOT**, of Burlington, Nov. 27, 1821, by Rev. Jonathan Cone — 1 — 12

Benjamin, m. Sally **KINNEY**, Sept. 12, 1837, by Harvey Husted — 1 — 116

Daniel, m. Sarah **WEBSTER**, Nov. 23, 1785 — TR1 — 489

Daniel, Jr., s. Capt. Daniel, b. Sept. 1, 1788 — TR1 — 500

Daniel, of Bristol, m. Laura **CURTISS**, of Burlington, Jan. 18, 1843, by S. W. Smith, Elder — 3 — 10

Decius Tullius Cicero, s. Capt. Daniel, b. Apr. 28, 1804 — TR1 — 500

Edward, of Addison, Vt., m. Eliza **NEWELL**, of Bristol, Oct. 5, 1830, by Rev. Noah Porter, of Farmington — 1 — 62

Electa, of Plymouth, m. Miles **SANFORD**, of Bristol, Feb. 16, 1834, by Rev. H. Stanwood — 1 — 94

Evelina, m. Dr. Charles **BYINGTON**, b. of Bristol, Dec. 6, 1821, by Rev. Jonathan Cone — 1 — 12

Fanny J., m. Samuel **HOLT**, b. of Bristol, Dec. 26, 1830, by Rev. H. Stanwood — 1 — 65

Giles, s. Capt. Daniel, b. Oct. 30, 1792 — TR1 — 500

	Vol.	Page
BARNES, BARNS, (cont.)		
Harriett, m. Henry **BEECHER**, Apr. 7, 1839, by Rev. David L. Parmelee	1	127
Henry Marcus, s. Capt. Daniel, b. Nov. 23, 1806	TR1	489
Hirum, [s. Seth & Elizabeth], b. Feb. 21, 1802	TR1	508
Horace, m. Almira **CARRINGTON**, b. of Bristol, Sept. 2, 1842, by Rev. Joseph S. Covell	3	8
John Bird, s. Capt. Daniel, b. Feb. 23, 1795	TR1	500
Joseph, s. Nathan, b. Apr. 15, 1797(?) (Conflicts with birth of "Lemon")	TR1	489
Josiah, Jr., of Bristol, m. Fanny **HORTON**, of Wolcott, Feb. 27, 1821, by Rev. Jonathan Cone	1	5
Lemon, s. Nathan, b. May 8, 1797(?) *(Conflicts with birth of "Joseph")	TR1	489
Marcus, s. Capt. Daniel, b. Feb. 17, 1787	TR1	500
Marcus, s. Capt. Daniel, d. Mar. 18, 1806	TR1	500
Martha, m. Leander B. **NORTON**, b. of Bristol, Dec. 28, 1845, by Rev. Orsamus Allen	3	26
Mary, d. Nathan, b. Sept. 8, 1880* *(Probably intended for "1800")	TR1	489
Monroe, of Bristol, m. Ann Eliza **TOLBERT**, of Burlington, Nov. 27, 1847, by Irenus Atkins	3	36
Oliver Ellsworth, s. Capt. Daniel, b. Jan. 12, 1803	TR1	500
Orville, s. Capt. Daniel, b. Feb. 26, 1797	TR1	500
Polly, d. Capt. Daniel, b. Nov. 12, 1790	TR1	500
Rhoda, of Plymouth, m. Mark **NORTON**, of Bristol, May 21, 1832, by Rev. H. Stanwood	1	70
Romulus, s. Capt. Daniel, b. Oct. 16, 1800	TR1	500
Sally, d. Seth [& Elizabeth], b. Nov. 14, 1798	TR1	508
Sally, m. Asa **BECKWITH**, May 28, 1821, by Rev. Jonathan Cone	1	6
Samuel, of Burlington, m. Sarah Maria **WILCOX**, of Bristol, Jan. 15, 1829, by Rev. Aaron Pearce	1	49
Sarah E., m. Charles L. **AVEREST**, b. of Bristol, Apr. 21, 1853, by Rev. Lester Lewis	3	64
Seth, m. Elizabeth **LEE**, d. William, Jan. 10, 1798	TR1	508
Thomas, m. Lucy Ann **CANDEE**, Oct. 23, 1836, by Rev. David L. Parmelee	1	107
Wallace, m. Eliza J. **FULLER**, b. of Bristol, Apr. 5, 1849, by Lester Lewis	3	47
BARNUM, Sarah A., m. Roswell **ATKINS**, b. of Bristol, Sept. 25, 1853, by Rev. Henry Fitch	3	67
BARRETT, Willard H., of New Hartford, m. Nancy **STEVENS**, of Bristol, Oct. 29, 1846, by Rev. A. S. Francis	3	32
BARTHOLOMEW, Asa, Jr., m. Mary L. **BIRGE**, Nov. 10, 1836, by Rev. David L. Parmelee	1	109
Asahel, s. Jacob, Jr., b. Feb. 22, 1795	TR1	489
Betsy, d. Jacob, Jr., b. July 31, 1799	TR1	489

	Vol.	Page
BARTHOLOMEW, (cont.)		
Charles, s. Jacob, Jr., b. Feb. 24, 1793	TR1	489
Charlotte Louisa, of Bristol, m. Austin **WILCOX**, of [ ],		
Mar. 30, 1847, by Rev. R. H. Seely	3	31
Chloe, d. Jacob, Jr., b. Mar. 25, 1791	TR1	489
Emily, m. George R. **UPSON**, Nov. 25, 1824, by Luther Hart	1	25
Gad, m. Phene **STONE**, d. William, of Harwinton, May 23,		
1804	TR1	534
George W., m. Angeline **IVES**, b. of Bristol, Jan. 13,		
1829, by Rev. Aaron Pearce	1	49
Harriet, m. Samuel **PECK**, Mar. 14, 1827, by Jonathan Cone,		
V. D. M.	1	38
Jacob, Jr., m. Rebeckah **BEACH**, Jan. 27, 1790	TR1	494
Jane C., m. Wellington **WINSTON**, b. of Bristol, Sept. 14,		
1842, by Rev. Joseph S. Covell	3	8
Jennet, m. Eli I. **MERRIMAN**, May 8, 1833, by Rev. David		
L. Parmelee	1	85
Nancy M., m. Alanson **WINSTON**, May 9, 1839, by Rev.		
David L. Parmelee	1	129
Pautince*, m. Alvin F. **ALPRESS**, Sept. 12, 1832, by Rev.		
David L. Parmelee *(Should be "Paulina". Corrected by		
G. W. Bartholomew)	1	75
Rebeca, d. Jacob, Jr., b. May 12, 1797	TR1	489
BASSETT, Edwin A., m. Mary Ann **WOOD**, Nov. 30, 1836, by		
Rev. David L. Parmelee	1	109
Harriet L., of Bristol, m. Norris **CLARK**, of Southington,		
Nov. 5, 1827, by Jonathan Cone, V. D. M.	1	43
BATES, Elizabeth, of Bristol, m. Jason **ALLEN**, of Davenport,		
N. Y., Dec. 21, 1851, by Irenus Atkins	3	56
Isaac, of Plymouth, m. Sybil **HORTON**, of Bristol, Nov. 30,		
1840, by Rev. Joseph S. Covill	1	143
William, of Watertown, m. Melissa **PLATT**, of Bristol,		
Sept. 3, 1829, by Rev. Henry Stanwood	1	57
BEACH, Charles, of Burlington, m. Mary **GRANNIS**, of		
Southington, Apr. 5, 1840, by E. S. Stout	1	143
Huldah A., m. Lewis **LOVELAND**, b. of Plymouth, last		
evening [Apr. 19, 1835], by Jeremiah Rice, J. P., at his		
house	1	100
James A., m. Adeline E. **WILCOX**, Jan. 10, 1841, by Rev.		
David L. Parmelee	3	1
Levi, m. Annette **COWLES**, b. of Bristol, Nov. 2, 1848,		
by Rev. R. H. Seeley	3	45
Mary L., m. Orange M. **FRARY**, July 14, 1842, by Rev.		
Merritt Richardson	3	6
Minerva A., of Bristol, m. Salmon P. **BURDICT**, of Ansonia,		
Nov. 7, 1853, by Rev. N. C. Lewis	3	68
Rebeckah, m. Jacob **BARTHOLOMEW**, Jr., Jan. 27, 1790	TR1	494
William, m. Mary **HILLS**, Sept. 3, 1828, by Jonathan Cone,		

	Vol.	Page
BEACH, (cont.)		
V. D. M.	1	46
BEARD, Ephrim, m. Mabel **PEARKS**, Aug. 6, 1789	TR1	494
Patty, d. Ephraim, b. May 27, 1792	TR1	489
Rebeckah, d. Epherim, b. June 15, 1790	TR1	489
BEARDSLEE, Lewis S., of Trumbull, m. Martha E. **COWD**, of		
Waterbury, Jan. 22, 1843, by Edward Savage	3	12
BECHSTEDL, Carl, m. Anna **SCHMIDT**, Oct. 27, 1850, by Rev.		
William H. Goodrich	3	51
BECKLEY, BECKLY, Henry C., m. Emily P. **BOTSFORD**, b. of		
Bristol, June 9, 1846, by Merrill Richardson. Int. Pub.		
June 7, 1846, by R. H. Seely	3	28
James H., of Bristol, m. Emeline A. **BLAKE**, of Middletown,		
Mar. 29, 1846, by Rev. A. S. Francis	3	27
BECKMON, David, of Columbia, Co., N. Y., m. Sarah **EASTMAN**,		
of Green Co., N. Y., Nov. 4, 1849, by Rev. Lester Lewis	3	46
BECKWITH, Abner, m. Rachel **LEDWELL**, June 23, 1800	TR4	519
Anson, m. Emily **PECK**, July 25, 1825, by Jonathan Cone,		
V. D. M.	1	29
Anson, of Bristol, m. Amelia F. **SCHUBERT**, of Schweinfurt,		
Germany, Sept. 13, 1852 by Rev. William H. Goodrich	3	62
Asa, m. Sally **BARNS**, May 28, 1821, by Rev. Jonathan Cone	1	6
Elenor E., of Bristol, m. Henry V. E. **HOTCHKISS**, of		
Prospect, July 10, 1849, by Rev. L. H. Pease	3	44
Emeline, m. Richard A. **IVES**, Aug. 18, 1825, by Jonathan		
Cone, V. D. M.	1	29
Henry, m. Charlotte M. **SKINNER**, b. of Bristol, July 14,		
1851, by Rev. Lester Lewis	3	54
Sidney, m. Belinda **GRIDLEY**, May 14, 1834, by Rev. David		
L. Parmelee	1	96
BEEBE, Alvin M., m. Lurenda F. **BLAKESLEE**, June 16, 1833, by		
Rev. David L. Parmelee	1	88
BEECHER, Henry, m. Harriett **BARNES**, Apr. 7, 1839, by Rev.		
David L. Parmelee	1	127
Sheldon C., of Edinburgh, N. Y., m. Martha E. **CANDEE**,		
of Bristol, Nov. 4, 1850, by Rev. Henry Fitch	3	51
BELDEN, Susan, of Burlington, m. Henry F. **RODEN**, of Bristol,		
June 8, 1845, by Rev. A. S. Francis	3	24
BENHAM, Abigail, of New Hartford, m. Thomas T.		
MELANTHAN, of Bristol, May 1, 1850, by Rev. Lester		
Lewis	3	49
Betsy, of Bristol, m. Horace **MUNSON**, of Plymouth, Sept. 11,		
1839, by F. B. Woodward	3	5
Hannah, of Waterbury, m. Garret P. **WARNER**, of Bristol,		
Dec. 28, 1845, by Rev. Joseph S. Covill	3	26
BENJAMIN, Almira, of Springfield, Mass., m. Morgan		
APPLETON, Aug. 4, 1839, by F. B. Woodward	3	5
BENNET, Smith, of New Hartford, m. Caroline **VORSE**, of New		

	Vol.	Page
BENNET, (cont.)		
Haven, Jan. 21, 1852, by Rev. Lester Lewis	3	58
BENTON, John, m. Polly Chena **UPSON**, d. Fremend, Oct. 13, 1802	TR1	534
BIDWELL, Adeline C., of Middletown, m. Alden A. **ATKINS**, of Bristol, Sept. 20, 1832, by Rev. Henry Stanwood	1	76
BIRD, Henry N., of Cincinnatti, O., m. Martha M. **HOOKER**, of Bristol, July 28, 1851, by Merrill Richardson	3	55
BIRGE, John, m. Mrs. Jerusha **JOHNSON**, Nov. 18, 1844, by R. H. Seely	3	19
Juliett, m. Abraham B. **DOOLITTLE**, Dec. 5, 1832, by Rev. David L. Parmelee	1	80
Mary L., m. Asa **BARTHOLOMEW**, Jr., Nov. 10, 1836, by Rev. David L. Parmelee	1	109
Nathan L., m. Adeline M. **SMITH**, b. of Bristol, May 19, 1852, by Rev. W. H. Goodrich	3	61
BISHOP, Hobart Henry, m. Helen Eliza **DOWNS**, b. of Bristol, June 6, 1852, by Rev. Henry Fitch	3	60
Homer, m. Martha **SMITH**, b. of Bristol, Nov. 18, 1829, by Rev. H. Stanwood	1	58
BLAKE, Emeline A., of Middletown, m. James H. **BECKLEY**, of Bristol, Mar. 29, 1846, by Rev. A. S. Francis	3	27
BLAKESLEE, BLAKESLY, BLAKSLEE, BLAKESLEY, BLACKESLEE, Amanda P., of Bristol, m. William H. **NEWELL**, of Cheshire, May 30, 1848, by Rev. R. H. Seeley	3	39
Amaryer, s. Jordan, b. June 5, 1779	TR1	489
Belinda, m. Hart **FENN**, Oct. 4, 1827, by Jonathan Cone, V.D.M.	1	43
Charles, of Litchfield, m. Lucy A. **CLARK**, of Plymouth, Apr. 8, 1849, by Rev. Lester Lewis	3	47
Charles W., m. Sarah A. **ATWOOD**, Dec. 15, 1844, by Rev. Andrew L. Stone	3	21
Elorretta A., m. Walter A. **JUDD**, b. of New Britain, Mar. 30, 1854, by Rev. William H. Goodrich	3	70
Eneas, of Bristol, m. Anna M. **BAILEY**, of Wolcott, Nov. 24, 1830, by Rev. Henry Stanwood	1	64
Erastus, m. Margaret F. **NORTON**, Oct. 17, 1832, by Rev. David L. Parmelee	1	77
Hareat, d. Sala, b. May 27, 1792	TR1	489
Julia Ann, of Bristol, m. Beecher **PERKINS**, of Woodbridge, Oct. 18, 1832, by Rev. Henry Stanwood	1	78
Jurdon, Jr., s. Jordan, b. May 21, 1775	TR1	489
Leander S., of Bristol, m. Abigail **PRICHARD**, of Waterbury, Oct. 6, 1833, by Rev. H. Stanwood	1	90
Lewis A., m. Maria **BANCROFT**, July 5, 1837, by Rev. David L. Parmelee	1	115
Lois R., of Bristol, m. Frisbie R. **NORTON**, of Plymouth, Jan. 5, 1834, by Rev. H. Stanwood	1	93

	Vol.	Page

BLAKESLEE, BLAKESLY, BLAKSLEE, BLAKESLEY,
BLACKESLEE, (cont.)

Lurenda F., m. Alvin M. **BEEBE**, June 16, 1833, by Rev.
   David L. Parmelee — 1 — 88

Martain, s. Jordon, b. July 15, 1781 — TR1 — 489

Martin R., of Bristol, m. Nancy R. **CARRINGTON**, of
   Southington, Aug. 24, 1829, by Rev. Irenus Atkins, of
   Southington — 1 — 55

Mary Ann, of Bristol, m. Almanza **ROBERTS**, of Burlington,
   Mar. 30, 1829, by Rev. Henry Stanwood — 1 — 51

Mary S., of Bristol, m. Francis B. **NORTON**, of Southington,
   Jan. 1, 1852, by Rev. Lester Lewis — 3 — 57

Molley, d. Jordan, b. Mar. 31, 1777 — TR1 — 489

Rufus, s. Jordan, b. Oct. 9, 1773 — TR1 — 489

Susan, of Bristol, m. Sidney **CLARK**, of Plymouth, July
   31, 1853, by Rev. Lester Lewis — 3 — 67

BLOOD, Ebenezer, m. Paulina **GILLIGAN**, Mar. 17, 1840, by Rev.
   Orsamus Allen — 1 — 138

BOARDMAN, Jane R., of Bristol, m. William L. **ROGERS**, of
   Tolland, Mass., Nov. 19, 1851, by Rev. William H.
   Goodrich — 3 — 59

Lydia E., of Bristol, m. Charles T. **FOOTE**, of Canton,
   Dec. 8, 1847, by Rev. R. H. Seeley — 3 — 36

Martha A., m. Theron **IVES**, Sept. 11, 1838, by Rev. David
   L. Parmelee — 1 — 122

Sarah C., m. Joseph A. **WELLS**, Nov. 22, 1832, by Rev.
   David L. Parmelee — 1 — 80

BODURTHA, Jerre A., of West Springfield, Mass., m. Helen M.
   GIBBS, of Blanford, Mass., Sept. 25, 1849, by Rev.
   Lester Lewis — 3 — 46

BONFOEY, A. C., of Haddam, m. Sarah E. **HOUGH**, of Bristol,
   July 24, 1852, by Rev. William H. Goodrich — 3 — 62

BOOTH, Hiram, m. Laura **BURWELL**, b. of Bristol, May 26, 1836,
   by Rev. Orsamus Allen — 1 — 107

BOTSFORD, Emily P., m. Henry C. **BECKLY**, b. of Bristol, June
   9, 1846, by Merrill Richardson, Int. Pub. June 7, 1846,
   by R. H. Seely — 3 — 28

Harriet, m. Philo **STEVENS**, b. of Bristol, May 20, 1827,
   by Henry Stanwood — 1 — 40

Hiram, m. Elizabeth H. **WHITMORE**, Jan. 16, 1839, by Rev.
   David L. Parmelee — 1 — 127

Huldah, of Meriden, m. Julius E. **PIERCE**, of Bristol, May
   30, 1849, by Rev. Lester Lewis — 3 — 47

Jane, of Bristol, m. Albro **ALFRED**, of Harwinton, Apr. 22,
   1833, by Rev. Grant Powers, of Goshen. Int. Pub. — 1 — 84

Lorenzo, m. Hannah **NORTON**, b. of Bristol, June 16, 1842,
   by Rev. Orsamus Allen — 3 — 7

Nancy, m. Elias **PERKINS**, 2nd, b. of Bristol, Dec. 4, 1827,

	Vol.	Page
BOTSFORD, (cont.)		
by Rev. Noah Porter	1	44
Ruth Ann, m. Otis **HOUSE**, Dec. 13, 1832, by Rev. David L. Parmelee	1	81
BRACKETT, Mary, of Bristol, m. Aurelious **PECK**, of Burlington, Feb. 8, 1821, by Datus Ensign, Elder	1	4
BRADLEY, Adolphus, of Bristol, m. Sarah Maria **SMITH**, of Mt. Washington, Mass., Mar. 22, 1847, by Rev. R. H. Seely	3	31
Harriet, of Plymouth, m. Bishop **SMITH**, of Bristol, Sept. 15, 1847, by Rev. Harvey Husted	3	34
Harvey, m. Betsey **STEELE**, b. of Bristol, Sept. 26, 1822, by Rev. Jonathan Cone	1	16
Jemima, of Bristol, m. Chauncy **HILLS**, Jr., of Farmington, Apr. 13, 1824, by Rev. Jonathan Cone	1	23
John, of Chesire, m. Angeline **MANROSS**, of Bristol, Sept. 1, 1845, by Rev. William Wright, of Farmington	3	24
Lucy, m. Isaac **HOTCHKISS**, b. of Bristol, Apr. 23, 1843, by Aaron C. Beech	3	12
Lyman G., m. Rhoda A. **NORTON**, June 28, 1840, by Rev. David L. Parmelee	1	137
Mariett, of Wolcott, m. Asahel **BROCKETT**, of Bristol, Mar. 24, 1844, by Edward Savage	3	16
Melenda, of Wolcott, m. Salmon **ALLEN**, of Bristol, Dec. 14, 1820, by Rev. Caleb Read	1	2
Wintworth H., of Bristol, m. Martha J. **DICKINSON**, of Waterbury, May 22, [1854], by Rev. Josiah T. Smith	3	69
BRAINARD, Catharine, of Bristol, m. William **LUM**, of Derby, Feb. 7, 1827, by Rev. Rodney Rossiter, of Plymouth	1	39
Susan C., m. William **McCRACKEN**, Feb. 12, 1838, by Rev. David L. Parmelee	1	119
BREWSTER, Julia, of Bristol, m. George **BRIGGS**, of New York, Oct. 10, 1854, by Rev. W[illia]m H. Goodrich	3	70
Lucy A., m. Joseph W. **CAMP**, Apr. 30, 1839, by Rev. David L. Parmelee	1	128
Martha J., m. Samuel P. **NEWELL**, Oct. 10, 1854, by Rev. William H. Goodrich	3	71
BRIGGS, George, of New York, m. Julia **BREWSTER**, of Bristol, Oct. 10, 1854, by Rev. W[illia]m H. Goodrich	3	70
BRISTOL, Mary S., m. Franklin **NEWELL**, Nov. 11, 1840, by Rev. David L. Parmelee	1	140
Thadeus, m. Elisa **STONE**, Nov. 8, 1848, by Rev. Charles Chittenden	3	41
BROCKETT, Asahel, of Bristol, m. Mariett **BRADLEY**, of Wolcott, Mar. 24, 1844, by Edward Savage	3	16
Calvin, of Bristol, m. Celestia I. **PLUMB**, of Wolcott, Apr. 14, 1844, by Edward Savage	3	16
BRONSON, BROWNSON, Charles, m. Falla **ROBERTS**, May 19, 1836, by Rev. David L. Parmelee	1	105

	Vol.	Page
BRONSON, BROWNSON, (cont.)		
Charles, of Waterbury, m. Rachel R. **PECK**, of Bristol,		
July 25, 1848, by Rev. Charles Chittenden	3	39
Chloe, d. Stepher, b. Apr. 26, 1787	TR1	503
Lorenda, d. Stepher, b. May 1, 1791	TR1	503
William S., m. Deadama **GAYLORD**, Mar. 24, 1841, by Rev.		
David L. Parmelee	3	1
BROOKS, Alvira L., of Bristol, m. Hiram H. **HOLT**, of Harwinton,		
Nov. 8, 1846, by Rev. Henry V. Gardner, of Plymouth	3	29
Amanda, see Amanda **MARKS**	1	16
Emily J., of Bristol, m. Sylvanus **BUTLER**, of Plymouth,		
Oct. 10, 1841, by Rev. Joseph S. Covell	1	144
Emily J., of Bristol, m. Sylvanus **BUTLER**, of Plymouth,		
Oct. 10, 1841, by Rev. Joseph S. Covill	3	4
Hannah, d. Samuel, d. June 19, 1783, in the 3rd y. of her age	TR1	536
Orrin, s. Abraham, b. Feb. 13, 1786	TR1	500
Ruth, w. Samuell, d. Apr. 25, 1804, in the 69th y. of her age	TR1	536
Ruth, of Bristol, m. Thomas **COOKE**, of Torrington, May 23,		
1824, by Rev. Jonathan Cone	1	24
BROWN, Hezekiah, m. Eliza M. **CLARK**, of Bristol, Aug. 26,		
1838, by Rev. E. S. Stout	1	126
Levi, m. Susanna **ALLEN**, of Plymouth, May 26, 1845, by		
Rev. Edward Savage	3	23
Lorene, Mrs., m. Abel **YALE**, b. of Bristol, June 28, 1821,		
by Rev. Jonathan Cone	1	7
Mary, of Plymouth, m. Burton **ALLEN**, May 30, 1847, by		
Rev. Lester Lewis	3	35
Mary E., of Bristol, m. John **ROOT**, of Berlin, Mar. 31,		
1833, by Rev. H. Stanwood	1	83
Mary J., m. John R. **POMEROY**, b. of Bristol, May 18, 1836,		
by Rev. Orsamus Allen	1	106
Samuel, of Harwinton, m. Malinda **CHURCHILL**, of Bristol,		
Nov. 16, 1831, by Rev. H. Stanwood	1	68
BULKLEY, BUCKLEY, Hannah, m. William B. **DUNBAR**, b. of		
Bristol, Mar. 22, 1835, by Rev. Orsamus Allen	1	98
Mahitable J., m. Noah E. **WETTON**,* July 12, 1832, by Rev.		
David L. Parmelee *(Welton"?)	1	73
BUNCE, Dorcas, of Southington, m. James **HITCHCOCK**, of		
Bristol, Oct. 4, 1849, by Rev. Lester Lewis	3	46
BUNNELL, BUNNEL, Allen, Capt., of Plymouth, m. Sally **PECK**,		
of Bristol, Oct. 3, 1822, by Rev. Jonathan Cone	1	16
Allen, m. Rhoda **ATWATER**, Feb. 8, 1826, by Rev. Daniel		
Wildman	1	32
Caroline, m. Franklin **STEELE**, Nov. 24, 1853, by Rev.		
William H. Goodrich	3	64
Charlottee E., of Burlington, m. Norman **ALLEN**, of Bristol,		
May 13, 1844, by Rev. Joseph S. Covill	3	17
Harriett N., m. Mortimer D. **HOLCOM**, b. of Terryville,		

	Vol.	Page
BUNNELL, BUNNEL, (cont.)		
Oct. 3, 1852, by Rev. William H. Goodrich	3	62
Harriet N., m. Mortimer D. **HOLCOMB**, Oct. 3, 1852, by Rev. William H. Goodrich	3	64
Jane Ellen, of Waterbury, m. James E. **MERRIAM**, of Meriden, Mar. 9, 1851, by Rev. Henry Fitch	3	52
Lysander M., of Plymouth, m. Jane P. **POTTER**, of Plymouth, Feb. 17, 1849, by Rev. S. J. Evens	3	42
Mary D., of Southington, m. William H. **YALE**, of Bristol, Nov. 25, 1841, by Rev. Joseph S. Covill	3	4
Parmelia, of Plymouth, m. Thomas **BUNNELL**, of Burlington, May 15, 1829, by Rev. Henry Stanwood	1	51
Perkins, of Burlington, m. Polly **SMITH**, of Bristol, Nov. 12, 1837, by Rev. Harvey Husted	1	118
Susan, of Burlington, m. David B. **CLARK**, of Derby, Oct. 31, 1833, by Rev. Henry Stanwood	1	91
Thomas, of Burlington, m. Parmelia **BUNNELL**, of Plymouth, May 15, 1829, by Rev. Henry Stanwood	1	51
BURDICT, Albert, of Bristol, m. Abigail L. **SHEPHERD**, of Southington, May 20, 1844, by R. H. Seely	3	17
Salmon P., of Ansonia, m. Minerva A. **BEACH**, of Bristol, Nov. 7, 1853, by Rev. N. C. Lewis	3	68
BURNHAM, Hezekiah M., m. Eleanor R. **UPSON**, b. of Bristol, Sept. 24, 1845, by Rev. A. S. Francis	3	25
BURR, Albert, m. Abigail **CURTISS**, b. of Bristol, Nov. 5, 1850, by Rev. Lester Lewis	3	51
BURWELL, John S., of New Hartford, m. Clarrissa M. **LEWIS**, of Bristol, Sept. 23, 1849, by Rev. Lester Lewis	3	45
Laura, m. Hiram **BOOTH**, b. of Bristol, May 26, 1836, by Rev. Orsamus Allen	1	107
BUTLER, Sylvanus, of Plymouth, m. Emily J. **BROOKS**, of Bristol, Oct. 10, 1841, by Rev. Joseph S. Covell	1	144
Sylvanus, of Plymouth, m. Emily J. **BROOKS**, of Bristol, Oct. 10, 1841, by Rev. Joseph S. Covill	3	4
BYINGTON, Asahel, s. Joseph, b. Feb. 16, 1780	TR1	500
Calista, m. Augustin **NORTON**, b. of Bristol, May [ ], 1849, by Rev. L. H. Pease	3	43
Charles, Dr., m. Evelina **BARNS**, b. of Bristol, Dec. 6, 1821, by Rev. Jonathan Cone	1	12
Chloe, d. Joseph, b. June 3, 1777	TR1	500
Clarissa, d. Joseph, b. Feb. 4, 1770	TR1	500
Delia, m. William **DAVIS**, b. of Bristol, Jan. 6, 1823, by Rev. Jonathan Cone	1	19
Enos, s. Joseph, b. Dec. 28, 1781	TR1	500
Hannah, d. Joseph, b. Nov. 10, 1773	TR1	500
Harriet, m. William **RUSSELL**, Aug. 20, 1848, by Rev. Charles Chittenden	3	40
Inez, of Bristol, m. Israel L. **GRAHAM**, of Canton, Mar. 10,		

	Vol.	Page
BYINGTON, (cont.)		
1852, by Rev. William H. Goodrich	3	60
Isaac, s. Joseph, b. Jan. 24, 1761	TR1	500
Isaiah, s. Joseph, b. Dec. 31, 1764	TR1	500
Joseph, Jr., s. Joseph, b. Oct. 14, 1778	TR1	500
Lauren, m. Honor **GRAHAM**, b. of Bristol, Feb. 11, 1829, by Rev. Aaron Pearce	1	52
Lauren, m. Julia P. **HART**, May 13, 1833, by Rev. David L. Parmelee	1	86
Margaret, m. David **REDFEARN**, b. of Bristol, Oct. 27, 1851, by Rev. Henry Fitch	3	56
Maria, of Bristol, m. Horace H. **JUDD**, of Farmington, May 8, 1822, by Rev. Jonathan Cone	1	15
Martin, s. Joseph, b. Nov. 13, 1767	TR1	500
Martin, d. Aug. 12, 1821, in the 54th y. of his age	2	20
Mary, m. Asahel H. **NORTON**, Jr., b. of Bristol, Apr. 2, 1827, by Henry Stanwood	1	38
Melisscent, d. Joseph, b. Aug. 20, 1775	TR1	500
Moses, of Wolcott, m. Susannah **ADAMS**, of Bristol, Apr. 12, 1826, by Jonathan Cone, V. D. M.	1	31
Newel, s. Joseph, b. Nov. 28, 1787	TR1	500
Newell, m. Electa **LEWIS**, Aug. 15, 1837, by Rev. David L. Parmelee	1	115
Noah, s. Joseph, b. Sept. 23, 1762	TR1	500
BYRON, Catharine Hale, of New York City, m. Philander Cook **HORTON**, of Bristol, July 19, 1847, by Rev. Harvey Husted	3	34
CADY, Annah I., m. John M. **WOODRUFF**, June 4, 1837, by Rev. David L. Parmelee	1	114
CAMP, Joseph W., m. Lucy A. **BREWSTER**, Apr. 30, 1839, by Rev. David L. Parmelee	1	128
CANDEE, Lucy Ann, m. Thomas **BARNES**, Oct. 23, 1836, by Rev. David L. Parmelee	1	107
Martha E., of Bristol, m. Sheldon C. **BEECHER**, of Edinburgh, N. Y., Nov. 4, 1850, by Rev. Henry Fitch	3	51
CAREY, Moses, m. Ann **GRANT**, Dec. 6, 1840, by Rev. David L. Parmelee	1	142
CARPENTER, William B., m. Henriette **IVES**, Nov. 6, 1834, by Rev. David L. Parmelee	1	96
CARRIER, Elizabeth P., of Glastonbury, m. Henry I. **WOODRUFF**, of Farmington, May 20, 1851, by Rev. Lester Lewis	3	54
CARRINGTON, Almira, m. Horace **BARNES**, b. of Bristol, Sept. 2, 1842, by Rev. Joseph S. Covell	3	8
Candace E., of Plymouth, m. George A. **ADAMS**, of Waterbury, July 16, 1848, by Rev. Samuel I. Evans	3	39
David, m. Maria **ROOT**, June 29, 1835, by Rev. David L. Parmelee	1	100

	Vol.	Page
CARRINGTON, (cont.)		
Esther, of Bristol, m. Josiah **HOTCHKISS**, of Farmington, Feb. 19, 1827, by Jonathan Cone, V. D. M.	1	37
Juliet M., of Bristol, m. Plina A. **JEWETT**, M. D., of New Haven, Nov. 10, 1847, by Rev. Joseph H. Nichols	3	37
Julius, of Bristol, m. Betsey **MANFORD**, of Danbury, July 21, 1844, by Edward Savage	3	18
Lois D., m. Oswald K. **NORTON**, b. of Southington, Aug. 24, 1829, by Rev. Irenus Atkins, of Southington	1	56
Mary, m. H. Burton **HINMAN**, b. of Bristol, Nov. 11, 1835, by Rev. G. C. V. Eastman	1	103
Nancy R., of Southington, m. Martin R. **BLAKESLEY**, of Bristol, Aug. 24, 1829, by Rev. Irenus Atkins, of Southington	1	55
Sylvia, m. Lott **JEROME**, b. of Bristol, Jan. 3, 1821, by Rev. Jonathan Cone	1	3
CARTER, Charles Lawson, [s. Luther F. & Betsey], b. Mar. 18, 1838	2	28
Henry J., m. Mary M. **ELTON**, Sept. 16, 1839, by Rev. David L. Parmelee	1	131
Mary E., m. Enos **HOLMES**, b. of Wethersfield, Sept. 4, 1842, by Rev. Joseph S. Covell	3	7
Selina D., m. Edward **TWITCHELL**, Sept. 3, 1835, by Rev. David L. Parmelee	1	102
CASE, Grove Griswold, [s. Leaverett G.], b. June 20, 1839	2	29
Mary Jane, m. James C. **LEWIS**, b. of Bristol, Sept. 13, 1852, by Rev. N. Whiting, of Bloomfield	3	62
CASTLE, Emiline, m. Isaac **GILLETT**, b. of Bristol, July 18, 1849, by Rev. Charles Chittenden	3	44
Randal A., m. Eunice **WHEELER**, Sept. 12, 1838, by Rev. E. S. Stout	1	125
CATHERWAY, Cynus, of Hartford, m. Aurilla **JONES**, of Bristol, Aug. 1, 1822, by Rev. Isaac Merriman	1	15
CATLIN, **CATLING**, Alfred R., of Collinsville, m. Emelie **DARROW**, of Bristol, June 1, 1847, by R. H. Seeley	3	33
Arumah, d. Timothy, b. Oct. 5, 1785	TR1	500
Timothy, m. Rebeckah **GOODEH**, May 17, 1785	TR1	494
CHAPIN, Atlas, of Manchester, m. Semantha **CLARK**, of Plymouth Jan. 18, 1852, by Rev. Lester Lewis	3	57
CHAPMAN, Eunice, d. Isiah, Jr., b. Sept. 23, 1793	TR1	499
Isaiah, 3rd, s. Isaiah, Jr., b. June 11, 1791	TR1	499
Salithial, Jr., s. Salathial, b. Aug. 4, 1788	TR1	491
CHURCH, Harriet Malissa, of Bloomfield, m. Andrew **JACKSON**, of Mass., Sept. 23, 1849, by Rev. Lester Lewis	3	45
CHURCHILL, **CHURCHELL**, Abigail, d. Benjamin, b. Apr. 15, 1770	TR1	499
Asahel, s. Benjamin, b. May 1, 1754	TR1	499
Benjamin, m. Abigael **BARNS**, Apr. 19, 1753	TR1	494

	Vol.	Page
CHURCHILL, CHURCHELL, (cont.)		
Benjamin, Jr., s. Benjamin, b. Mar. 16, 1769	TR1	499
Electa, of Bristol, m. Henry A. **SEYMOUR**, of New Hartford, July 28, 1844, by R. H. Seely, Int. Pub.	3	19
Ira, s. Benjamin, b. Apr. 9, 1764	TR1	499
Ira, Jr., m. Betsey **MATTHEWS**, b. of Bristol, Nov. 27, 1822, by Rev. Jonathan Cone	1	17
Jedediah, s. Benjamin, b. Mar. 27, 1766	TR1	499
Joel N., of Bristol, m. Abigail **ALLEN**, of Plymouth, [Nov.] 12, [1827], by Rev. Noah Porter, of Farmington	1	45
John, m. Eliza Ann **HENDRICK**, Nov. 4, 1841, by Rev. C. D. Cowles	3	4
Lydia, d. Benjamin, b. Sept. 3, 1756	TR1	499
Malinda, of Bristol, m. Samuel **BROWN**, of Harwinton, Nov. 16, 1831, by Rev. H. Stanwood	1	68
Samuell, s. Benjamin, b. Aug. 7, 1761	TR1	499
Sarah, m. Forrest W. **MILLS**, b. of Bristol, Apr. 3, 1823, by Rev. Jonathan Cone	1	21
CLAPP, Henry, of Hartford, m. Ann **ELY**, of Harwinton, Apr. 28, 1844, by R. H. Seely. Int. Pub. Apr. 14, 1844	3	16
Rosannah, m. Sylvester **SHEPARD**, b. of Farmington, Nov. 27, 1846, by Charles G. Ives, J. P.	3	30
CLARK, CLARKE, Antionette M., m. David S. **MALLORY**, May 7, 1840, by Rev. David L. Parmelee	1	136
Beulah, m. Noadiah **HART**, Sept. 25, 1785	TR1	494
Charles E., of Great Bend, N. Y., m. Hannah S. **KELSEY**, of Bristol, Apr. 22, 1852, by Rev. William H. Goodrich	3	60
David B., of Derby, m. Susan **BUNNELL**, of Burlington, Oct. 31, 1833, by Rev. Henry Stanwood	1	91
Eliza M., m. Hezekiah **BROWN**, Aug. 26, 1838, by Rev. E. S. Stout	1	126
Henry A., of Southington, m. Sarah **CURTISS**, of Bristol, Nov. 14, 1832, by David L. Odgen	1	79
Lucy A., of Plymouth, m. Charles **BLAKESLY**, of Litchfield, Apr. 8, 1849, by Rev. Lester Lewis	3	47
Mary, m. Julius R. **SHIPMAN**, Jan. 1, 1852, by Rev. W. H. Goodrich	3	59
Mary Ann, m. Charles H. **FASSAUR**, b. of Bristol, May 8, 1842, by Rev. Joseph S. Covell	3	6
Norris, of Southington, m. Harriet L. **BASSETT**, of Bristol, Nov. 5, 1827, by Jonathan Cone, V. D. M	1	43
Orffy, of Farmington, m. Boylston **WHITNEY**, of Bristol, Oct. 11, 1845, by Rev. A. S. Francis	3	25
Semantha, of Plymouth, m. Atlas **CHAPIN**, of Manchester, Jan. 18, 1852, by Rev. Lester Lewis	3	57
Sarah M., m. Rodney **LANE**, Sept. 30, 1844, by R. H. Seely	3	20
Sidney, of Plymouth, m. Susan **BLAKESLEE**, of Bristol, July 31, 1853, by Rev. Lester Lewis	3	67

	Vol.	Page
CLARK, CLARKE, (cont.)		
Sophia, of Bristol, m. James **LEWIS**, of Southington, Oct. 4, 1826, by Jonathan Cone, V. D. M.	1	35
Sylvia, of Southington, m. William **POGUE**, of Albany, N. Y., Feb. 12, 1829, by Rev. Henry Stanwood	1	50
COLTON, Sarah, of Burlington, m. William P. **GOODSELL**, Apr. 21, 1847, by Rev. Lester Lewis	3	35
CONE, Abigail Cleveland, [d. Jonathan & Abbe C.], b. Apr. 13, 1819	2	21
Cephas, m. Ialla **PARMELE**, June 19, 1826, by Luther Hart	1	34
Jonathan Revilo, [s. Jonathan & Abbe C.], b. June 17, 1817	2	21
Nancy Usher, [d. Jonathan & Abbe C.], b. Jan. 31, 1815	2	21
Norris Holmes, [s. Jonathan & Abbe C.], b. Apr. 21, 1822	2	21
Sarah Anne, [d. Jonathan & Abbe C.], b. Feb. 9, 1813	2	21
CONGELMAN, Christian, m. Catharine **SCHEEGEL**, Sept. 28, 1851, by Rev. W. H. Goodrich	3	55
COOK, COOKE, Rachel, m. Julius **NOTT**, Oct. 29, 1844, by R. H. Seely	3	20
Sophia M., of Waterbury, m. William **FEURDEN**, of New Haven, Jan. 1, 1846, by Rev. Edward Savage	3	26
Thomas, of Torrington, m. Ruth **BROOKS**, of Bristol, May 23, 1824, by Rev. Jonathan Cone	1	24
COSTELL, Clara, m. Joel **GRIDLEY**, of Harwinton, Sept. 13, 1827, by Jonathan Cone, V. D. M.	1	42
COTT, Huldah, m. Silas **GRIDLEY**, Jr., Nov. 2, 1803, at Harwinton, by Rev. Joshua Williams (Perhaps "Huldah **COLT**"?)	2	18
COVEY, Lois, m. Rogers **DAVIS**, Aug. 28, 1788	TR1	494
COWD, Martha E., of Waterbury, m. Lewis S. **BEARDSLEE**, of Trumbull, Jan. 22, 1843, by Edward Savage	3	12
COWLES, Annette, m. Levi **BEACH**, b. of Bristol, Nov. 2, 1848, by Rev. R. H. Seeley	3	45
Deama, d. Isaac, b. July 11, 1794	TR1	491
Jenett, m. Berkley D. **PARSONS**, Jan. 2, 1850, by Rev. Merrill Richardson	3	48
John G., m. Annis **WINSTON**, Nov. [ ], 1838, by Rev. David L. Parmelee	1	126
Lucy, d. Isaac, b. May 12, 1788	TR1	491
Maria, of Southington, m. Elisha **MANROSS**, of Bristol, [Jan.] 29, 1821, by Rev. Jonathan Cone	1	4
Martha, m. Joseph **GRIDLEY**, Aug. 26, 1838, by Rev. David L. Parmelee	1	122
Olive, m. Pardon **POTTER**, June 13, 1833, by Rev. David L. Parmelee	1	87
Sophrona, d. Isaac, b. Mar. 7, 1802	TR1	491
Theron, s. Isaac, b. May 25, 1798	TR1	491
COY, Charles F., of Munson, Mass., m. Julia A. **LEWIS**, of Bristol, July 30,* 1847, by Rev. R. H. Seeley *(Probably "13th")	3	34

	Vol.	Page
CRAMER, Charles, m. Nancy ROOT, Jan. 4, 1840, by Rev. David L. Parmelee	1	136
Nathaniel, m. Almira A. MOORE, b. of Bristol, May 28, 1837, by Rev. Harvey Husted	1	114
CRAMPTON, Ruth Ann, m. Samuel STANLEY, June 6, 1832, by Rev. David S. Parmelee	1	72
CRANDALL, John, of Burlington, m. Julia ATWATER, of Bristol, Aug. 21, 1844, by Edward Savage	3	18
CRANE, Marilla N., of Winsted, m. Albert P. WOODRUFF, of Bristol, Sept. 15, 1853, by Rev. Lester Lewis	3	63
CROMACK, Charles, of New Hartford, m. Betsy RADCLIFFE, of Bristol, Oct. 17, 1852, by D. Ives	3	62
CULVER, Abel G., of Bristol, m. Chloe CURTIS, of Burlington, Dec. 1, 1836, by Rev. Harvey Husted	1	110
CUMMINGS, Caroline, m. John W. DOOLITTLE, Oct. 9, 1848, by Rev. Charles Chittenden	3	40
Elizaantha, m. Josiah GRISWOLD, b. of Bristol, Feb. 8, 1841, by Rev. Parmelee Chamberlin	3	1
Frederick E., of Bristol, m. Jane L. HADSELL, of Burlington, Nov. 3, 1846, by Rev. A. S. Francis	3	32
Ruth A., of Bristol, m. Isaac GILLETT, Jr., of Burlington, Mar. 16, 1847, by Rev. A. S. Francis	3	33
CURTIS, CURTISS, Abigail, m. Albert BURR, b. of Bristol, Nov. 5, 1850, by Rev. Lester Lewis	3	51
Charlotte, m. Philo CURTISS, b. of Burlington, Sept. 3, 1829, by William Marks, J. P.	1	55
Chloe, of Burlington, m. Abel G. CULVER, of Bristol, Dec. 1, 1836, by Rev. Harvey Husted	1	110
Corydon, of Burlington, m. Mary Ann DAYTON, of Bristol, Sept. 3, 1843, by Rev. Joseph S. Covell	3	14
Ellen, m. Lafayette HILLS, b. of Bristol, June 16, 1851, by Rev. William H. Goodrich	3	53
Eunice, of Bristol, m. Simeon STEPHENS, of Litchfield, Dec. 22, 1825, by Erastus Clapp, V. D. M.	1	30
George W., of Burlington, m. Lydia M. WARNER, of Southington, Aug. 2, 1826, by Jonathan Cone, V. D. M	1	34
John, of Wolcott, m. Sarah ALLEN, of Bristol, Nov. 30, 1826, by Jonathan Cone, V. D. M.	1	36
Laura, of Burlington, m. Daniel BARNES, of Bristol, Jan. 18, 1843, by S. W. Smith, Elder	3	10
Lucinda, m. Edwin N. LEWIS, Nov. 27, 1833, by Rev. David L. Parmelee	1	92
Philo, m. Charlotte CURTISS, b. of Burlington, Sept. 3, 1829, by William Marks, J. P.	1	55
Phineas, m. Janet LEWIS, June 15, 1842, by Merritt Richardson	3	6
Polly, m. Edwin GILMAN, b. of Bristol, Nov. 27, 1846, by Irenus Atkins	3	31

	Vol.	Page
CURTIS, CURTISS, (cont.)		
Samuel, m. Alvira **ALLEN**, b. of Bristol, Apr. 18, 1843, by Rev. Joseph S. Covell	3	11
Sarah, of Bristol, m. Henry A. **CLARK**, of Southington, Nov. 14, 1832, by David L. Ogden	1	79
Sarah E., m. Franklin **WOOLWORTH**, b. of Bristol, Apr. 6, 1853, by E. C. Jones	3	68
Thomas, Jr., m. Harriet **STEPHENS**, b. of Bristol, May 5, 1830, by Rev. Irenus Atkins, of Southington	1	61
DANSON, Marilla E., of New Hartford, m. George H. **EVENS**, of Chatham, Nov. 22, 1848, by Rev. Charles Chittenden	3	41
DARROW, Emelie, of Bristol, m. Alfred R. **CATLIN**, of Collinsville, June 1, 1847, by Rev. R. H. Seeley	3	33
Esther W., m. Alanson S. **PLATT**, Nov. 19, 1840, by Rev. David L. Parmelee	1	141
Francis V., m. Julia A. **ROBERTS**, b. of Bristol, Nov. 10, 1850, by Rev. Lester Lewis	3	51
Julia, of Bristol, m. Jerome B. **HUBBARD**, of Haddam, May 31, 1848, by Rev. R. H. Seeley	3	39
Mary, m. Isaac M. **STAGG**, Nov. 29, 1838, by Rev. E. S. Stout	1	125
Sarah A., of Bristol, m. Lucius **HATCH**, of Tolland, Sept. 26, 1841, by Rev. I. S. Ward	3	3
DART, Smith, of Vernon, m. Chloe **TUTTLE**, of Bristol, Jan. 12, 1843, by Edward Savage	3	12
DAVIS, DAVICE, Harriet E., m. Hiram **HARKNESS**, b. of Bristol, Dec. 5, 1852, by Rev. Stephen Rushmore	3	65
John, Elder, d. Aug. 29, 1792	TR1	537
Nelson, of Bristol, m. Mary Frances **PEMBLETON**, of Southington, Dec. 19, 1850, by Henry A. Mitchell, J. P.	3	52
Pardon, s. Roger, b. Mar. 21, 1791	TR1	492
Polly, d. Rogers, b. July 16, 1789	TR1	492
Rogers, m. Lois **COVEY**, Aug. 28, 1788	TR1	494
William, m. Delia **BYINGTON**, b. of Bristol, Jan. 6, 1823, by Rev. Jonathan Cone	1	19
DAWSON, Sybel P., of New Hartford, m. Joseph **SIGOURNEY**, of Bristol, June 9, 1845, by Rev. E. Savage	3	23
DAYTON, Abagail, of Bristol, m. Asahel **WARNER**, of Waterbury, Dec. 4, 1842, by Rev. Joseph S. Covel	3	10
Lydia, m. Samuel **HOLT**, b. of Bristol, Mar. 15, 1846, by Rev. A. S. Francis	3	27
Mary Ann, of Bristol, m. Corydon **CURTISS**, of Burlington, Sept. 3, 1843, by Rev. Joseph S. Covell	3	14
DEALLING, Benjamin, of Middletown, m. Eunice **WINSTON**, of Bristol, Oct. 30, 1822, by Rev. Jonathan Cone	1	17
DEAN, Lucy E., m. Constantine **JEROME**, b. of Bristol, Jan. 9, 1854, by Rev. W[illia]m H. Goodrich	3	70
DeFOREST, Charles, m. Minerva **POTTER**, Aug. 9, 1835, by Rev.		

	Vol.	Page
DeFOREST, (cont.)		
Chester W. Turner	1	101
DEMING, Henry, of Woodbury, m. Almira **HINMAN**, of Bristol,		
Dec. 20, 1829, by Rev. H. Stanwood	1	59
DEWEY, Maria P., m. Ambrose **PECK**, Mar. 29, 1846, by R. H.		
Seely	3	26
Martha, of Chesire, m. Leonard **NORTON**, of Bristol, Aug.		
8, 1847, by Rev. Lester Lewis	3	35
DICKINSON, Eliada, m. Lois B. **FANCHER**, Nov. 24, 1833, by		
Rev. David L. Parmelee	1	91
Martha J., of Waterbury, m. Wintworth H. **BRADLEY**, of		
Bristol, May 22, [1854], by Rev. Josiah T. Smith	3	69
DOLBEAR, Harriet E., of Montville, m. John **JONES**, of East		
Windsor, June 16, 1844, by R. H. Seely	3	17
DOOLITTLE, Abraham B., m. Juliett **BIRGE**, Dec. 5, 1832, by		
Rev. David L. Parmelee	1	80
John W., m. Caroline **CUMMINGS**, Oct. 9, 1848, by		
Rev Charles Chittenden	3	40
Maryett, [d. Ira & Lowly], b. Sept. 27, 1821	2	19
Sarah, of New Haven, m. Silas Coolidge **McCLARY**, of		
Michigan, Aug. 11, 1850, in Trinity Church, by Rev.		
Harry Croswell, of New Haven	3	50
DOWNES, DOWNS, Chloe Adaline, [d. Ephraim & Chloe], b. Feb.		
18, 1830	2	23
D. Adelaide, m. William I. **MORGAN**, b. of Bristol, June		
6, 1853, by Rev. Henry Fitch	3	66
Franklin, s. Ephraim & Chloe, b. June 12, 1824, in Plymouth	2	23
George, [s. Ephraim & Chloe], b. Mar. 6, 1826	2	23
George, of Bristol, m. Henrietta **PAYNE**, of Burlington,		
Jan. 3, 1849, by Rev. S. J. Evans	3	41
Helen Eliza, m. Hobart Henry **BISHOP**, b. of Bristol, June		
6, 1852, by Rev. Henry Fitch	3	60
Robert Carlton, [s. Ephraim & Chloe], b. Apr. 19, 1828	2	23
DRAKE, Adna W., m. Cornelia **SPENCER**, b. of Farmington, Apr.		
8, 1849, by Rev. Lester Lewis	3	47
DUDLEY, Timothy, of Guilford, m. Flora M. **HAWLEY**, of		
Burlington, Feb. 21, 1850, by Rev. Lester Lewis	3	48
DUNBAR, Ransom A., of Wolcottville, m. Polly M. **PERKINS**, of		
Bristol, Aug. 20, 1837, by Rev. Harvey Husted	1	116
William B., m. Hannah **BULKLEY**, b. of Bristol, Mar. 22,		
1835, by Rev. Orsamus Allen	1	98
DUTTON, Candace R., of Bristol, m. Thadeus **SMITH**, of		
Plymouth, May 12, 1830, by Rev. Abner J. Leavenworth	1	61
EASTMAN, Sarah, of Green Co., N. Y., m. David **BECKMON**, of		
Columbia Co., N. Y., Nov. 4, 1849, by Rev. Lester Lewis	3	46
EDDY, Hannah, m. Samuel **OSBORN**, b. of Bristol, Jan. 2, 1853,		
by Rev. Henry Fitch	3	63
EDMONDS, Amelia, of Bristol, m. Elisha **MIX**, of Terrysville,		

	Vol.	Page
EDMONDS, (cont.)		
July 10, 1843, by Rev. Merrill Richardson. Int. Pub.	3	14
ELKEY. Jane A., m. Charles H. **TREADWELL**, Mar. 3, 1853, by		
Rev. William H. Goodrich	3	66
ELTON, Mary M., m. Henry J. **CARTER**, Sept. 16, 1839, by Rev.		
David L. Parmelee	1	131
ELWELL, Harrison, m. Eliza **MATTHEWS**, July 9, 1845, by R. H.		
Seeley	3	23
ELY, Ann, of Harwinton, m. Henry **CLAPP**, of Hartford, Apr. 28,		
1844, by R. H. Seely. Int. Pub. Apr. 14, 1844	3	16
Mary, of Harwinton, m. Alphonso **BARNES**, of Bristol, Jan.		
26, 1841, by Rev. Parmelee Chamberlin	3	1
EVENS, George H., of Chatham, m. Marilla E. **DANSON**, of New		
Hartford, Nov. 22, 1848, by Rev. Charles Chittenden	3	41
FANCHER, Lois B., m. Eliada **DICKINSON**, Nov. 24, 1833, by		
Rev. David L. Parmelee	1	91
FARNSWORTH, Jesse H., of Burlington, m. Harriet E.		
ATWATER, of Bristol, July 19, 1843, by Edward Savage	3	13
William, of New Hartford, m. Salome **OLMSTED**, of		
Plymouth, Jan. 17, 1853, by Rev. Lester Lewis	3	64
FARRELL, Malenna, of Waterbury, m. Chester A.		
WOOLWORTH, of Bristol, May 19, 1841, by Rev.		
James Squier	3	2
FASSAUR, Charles H., m. Mary Ann **CLARK**, b. of Bristol, May		
8, 1842, by Rev. Joseph S. Covell	3	6
FENN, Elam A., of Plymouth, m. Mary J. **BARKER**, of Bristol,		
Oct. 15, 1842, by Rev. Merritt Richardson. Int. Pub. Oct.		
9, 1842, Plymouth	3	9
Hart, m. Belinda **BLAKESLEE**, Oct. 4, 1827, by Jonathan		
Cone. V. D. M.	1	43
Henry, m. Silence **LEE**, Oct. 11, 1832, by Rev. David L.		
Parmelee	1	77
Hiram H., of Jersey City, m. Martha E. **MIX**, of Bristol,		
July 28, 1851, by Irenus Atkins	3	57
FENTON, Ann, of Plymouth, m. Levi **PARSONS**, of Southington,		
July 29, 1829, by Rev. Irenus Atkins, of Southington	1	54
Roxana, of Plymouth, m. William H. **SHEPHERD**, of		
Southington, Apr. 7, 1833, by Rev. H. Stanwood	1	84
FEURDEN, William, of New Haven, m. Sophia M. **COOK**, of		
Waterbury, Jan. 1, 1846, by Rev. Edward Savage	3	26
FISH, Miller, of Bloomfield, m. Mrs. Celista **McKEE**, of Bristol,		
Nov. 13, 1842, by S. W. Smith, Elder	3	8
FOOTE, FOOT, Charles T., of Canton, m. Lydia E. **BOARDMAN**,		
of Bristol, Dec. 8, 1847, by Rev. R. H. Seeley	3	36
Ira, of Burlington, m. Nancy **MIX**, of Bristol, Dec. 25,		
1822, by Rev. Jonathan Cone	1	18
FORBES, Lucy M., of Bristol, m. Joel **WOODRUFF**, of		
Southington, Sept. 1, 1845, by Rev. Edward Savage	3	24

	Vol.	Page
FOSTER, Erastus, of East Windsor, m. Ann Maria **GAYLORD**, of		
Bristol, Jan. 18, 1837, by Rev. Harvey Husted	1	111
Frances, m. George S. **ATKINS**, Dec. 5, 1850, by Rev.		
William H. Goodrich	3	52
Seth, m. Sarah **POND**, Apr. 30, 1833, by Rev. David L.		
Parmelee	1	85
Thomas Y., m. Sarah **GAYLORD**, Jan. 15, 1834, by Rev.		
David L. Parmelee	1	92
FRARY, Orange M., m. Mary L. **BEACH**, July 14, 1842, by Rev.		
Merritt Richardson	3	6
FRISBIE, Esther B., of Bristol, m. Tertius D. **POTTER**, of		
Plymouth, Jan. 30, 1828, by Jonathan Cone, V. D. M.	1	44
Laura, m. Seth **STILES**, b. of Bristol, Feb. 9, 1834, by		
Rev. H. Stanwood	1	94
Ruth, m. Josiah C. **USHER**, Sept. 9, 1828, by Jonathan Cone,		
V. D. M.	1	46
Sarah, m. Bryan **RICHARDS**, July 16, 1832, by Rev. David		
L. Parmelee	1	73
FROST, David H. Jr., of Wolcott, m. Levia **ATKINS**, of Bristol,		
Jan. 1, 1822, by Rev. Isaac Merriam	1	13
FULLER, Eliza J., m. Wallace **BARNES**, b. of Bristol, Apr. 5,		
1849, by Lester Lewis	3	47
Nancy, m. Bryan **HOOKER**, Oct. 7, 1804	TR1	517
Rhoda Ann, b. Sept. 22, 1796	TR1	517
Sarah, of Simsbury, m. Austin **WILCOX**, Jan. 18, 1851, by		
Rev. William H. Goodrich	3	59
Thomas F., b. Apr. 29, 1798	TR1	517
Thomas Franklin, m. Eunice* **WINSTONE**, [Aug.] 29, 1821,		
by Rev. Jonathan Cone *(Written in pencil "Lucy"?)	1	9
FULLERTON, David O., of New Haven, m. Jane L. **HART**, of		
Bristol, June 7, 1852, by Rev. W. H. Goodrich	3	61
FUNCK, Dora Augusta, of Bristol, m. John Conrad **HAUSST***, of		
Farmington, Oct. 16, 1851, by Rev. Lester Lewis		
*(Written over "**HAUFTER**"?)	3	55
GAMBLE, Henry, of Ireland, m. Mary Ann **STEVENS**, of Bristol,		
Oct. 29, 1849, by Rev. S. J. Evans	3	54
GATES, Horatio V., of New York, m. Melissa C. **HART**, of Conn.,		
Oct. 29, 1854, by Rev. L. C. Cheeney	3	71
GAYLORD, Ann Maria, of Bristol, m. Erastus **FOSTER**, of East		
Windsor, Jan. 18, 1837, by Rev. Harvey Husted	1	111
Annah, of Bristol, m. Orrin **JUDSON**, of Plymouth, Mar. 24,		
1825, by Rev. Isaac Merriam	1	26
Deadama, m.. William S. **BRONSON**, Mar. 24, 1841, by Rev.		
David L. Parmelee	3	1
Eliza Ann, m. Salmon **ROOT**, Apr. 14, 1841, by Rev. David		
L. Parmelee	3	2
Franklin W., m. Eliza Ann **NETTLETON**, Sept. 10, 1839, by		
Rev. David L. Parmelee	1	130

	Vol.	Page
GAYLORD, (cont.)		
Jesse, Capt., m. Mrs. Elizabeth **JOHNSON**, b. of Bristol, July 3, 1821, by Rev. Jonathan Cone	1	7
Lucina, of Bristol, m. Orrin **HART**, of Waterloo, N. Y., Jan. 7, 1844, by Rev. Henry Lownsbery	3	15
Lydia, m. Alexander **POND**, Apr. 6, 1834, by Rev. David L. Parmelee	1	95
Nancy, of Bristol, m. Leonard **HORTON**, of Wolcott, June 1, 1825, by Rev. Jonathan Cone	1	28
Prudence, w. Eleazer, d. May 28, 1804	TR1	507
Rachel M., of Bristol, m. Eron N. **THOMAS**, of Rose Wayne Cty., N. Y., Sept. 15, 1844, by Rev. Henry F. Roberts	3	19
Sarah, m. Thomas Y. **FOSTER**, Jan. 15, 1834, by Rev. David L. Parmelee	1	92
Thankfull, m. Moses **PECKHAM**, Mar. 26, 1823, by Rev. Jonathan Cone	1	21
Willard, of Goshen, m. Amy **HOOKER**, of Bristol, Apr. 27, 1825, by Rev. Jonathan Cone	1	27
GIBBS, Helen M., of Blanford, Mass., m. Jerre A. **BODURTHA**, of West Springfield, Mass., Sept. 25, 1849, by Rev. Lester Lewis	3	46
GILBERT, Harriet, m. William **THORP**, Nov. 10, 1831, by Rev. H. Stanwood	1	67
GILLETT, GILLET, Caroline, of Windsor, m. Abel S. **LEACH**, of Torrington, June 5, 1822, by Rev. Isaac Merriam	1	19
Isaac, Jr., of Burlington, m. Ruth A. **CUMMINGS**, of Bristol, Mar. 16, 1847, by Rev. A. S. Francis	3	33
Isaac, m. Emiline **CASTLE**, b. of Bristol, July 18, 1849, by Rev. Charles Chittenden	3	44
GILLIGAN, Paulina, m. Ebenezer **BLOOD**, Mar. 17, 1840, by Rev. Orsamus Allen	1	138
GILMAN, Edwin, m. Polly **CURTIS**, b. of Bristol, Nov. 27, 1846, by Irenus Atkins	3	31
GLADDING, Jane A., of Berlin, m. James A. **RONDEN**, of Bristol, Sept. 10, 1849, by Rev. Lester Lewis	3	45
Timothy, of Wethersfield, m. Mary **BACON**, of Waterbury, July 1, 1850, by William H. Goodrich	3	49
GLASSON, James, m. Lavinia **MATTHEWS**, b. of Bristol, formerly of England, Jan. 30, 1848, by Rev. Joseph H. Nichols	3	37
Jane, m. David **POPE**, Apr. 14, 1850, by Rev. William H. Goodrich	3	49
GLOVER, Nancy H., Mrs. of Coventry, m. John **SWAN**, of Hebron, Feb. 23, 1847, by Rev. R. H. Seely	3	30
GOLDSMITH, Esther Eliza, of Plymouth, m. Addin C. **LEWIS**, of Southington, Apr. 23, 1849, by Rev. S. J. Evens	3	43
GOODEH, Rebeckah, m. Timothy **CATLING**, May 17, 1785	TR1	494
GOODRICH, David W., of Millbury, Mass., m. Mary L. **STONE**,		

	Vol.	Page
GOODRICH, (cont.)		
of Terryville, Dec. 29, 1844, by Rev. Henry F. Roberts.		
Witnesses: Elijah Stone & Elvira Stone, [ ] Foster	3	20
George, m. Charlotte S. **IVES**, May 21, 1828, by Luther Hart	1	58
Jared, of Glastonbury, m. Sophronia **PIERCE**, of Bristol,		
Nov. 10, 1839, by Rev. Simon Shailer	1	133
GOODSELL, Lewis A., of Southington, m. Julia H. **HOUGH**, of		
Bristol, Apr. 18, 1852, by Rev. William H. Goodrich	3	60
William P., m. Sarah **COLTON**, of Burlington, Apr. 21, 1847,		
by Rev. Lester Lewis	3	35
GOODWIN, Edwin O., m. Mrs. Harriet **POMEROY**, b. of Bristol,		
Sept. 13, 1848, by Rev. R. H. Seeley	3	45
GRAHAM, Edward, m. Caroline **HART**, b. of Bristol, May 7, 1843,		
by Rev. Samuel W. Smith	3	11
Honor, m. Lauren **BYINGTON**, b. of Bristol, Feb. 11, 1829,		
by Rev. Aaron Pearce	1	52
Isaac, m. Honor **RUST**, b. of Bristol, May 3, 1826, by Jared		
W. Pardee, J. P.	1	31
Israel L., of Canton, m. Inez **BYINGTON**, of Bristol, Mar.		
10, 1852, by Rev. William H. Goodrich	3	60
GRANNISS, **GRANNIS**, Lydia, of Southington, m. Miles F.		
NORTON, of Bristol, Oct. 12, 1831, by Rev. H.		
Stanwood	1	67
Mary, of Southington, m. Charles **BEACH**, of Burlington,		
Apr. 5, 1840, by E. S. Stout	1	143
GRANT, Ann, m. Moses **CAREY**, Dec. 6, 1840, by Rev. David L.		
Parmelee	1	142
Charles S., m. Harriet B. **ATKINS**, July 24, 1844, by		
Edward Savage	3	18
Emily M., m. Edwin **MATTHEWS**, Apr. 4, 1832, by Rev.		
David S. Parmelee	1	69
GRAY, Horace, m. Julia B. **PERRY**, b. of Bristol, June 26, 1854,		
by Rev. Josiah T. Smith	3	69
GREEN, Mary, Mrs., m. Joel **HART**, b. of Bristol, July 1, 1838,		
by Rev. Orsamus Allen	1	121
Mary, of Bristol, m. Ara **HAWLEY**, of Farmington, Apr. 16,		
1845, by Rev. Edward Savage	3	22
S. E., of Bristol, m. L. A. **MOORE**, of Harwinton, May 3,		
1848, by Rev. L. Lewis	3	38
GREINER, Augusta, m. Louis **SUHER**, b. of Germany, Oct. 15,		
1854, by Rev. L. C. Cheeney	3	71
GRIDLEY, Belinda, m. Sidney **BECKWITH**, May 14, 1834, by		
Rev. David L. Parmelee	1	96
Eliza, [d. Silas, Jr. & Huldah], b. Dec. 4, 1804, at Harwinton	2	18
Eliza, of Bristol, m. Romantee Orlando **PLUMB**, of Wolcott,		
Jan. 27, 1825, by Rev. Jonathan Cone	1	26
Henry, m. Harriett **NORTON**, Sept. 9, 1840, by Rev. David		
L. Parmelee	1	139

	Vol.	Page
GRIDLEY, (cont.)		
Huldah Belinda, [d. Silas, Jr. & Huldah], b. Mar. 13, 1809, at Plymouth	2	18
Joel, of Harwinton, m. Clara **COSTELL**, Sept. 13, 1827, by Jonathan Cone, V. D. M	1	42
Joseph, m. Martha **COWLES**, Aug. 26, 1838, by Rev. David L. Parmelee	1	122
Mary, of Bristol, m. Luther A. **REED**, of Plymouth, May 3, 1842, by Rev. Orsimus Allen	3	17
Sally, [d. Silas, Jr. & Huldah], b. Mar. 23, 1807, at Plymouth	2	18
Silas, Jr., m. Huldah **COTT**, Nov. 2, 1803, at Harwinton, by Rev. Joshua Williams (Perhaps "Huldah **COLT**"?)	2	18
Silas Riley, [s. Silas, Jr. & Huldah], b. Sept. 10, 1820	2	18
GRIFFIN, [see also **GRIFFIS**], Warren A., m. Malinda **LOVELL**, b. of Bristol, Sept. 17, 1848, by Rev. L. Lewis	3	40
GRIFFIS, [see also **GRIFFIN**], Daniel, s. John, b. July 6, 1798	TR1	504
Elizabeth, d. John, b. Sept. 20, 1802	TR1	504
John, s. John, b. Nov. 8, 1799	TR1	504
GRIGGS, Mary, of Plymouth, m. Calvin **WOODIN**, 2nd, of Harwinton, Feb. 28, 1827, by Charles G. Ives, J. P.	1	37
GRISWOLD, Augusta L., of Plainville, m. Willard **HUNT**, of Bolton, June 19, 1849, by Rev. Charles Chittenden	3	44
Josiah, m. Elizaantha **CUMMINGS**, b. of Bristol, Feb. 8, 1841, by Rev. Parmelee Chamberlin	3	1
Wait R., of Wethersfield, m. Piera L. **ROBERTS**, of Bristol, Sept. 1, 1846, by R. H. Seely	3	28
GUNN, Lewis, m. Ann E. **HALL**, b. of New Haven, Mar. 2, 1848, by Rev. L. Lewis	3	38
HADSELL, Jane L., of Burlington, m. Frederick E. **CUMMINGS**, of Bristol, Nov. 3, 1846, by Rev. A. S. Francis	3	32
HALL, Ann E., m. Lewis **GUNN**, b. of New Haven, Mar. 2, 1848, by Rev. L. Lewis	3	38
Antoinette S., of Southington, m. Henry L. **WELCH**, of Bristol, June 24, 1840, by Rev. Simon Shailor	1	137
Basinah, d. [Isaac], b. Nov. 10, 177[ ]* *(Probably "1777")	TR1	505
Elihu, s. [Isaac], b. Dec. 14, 1784	TR1	505
Isaac, Jr., s. Isaac, b. May 13, 1781	TR1	505
Levi, of Wolcott, m. Hannah **WARNER**, of Bristol, May 1, 1844, by Rev. Joseph S. Covill	3	16
Maria, d. Isaac, b. Jan. 14, 1775	TR1	505
Rhoda, d.[Isaac], b. July 29, 1779	TR1	505
Sarah, d. Isaac, b. May 5, 1776	TR1	505
HAMLIN, Maria, of Bristol, m. John **HITCHCOCK**, of Madison, N. Y., Oct. 28, 1849, by Rev. Lester Lewis	3	46
HANSON, John H., Rev. of New York City, m. Caroline A. **RICH**, of Bristol, Aug. 15, 1843, by Rev. Joseph S. Cowell	3	13
HARD, Justus P., m. Charlotte **BALDWIN**, May 16, 1826, by Jonathan Cone, V. D. M.	1	33

	Vol.	Page
HARKABUS, Rosesatte, owned by Samuel **ADAMS**, or his w.		
Elezebeth, was b. Sept. 1, 1782	TR1	1
HARKNESS, Hiram, m. Harriet E. **DAVIS**, b. of Bristol, Dec. 5,		
1852, by Rev. Stephen Rushmore	3	65
HARRISON, Epaphroditus, m. Mary **TREADWELL**, Mar. 17,		
1853, by William H. Goodrich	3	66
HART, Adna, of Burlington, m. Rosey Anne **YALE**, of Bristol,		
Feb. 5, 1821, by Rev. Jonathan Cone	1	4
Alma, d. Ambrose, b. Apr. 10, 1791	TR1	505
Amanda, m. Arel **HART**, b. of Bristol, Jan. 3, 1831, by		
Rev. H. Stanwood	1	66
Ambrose, Jr., s. Ambrose, b. Oct. 3, 1793	TR1	505
Amos Bushnell, [s. Ard & Amanda], b. May 10, 1832	2	27
Ard Benton, [s. Ard & Amanda], b. Apr. 6, 1836	2	27
Arel, m. Amanda **HART**, b. of Bristol, Jan. 3, 1831, by		
Rev. H. Stanwood	1	66
Caroline, m. Edward **GRAHAM**, b. of Bristol, May 7, 1843,		
by Rev. Samuel W. Smith	3	11
Cornelia M., of Bristol, m. George H. **LANGDON**, of		
Burlington, Apr. 20, 1834, by Erastus Scranton, V. D. M.	1	97
Cornelia Mercy, [d. Orrin & Eunice], b. Sept. 5, 1814	2	21
Cornelia Mercy, [d. Orrin & Eunice], b. Sept. 5, 1814	2	24
Emeline, m. Linus **WILCOX**, Feb. 13, 1825, by Rev. Jonathan		
Cone	1	26
Enos Ives, [s. Orrin & Eunice], b. Sept. 14, 1822	2	21
Enos Ives, [s. Orrin & Eunice], b. Sept. 14, 1822	2	24
Esther, d. Thomas, of Farmington, m. Zebulon **PECK**, Jr.		
Nov. 2, 1769; d. Oct. 27, 1777, in the 26th y. of her age	TR1	536
Esther Ann, m. Henry **LEWIS**, b. of Bristol, Apr. 3, 1853,		
by Rev. Lester Lewis	3	64
George, [s. Orrin & Eunice], b. Feb. 20, 1816	2	21
George, [s. Orrin & Eunice], b. Feb. 20, 1816	2	24
Harriet Ives, [twin with Henry Cowles], [d. Orrin & Eunice],		
b. Aug. 19, 1818	2	21
Harriet Ives, [twin with Henry Cowles, d. Orrin & Eunice],		
b. Aug. 19, 1818	2	24
Henry Cowles, [twin with Harriet Ives, s. Orrin & Eunice], b.		
Aug. 19, 1818	2	21
Henry Cowles, [twin with Harriet Ives, s. Orrin & Eunice],		
b. Aug. 19, 1818	2	24
James, m. Betsey **JOHNSON**, b. of Bristol, Jan. 1, 1821,		
by Rev. Jonathan Cone	1	3
Jane L., of Bristol, m. David O. **FULLERTON**, of New		
Haven, June 7, 1852, by Rev. W. H. Goodrich	3	61
Jason Harvilah, [s. Ard & Amanda], b. Feb. 20, 1834	2	27
Joel, m. Mrs. Mary **GREEN**, b. of Bristol, July 1, 1838,		
by Rev. Orsamus Allen	1	121
John, s. Ambrose, b. May 27, 1787	TR1	505

	Vol.	Page

HART, (cont.)

Julia P., m. Lauren **BYINGTON**, May 13, 1833, by Rev.
David L. Parmelee — 1 — 86

Lucy, d. Noadiah, b. June 21, 1786 — TR1 — 505

Lucy A., m. Elmore **YALE**, b. of Bristol, Apr. 16, 1843,
by S. W. Smith, Elder — 3 — 11

Marcus, m. Rhoda **WIERD**, d. Seth, Jan. 17, 1786 — TR1 — 494

Martin, s. Ambrose, b. June 10, 1783 — TR1 — 505

Melissa C., of Conn., m. Horatio V. **GATES**, of New York,
Oct. 29, 1854, by Rev. L. C. Cheeney — 3 — 71

Noadiah, m. Beulah **CLARK**, Sept. 25, 1785 — TR1 — 494

Orail, s. Ambrose, b. May 5, 1789 — TR1 — 505

Orrin, of Waterloo, N. Y., m. Lucina **GAYLORD**, of Bristol,
Jan. 7, 1844, by Rev. Henry Lownsbery — 3 — 15

Purlina S., of Bristol, m. Jesse B. **ROSE**, of Wolcott,
Apr. 15, 1840, by Rev. Aaron S. Hill — 1 — 135

Roswell, m. Phebe **JOHNSON**, June 27, 1820, by Rev.
Jonathan Coe — 1 — 1

Roxanna, of Bristol, m. George **ATWOOD**, of Milford, July
5, 1846, by Rev. A. S. Francis — 3 — 32

Sarah, d. Ambrose, b. Oct. 3, 1784 — TR1 — 505

Seth, of Bristol, m. Mrs. Charlotte **ORVIS**, of Harwinton,
July 1, 1839, by William Marks, J. P. — 1 — 129

Sylvester C., m. Paulina **NORTON**, Jan. 19, 1842, by Rev.
Orsamus Allen — 3 — 7

William Henry, [s. Ard & Amanda], b. Sept. 8, 1830 — 2 — 27

HATCH, Lucius, of Tolland, m. Sarah A. **DARROW**, of Bristol,
Sept. 26, 1841, by Rev. I. S. Ward — 3 — 3

HAUSST*, John Conrad, of Farmington, m. Dora Augusta **FUNCK**,
of Bristol, Oct. 16, 1851, by Rev. Lester Lewis *(Written
over "HAUFTER"?) — 3 — 55

HAWLEY, Ara, of Farmington, m. Mary **GREEN**, of Bristol, Apr.
16, 1845, by Rev. Edward Savage — 3 — 22

David, of Farmington, m. Adeline **RICH**, of Bristol, Feb. 6,
1832, by Rev. Noah Porter, of Farmington — 1 — 69

Flora M., of Burlington, m. Timothy **DUDLEY**, of Guilford,
Feb. 21, 1850, by Rev. Lester Lewis — 3 — 48

George, of Farmington, m. Emeline **LEE**, of Bristol, Feb.
12, 1827, by Jonathan Cone, V. D. M. — 1 — 37

George, m. Sarah **JEROME**, Apr. 7, 1840, by Rev. David L.
Parmelee — 1 — 135

Louisa A., m. Miles **SANFORD**, May 30, 1841, by Rev.
Orsamus Allen — 3 — 2

Lucy E., of Sandisfield, Mass., m. Hiram **BALL**, of Bristol,
Dec. 3, 1851, by Rev. Henry Fitch — 3 — 56

Lydia J., of Bristol, m. Pliny **HITCHCOCK**, of Springfield,
Mass., Apr. 4, 1832, by Rev. H. Stanwood — 1 — 70

Mary, d. Ebenezer, of Farmington, m. Zebulon **PECK**, Jr.,

	Vol.	Page
HAWLEY, (cont.)		
June 11, 1778	TR1	536
Nathan E., m. Mary Ann **BALL**, b. of Bristol, June 11,		
1851, by Rev. Henry Fitch	3	53
Roswell, of New Britain, m. Jane B. **RICH**, of Bristol,		
Sept. 13, 1853, by Rev. William H. Goodrich	3	67
HAYDEN, HAYDON, Hannah, of New Haven, m. George W.		
MATTHEWS, of Bristol, June 23, 1833, by Rev.		
Augustus Bolles	1	86
Mindwell, d. David, of Harwinton, m. Zebulon **PECK**, Jr.,		
May 21, 1794	TR1	536
HAYES, Charles R., of New Haven, m. Jane **THOMAS**, Feb. 11,		
1849, by Rev. Charles Chittenden	3	42
Milly I., of Hartland, m. Selah W. **NOTT**, of Bristol,		
June 15, 1851, by Rev. William H. Goodrich	3	53
HENDERSON, Jane Manerva, m. Samuel Emerson **ROOT**, b. of		
Bristol, Nov. 5, 1845, by R. H. Seely	3	25
HENDRICK, HENDRICKS, Eliza Ann, m. John **CHURCHILL**,		
Nov. 4, 1841, by Rev. C. D. Cowles	3	4
Horis, s. Abel, b. Mar. 8, 1792	TR1	505
John, m. Nancy **ATKINS**, b. of Bristol, Sept. 23, 1830,		
by Rev. Henry Stanwood	1	62
Lucy C., m. Robert C. **MANROSS**, b. of Bristol, May 11,		
1842, by Rev. C. D. Cowles, of Plainville	3	6
Mary, m. Horatio N. **SPERRY**, b. of Bristol, Mar. 23, 1836,		
by Rev. Orsamus Allen	1	104
Norman Barns, s. Abel, b. June 28, 1797	TR1	505
Wyllys, s. Abel, b. May 28, 1794	TR1	505
Wyllys, s. Abel, b. Mar. 8, 1800	TR1	505
HERBOLD, Henry, m. Catharine **IAGER**, Sept. 14, 1851, by Rev.		
William H. Goodrich	3	55
HILL, HILLS, Benjamin W., of Providence, R. I., m. Margaret		
D. **SMART**, of Bristol, May 18, 1836, by Rev. Orsamus		
Allen	1	106
Chauncy, Jr., of Farmington, m. Jemima **BRADLEY**, of		
Bristol, Apr. 13, 1824, by Rev. Jonathan Cone	1	23
Ely, of Hanover, Mass., m. Zelinda **WELCH**, of Bristol,		
Jan. 1, 1840, by Rev. Simon Shailer	1	133
Helen A., of Bristol, m. Jacob **STRICKLAND**, of New Britain,		
Jan. 19, 1848, by Rev. R. H. Seeley	3	37
Jane A., m. George H. **PARKER**, b. of Bristol, Apr. 10,		
1842, by Rev. Joseph S. Covell	3	5
Jane B., m. Edmund **PLUMB**, b. of Bristol, June 1, 1851,		
by Rev. Lester Lewis	3	54
Julia, m. Walter **KILBY**, b. of Hartford, Oct. 13, 1823, by Rev.		
Jonathan Cone	1	22
Lafayette, m. Ellen **CURTISS**, b. of Bristol, June 16, 1851, by		
Rev. William H. Goodrich	3	53

	Vol.	Page
HILL, HILLS, (cont.)		
Mary, m. William **BEACH**, Sept. 3, 1828, by Jonathan Cone, V. D. M.	1	46
Mary Ann, of Bristol, m. Alvah **WEST**, of Stafford, [ ], by Rev. Lester Lewis	3	50
Sally, m. Daniel **TUTTLE**, b. of Bristol, Nov. 26, 1822, by Rev. Jonathan Cone	1	17
Sarah, d. Darkiss **PARSONS**, b. July 15, 1792	TR1	507
William, of Troy, N. Y., m. Nancy **HOOKER**, of Bristol, Sept. 20, 1831, by Rev. Abner J. Leaven worth	1	67
HINMAN, Almira, of Bristol, m. Henry **DEMING**, of Woodbury, Dec. 20, 1829, by Rev. H. Stanwood	1	59
Daniel B., m. Sarah **ANDRUSS**, b. of Bristol, Oct. 13, 1825, by Rev. Daniel Wildman	1	30
Elvina, m. Philo **RICHARDSON**, b. of Bristol, July 15, 1829, by Rev. Henry Stanwood	1	53
H. Burton, m. Mary **CARRINGTON**, b. of Bristol, Nov. 11, 1835, by Rev. G. C. V. Eastman	1	103
Mary, m. Alphonso **BARNES**, Jan. 20, 1845, by R. H. Seely	3	21
Willys, of Plymouth, m. Olive **ATWATER**, of Bristol, Apr. 9, 1823, by Rev. Rodney Rossiter, of Plymouth	1	20
HINSDALE, HINDSALE, Emily, Mrs., m. Ira **MASON**, Apr. 4, 1822, by Rev. Jonathan Cone	1	14
Gilman, m. Ann **RICHARDS**, Sept. 10, 1840, by David L. Parmelee	1	139
Isaac O., of Burlington, m. Luanna B. **SPERRY**, of Bristol, Jan. 14, 1838, by Rev. Henry Husted	1	118
HITCHCOCK, Amanda, Mrs., of Bristol, m. Charles B. **WILDMAN**, of Danbury, Aug. 30, 1835, by Rev. Orsamus Allen	1	102
Asa, of Chesire, m. Thankfull **THORP**, of Bristol, Feb. 20, 1828, by Jonathan Cone, V. D. M.	1	44
James, of Bristol, m. Dorcas **BUNCE**, of Southington, Oct. 4, 1849, by Rev. Lester Lewis	3	46
John, of Madison, N. Y., m. Maria **HAMLIN**, of Bristol, Oct. 28, 1849, by Rev. Lester Lewis	3	46
Pliny, of Springfield, Mass., m. Lydia J. **HAWLEY**, of Bristol, Apr. 4, 1832, by Rev. H. Stanwood	1	70
HOLCOMB, HOLCOM, Mortimer D., m. Harriett N. **BUNNEL**, b. of Terryville, Oct. 3, 1852, by Rev. William H. Goodrich	3	62
Mortimer D., m. Harriet N. **BUNNELL**, Oct. 3, 1852, by Rev. William H. Goodrich	3	64
HOLMES, Enos, m. Mary E. **CARTER**, b. of Wethersfield, Sept. 4, 1842, by Rev. Joseph S. Covell	3	7
John, m. Elmina **HUBBARD**, Jan. 7, 1833, by Rev. David L. Parmelee	1	81
HOLT, Abigail, of Bristol, m. Ransom **SCARRET**, of Wolcott, Mar. 28, 1825, by Rev. Jonathan Cone	1	27

	Vol.	Page
HOLT, (cont.)		
Candanc M., of Bristol, m. William **NICKOLS**, of Middlebury,		
Mar. 22, 1835, by Rev. Orsamus Allen	1	99
Hiram H., of Harwinton, m. Alvira L. **BROOKS**, of Bristol,		
Nov. 8, 1846, by Rev. Henry V. Gardner, of Plymouth	3	29
Josiah, s. Vine & Susannah, b. Nov. 21, 1794	TR1	506
Mary Scofield, d. Vine & Susannah, b. Feb. 27, 1797	TR1	506
Mary Scofield, m. William **JOHNSON**, of Colchester, July		
6, 1821, by Rev. Orra Martin	1	8
Polly Ann, of Waterbury, m. Arden **HOTCHKISS**, Oct. 22,		
1847, by Rev. Lester Lewis	3	35
Samuel, m. Fanny J. **BARNES**, b. of Bristol, Dec. 26, 1830,		
by Rev. H. Stanwood	1	65
Samuel, m. Lydia **DAYTON**, b. of Bristol, Mar. 15, 1846,		
by Rev. A. S. Francis	3	27
Zilia, s. Vine, b. Jan. 18, 1800	TR1	506
HOOKER, Amy, of Bristol, m. Willard **GAYLORD**, of Goshen,		
Apr. 27, 1825, by Rev. Jonathan Cone	1	27
Bryan, m. Lydia **LEWIS**, Oct. 7, 1790	TR1	517
Bryan, m. Nancy **FULLER**, Oct. 7, 1804	TR1	517
Caroline, of Bristol, m. Cornelius R. **WILLIAMS**, of		
Wethersfield, Sept. 4, 1831, by Rev. Abner J.		
Leavenworth	1	66
Eliza Ann M., m. Anson L. **ATWOOD**, Nov. 18, 1840, by		
Rev. David L. Parmelee	1	141
Julia E., of Bristol, m. Andrew **STOUGHTON**, of Plymouth,		
Sept. 30, 1824, by Rev. Jonathan Cone	1	24
Lurena, m. George H. **MITCHELL**, Oct. 16, 1833, by Rev.		
David L. Parmelee	1	90
Lydia, w. Bryan, d. Apr. 20, 1804	TR1	517
Lydia L., [d. Bryan & Nancy], b. Aug. 8, 1805	TR1	517
Lydia Lewis, m. Cyrus Porter **SMITH**, Sept. 5, 1826, by		
Jonathan Cone, V. D. M.	1	35
Martha M., of Bristol, m. Henry N. **BIRD**, of Cincinnatti,		
O., July 28, 1851, by Merrill Richardson	3	55
Nancy, [d. Bryan & Nancy], b. July 24, 1809	TR1	517
Nancy, of Bristol, m. William **HILL**, of Troy, N. Y., Sept.		
20, 1831, by Rev. Abner J. Leavenworth	1	67
HOPKINS, Amy Ann, of New Haven, m. Orren **SMITH**, July 30,		
1843, by Edward Savage	3	13
HORE, Henry, of England, m. Elizabeth **ALLEN**, of Seedgoam,		
Eng., Nov. 15, 1849, by Rev. S. J. Evans	3	54
HORTON, Alfred, of Wolcott, m. Julian **NORTON**, of Bristol, July		
7, 1829, by Rev. Irenus Atkins, of Southington	1	54
Everett, m. Almira C. **ATWATER**, b. of Bristol, July 2, 1854,		
by Rev. Josiah T. Smith	3	70
Fanny, of Wolcott, m. Josiah **BARNS**, Jr., of Bristol, Feb. 27,		
1821, by Rev. Jonthan Cone	1	5

	Vol.	Page

HORTON, (cont.)

Leonard, of Wolcott, m. Nancy **GAYLORD**, of Bristol, June
    1, 1825, by Rev. Jonathan Cone — 1 — 28

Mary, m. Merit W. **ATKINS**, b. of Bristol, May 4, 1825, by
    Rev. Isaac Merriman — 1 — 27

Nancy R., m. Henry H. **PORTER**, May 1, 1832, by Rev.
    David S. Parmelee — 1 — 71

Phebe N., of Wolcott, m. John **NORTON**, of Bristol, Sept.
    22, 1833, by Rev. H. Stanwood — 1 — 89

Philander Cook, of Bristol, m. Catharine Hale **BRYON**,
    of New York City, July 19, 1847, by Rev. Harvey
    Husted — 3 — 34

Sarah A., m. Garry **ALLEN**, b. of Bristol, Oct. 16, 1853,
    by Rev. Lester Lewis — 3 — 67

Sybil, of Bristol, m. Isaac **BATES**, of Plymouth, Nov. 30,
    1840, by Rev. Joseph S. Covill — 1 — 143

William H., m. Charlotte A. **PARKER**, b. of Bristol, Apr.
    11, 1849, by Rev. Lester Lewis — 3 — 47

HOTCHKISS, Arden, m. Polly Ann **HOLT**, of Waterbury, Oct. 22,
    1847, by Rev. Lester Lewis — 3 — 35

Henry V. E., of Prospect, m. Elenor E. **BECKWITH**, of
    Bristol, July 10, 1849, by Rev. L. H. Pease — 3 — 44

Isaac, m. Lucy **BRADLEY**, b. of Bristol, Apr. 23, 1843, by
    Aaron C. Beach — 3 — 12

Jason, m. Almira **NORTON**, b. of Bristol, Oct. 29, 1823,
    by Jared W. Pardee, J. P. — 1 — 22

Josiah, of Farmington, m. Esther **CARRINGTON**, of Bristol,
    Feb. 19, 1827, by Jonathan Cone, V. D. M. — 1 — 37

Lavina, of Norfolk, m. Lucius **WILMOT**, of Burlington,
    Jan. 4, 1829, by Rev. Henry Stanwood — 1 — 48

HOUGH, Andrew, m. Hannah Ann **SPERRY**, Dec. 21, 1834, at the
    house of Mrs. Sperry, by Rev. G. C. V. Eastman — 1 — 97

Jane, m. Isaac H. **POTTER**, June 2, 1845, by R. H. Seely — 3 — 22

Julia H., of Bristol, m. Lewis A. **GOODSELL**, of Southington,
    Apr. 18, 1852, by Rev. William H. Goodrich — 3 — 60

Lucy M., of Wolcott, m. Isaac I. **HUBBARD**, of Meriden, Apr.
    23, 1846, by Aaron C. Beach — 3 — 28

Reuben, m. Ruth **LEWIS**, Jan. 1, 1812 — TR1 — 519

Sarah E., of Bristol, m. A. C. **BONFOEY**, of Haddam, July
    24, 1852, by Rev. William H. Goodrich — 3 — 62

Stanly Parmelee, [s. Reuben & Ruth], b. Jan. 15, 1814 — TR1 — 519

HOUSE, L. D., m. Ellen M. **IVES**, b. of Bristol, May 9, 1854,
    by Rev. W[illia]m H. Goodrich — 3 — 70

Otis, m. Ruth Ann **BOTSFORD**, Dec. 13, 1832, by Rev. David
    L. Parmelee — 1 — 81

HUBBARD, Elmina, m. John **HOLMES**, Jan. 7, 1833, by Rev.
    David L. Parmelee — 1 — 81

Esther J., m. Alfred **WAY**, Jan. 13, 1829, by Jonathan

	Vol.	Page
HUBBARD, (cont.)		
Cone, V. D. M	1	48
Isaac I., of Meriden, m. Lucy M. **HOUGH**, of Wolcott, Apr. 23, 1846, by Aaron C. Beach	3	28
Jerome B., of Haddam, m. Julia **DARROW**, of Bristol, May 31, 1848, by Rev. R. H. Seeley	3	39
HUBBELL, HUBBEL, Richard R., m. Amelia E. **ROBERT**, b. of Bristol, Oct. 26, 1851, by Rev. William H. Goodrich	3	59
Ruth L., m. Ralph E. **TERRY**, Oct. 9, 1844, by R. H. Seely	3	20
HUBBERT, Oscar, of Rochester, m. Almira A. **NORTON**, of Bristol, Sept. 26, 1841, by Rev. I. S. Ward	3	3
HUMPHREY, Adaline Julia, m. Rev. Orsamus **ALLEN**, b. of Bristol, July 12, 1835, by Rev. George Phippit, of Canton	1	101
Candace, d. Solomon, b. July 11, 1792	TR1	530
Clarrinda, d. Solomon, b. Feb. 18, 1789	TR1	530
Electa, d. Solomon, b. Feb. 28, 1799	TR1	530
Elizebeth, d. Giles, b. June 3, 1785	TR1	506
Flora, of Bristol, m. Asahel **WOODFORD**, of Farmington, Sept. 12, 1827, by Charles G. Ives, J. P.	1	41
Hannah, d. Solomon, b. Dec. 4, 1796	TR1	530
Harriet, d. Solomon, b. Feb. 28, 1803	TR1	530
Heman, s. Solomon, b. Mar. 26, 1779	TR1	530
Lucy, d. Solomon, b. Sept. 19, 1780	TR1	530
Luther, s. Solomon, b. Oct. 7, 1783	TR1	530
Lydia, d. Giles, b. Nov. 29, 1787	TR1	506
Lyman, s. Giles, b. Feb. 11, 1791	TR1	506
Merrils, of Bristol, m. Rachel **SNATH**, of Burlington, May 4, 1826, by Rev. Noah Porter, of Farmington	1	33
Naoma, d. Solomon, b. Sept. 28, 1794	TR1	530
Norman, s. Giles, b. May 17, 1781	TR1	506
Salley, d. Giles, b. Apr. 4, 1783	TR1	506
Sula, d. Giles, b. Aug. 1, 1794	TR1	506
HUNGERFORD, Benjamin, m. Idde **NEWELL**, d. Ens. David, Jan. 18, 1798	TR1	507
Benjamin, Jr., twin with Prudence, s. Benjamin, b. June 18, 1804	TR1	507
Benjamin, Jr., s. Benjamin, d. Sept. 22, 1804	TR1	507
Benjamin, [twin with Newell], b. Mar. 20, 1808	TR1	507
Benjamin, d. Mar. 4, 1814	TR1	507
Benjamin, m. Fanny **LEWIS**, May 13, 1832, by Rev. David S. Parmelee	1	71
Henry, s. Benjamin, b. Nov. 20, 1798	TR1	507
Kezia, d. Benjamin, b. Mar. 28, 1801	TR1	507
Kiziah, of Bristol, m. Timothy S. **WILLIAMS**, of Middletown, Dec. 24, 1826, by Jonathan Cone, V. D. M.	1	36
Leander, m. Janet **JONES**, b. of Bristol, probably Apr. 13, 1836, by G. C. V. Eastman	1	105
Leander G., of Bristol, m. Jennell **ANDRUS**, of Farmington,		

	Vol.	Page

HUNGERFORD, (cont.)

	Vol.	Page
Feb. 25, 1849, by Rev. Charles Chittenden	3	42
Louisa A., of Bristol, m. Lockwood **TUTTLE**, of Burlington,		
Feb. 1, 1846, by Rev. A. S. Francis	3	27
Newell, [twin with Benjamin], b. Mar. 20, 1808	TR1	507
Prudence, twin with Benjamin, Jr., d. Benjamin, b. June		
18, 1804	TR1	507
Zadah, m. James **LEE**, b. of Bristol, Oct. 15, 1826, by		
Jonathan Cone, V. D. M.	1	35

HUNT, Willard, of Bolton, m. Augusta L. **GRISWOLD**, of

	Vol.	Page
Plainville, June 19, 1849, by Rev. Charles Chittenden	3	44

HUSTED, Harvey, Rev., m. Almira **LEWIS**, b. of Bristol, June 4,

	Vol.	Page
1848, by Rev. Oliver Sykes	3	38

HYETT, Adeline, m. Milo **LEWIS**, Mar. 24, 1837, by Rev. David

	Vol.	Page
L. Parmelee	1	111

IAGER, Catharine, m. Henry **HERBOLD**, Sept. 14, 1851, by Rev.

	Vol.	Page
William H. Goodrich	3	55

IVES, Angelina, d. Charles G. [& Parthena], b. Mar. 20, 1807

	Vol.	Page
	TR1	530
Angeline, m. George W. **BARTHOLOMEW**, b. of Bristol,		
Jan. 13, 1829, by Rev. Aaron Pearce	1	49
Belinda, d. Lent, b. Dec. 31, 1791	TR1	509
Celestia, d. Joseph & Almenia, b. Nov. 25, 1809	TR1	530
Charles G., m. Parthena **RICH**, May 14, 1806	TR1	530
Charles G., Dea., d. May 7, 1867, ae 86 y.	TR1	530
Charles Granddason, s. Enos, b. Oct. 22, 1781	TR1	509
Charlotte S., m. George **GOODRICH**, May 21, 1828, by		
Luther Hart	1	58
Chauncy, s. Amasa, b. June 28, 1787	TR1	509
Elizabeth, of Bristol, m. Charles **LOCKWOOD**, of New		
Milford, Nov. 18, 1824, by Rev. Jonathan Cone	1	25
Ellen M., m. L. D. **HOUSE**, b. of Bristol, May 9, 1854,		
by Rev. W[illia]m H. Goodrich	3	70
Emaline, d. Moses, b. Sept. 1, 1802	TR1	509
Enos, Jr., s. Enos, b. May 21, 1793	TR1	509
Eunice, d. Enos, b. Mar. 11, 1780	TR1	509
Eveline S., m. Samuel B. **TUTTLE**, Apr. 7, 1835, by Rev.		
David L. Parmelee	1	99
Harriet, d. Charles G.[& Parthena], b. Dec. 30, 1810	TR1	530
Harriet A., [d. Joseph & Almenia], b. Sept. 15, 1816	TR1	530
Hennetta, [d. Joseph & Almenia], b. Oct. 6, 1812	TR1	530
Henriette, m. William B. **CARPENTER**, Nov. 6, 1834, by		
Rev. David L. Parmelee	1	96
Hiram, s. Moses, b. Nov. 8, 1799	TR1	509
Jared, s. Lent, b. Aug. 22, 1786	TR1	509
John, of Chesire, m. Leanora **TUTTLE**, of Bristol, Oct.		
27, 1842, by Rev. Joseph S. Covell	3	9
Joseph, m. Almenia **RICH**, Sept. 29, 1805	TR1	530
Keturah, d. Enos, b. Aug. 6, 1778, at Wallingford	TR1	509

	Vol.	Page
IVES, (cont.)		
Newton, s. Moses, b. Dec. 29, 1794	TR1	509
Ophelia Clarrissa, [d. Richard A. & Emaline], b. Jan. 26, 1827	2	25
Orrin, s. Enos, b. Sept. 1, 1797	TR1	509
Orren, m. Angeline **PECK**, Dec. 22, 1824, by Rev. Jonathan		
Cone	1	25
Philothela, d. Amasa, b. Apr. 12, 1790	TR1	509
Piera, d. Amasa, b. June 30, 1792	TR1	509
Porteus Rowlet, s. Joseph [& Almenia], b. Nov. 8, 1806	TR1	530
Richard A., m. Emeline **BECKWITH**, Aug. 18, 1825, by		
Jonathan Cone, V. D. M.	1	29
Romante, s. Moses, b. Feb. 13, 1797	TR1	509
Sarah, d. Enos, b. Sept. 24, 1789	TR1	509
Shaler, s. Amasa, b. July 4, 1785	TR1	509
Thelus, s. Lent, b. Feb. 17, 1789	TR1	509
Theron, m. Martha A. **BOARDMAN**, Sept. 11, 1838, by Rev.		
David L. Parmelee	1	122
JACKSON, Andrew, of Mass., m. Harriet Malissa **CHURCH**, of		
Bloomfield, Sept. 23, 1849, by Rev. Lester Lewis	3	45
Sybel, of Farmington, m. Charles **PETERSON**, of New Haven,		
Nov. 20, 1830, by Noah Porter, of Farmington	1	65
JEROME, Ann J., of Bristol, m. J. D. **RHOADES**, of Wethersfield,		
June 17, 1838, by Rev. Orsamus Allen	1	120
Augusta I., of Bristol, m. James W. **MUNROE**, of Warren,		
May 16, 1852, by Rev. W. H. Goodrich	3	61
Candace, m. Samuel W. **ALLEN**, Oct. 5, 1840, by Rev. David		
L. Parmelee	1	140
Constantine, m. Lucy E. **DEAN**, b. of Bristol, Jan. 9, 1854,		
by Rev. W[illia]m H. Goodrich	3	70
Juliana H., m. Samuel **PARDEE**, June 15, 1825, by Jonathan		
Cone, V. D. M.	1	28
Lott, m. Sylvia **CARRINGTON**, b. of Bristol, Jan. 3, 1821,		
by Rev. Jonathan Cone	1	3
Noble, m. Fanny **PECK**, Dec. 11, 1823, by Rev. Jonathan		
Cone	1	23
Sarah, m. George **HAWLEY**, Apr. 7, 1840, by Rev. David L.		
Parmelee	1	135
Thomas, m. Mrs. Ruth **TAYLOR**, b. of Bristol, Feb. 18,		
1823, by Rev. Jonathan Cone	1	20
JEWETT, Plina A., M. D., of New Haven m. Juliet M.		
CARRINGTON, of Bristol, Nov. 10, 1847, by Rev.		
Joseph H. Nichols	3	37
JOHNSON, Betsey, m. James **HART**, b. of Bristol, Jan. 1, 1821,		
by Rev. Jonathan Cone	1	3
Calvin, of Farmington, m. Isabel **LARDNER**, of Bristol,		
Dec. 24, 1849, by Rev. S. J. Evans	3	48
Chelsea, s. Chanler, b. Jan. 15, 1792	TR1	510
Cordelia, of Wolcott, m. Garry **ALLEN**, of Bristol, Nov. 25,		

	Vol.	Page
JOHNSON, (cont.)		
1832, by Rev. Henry Stanwood	1	82
Cornelia, of New Haven, m. William H. **LEWIS**, of Bristol,		
Mar. 1, 1852, by Rev. William H. Goodrich	3	59
Daniel, Jr., s. Daniel, b. Oct. 21, 1795	TR1	509
Dennis, s. Amos & Eunice, b. Aug. 14, 1790	TR1	509
Eli, of Lyons, N. Y., m. Betsey **BALDWIN**, of Bristol,		
Sept, 17, 1827, by Jonathan Cone, V. D. M.	1	42
Elizabeth, d. Daniel, b. Oct. 27, 1792	TR1	509
Elizabeth, Mrs., m. Capt. Jesse **GAYLORD**, b. of Bristol,		
July 3, 1821, by Rev. Jonathan Cone	1	7
Esther, d. Daniel, b. Apr. 18, 1786	TR1	509
Hannah, of Plymouth, m. Ebenezer **PRITCHARD**, of		
Waterbury, Oct. 27, 1830, by Rev. H. Stanwood	1	63
Jerusha, d. Daniel, b. Apr. 16, 1790	TR1	509
Jerusha, Mrs., m. John **BIRGE**, Nov. 18, 1844, by R. H. Seely	3	19
Josiah, s. Chanler, b. May 23, 1787	TR1	510
Julia, of Bristol, m. Asahel **LEE**, of Lebanon, Jan. 25,		
1822, by Rev. Jonathan Cone	1	14
Julia, of Plymouth, m. David **SHERMAN**, of Bristol, June		
29, 1829, by Rev. Henry Stanwood	1	53
Julia, of Bristol, m. James **SCARRITT**, of Wolcott, May		
31, 1843, by Edward Savage	3	12
Lorree, d. Chanler, b. June 21, 1789	TR1	510
Mary Ann, m. Francis S. **LOBB**, b. of Bristol, May 3, 1837,		
by Rev. Joseph S. Covill	1	113
Phebe, m. Roswell **HART**, June 27, 1820, by Rev. Jonathan		
Coe	1	1
Raphel, s. Chanler, b. Mar. 4, 1785	TR1	510
Sharmon, s. Daniel, b. Mar. 5, 1782	TR1	509
Wealthy, m. Miles F. **ALLEN**, b. of Bristol, Dec. 25, 1836,		
by Rev. Orsamus Allen	1	112
William, s. Amos, b. Oct. 4, 1793	TR1	516
William, of Colchester, m. Mary Scofield, **HOLT**, July 6,		
1821, by Rev. Orra Martin	1	8
Zaroiah, d. Daniel, b. Dec. 7, 1783	TR1	509
JONES, Aurilla, of Bristol, m. Cynus **CATHERWAY**, of Hartford,		
Aug. 1, 1822, by Rev. Isaac Marriman	1	15
Daniel, m. Phebe **LEWIS**, Feb. 12, 1840, by Rev. David L.		
Parmelee	1	134
Janet, m. Leander **HUNGERFORD**, b. of Bristol, probably		
Apr. 13, 1836, by G. C. V. Eastman	1	105
John, of East Windsor, m. Harriet E. **DOLBEAR**, of Montville,		
June 16, 1844, by R. H. Seely	3	17
JUDD, Horace H., of Farmington, m. Maria **BYINGTON**, of Bristol,		
May 8, 1822, by Rev. Jonathan Cone	1	15
Loring F., of New Britain, m. Josephine **LEE**, of Bristol,		
May 19, 1842, by Rev. Joseph S. Covell	3	5

	Vol.	Page

JUDD, (cont.)

Martin, of Avon, m. Jane **WINTHERBURY**, of Ohio, Dec. 2, 1849, by Rev. Lester Lewis — 3 — 46

Oliver, m. Emily A. **LEWIS**, Apr. 15, 1839, by Rev. David L. Parmelee — 1 — 128

Walter A., m. Elorretta A. **BLAKESLEE**, b. of New Britain, Mar. 30, 1854, by Rev. William H. Goodrich — 3 — 70

JUDSON, Orrin, of Plymouth, m. Annah **GAYLORD**, of Bristol, Mar. 24, 1825, by Rev. Isaac Merriam — 1 — 26

Rebeca, of Bristol, m. Justus R. **LOOMIS**, of Torrington, Feb. 24, 1833, by Irenus Atkins — 1 — 82

KEARNEY, Hugh, m. Mrs. Amanda **MARKS**, (alias **BROOKS**), b. of Torrington, Oct. 22, 1822, by Rev. Jonathan Cone — 1 — 16

KELSEY, Hannah S., of Bristol, m. Charles E. **CLARK**, of Great Bend, N. Y., Apr. 22, 1852, by Rev. William H. Goodrich — 3 — 60

Pinney, of Bloomfield, m. Hannah **TUTTLE**, of Bristol, June 1, 1843, by Edward Savage — 3 — 13

KEYS, Daniel W., of Russia, N. Y., m. Jane E. **STEELE**, of Bristol, July 26, 1853, by Rev. Lester Lewis — 3 — 66

KILBOURN, Henry H., m. Mary M. **STEELE**, b. of Bristol, Apr. 30, 1851, by Rev. William H. Goodrich — 3 — 55

KILBY, Walter, m. Julia **HILLS**, b. of Hartford, Oct. 13, 1823, by Rev. Jonathan Cone — 1 — 22

KILLPATRICK, Elihu, of Washington Cty., Miss., m. Mrs. Jerusha A. **THOMPSON**, of Bristol, Aug. 11, 1848, by Rev. Lester Lewis — 3 — 40

KINNEY, Sally, m. Benjamin **BARNES**, Sept. 12, 1837, by Harvey Husted — 1 — 116

LANE, Rodney, m. Sarah M. **CLARK**, Sept. 30, 1844, by R. H. Seely — 3 — 20

LANGDON, Asahel, m. Mamre **LOWREY**, Oct. 3, 1827, by Jonathan Cone, V. D. M. — 1 — 43

George H., of Burlington, m. Cornelia M. **HART**, of Bristol, Apr. 20, 1834, by Erastus Scranton, V. D. M. — 1 — 97

Julia Ann, m. Moses **PECKINGHAM**, b. of Bristol, Sept. 30, 1829, by Rev. Henry Stanwood — 1 — 57

Perry, of Southington, m. Mrs. Lucy **MORSE**, of Bristol, June 18, 1851, by Rev. William H. Goodrich — 3 — 53

LARDNER, Daniel S., m. Jane E. **RICHARDS**, b. of Bristol, Sept. 20, 1848, by Rev. R. H. Seeley — 3 — 45

Isabel, of Bristol, m. Calvin **JOHNSON**, of Farmington, Dec. 24, 1849, by Rev. S. J. Evans — 3 — 48

LARKIN, Julia Ann, of Bristol, m. Jason **WATTON**, of South Coventry, Jan. 5, 1834, by Rev. H. Stanwood — 1 — 93

Lemuel, m. Abigail **MATTHEWS**, b. of Bristol, June 27, 1833, by Rev. H. Stanwood — 1 — 87

Levi T., m. Delia **RIBBY**, Aug. 9, 1827, by Jonathan Cone, V. D. M. — 1 — 41

	Vol.	Page
LEACH, Abel S., of Torrington, m. Caroline **GILLET**, of		
Windsor, June 5, 1822, by Rev. Isaac Merriam	1	19
LEDWELL, Rachel, m. Abner **BECKWITH**, June 23, 1800	TR4	519
LEE, Asahel, of Lebanon, m. Julia **JOHNSON**, of Bristol, Jan.		
25, 1822, by Rev. Jonathan Cone	1	14
Charles, s. William, b. May 29, 1785	TR1	510
Elizabeth, d. William, m. Seth **BARNES**, Jan. 10, 1798	TR1	508
Emeline, of Bristol, m. George **HAWLEY**, of Farmington,		
Feb. 12, 1827, by Jonathan Cone, V. D. M.	1	37
James, m. Zadah **HUNGERFORD**, b. of Bristol, Oct. 15, 1826,		
by Jonathan Cone, V. D. M.	1	35
Josephine, of Bristol, m. Loring F. **JUDD**, of New Britain,		
May 19, 1842, by Rev. Joseph S. Covell	3	5
Nelson, m. Bristol, m. Abbe **WHITMAN**, of Southington, Oct.		
5, 1820, by Rev. Jonathan Coe	1	1
Silence, m. Henry **FENN**, Oct. 11, 1832, by Rev. David L.		
Parmelee	1	77
LEWIS, Addin C., of Southington, m. Esther Eliza **GOLDSMITH**,		
of Plymouth, Apr. 23, 1849, by Rev. S. J. Evens	3	43
Almira, m. Rev. Harvey **HUSTED**, b. of Bristol, June 4, 1848,		
by Rev. Oliver Sykes	3	38
Amy, of Bristol, m. Theodore **BARNARD**, of Hartford, Feb.		
6, 1823, by Rev. Jonathan Cone	1	19
Anson, s. Samuell, b. Apr. 17, 1784	TR1	510
Charles, s. Samuell, b. June 4, 1780	TR1	510
Chancy, s. Samuel, b. Feb. 8, 1775	TR1	510
Clarrissa M., of Bristol, m. John S. **BURWELL**, of New		
Hartford, Sept. 23, 1849, by Rev. Lester Lewis	3	45
Edward, m. Sylvia **RICHARDS**, May 7, 1821, by Noah		
Porter, V. D. M.	1	10
Edward, of Wolcott, m. Jennet **WIGHTMAN**, of Southington,		
Nov. 24, 1828, by Rev. Irenus Atkins, of Southington	1	47
Edwin N., m. Lucinda **CURTISS**, Nov. 27, 1833, by Rev.		
David L. Parmelee	1	92
Edwin S., m. Mary A. **TUTTLE**, Nov. 4, 1830, by Rev. Abner		
J. Leavenworth	1	63
Electa, m. Newell **BYINGTON**, Aug. 15, 1837, by Rev. David		
L. Parmelee	1	115
Emily A., m. Oliver **JUDD**, Apr. 15, 1839, by Rev. David		
L. Parmelee	1	128
Ezekiel Thompson, s. Samuel, b. May 31, 1771	TR1	510
Fanny, m. Benjamin **HUNGERFORD**, May 13, 1832, by Rev.		
David S. Parmelee	1	71
Frederick, s. Enos. b. Mar. 13, 1787	TR1	510
Henry, m. Esther Ann **HART**, b. of Bristol, Apr. 3, 1853,		
by Rev. Lester Lewis	3	64
Ira, of Bristol, m. Laura **ANDRUS**, of Southington, Jan.		
10, 1822, by Rev. Jonathan Cone	1	13

	Vol.	Page

LEWIS, (cont.)

James, of Southington, m. Sophia **CLARKE**, of Bristol,
Oct. 4, 1826, by Jonathan Cone, V. D. M. — 1 — 35

James C., m. Mary Jane **CASE**, b. of Bristol, Sept. 13,
1852, by Rev. N. Whiting, of Bloomfield — 3 — 62

Jane, of Southington, m. Seth **WINCHELL**, of Bristol, Apr.
14, 1850, by Rev. Harvey Camp — 3 — 49

Janet, m. Phineas **CURTISS**, June 15, 1842, by Merritt
Richardson — 3 — 6

Julia A., of Bristol, m. Charles F. **COY**, of Munson, Mass.,
July 30*, 1847, by Rev. R. H. Seeley *(Probably "13th") — 3 — 34

Katherine Hecocks, d. Samuell, b. Mar. 5, 1778 — TR1 — 510

Laura Ann, m. Gilbert **PENFIELD**, May 6, 1845, by R. H.
Seely — 3 — 22

Lydia, m. Bryan **HOOKER**, Oct. 7, 1790; d. Apr. 20, 1804 — TR1 — 517

Milo, m. Adeline **HYETT**, Mar. 24, 1837, by Rev. David L.
Parmelee — 1 — 111

Nathaniel C., of Wolcott, m. Lucy N. **ADAMS**, of Bristol,
Apr. 18, 1823, by Rev. Jonathan Cone — 1 — 20

Phebe, m. Daniel **JONES**, Feb. 12, 1840, by Rev. David L.
Parmelee — 1 — 134

Ruth, m. Reuben **HOUGH**, Jan. 1, 1812 — TR1 — 519

Sabra, d. Enos, b. June 3, 1791 — TR1 — 510

Sabrina, d. Enos, b. Aug. 31, 1795 — TR1 — 510

Samuel, m. Elinor **THOMPSON**, Jan. 17, 1770 — TR1 — 494

Thomas, of Wolcott, m. Semanthy **SEELY**, of Waterbury, Nov.
16, 1842, by Rev. Joseph S. Covell — 3 — 9

Trumah, s. Samuel, b. Nov. 21, 1772 — TR1 — 510

William H., of Bristol, m. Cornelia **JOHNSON**, of New Haven,
Mar. 1, 1852, by Rev. William H. Goodrich — 3 — 59

LOBB, Francis S., m. Mary Ann **JOHNSON**, b. of Bristol, May 3,
1837, by Rev. Joseph S. Covill — 1 — 113

LOCKWOOD, Charles, of New Milford, m. Elizabeth **IVES**, of
Bristol, Nov. 18, 1824, by Rev. Jonathan Cone — 1 — 25

LOOMIS, Henry, m. Chloe **STEELE**, Sept. 7, 1825, by Jonathan
Cone, V. D. M. — 1 — 29

Justus R., of Torrington, m. Rebeca **JUDSON**, of Bristol,
Feb. 24, 1833, by Irenus Atkins — 1 — 82

LOVELAND, Lewis, m. Huldah A. **BEACH**, b. of Plymouth, last
evening, [Apr. 19, 1835], by Jeremiah Rice, J. P., at his
house — 1 — 100

LOVELL, Malinda, m. Warren A. **GRIFFIN**, b. of Bristol, Sept. 17,
1848, by Rev. L. Lewis — 3 — 40

LOWREY, Anna, d. Samuell, b. Oct. 5, 1796 — TR1 — 510

David, s. Samuel, b. Sept. 14, 1786 — TR1 — 510

Isaac, s. Samuell, b. Mar. 14, 1781 — TR1 — 510

Lois, d. Samuell, b. Sept. 30, 1783 — TR1 — 510

Lydia, d. Samuell, b. Feb. 9, 1791 — TR1 — 510

	Vol.	Page

LOWREY, (cont.)

Mamre, m. Asahel **LANGDON**, Oct. 3, 1827, by Jonathan
    Cone, V. D. M.   1   43

Mark, s. Samuell, b. July 14, 1798   TR1   510

Richard, s. Samuel, b. July 27, 1776   TR1   510

Roswell, s. Samuell, b. Aug. 4, 1793   TR1   510

Samuell, Jr., s. Samuell, b. Aug. 25, 1778   TR1   510

Sarah, d. Samuell, b. Jan. 17, 1789   TR1   510

LUM, William, of Derby, m. Catharine **BRAINARD**, of Bristol,
    Feb. 7, 1827, by Rev. Rodney Rossiter, of Plymouth   1   39

McCLARY, Silas Coolidge, of Michigan, m. Sarah **DOOLITTLE**,
    of New Haven, Aug. 11, 1850, in Trinity Church, by Rev.
    Harry Croswell, of New Haven   3   50

McCRACKEN, William, m. Susan C. **BRAINARD**, Feb. 12, 1838,
    by Rev. David L. Parmelee   1   119

MACK, John C., m. Jane E. **AVERY**, Nov. 21, 1849, by Rev.
    Lester Lewis   3   46

McKEE, Celista, Mrs. of Bristol, m. Miller **FISH**, of Bloomfield,
    Nov. 13, 1842, by S. W. Smith, Elder   3   8

McKNIGHT, John F., m. Cynthia A. **PETTIBONE**, Oct. 30, 1836,
    by Rev. David L. Parmelee   1   108

McTHEY, Electa, of Bristol, m. Lecister **SMITH**, of Plymouth,
    July 31, 1823, by Rev. Jonathan Cone   1   22

MALLORY, Catharine, of Bristol, m. Heman **WHITE**, of
    Montgomery, Ala., Oct. 17, 1842, by Rev. Joseph S.
    Covell   3   8

David S., m. Antoinette M. **CLARK**, May 7, 1840, by Rev.
    David L. Parmelee   1   136

MALTBY, Ephraim S., m. Cynthia **MIX**, Mar. 25, 1840, by David
    L. Parmelee   1   134

MANFORD, Betsey, of Danbury, m. Julius **CARRINGTON**, of
    Bristol, July 21, 1844, by Edward Savage   3   18

MANROSS, [see also **MUNROE**], Angeline, of Bristol, m. John
    BRADLEY, of Chesire, Sept. 1, 1845, by Rev. William
    Wright, of Farmington   3   24

Elisha, of Bristol, m. Maria **COWLES**, of Southington,
    [Jan.] 29, 1821, by Rev. Jonathan Cone   1   4

Hannah, m. Samuel **PECK**, June 9, 1791   TR4   530

Hannah, m. Samuel **PECK**, June 9, 1791   2   10

Robert C., m. Lucy C. **HENDRICK**, b. of Bristol, May 11,
    1842, by Rev. C. D. Cowles, of Plainville   3   6

MARKLAND, Mary, of Bristol, m. Asahel **ROOT**, of Farmington,
    Mar. 20, 1849, by Rev. Lester Lewis   3   47

MARKS, Amanda, alias **BROOKS**, Mrs., of Torrington, m. Hugh
    KEARNEY, b. of Torrington, Oct. 22, 1822, by Rev.
    Jonathan Cone   1   16

MARSH, Irrom, of Northfield, m. Evaline **ROPER**, of Bristol,
    Oct. 7, 1841, by Rev. Joseph S. Covell   1   144

	Vol.	Page
MARSH, (cont.)		
T., of Northfield, m. Evaline **ROPER**, of Bristol, Oct.		
7, 1841, by Rev. Joseph S. Covell	3	3
MARTIN, Ebenezer, [s. Orra & Polly Smith], b. Apr. 18, 1820	2	8
Emelia, [w. Orra], d. Jan. 8, 1817	2	8
Emelia, w. Rev. Orra, d. Jan. 8, 1817	TR4	529
George Phelps, s. Orra & Emelia, b. Jan. 7, 1817	TR4	529
George Phelps, [s. Orra & Emelia], b. Jan. 7, 1817	2	8
Julius Mitchell, [s. Orra & Polly Smith], b. Sept. 26, 1818	2	8
Orra, of Windsor, m. Emelia **PHELPS**, of Simsbury, Nov.		
15, 1815, at Simsbury, by Rev. Elisha Cushman, Hartford	TR4	529
Orra, of Windsor, m. Emelia **PHELPS**, of Simsbury, Nov.		
15, 1815, at Simsbury, by Rev. Elisha Cushman	2	8
Orra, m. Polly Smith **MITCHELL**, Sept. 10, 1817	2	8
Samuel Augustus, s. Elder Orra [& Polly Smith], b. Aug.		
21, 1822	2	8
MASON, Ira, m. Mrs. Emily **HINSDALE**, Apr. 4, 1822, by Rev.		
Jonathan Cone	1	14
Ruth Frisbie, [d. Ira & Emila], b. July 12, 1823	2	22
Ruth Ann, [d. Ira & Emila], b. July 11, 1825	2	22
MATTHEWS, MATHEWS, MATTHEW, Abigail, m. Lemuel		
LARKIN, b. of Bristol, June 27, 1833, by Rev. H.		
Stanwood	1	87
Bela, s. John, b. July 12, 1791	TR1	511
Belinda, d. Caleb, Jr., b. Oct. 12, 1801	TR1	512
Belinda, d. Caleb, Jr., d. Apr. 21, 1805, ae 3 y. 6 m. 9 d.	TR1	512
Betsey, d. John, b. Dec. 26, 1788	TR1	511
Betsey, m. Ira **CHURCHILL**, Jr., b. of Bristol, Nov. 27,		
1822, by Rev. Jonathan Cone	1	17
Caleb, Jr., m. Sarah **NEWELL**, d. David, Jan. 22, 1794	TR1	511
Caleb Newell, s. Caleb, Jr., b. Oct. 20, 1796	TR1	512
Clarisse, d. Abel, b. Oct. 16, 1787	TR1	511
Edwin, m. Emily M. **GRANT**, Apr. 4, 1832, by Rev. David		
S. Parmelee	1	69
Eliza, m. Harrison **ELWELL**, July 9, 1845, by R. H. Seeley	3	23
Elleh, d. John, b. Nov. 19, 1785	TR1	511
George W., of Bristol, m. Hannah **HAYDEN**, of New Haven,		
June 23, 1833, by Rev. Augustus Bolles	1	86
Henry, of Bristol,m. Ollivia **PARDEE**, of Southington,		
Sept. 9, 1838, by Orsamus Allen	1	123
Horatio Nelson, s. Caleb, Jr., b. Mar. 29, 1799	TR1	512
Lavinia, m. James **GLASSON**, b. of Bristol, formerly of		
England, Jan. 30, 1848, by Rev. Joseph H. Nichols	3	37
Lois, d. John, b. Sept. 7, 1783	TR1	511
Mary Ann, of Bristol, m. Henry Egbert **REED**, of Plymouth,		
May 1, 1849, by Rev. S. J. Evens	3	43
Mahitabel, d. John, b. July 28, 1794	TR1	511
Merriman, m. Ann **PENFIELD**, b. of Bristol, Jan. 9, 1853,		

	Vol.	Page
MATTHEWS, MATHEWS, MATTHEW, (cont.)		
by Rev. Henry Fitch	3	63
Orra, of Bristol, m. Leicester C. WELTON, of Harwinton,		
Oct. 28, 1845, by Rev. Joseph S. Covill	3	25
Phebe R., of Bristol, m. Wilson SHELDON, of Branford,		
Oct. 17, 1830, by Rev. H. Stanwood	1	63
Polly A., of Bristol, m. Almerin SANFORD, of Hamden, Oct.		
10, 1832, by Rev. Henry Stanwood	1	76
Sarah, d. Caleb, Jr., b. Dec. 9, 1794	TR1	512
MEACHAM, Dianthe, d. Jeremiah, b. Sept. 18, 1791	TR1	511
Jeremiah, Jr., s. Jeremiah, b. Dec. 6, 1792	TR1	511
Mariah, d. Jeremiah, b. Mar. 27, 1795	TR1	511
Marilla, d. Jeremiah, b. Feb. 28, 1797	TR1	511
Rhoda, d. Jeremiah, b. Aug. 31, 1788	TR1	511
Roxana, d. Jeremiah, b. Dec. 14, 1789	TR1	511
MELANATHAN, Thomas T., of Bristol, m. Abigail BENHAM, of		
New Hartford, May 1, 1850, by Rev. Lester Lewis	3	49
MERRILL, Daniel, of Canton, m. Lydia RICHARDS, of Bristol,		
Mar. 30, 1830, by Rev. Noah Porter, of Farmington	1	60
MERRIMAN, MERRIAM, Asahel, s. Josiah, b. June 27, 1803	TR1	512
Caroline N. I., of Bristol, m. Roswell STONE, of Warren, O.,		
[Sept.] 16, 1822, by Rev. Jonathan Cone	1	16
Eli I., m. Jennet BARTHOLOMEW, May 8, 1833, by Rev.		
David L. Parmelee	1	85
George E., m. Almira Ann PECK, Nov. 20, 1832, by Rev.		
David L. Parmelee	1	79
James E., of Meriden, m. Jane Ellen BUNNEL, of Waterbury,		
Mar. 9, 1851, by Rev. Henry Fitch	3	52
Jonathan, s. Isaac & Mary, b. July 28, 1825	2	23
Lydia, m. Elizur PLATT, b. of Bristol, Apr. 25, 1825,		
by Rev. Daniel Wildman	1	28
Martha Ann, of Southington, m. Edward H. RUSSEL, of		
Wolcott, Dec. 17, 1827, by Irenus Atkins	1	45
Titus, Dr., m. Mrs. Katharine THORP, May 3, 1827, by		
Jonathan Cone, V. D. M.	1	39
MILLARD, Calvin, of Bristol, m. Mrs. Sarah WARFIELD, of		
Springfield, Sept. 1, 1841, by Charles G. Ives, J. P.	3	3
MILLER, Ebenezer, s. Rev. Jonathan, b. Oct. 23, 1799	TR1	511
Elizabeth, d. Rev. Jonathan, b. Feb. 16, 1796	TR1	511
Experience, d. Rev. Jonathan, b. Aug. 3, 1783	TR1	511
Jonathan Gaylord, s. Rev. Jonathan, [b.] Aug. 22, 1790	TR1	511
Ruel, s. Rev. Jonathan, b. Feb. 4, 1794	TR1	511
Sophia, d. Rev. Jonathan, b. July 12, 1787	TR1	511
Sophia, d. Rev. Jonathan, m. Richard PECK, June 28, 1815,		
at Burlington, by Rev. Mr. Miller	TR1	522
MILLS, Forrest W., m. Sarah CHURCHILL, b. of Bristol, Apr.		
3, 1823, by Rev. Jonathan Cone	1	21
Revilo, m. Chloe NORTON, May 2, 1837, by Rev. David L.		

	Vol.	Page
MILLS, (cont.)		
Parmelee	1	113
MITCHELL, George H., m. Lurena **HOOKER,** Oct. 16, 1833, by		
Rev. David L. Parmelee	1	90
Julius R., m. Drucilla **WELCH,** Jan. 21, 1845, by Rev.		
Edward Savage	3	21
Mariette, m. Austin **WOODIN,** b. of Bristol, Dec. 6, 1829,		
by Rev. Henry Stanwood	1	58
Polly Smith, m. Orra **MARTIN,** Sept. 10, 1817	2	8
MIX, Asahel, s. Ashbel, b. Nov. 12, 1795	TR1	512
Ashbel, Jr., s. Ashbel, b. May 15, 1801	TR1	512
Cynthia, m. Ephraim S. **MALTBY,** Mar. 25, 1840, by David		
L. Parmelee	1	134
Elisha, of Terrysville, m. Amelia **EDMONDS,** of Bristol,		
July 10, 1843, by Rev. Merrill Richardson, Int. Pub.	3	14
Lyman, s. Ashbel, b. July 19, 1797	TR1	512
Martha E., of Bristol, m. Hiram H. **FENN,** of Jersey City,		
July 28, 1851, by Irenus Atkins	3	57
Minerva, m. Isaac **MUZZY,** Jr., b. of Bristol, Nov. 23,		
1823, by Rev. Jonathan Cone	1	23
Minerva Hannah, d. Ashbel, b. Apr. 28, 1805	TR1	512
Nancy, of Bristol, m. Ira **FOOT,** of Burlington, Dec. 25,		
1822, by Rev. Jonathan Cone	1	18
Nancy Chloe, d. Ashbel, b. Dec. 25, 1793	TR1	512
Noble, s. Ashbel, b. Oct. 1, 1798	TR1	512
MONROE, MUNROE, [see also **MANROSS**], James W., of		
Warren, m. Augusta I. **JEROME,** of Bristol, May 16,		
1852, by Rev. W. H. Goodrich	3	61
MOORE, Almira A., m. Nathaniel **CRAMER,** b. of Bristol, May		
28, 1837, by Rev. Harvey Husted	1	114
L. A., of Harwinton, m. S. E. **GREEN,** of Bristol, May 3,		
1848, by Rev. L. Lewis	3	38
MORGAN, William I., m. D. Adelaide **DOWNS,** b. of Bristol, June		
6, 1853, by Rev. Henry Fitch	3	66
MORSE, Annis J., formerly of Avon, m. Adin **PIPPLES,** formerly		
of Glastenbury, Nov. 19, 1844, by Tracy Peck, J. P.	3	20
Lucy, Mrs., of Bristol, m. Perry **LANGDON,** of Southington,		
June 18, 1851, by Rev. William H. Goodrich	3	53
Willis, m. Lois **SCOVILL,** b. of Plymouth, Jan. 6, 1830,		
by Abner J. Leavenworth	1	59
MOSES, Richard, m. Rachel **NORTON,** Apr. 19, 1836, by Rev.		
David L. Parmelee	1	104
MUNSON, Horace, of Plymouth, m. Betsy **BENHAM,** of Bristol,		
Sept. 11, 1839,. by F. B. Woodward	3	5
MURPHY, Abigail, Mrs., m. Milo **TERRY,** Sept. 20, 1838, by Rev.		
David L. Parmelee	1	123
Benjamin, of East Hartford, m. Abigail **PARSONS,** of Bristol,		
Dec. 8, 1830, by Rev. Abner J. Leavenworth	1	64

	Vol.	Page
MUZZY, Hannah M., m. Josiah **PIERCE**, May 2, 1848, by Rev. R. H. Seeley	3	38
Isaac, Jr., m. Minerva **MIX**, b. of Bristol, Nov. 23, 1823, by Rev. Jonathan Cone	1	23
Jane C., m. Hiram J. **SPELLMAN**, Oct. 2, 1845, by R. H. Seely	3	24
NEALE, NEAL, Esther, m. Voluntine **WIGHTMAN**, b. of Southington, May 2, 1842, by Rev. James Squire	3	7
Harriet, of Southington, m. Ambrose **PRATT**, of Ashford, May 5, 1850, by Rev. Lester Lewis	3	50
Roswell A., of Springfield, N. Y., m. Eunice **ATKINS**, of Bristol, Apr. 14, 1846, by Edward Savage	3	28
NETTLETON, Eliza Ann, m. Franklin W. **GAYLORD**, Sept. 10, 1839, by Rev. David L. Parmelee	1	130
Wilford H., m. Harriet N. **TUTTLE**, b. of Bristol, June 9, 1847, by Rev. R. H. Seeley	3	33
NEWELL, Eliza, of Bristol, m. Edward **BARNS**, of Addison, Vt., Oct. 5, 1830, by Rev. Noah Porter, of Farmington	1	62
Franklin, m. Mary S. **BRISTOL**, Nov. 11, 1840, by Rev. David L. Parmelee	1	140
Idde, d. Ens. David, m. Benjamin **HUNGERFORD**, Jan. 18, 1798	TR1	507
Samuel P., m. Martha J. **BREWSTER**, Oct. 10, 1854, by Rev. William H. Goodrich	3	71
Sarah, d. David, m. Caleb **MATTHEWS**, Jr., Jan. 22, 1794	TR1	511
William H., of Chesire, m. Amanda P. **BLAKESLEE**, of Bristol, May 30, 1848, by Rev. R. H. Seely	3	39
NICHOLS, NICKOLS, David, of Middlebury, m. Mrs. Sylvia **POGUE**, of Bristol, Jan. 6, 1835, by Tracy Peck, J. P.	1	98
Horace W., of Waterbury, m. Abigail H. **SCARRITT**, of Bristol, Jan. 2, 1831, by Rev. H. Stanwood	1	65
Orra C., m. Sheldon S. **NORTON**, b. of Bristol, Aug. 5, 1838, by Rev. James D. Chapman, of Wolcott	1	121
William, of Middlebury, m. Candanc M. **HOLT**, of Bristol, Mar. 22, 1835, by Rev. Orsamus Allen	1	99
NOON, Edward, of Bristol, m. Susannah **STONE**, of Litchfield, Jan. 2, 1853, by Rev. Lester Lewis	3	63
NORTH, Cornelia N., of Bristol, m. Abiram S. **ATWOOD**, of Woodbury, Jan. 1, 1846, by Rev. A. S. Francis	3	27
Loomis, m. Ann E. **RICH**, May 17, 1852, by Rev. William H. Goodrich	3	61
NORTON, Adaline, m. George D. **ATWATER**, Aug. 15, 1832, by Rev. David L. Parmelee	1	74
Almira, m. Jason **HOTCHKISS**, b. of Bristol, Oct. 29, 1823, by Jared W. Pardee, J. P.	1	22
Almira A., of Bristol, m. Oscar **HUBBERT**, of Rochester, Sept. 26, 1841, by Rev. I. S. Ward	3	3
Angelina, m. Lucius **ATWATER**, Jr., b. of Bristol, Oct. 11,		

	Vol.	Page
NORTON, (cont.)		
1820, by Rev. Jonathan Coe	1	2
Asahel H., Jr., m. Mary **BYINGTON**, b. of Bristol, Apr. 2, 1827, by Henry Stanwood	1	38
Augustin, m. Calista **BYINGTON**, b. of Bristol, May [ ], 1849, by Rev. L. H. Pease	3	43
Augustus, m. Nancy **TREAT**, Nov. 20, 1839, by Rev. Orsamus Allen	1	138
Catharine R., m. John M. **THOMAS**, Jan. 31, 1844, by R. H. Seely. Int. Pub. Jan. 28, 1844	3	15
Chloe, m. Revilo **MILLS**, May 2, 1837, by Rev. David L. Parmelee	1	113
Cornelia, of Bristol,m. Luther **ADAMS**, of Waterbury, Nov. 20, 1851, by Rev. W. H. Goodrich	3	59
Daniel E., m. Emily **ALLEN**, b. of Bristol, Aug. 19, 1832, by Rev. Henry Stanwood	1	75
Eliza, [d. Ezra & Sylvia], b. Jan. 15, 1804	TR1	513
Eliza, [d. Ezra & Sylvia], b. Jan. 15, 1804	2	12
Ezra, m. Harriet **SMITH**, b. of Bristol, Feb. 19, 1821, by Rev. Orra Martin	1	5
Francis B., of Southington, m. Mary S. **BLAKESLEE**, of Bristol, Jan. 1, 1852, by Rev. Lester Lewis	3	57
Frisbie R., of Plymouth, m. Lois R. **BLAKESLEE**, of Bristol, Jan. 5, 1834, by Rev. H. Stanwood	1	93
Hannah, m. Lorenzo **BOTSFORD**, b. of Bristol, June 16, 1842, by Rev. Orsamus Allen	3	7
Harriet, [d. Ezra & Sylvia], b. Nov. 25, 1806	TR1	513
Harriet, [d. Ezra & Sylvia], b. Nov. 25, 1806	2	12
Harriett, m. Henry **GRIDLEY**, Sept. 9, 1840, by Rev. David L. Parmelee	1	139
Harriet E., Mrs., m. Munson **WILCOX**, b. of Bristol, Apr. 18, 1847, by Rev. Lester Lewis	3	34
Helen, [d. Ezra & Sylvia], b. Apr. 19, 1812; d. Nov. [ ], 1812	TR1	513
Helen, [d. Ezra & Sylvia], b. Apr. 19, 1812; d. Nov. [ ], 1812	2	12
Hiram, m. Flora **YALE**, b. of Bristol, Nov. 24, 1831, by Charles G. Ives, J. P.	1	68
Jane, [d. Ezra & Sylvia], b. Nov. 29, 1814	TR1	513
Jane, [d. Ezra & Sylvia], b. Nov. 29, 1814	2	12
Jane J., of Bristol, m. Leveret C. **AUSTIN**, of Waterbury, Oct. 23, 1835, by Rev. Orsamus Allen	1	103
Jerusha I., m. Austin **SANFORD**, Mar. 10, 1833, by Rev. David L. Parmelee	1	83
John, of Bristol, m. Phebe N. **HORTON**, of Wolcott, Sept. 22, 1833, by Rev. H. Stanwood	1	89
Julian, of Bristol, m. Alfred **HORTON**, of Wolcott, July 7, 1829, by Rev. Irenus Atkins, of Southington	1	54
Leander B., m. Martha **BARNES**, b. of Bristol, Dec. 28, 1845, by Rev. Orsamus Allen	1	26

	Vol.	Page
NORTON, (cont.)		
Leonard, of Bristol, m. Martha **DEWEY**, of Chesire, Aug.		
8, 1847, by Rev. Lester Lewis	3	35
Margaret F., m. Erastus **BLAKESLEE**, Oct. 17, 1832, by Rev.		
David L. Parmelee	1	77
Mark, of Bristol, m. Rhoda **BARNES**, of Plymouth, May 21,		
1832, by Rev. H. Stanwood	1	70
Miles F., of Bristol, m. Lydia **GRANNISS**, of Southington,		
Oct. 12, 1831, by Rev. H. Stanwood	1	67
Nancy Pierce, [d. Salmon & Sally], b. Apr. 16, 1804	TR1	513
Oswald K., m. Lois D. **CARRINGTON**, b. of Southington,		
Aug. 24, 1829, by Rev. Irenus Atkins, of Southington	1	56
Paulina, m. Sylvester C. **HART**, Jan. 19, 1842, by Rev.		
Orsamus Allen	3	7
Porter A., m. Mary **TODD**, b. of Bristol, Sept. 18, 1828,		
by Rev. Henry Stanwood	1	46
Rachel, m. Richard **MOSES**, Apr. 19, 1836, by Rev. David		
L. Parmelee	1	104
Rhoda A., m. Lyman G. **BRADLEY**, June 28, 1840, by Rev.		
David L. Parmelee	1	137
Salmon, m. Sally **PIERCE**, d. Abraham, Nov. 16, 1800	TR1	513
Salome, [d. Salmon & Sally], b. Feb. 3, 1806	TR1	513
Sarah, of Bristol, m. Thomas **WILDMAN**, of Danbury, Oct.		
8, 1821, by Rev. Daniel Wildman	1	10
Sheldon S., m. Orra C. **NICHOLS**, b. of Bristol, Aug. 5,		
1838, by Rev. James D. Chapman, of Wolcott	1	121
Thomas, [s. Ezra & Sylvia], b. Jan. 7, 1809	TR1	513
Thomas, [s. Ezra & Sylvia], b. Jan. 7, 1809	2	12
NOTT, Edward, m. Mary F. **ROPER**, of Bristol, Mar. 30, 1847,		
by Rev. R. H. Seely	3	31
Julius, m. Rachel **COOK**, Oct. 29, 1844, by R. H. Seely	3	20
Selah W., of Bristol, m. Milly I. Hayes, of Hartland,		
June 15, 1851, by Rev. William H. Goodrich	3	53
OAKLY, Junius, of Winsted, m. Mary Ann **ATKINS**, of Bristol,		
Sept. 19, 1852, by Rev. Lester Lewis	3	63
ODGERS, Richard, m. Mary Ann **OULDS**, b. of England, Apr. 23,		
1850, by Rev. S. J. Evans	3	49
OLMSTED, Julius A., of Canton, m. Salome **TUTTLE**, of		
Plymouth, Nov. 17, 1843, by Edward Savage	3	14
Salome, of Plymouth, m. William **FARNSWORTH**, of New		
Hartford, Jan. 17, 1853, by Rev. Lester Lewis	3	64
ORVIS, Charlotte, Mrs. of Harwinton, m. Seth **HART**, of Bristol,		
July 1, 1839, by William Marks, J. P.	1	129
OSBORN, Samuel, m. Hannah **EDDY**, b. of Bristol, Jan. 2, 1853,		
by Rev. Henry Fitch	3	63
OULDS, Mary Ann, m. Richard **ODGERS**, b. of England, Apr. 23,		
1850, by Rev. S. J. Evans	3	49
PALMER, Maria, m. Phillip **POND**, b. of Bristol, Mar. 13, 1843,		

	Vol.	Page
PALMER, (cont)		
by Rev. Orsamus Allen	3	10
Stephen F., Gen. of Ashford, m. Statira H. **USHER**, of		
Hartford, June 18, 1827, by Jonathan Cone, V. D. M	1	40
PARDEE, Czrena Elizabeth, of Bristol, m. Asa Champion		
RUSSELL, of Great Barrington, Mass., Aug. 25, 1840,		
by Joseph S. Covell	1	142
Jared W., Dr., d. Jan. 9, 1867, ae 75 y.	TR1	523
Laura Ann, of Bristol, m. Amos **PARSONS**, of Longmeadow,		
Mass., Jan. 2, 1842, by Rev. Harvey D. Ketchel	3	4
Ollivia, of Southington, m. Henry **MATTHEWS**, of Bristol,		
Sept. 9, 1838, by Rev. Orsamus Allen	1	123
Samuel, m. Juliana H. **JEROME**, June 15, 1825, by Jonathan		
Cone, V. D. M.	1	28
PARKER, Albert J., of Wallingford, m. Rachel S. **THORP**, of		
North Haven, Sept. 20, 1846, by Edward Savage	3	29
Charlotte A., m. William H. **HORTON**, b. of Bristol, Apr.		
11, 1849, by Rev. Lester Lewis	3	47
George H., m. Jane A. **HILLS**, b. of Bristol, Apr. 10,		
1842, by Rev. Joseph S. Covell	3	5
Hannah A., m. Abner **TUTTLE**, May 27, 1838, by Rev. David		
L. Parmelee	1	120
Jane A., of Bristol, m. Charles G. **WIGHTMAN**, of		
Philadelphia, Apr. 10, 1854, by Irenus Atkins	3	68
PARKHURST, C., of Springfield, Mass., m. Emily A. **BAILEY**, of		
Harwinton, Oct. 11, 1846, by Rev. Edward Savage	3	29
PARLIN, Samuel, of Action, Mass., m. Lucy **ROYCE**, of Wolcott,		
Jan. 2, 1832, by Rev. Henry Stanwood	1	68
PARMELEE, PARMELE, Clarissa, m. John E. **TUBBS**, b. of New		
Britain, Jan. 11, 1852, by Rev. Henry Fitch	3	58
Ialla, m. Cephas **CONE**, June 19, 1826, by Luther Hart	1	34
Samuel, of New Britain, m. Amelia H. **SHEPHERD**, of		
Bristol, Jan. 11, 1852, by Rev. Henry H. Fitch	3	57
PARSONS, Abigail, of Bristol, m. Benjamin **MURPHY**, of East		
Hartford, Dec. 8, 1830, by Rev. Abner J. Leavenworth	1	64
Amos, of Longmeadow, Mass., m. Laura Ann **PARDEE**, of		
Bristol, Jan. 2, 1842, by Rev. Harvey D. Ketchel	3	4
Berkley D., m. Jenett **COWLES**, Jan. 2, 1850, by Rev.		
Merrill Richardson	3	48
Darkiss, had d. Sarah **HILLS**, b. July 15, 1792	TR1	507
Harvy Prichard, s. Darias, b. Mar. 9, 1787	TR1	514
Levi, of Southington, m. Ann **FENTON**, of Plymouth, July		
29, 1829, by Rev. Irenus Atkins, of Southington	1	54
Merina A., m. Ebenezer W. **STRONG**, Dec. 22, 1841, by		
Merrill Richardson	3	4
PAYNE, Henrietta, of Burlington, m. George **DOWNS**, of Bristol,		
Jan. 3, 1849, by Rev. S. J. Evans	3	41
Stephen Johnson, of Prospect, m. Mary **ROSE**, of Wolcott,		

	Vol.	Page
PAYNE, (cont.)		
May 2, 1841, by Rev. Parmele Chamberlin	3	2
PEARKS, Mabel, m. Ephrim **BEARD,** Aug. 6, 1789	TR1	494
PECK, Abby Miller, [d. Richard & Sophia], b. Dec. 12, 1818	TR1	522
Abel Gaylord, [s. Samuel & Hannah], b. June 8, 1807	TR4	530
Abel Gaylord, [s. Samuel & Hannah], b. June 8, 1807	2	10
Adine, of Bristol, m. Elisha J. **THOMPSON,** of Southington,		
Apr. 30, 1843, by Irenus Atkins	3	11
Almira Ann, m. George E. **MERRIMAN,** Nov. 20, 1832, by		
Rev. David L. Parmelee	1	79
Ambrose, m. Maria P. **DEWEY,** Mar. 29, 1846, by R. H.		
Seely	3	26
Amia, d. Caleb, b. Feb. 28, 1792	TR1	514
Amia, w. Caleb, d. Dec. 7, 1795, in the 35th y. of her age	TR1	514
Angelina, [d. Samuel & Hannah], b. May 28, 1799	TR4	530
Angelina, [d. Samuel & Hannah], b. May 28, 1799	2	10
Angeline, m. Orren **IVES,** Dec. 22, 1824, by Rev.		
Jonathan Cone	1	25
Annar, d. Caleb, b. Sept. 14, 1789	TR1	514
Anthony, s. Zebulon, & Mary, b. Mar. 19, 1786	TR1	535
Aurelious, of Burlington, m. Mary **BRACKETT,** of Bristol,		
Feb. 8, 1821, by Datus Ensign, Elder	1	4
Avaristo, of Burlington, m. Mary J. **YALE,** of Bristol,		
Mar. 26, 1846, by Edward Savage	3	30
Betsey, d. Lycias, b. Apr. 8, 1794	TR1	514
Beulah, d. Zebulon & Esther, b. Mar. 12, 1774	TR1	535
Beulah, d. Zebulon & Esther, d. Dec. 1, 1786, in the		
13th y. of her age	TR1	536
Bulah, d. Zebulon & Mary, b. Mar. 23, 1789	TR1	535
Eliza Jane, [d. Tracy & Sally], b. Aug. 19, 1828	TR1	521
Eliza Jane, d. Tracy & Sally, d. July 17, 1847, ae 19 y.	TR1	524
Elizabeth Gaylord, [d. Richard & Sophia], b. Nov. 14, 1816	TR1	522
Emila, [d. Samuel & Hannah], b. Apr. 21, 1797	TR4	530
Emila, [child of Samuel & Hannah], b. Apr. 21, 1797	2	10
Emila, 2nd, [child of Samuel & Hannah], b. Mar. 9, 1805	TR4	530
Emila, 2nd, [child of Samuel & Hannah], b. Mar. 9, 1805	2	10
Emily, m. Anson **BECKWITH,** July 25, 1825, by Jonathan		
Cone, V. D. M.	1	29
Ephaphroditus, s. Lement [& Rachel], b. Oct. 26, 1791	TR1	534
Epaphroditus, s. [Tracy & Sally], b. Nov. 13, 1812	TR1	521
Esther, w. Zebulon, Jr., d. Oct. 27, 1777, in the 26th		
y. of her age	TR1	536
Esther, d. Zebulon & Mary, b. Apr. 7, 1781	TR1	535
Fanny, m. Noble **JEROME,** Dec. 11, 1823, by Rev. Jonathan		
Cone	1	23
Fayette Monroe, [s. Sylvester & Fanny], b. Jan. 22, 1822	2	11
Francis Newman, s. Newmah & Sarah, b. July 21, 1830	2	26
Henry Adams, [s. Tracy & Sally], b. July 26, 1832	TR1	521

	Vol.	Page
PECK, (cont.)		
Isaac, s. Zebulon & Esther, b. Nov. 23, 1771	TR1	535
James Goreham, s. Lement [& Rachel], b. June 24, 1800;		
d. Apr. 12, 1874, ae 74 y.	TR1	534
Joseph Adams, [s. Tracy & Sally], b. Oct. 9, 1820	TR1	521
Joseph Adams, [s. Tracy & Sally], d. Dec. 4, 1822, ae 26 m.	TR1	521
Joseph Adams, [s. Tracy & Sally], b. Feb. 18, 1824	TR1	521
Josiah T., m. Ellen S. **BARNARD**, b. of Bristol, Nov. 23,		
1847, by Rev. R. H. Seeley	3	36
Josiah Tracy, [s. Tracy & Sally], b. Aug. 3, 1826	TR1	521
Kezia, [d. Tracy & Sally], b. Nov. 25, 1834	TR1	521
Lement, m. Rachel **TRASCY**, Sept. 23, 1782	TR1	534
Levi N., of Cheshire, m. Esther Ann **TODD**, of Plymouth,		
Nov. 6, 1836, by Rev. Joseph S. Covill	1	110
Loma, d. Zebulon & Mary, b. June 4, 1784	TR1	535
Lydia, d. Lycias, b. Apr. 11, 1788	TR1	514
Mary, [twin with Zebulon], d. Zebulon & Mary, b. Mar.		
24, 1779	TR1	535
Mary, d. Zebulon & Mary, d. Mar. 30, 1779, in the 1st		
y. of her age	TR1	536
Mary, w. Zebulon, Jr., d. Nov. 18, 1791, in the 45th y.		
of her age	TR1	536
Miles, s. Caleb, b. June 17, 1784, at Woodbridge, Soc. of		
Bathany; moved to Bristol, 1785	TR1	514
Nancy, d. Lycias, b. Feb. 23, 1792	TR1	514
Nehemiah, s. Lement [& Rachel], b. Sept. 26, 1793	TR1	534
Newman, s. Lement [& Rachel], b. Nov. 25, 1795	TR1	534
Ozias, m. Harriet A. **POND**, Nov. 8, 1832, by Rev. David		
L. Parmelee	1	78
Polly, d. Lycias, b. Feb. 27, 1796	TR1	514
Rachel, d. Lement [& Rachel], b. Dec. 25, 1797	TR1	534
Rachel, of Bristol, m. Israel **RUSSELL**, of Middletown, Jan.		
31, 1827, by Jonathan Cone, V. D. M.	1	36
Rachel R., of Bristol, m. Charles **BRONSON**, of Waterbury,		
July 25, 1848, by Rev. Charles Chittenden	3	39
Rachel Ripley, [d. Tracy & Sally], b. Sept. 27, 1818	TR1	521
Richard, s. Lement [& Rachel], b. Dec. 15, 1786	TR1	534
Richard, m. Sophia **MILLER**, d. Rev. Jonathan, June 28, 1815,		
at Burlington, by Rev. Mr. Miller	TR1	522
Roxani, d. Zebulon & Esther, b. Apr. 14, 1770	TR1	535
Sally, d. Caleb, b. Apr. 1, 1782, at the town of New Haven,		
Parish of Bathany; moved to Bristol, 1785	TR1	514
Sally, of Bristol, m. Capt. Allen **BUNNEL**, of Plymouth,		
Oct. 3, 1822, by Rev. Jonathan Cone	1	16
Sally Hannah Selden, [d. Tracy & Sally], b. Mar. 17, 1815;		
d. Dec. 9, 1815	TR1	521
Samuel, m. Hannah **MANROSS**, June 9, 1791	TR4	530
Samuel, m. Hannah **MANROSS**, June 9, 1791	2	10

	Vol.	Page
PECK, (cont.)		
Samuel, [s. Samuel & Hannah], b. June 10, 1801	TR4	530
Samuel, [s. Samuel & Hannah], b. June 10, 1801	2	10
Samuel, 2nd, [s. Samuel & Hannah], b. May 3, 1803	TR4	530
Samuel, 2nd, [s. Samuel & Hannah], b. May 3, 1803	2	10
Samuel, m. Harriet **BARTHOLOMEW**, Mar. 14, 1827, by		
Jonathan Cone, V. D. M.	1	38
Sanson, s. Caleb, b. May 1, 1787	TR1	514
Sarah, d. Lement [& Rachel], b. Feb. 7, 1784	TR1	534
Sarah T., m. Charles E. **SMITH**, Sept. 26, 1839, by Rev.		
David L. Parmelee	1	132
Sarah Tracy, [d. Tracy & Sally], b. Nov. 5, 1816	TR1	521
Silas, s. Zebulon & Esther, b. Mar. 30, 1776	TR1	535
Silva, d. Zebulon & Mary, b. July 23, 1782	TR1	535
Silva, d. Zebulon & Mary, d. Mar. 12, 1794, in the 12th		
y. of her age	TR1	536
Sophia M., m. Charles **ROOT**, b. of Bristol, Dec. 20, 1843,		
by R. H. Seely. Int. Pub. Dec. 17, 1843	3	15
Susannah, d. Lement [& Rachel], b. Aug. 31, 1788	TR1	534
Sylvester, [s. Samuel & Hannah], b. Aug. 12, 1794	2	10
Sylvester, [s. Samuel & Hannah], b. Aug. 12, 1794	TR4	530
Tracy, s. Lement [& Rachel], b. Apr. 5, 1785	TR1	534
Tracy, m. Sally **ADAMS**, d. Joseph, Feb. 3, 1812, at		
Litchfield, by Rev. Lyman Beecher	TR1	521
Tracy & Sally, had s. [ ], b. July 6, 1822; d. July 12, 1822	TR1	521
Tracy, Jr., [s. Tracy & Sally], b. May 24, 1838	TR1	521
Tracy, d. Feb. 12, 1862, ae 76 y. 10 m. 7 d.	TR1	524
William, [s. Samuel & Hannah], b. Dec. 27, 1809	TR4	530
William, [s. Samuel & Hannah], b. Dec. 27, 1809	2	10
Zebulon, Jr., m. Esther **HART**, d. Thomas, of Farmington,		
Nov. 2, 1769	TR1	536
Zebulon, Jr., m. Mary **HAWLEY**, d. Ebenezer, of Farmington,		
June 11, 1778	TR1	536
Zebulon, [twin with Mary], s. Zebulon & Mary, b. Mar.		
24, 1779	TR1	535
Zebulon, Jr., m. Mindwell **HAYDON**, d. David, of Harwinton,		
May 21, 1794	TR1	536
PECKHAM, Moses, m. Thankfull **GAYLORD**, Mar. 26, 1823, by		
Rev. Jonathan Cone	1	21
PECKINGHAM, Moses, m. Julia Ann **LANGDON**, b. of Bristol,		
Sept. 30, 1829, by Rev. Henry Stanwood	1	57
PEMBLETON, Mary Frances, of Southington, m. Nelson **DAVIS**,		
of Bristol, Dec. 19, 1850, by Henry A. Mitchell, J. P.	3	52
PENFIELD, Ann, m. Merriman **MATTHEW**, b. of Bristol, Jan. 9,		
1853, by Rev. Henry Fitch	3	63
Gilbert, m. Laura Ann **LEWIS**, May 6, 1845, by R. H. Seely	3	22
PERKINS, Beecher, of Woodbridge, m. Julia Ann **BLAKESLEE**,		
of Bristol, Oct. 18, 1832, by Rev. Henry Stanwood	1	78

	Vol.	Page
PERKINS, (cont.)		
Caroline M., of Bristol, m. Willis S. **STONE**, of Burlington, Nov. 17, 1852, by Rev. Stephen Rushmore	3	65
Elias, 2nd, m. Nancy **BOTSFORD**, b. of Bristol, Dec. 4, 1827, by Rev. Noah Porter	1	44
Polly M., of Bristol, m. Ransom A. **DUNBAR**, of Wolcottville, Aug. 20, 1837, by Rev. Harvey Husted	1	116
Ursula, m. Elbridge **WIGHTMAN**, b. of Bristol, June 17, 1829, by Rev. Henry Stanwood	1	52
PERRY, Julia B., m. Horace **GRAY**, b. of Bristol, June 26, 1854, by Rev. Josiah T. Smith	3	69
PETERSON, Charles, of New Haven, m. Sybel **JACKSON**, of Farmington, Nov. 20, 1830, by Noah Porter, of Farmington	1	65
PETTIBONE, PETTEBONE, Abraham, m. Amelia **SMITH**, May 21, 1778	TR1	514
Abraham, Jr., s. Abraham [& Amelia], b. Apr. 21, 1781	TR1	514
Abraham, 3rd, s. Capt. Abraham, Jr., b. Apr. 24, 1781	TR1	500
Abraham, m. Huldah **PRINDLE**, of Harwinton, Mar. 23, 1797	TR1	514
Amelia, 2nd, d. Abraham [& Amelia], b. Nov. 7, 1791	TR1	514
Amelia, 2nd, d. Abraham [& Amelia], d. Mar. 8, 1794	TR1	514
Amelia, w. Abraham, d. May 19, 1796, in the 38th y. of her age	TR1	514
Casal, s. Abraham [& Amelia], b. Apr. 19, 1793	TR1	514
Cynthia A., m. John F. **McKNIGHT**, Oct. 30, 1836, by Rev. David L. Parmelee	1	108
Foris, s. Abraham [& Amelia], b. May 13, 1796	TR1	514
PHELPS, Emelia, of Simsbury, m. Orra **MARTIN**, of Windsor, Nov. 15, 1815, at Simsbury, by Rev. Elisha Cushman, Hartford	TR4	529
Emelia, of Simsbury, m. Orra **MARTIN**, of Windsor, Nov. 15, 1815, at Simsbury, by Rev. Elisha Cushman	2	8
John, Jr., m. Sarah Ann **YOUNG**, July 8, 1832, by Rev. David S. Parmelee	1	72
PICKET, Caroline, m. William **WESTON**, b. of Bristol Jan. 29, 1853, by Rev. Stephen Rushmore	3	65
PIERCE, Edward N., m. Henrietta L. **THOMPSON**, Oct. 23, 1837, by Rev. David L. Parmelee	1	117
Elizabeth, m. Titus **PIERCE**, Sept. 18, 1839, by Rev. David L. Parmelee	1	132
Josiah, m. Hannah M. **MUZZY**, May 2, 1848, by Rev. R. H. Seeley	3	38
Juliaett, m. Theodore **TERRY**, b. of Bristol, Mar. 24, 1830, by Rev. A. J. Leavenworth	1	60
Julius E., of Bristol, m. Huldah **BOTSFORD**, of Meriden, May 30, 1849, by Rev. Lester Lewis	3	47
Sally, d. Abraham, m. Salmon **NORTON**, Nov. 16, 1800	TR1	513
Sophronia, of Bristol, m. Jared **GOODRICH**, of Glastonbury,		

	Vol.	Page
PIERCE, (cont.)		
Nov. 10, 1839, by Rev. Simon Shailer	1	133
Titus, m. Elizabeth **PIERCE**, Sept. 18, 1839, by Rev.		
David L. Parmelee	1	132
PIPPLES, Adin, of Glastenbury, m. Annis J. **MORSE**, of Avon,		
Nov. 19, 1844, by Tracy Peck, J. P.	3	20
PLATT, Alanson S., m. Esther W. **DARROW**, Nov. 19, 1840, by		
Rev. David L. Parmelee	1	141
Elizur, m. Lydia **MERRIMAN**, b. of Bristol, Apr. 25, 1825,		
by Rev. Daniel Wildman	1	28
Melissa, of Bristol, m. William **BATES**, of Watertown,		
Sept. 3, 1829, by Rev. Henry Stanwood	1	57
PLUMB, Celestia I., of Wolcott, m. Calvin **BROCKETT**, of Bristol,		
Apr. 14, 1844, by Edward Savage	3	16
Edmund, m. Jane B. **HILLS**, b. of Bristol, June 1, 1851,		
by Rev. Lester Lewis	3	54
Romantee Orlando, of Wolcott, m. Eliza **GRIDLEY**, of Bristol,		
Jan. 27, 1825, by Rev. Jonathan Cone	1	26
POGUE, Sylvia, Mrs. of Bristol, m. David **NICHOLS**, of		
Middlebury, Jan. 6, 1835, by Tracy Peck, J. P.	1	98
William, of Albany, N. Y., m. Sylvia **CLARK**, of Southington,		
Feb. 12, 1829, by Rev. Henry Stanwood	1	50
POMEROY, Harriet, Mrs., m,. Edwin O. **GOODWIN**, b. of Bristol,		
Sept. 13, 1848, by Rev. R. H. Seeley	3	45
John R., m. Mary J. **BROWN**, b. of Bristol, May 18, 1836,		
by Rev. Orsamus Allen	1	106
POND, Alexander, m. Lydia **GAYLORD**, Apr. 6, 1834, by Rev.		
David L. Parmelee	1	95
Harriet A., m. Ozias **PECK**, Nov. 8, 1832, by Rev. David		
L. Parmelee	1	78
Phillip, m. Maria **PALMER**, b. of Bristol, Mar. 13, 1843,		
by Rev. Orsamus Allen	3	10
Sarah, m. Seth **FOSTER**, Apr. 30, 1833, by Rev. David L.		
Parmelee	1	85
POPE, David, m. Jane **GLASSON**, of Bristol, Apr. 14, 1850, by		
Rev. William H. Goodrich	3	49
PORTCH, John, of Bristol, m. Eliza **WILSON**, of Hartford, Apr.		
2, 1847, by Rev. R. H. Seely	3	32
PORTER, Curtis, of Farmington, m. Emma **UPSON**, of Bristol,		
Dec. 21, 1828, by Rev. Irenus Atkins, of Southington	1	47
Henry H., m. Nancy R. **HORTON**, May 1, 1832, by Rev.		
David S. Parmelee	1	71
POTTER, Isaac H., m. Jane **HOUGH**, June 2, 1845, by R. H. Seely	3	22
Jane P., m. Lysander M. **BUNNELL**, b. of Plymouth, Feb. 17,		
1849, by Rev. S. J. Evens	3	42
Minerva, m. Charles **DeFOREST**, Aug. 9, 1835, by Rev.		
Chester W. Turner	1	101
Pardon, m. Olive **COWLES**, June 13, 1833, by Rev.		

	Vol.	Page
POTTER, (cont.)		
David L. Parmelee	1	87
Tertius D., of Plymouth, m. Esther B. **FRISBIE**, of Bristol,		
Jan. 30, 1828, by Jonathan Cone, V. D. M.	1	44
PRATT, Ambrose, of Ashford, m. Harriet **NEALE**, of Southington,		
May 5, 1850, by Rev. Lester Lewis	3	50
PRINDLE, Huldah, of Harwinton, m. Abraham **PETTEBONE**, Mar.		
23, 1797	TR1	514
PRITCHARD, PRICHARD, Abigail, of Waterbury, m. Leander S.		
BLAKESLEE, of Bristol, Oct. 6, 1838, by Rev. H.		
Stanwood	1	90
Ebenezer, of Waterbury, m. Hannah **JOHNSON**, of Plymouth,		
Oct. 27, 1830, by Rev. H. Stanwood	1	63
Edward, of Waterbury, m. Elmina **BALL**, of Bristol, Nov.		
25, 1847, by Rev. Joseph H. Nichols	3	37
Luther, m. Almera A. **TODD**, Sept. 8, 1833, by Rev. David		
L. Parmelee	1	89
Rebeckah, m. Norman **ALLEN**, b. of Waterbury, Aug. 4, 1833,		
by Rev. Augustus Bolles	1	88
RADCLIFFE, Alice, of Bristol, m. George W. **TOMPKINS**, of		
Waterbury, July 22, 1852, by Tracy Peck, J. P.	3	61
Betsy, of Bristol, m. Charles **CROMACK**, of New Hartford,		
Oct. 17, 1852, by D. Ives	3	62
REDFEARN, David, m. Margaret **BYINGTON**, b. of Bristol, Oct.		
27, 1851, by Rev. Henry Fitch	3	56
REED, Henry Egbert, of Plymouth, m. Mary Ann **MATHEWS**, of		
Bristol, May 1, 1849, by Rev. S. J. Evens	3	43
Luther A., of Plymouth, m. Mary **GRIDLEY**, of Bristol,		
May 3, 1842, by Rev. Orsimus Allen	3	17
RHOADES, J. D., of Wethersfield, m. Ann J. **JEROME**, of Bristol,		
June 17, 1838, by Rev. Orsamus Allen	1	120
RIBBY, Delia, m. Levi T. **LARKIN**, Aug. 9, 1827, by Jonathan		
Cone, V. D. M.	1	41
RICE,[see uner **ROYCE**]		
RICH, Adeline, of Bristol, m. David **HAWLEY**, of Farmington,		
Feb. 6, 1832, by Rev. Noah Porter, of Farmington	1	69
Almenia, m. Joseph **IVES**, Sept. 29, 1805	TR1	530
Ann E., m. Loomis **NORTH**, May 17, 1852, by Rev. William		
H. Goodrich	3	61
Caroline A., of Bristol, m. Rev. John H. **HANSON**, of New		
York City, Aug. 15, 1843, by Rev. Joseph S. Cowell	3	13
Jane B., of Bristol, m. Roswell **HAWLEY**, of New Britain,		
Sept. 13, 1853, by Rev. William H. Goodrich	3	67
Parthena, m. Charles G. **IVES**, May 14, 1806	TR1	530
RICHARDS, Ann, m. Gilman **HINSDALE**, Sept. 10, 1840, by		
David L. Parmelee	1	139
Bryan, m. Sarah **FRISBIE**, July 16, 1832, by Rev. David		
L. Parmelee	1	73

	Vol.	Page

RICHARDS, (cont.)

Jane E., m. Daniel S. **LARDNER**, b. of Bristol, Sept. 20,
  1848, by Rev. R. H. Seeley — 3, 45

Lydia, of Bristol, m. Daniel **MERRILL**, of Canton, Mar. 30,
  1830, by Rev. Noah Porter, of Farmington — 1, 60

Mary H., m. Ezra **BALDWIN**, Apr. 10, 1834, by Rev. David
  L. Parmelee — 1, 95

Sarah A., m. Hiram P. **THOMPSON**, b. of Bristol, Feb. 14,
  1851, by Rev. William H. Goodrich — 3, 52

Sylvia, m. Edward **LEWIS**, May 7, 1821, by Noah Porter,
  V. D. M. — 1, 10

RICHARDSON, Philo, m. Elvina **HINMAN**, b. of Bristol, July 15,
  1829, by Rev. Henry Stanwood — 1, 53

ROBERTS, ROBERT, Almanza, of Burlington, m. Mary Ann
  BLAKESLEE, of Bristol, Mar. 30, 1829, by Rev. Henry
  Stanwood — 1, 51

Amelia E., m. Richard R. **HUBBEL**, b. of Bristol, Oct. 26,
  1851, by Rev. William H. Goodrich — 3, 59

Chloe, m. Ferdinand **ROBERTS**, b. of Bristol, July 12,
  1821, by Rev. Orra Martin — 1, 8

Falla, m. Charles **BRONSON**, May 19, 1836, by Rev. David
  L. Parmelee — 1, 105

Ferdinand, m. Chloe **ROBERTS**, b. of Bristol, July 12,
  1821, by Rev. Orra Martin — 1, 8

Julia A., m. Francis V. **DARROW**, b. of Bristol, Nov. 10,
  1850, by Rev. Lester Lewis — 3, 51

Molly, m. James **STONE**, Apr. 27, 1780 — TR1, 494

Piera L., of Bristol, m. Wait R. **GRISWOLD**, of Wethersfield,
  Sept. 1, 1846, by R. H. Seely — 3, 28

RODEN, Henry F., of Bristol, m. Susan **BELDEN**, of Burlington,
  June 8, 1845, by Rev. A. S. Francis — 3, 24

ROGERS, William L., of Tolland, Mass., m. Jane R. **BOARDMAN**,
  of Bristol, Nov. 19, 1851, by Rev. William H. Goodrich — 3, 59

RONDEN, James A., of Bristol, m. Jane A. **GLADDING**, of Berlin,
  Sept. 10, 1849, by Rev. Lester Lewis — 3, 45

ROOT, Asahel, of Farmington, m. Mary **MARKLAND**, of Bristol,
  Mar. 20, 1849, by Rev. Lester Lewis — 3, 47

Charles, m. Sophia M. **PECK**, b. of Bristol, Dec. 20, 1843,
  by R. H. Seely. Int. Pub. Dec. 17, 1843 — 3, 15

Edward, m. Lydia **YALE**, Oct. 17, 1838, by Rev. David L.
  Parmelee — 1, 124

Hezekiah, m. Azuba **RUSSELL**, b. of Bristol, [Apr.] 23,
  1821, by Rev. Jonathan Cone — 1, 6

John, of Berlin, m. Mary E. **BROWN**, of Bristol, Mar. 31,
  1833, by Rev. H. Stanwood — 1, 83

Maria, m. David **CARRINGTON**, June 29, 1835, by Rev.
  David L. Parmelee — 1, 100

Nancy, m. Charles **CRAMER**, June 4, 1840, by Rev. David

	Vol.	Page
ROOT, (cont.)		
L. Parmelee	1	136
Salmon, m. Eliza Ann **GAYLORD**, Apr. 14, 1841, by Rev. David L. Parmelee	3	2
Samuel Emerson, m. Jane Manerva **HENDERSON**, b. of Bristol, Nov. 5, 1845, by R. H. Seely	3	25
ROPER, Evaline, of Bristol, m. Irrom **MARSH**, of Northfield, Oct. 7, 1841, by Rev. Joseph S. Covell	1	144
Evaline, of Bristol, m. T. **MARSH**, of Northfield, Oct. 7, 1841, by Rev. Joseph S. Covell	3	3
Mary F., m. Edward **NOTT**, Mar. 30, 1847, by Rev. R. H. Seely	3	31
ROSE, Henry I., of Wolcott, m. Harriet **SEELY**, of Waterbury, Sept. 1, 1844, by Rev. Joseph S. Covill	3	19
Jesse B., of Wolcott, m. Purlina S. **HART**, of Bristol, Apr. 15, 1840, by Rev. Aaron S. Hill	1	135
Mary, of Wolcott, m. Stephen Johnson **PAYNE**, of Prospect, May 2, 1841, by Rev. Parmele Chamberlin	3	2
ROSSITER, Lucius G., of Bristol, m. Mary E. **ALLEN**, of Hartford, Oct. 31, 1849, by Rev. Lester Lewis	3	46
ROWE, ROW, Ira, s. Stephan, b. Dec. 25, 1785	TR1	515
John, s. Stephan, b. Feb. 21, 1795	TR1	515
Levi, s. Ari, b. Sept. 8, 1791	TR1	515
Loyra, d. Ari, b. May 7, 1793	TR1	515
Rendah, d. Stephan, b. July 3, 1790	TR1	515
Stephan, m. Leve Rende **ADAMES**, Feb. 5, 1783	TR1	494
Stephan, Jr., s. Stephan, b. Feb. 7, 1788	TR1	515
Truman, s. Stephan, b. Mar. 22, 1784	TR1	515
ROYCE, RICE, Abel, s. Lent, b. Feb. 23, 1797	TR1	515
Ada, d. Lent, b. Mar. 16, 1795	TR1	515
Amanda, d. Lent, b. Aug. 16, 1801	TR1	515
Amia, d. Lent, b. Feb. 11, 1793	TR1	515
Jane E., of Bristol, m. Philemon **TUTTLE**, of Prospect, Mar. 27, 1842, by Rev. Joseph S. Covell	3	5
Jeremiah, s. Lent, b. Sept. 4, 1788	TR1	515
Lucy, of Wolcott, m. Samuel **PARLIN**, of Action, Mass., Jan. 2, 1832, by Rev. Henry Stanwood	1	68
Rhoda, w. Nehemiah, d. Aug. 29, 1786	TR1	537
Rosannah, d. Lent, b. May 31, 1790	TR1	515
Truman Lent, s. Lent, b. June 8, 1799	TR1	515
RUSSELL, RUSSEL, Abel Chauncy, s. Abel, b. July 27, 1807	TR1	515
Abel Chauncy, [s. Abel], b. July 27, 1807	2	13
Asa Champion, of Great Barrington, Mass., m. Czrena Elizabeth **PARDEE**, of Bristol, Aug. 25, 1840, by Joseph S. Covell	1	142
Azuba, d. Abel, b. Apr. 6, 1795	TR1	515
Azuba, [d. Abel], b. Apr. 6, 1795	2	13
Azuba, m. Hezekiah **ROOT**, b. of Bristol, [Apr.] 23, 1821,		

	Vol.	Page
RUSSELL, RUSSEL, (cont.)		
by Rev. Jonathan Cone	1	6
Bridget, of Bristol, m. George W. **BALDWIN**, of Litchfield,		
Oct. 9, 1853, by Rev. N. C. Lewis	3	68
Cyntha Selinda, d. Abel, b. June 20, 1809	TR1	515
Cynthia Selinda, [d. Abel], b. June 20, 1809	2	13
Daniel, s. Abel, b. Nov. 15, 1799	TR1	515
Daniel, [s. Abel], b. Nov. 15, 1799	2	13
Daniel L., m. Rhoda C. **SANFORD**, b. of Waterbury, Aug.		
11, 1832, by Rev. Irenus Atkins, of Southington	1	74
Edward H., of Wolcott, m. Martha Ann **MERRIMAN**, of		
Southington, Dec. 17, 1827, by Irenus Atkins	1	45
Israel, of Middletown, m. Rachel **PECK**, of Bristol, Jan. 31,		
1827, by Jonathan Cone, V. D. M	1	36
Lydia, d. Abel, b. May 19, 1802	TR1	515
Lydia, [d. Abel], b. May 19, 1802	2	13
Phebe Philoma, d. Abel, b. July 6, 1811	TR1	515
Phebe Philoma, [d. Abel], b. July 6, 1811	2	13
Sally Sophrona, d. Abel, b. June 25, 1813	TR1	515
Sally Saphrona, [d. Abel], b. June 25, 1813	2	13
Samuel S., s. Abel, b. July 29, 1804	TR1	515
Samuel Seymour, [s. Abel], b. July 29, 1804	2	13
William, m. Harriet **BYINGTON**, Aug. 20, 1848, by Rev.		
Charles Chittenden	3	40
RUST, Honor, m. Isaac **GRAHAM**, b. of Bristol, May 3, 1826,		
by Jared W. Pardee, J. P.	1	31
SADD, George F., of Austinburgh, O., m. Jane R. **STRONG**, of		
New Hartford, May 31, 1847, by Rev. R. H. Seely	3	33
SANFORD, Almerin, of Hamden, m. Polly A. **MATTHEWS**, of		
Bristol, Oct. 10, 1832, by Rev. Henry Stanwood	1	76
Austin, m. Jerusha I. **NORTON**, Mar. 10, 1833, by Rev.		
David L. Parmelee	1	83
Miles, of Bristol, m. Electa **BARNES**, of Plymouth, Feb.		
16, 1834, by Rev. H. Stanwood	1	94
Miles, m. Louisa A. **HAWLEY**, May 30, 1841, by Rev.		
Orsamus Allen	3	2
Rhoda C., m. Daniel L. **RUSSELL**, b. of Waterbury, Aug. 11,		
1832, by Rev. Irenus Atkins, of Southington	1	74
SCARRITT, SCARRET, Abigail H., of Bristol, m. Horace W.		
NICHOLS, of Waterbury, Jan. 2, 1831, by Rev. H.		
Stanwood	1	65
James, of Wolcott, m. Julia **JOHNSON**, of Bristol, May 31,		
1843, by Edward Savage	3	12
Ransom, of Wolcott, m. Abigail **HOLT**, of Bristol, Mar.		
28, 1825, by Rev. Jonathan Cone	1	27
SCHEEGEL, Catharine, m. Christian **CONGELMAN**, Sept. 28,		
1851, by Rev. W. H. Goodrich	3	55
SCHMIDT, Anna, m. Carl **BECHSTEDL**, Oct. 27, 1850, by Rev.		

	Vol.	Page

SCHMIDT, (cont.)

William H. Goodrich — 3 — 51

SCHUBERT, Amelia F., of Schweinfurt, Germany, m. Anson
BECKWITH, of Bristol, Sept. 13, 1852, by Rev. William
H. Goodrich — 3 — 62

SCOVILL, Lois, m. Willis MORSE, b. of Plymouth, Jan. 6, 1830,
by Abner J. Leavenworth — 1 — 59

SEELY, Harriet, of Waterbury, m. Henry I. ROSE, of Wolcott,
Sept. 1, 1844, by Rev. Joseph S. Covill — 3 — 19

Semanthy, of Waterbury, m. Thomas LEWIS, of Wolcott,
Nov. 16, 1842, by Rev. Joseph S. Covell — 3 — 9

SEYMOUR, Henry A. of New Hartford, m. Electa CHURCHILL,
of Bristol, July 28, 1844, by R. H. Seely. Int. Pub. — 3 — 19

SHELDON, Wilson, of Branford, m. Phebe R. MATTHEWS, of
Bristol, Oct. 17, 1830, by Rev. H. Stanwood — 1 — 63

SHEPHERD, SHEPARD, Abigail L., of Southington, m. Albert
BURDICT, of Bristol, May 20, 1844, by R. H. Seely — 3 — 17

Amelia H., of Bristol, m. Samuel PARMELEE, of New
Britain, Jan. 11, 1852, by Rev. Henry H. Fitch — 3 — 57

Harriet, of Portland, m. Merritt BALDWIN, of Westville,
Nov. 20, 1842, by Rev. Joseph S. Covell — 3 — 10

Sylvester, m. Rosannah CLAPP, b. of Farmington, Nov. 27,
1846, by Charles G. Ives, J. P. — 3 — 30

William H., of Southington, m. Roxana FENTON, of
Plymouth, Apr. 7, 1833, by Rev. H. Stanwood — 1 — 84

SHERMAN, David, of Bristol, m. Julia JOHNSON, of Plymouth,
June 29, 1829, by Rev. Henry Stanwood — 1 — 53

SHIPMAN, Julius R., m. Mary CLARK, Jan. 1, 1852, by Rev.
W. H. Goodrich — 3 — 59

SIGOURNEY, Joseph, of Bristol, m. Sybel P. DAWSON, of New
Hartford, June 9, 1845, by Rev. E. Savage — 3 — 23

SKINNER, Charlotte M., m. Henry BECKWITH, b. of Bristol,
July 14, 1851, by Rev. Lester Lewis — 3 — 54

Edgar, m. Christiana R. THOMPSON, May 2, 1838, by Rev.
David L. Parmelee — 1 — 119

SMART, Margaret D., of Bristol, m. Benjamin W. HILL, of
Providence, R. I., May 18, 1836, by Rev. Orsamus Allen — 1 — 106

SMITH, Adeline M., m. Nathan L. BIRGE, b. of Bristol, May 19,
1852, by Rev. W. H. Goodrich — 3 — 61

Amelia, m. Abraham PETTEBONE, May 21, 1778 — TR1 — 514

Bishop, of Bristol, m. Harriet BRADLEY, of Plymouth,
Sept. 15, 1847, by Rev. Harvey Husted — 3 — 34

Charles E., m. Sarah T. PECK, Sept. 26, 1839, by Rev.
David L. Parmelee — 1 — 132

Cyrus Porter, m. Lydia Lewis HOOKER, Sept. 5, 1826, by
Jonathan Cone, V. D. M. — 1 — 35

Erastus, s. John, b. Jan. 21, 1785 — TR1 — 518

Genet, of Southington, m. Simon C. SWEET, of Farmington,

	Vol.	Page
SMITH, (cont.)		
Sept. 20, 1829, by Charles G. Ives, J. P.	1	56
Harriet, m. Ezra **NORTON**, b. of Bristol, Feb. 19, 1821,		
by Rev. Orra Martin	1	5
James R., of Southington, m. Seraphina **WATERS**, of Bristol,		
Sept. 18, 1851, by Rev. Lester Lewis	3	56
Lecister, of Plymouth, m. Electa **McTHEY**, of Bristol, July 31,		
1823, by Rev. Jonathan Cone	1	22
Martha, m. Homer **BISHOP**, b. of Bristol, Nov. 18, 1829, by		
Rev. H. Stanwood	1	58
Orren, m. Amy Ann **HOPKINS**, of New Haven, July 30, 1843,		
by Edward Savage	3	13
Phebe, of Southington, m. Elias **WILCOX**, Mar. 4, 1798	TR1	537
Polly, of Bristol, m. Perkins **BUNNELL**, of Burlington,		
Nov. 12, 1837, by Rev. Harvey Husted	1	118
Polly, of Waterbury, m. Edward **WELTON**, of Bristol, July 4,		
1844, by Edward Savage	3	18
Samuel B., m. Hannah M. **TERRY**, b. of Bristol, May 5, 1830,		
by Rev. Abner J. Leavenworth	1	61
Sarah Maria, of Mt. Washington, Mass., m. Adolphus		
BRADLEY, of Bristol, Mar. 22, 1847, by Rev. R. H.		
Seely	3	31
Thadeus, of Plymouth, m. Candance R. **DUTTON**, of Bristol,		
May 12, 1830, by Rev. Abner J. Leavenworth	1	61
SNATH, Rachel, of Burlington, m. Merrils **HUMPHREY**, of		
Bristol, May 4, 1826, by Rev. Noah Porter, of Farmington	1	33
SPELLMAN, Esther L., of Granville, Mass., m. Reuben A.		
SPENCER, of Bristol, July 4, 1852, by Rev. William H.		
Goodrich	3	61
Hiram J., m. Jane C. **MUZZY**, Oct. 2, 1845, by R. H. Seely	3	24
SPENCER, Adison, of New Hartford, m. Cornelia E. **WRIGHT**, of		
Bristol, Oct. 24, 1843, by Edward Savage	3	14
Cornelia, m. Adna W. **DRAKE**, b. of Farmington, Apr. 8,		
1849, by Rev. Lester Lewis	3	47
Reuben A., of Bristol, m. Esther L. **SPELLMAN**, of Granville,		
Mass., July 4, 1852, by Rev. William H. Goodrich	3	61
SPERRY, Hannah Ann, m. Andrew **HOUGH**, Dec. 21, 1834, at the		
house of Mrs. Sperry, by Rev. G. C. V. Eastman	1	97
Horatio N., m. Mary **HENDRICK**, b. of Bristol, Mar. 23,		
1836, by Rev. Orsamus Allen	1	104
Luanna B., of Bristol, m. Isaac O. **HINDSALE**, of Burlington,		
Jan. 14, 1838, by Rev. Henry Husted	1	118
STAGG, Isaac M., m. Mary **DARROW**, Nov. 29, 1838, by Rev. E.		
S. Stout	1	125
STANLEY, Samuel, m. Ruth Ann **CRAMPTON**, June 6, 1832, by		
Rev. David S. Parmelee	1	72
STEELE, STEAL, STEEL, Betsey, d. James, b. Dec. 12, 1797	TR1	518
Betsey, m. Harvey **BRADLEY**, b. of Bristol, Sept. 26, 1822,		

	Vol.	Page
STEELE, STEAL, STEEL, (cont.)		
by Rev. Jonathan Cone	1	16
Chloe, m. Henry **LOOMIS**, Sept. 7, 1825, by Jonathan Cone,		
V. D. M	1	29
David, m. Nancy **WILCOX**, b. of Bristol, Nov. 28, 1822,		
by Rev. Jonathan Cone	1	18
Franklin, m. Caroline **BUNNELL**, Nov. 24, 1853, by Rev.		
William H. Goodrich	3	64
Jane E., of Bristol, m. Daniel W. **KEYS**, of Russia, N. Y.,		
July 26, 1853, by Rev. Lester Lewis	3	66
Mary M., m. Henry H. **KILBOURN**, b. of Bristol, Apr. 30,		
1851, by Rev. William H. Goodrich	3	55
STEVENS, STEPHENS, Harriet, m. Thomas **CURTISS**, Jr., b. of		
Bristol, May 5, 1830, by Rev. Irenus Atkins, of		
Southington	1	61
Joshua, on May 5, 1791, entered his sentiments of his		
christian religion on record (viz) Annabablist	TR1	499
Mary Ann, of Bristol, m. Henry **GAMBLE**, of Ireland, Oct.		
29, 1849, by Rev. S. J. Evans	3	54
Nancy, of Bristol, m. Willard H. **BARRETT**, of New Hartford,		
Oct. 29, 1846, by Rev. A. S. Francis	3	32
Philo, m. Harriet **BOTSFORD**, b. of Bristol, May 20, 1827,		
by Henry Stanwood	1	40
Simeon, of Litchfield, m. Eunice **CURTIS**, of Bristol,		
Dec. 22, 1825, by Erastus Clapp, V. D. M.	1	30
STILES, Seth, m. Laura **FRISBIE**, b. of Bristol, Feb. 9, 1834,		
by Rev. H. Stanwood	1	94
STILLMAN, Almeron, s. Amos, b. Feb. 27, 1793	TR1	516
Amos, Jr., s. Amos, b. Jan. 17, 1783	TR1	516
Betsey, d. Amos, b. June 27, 1787	TR1	516
Elenor, d. Amos, b. Mar. 13, 1784	TR1	516
John Davis, s. Amos, b. Mar. 29, 1789	TR1	516
John W., m. Frances J. **AVERRY**, b. of Bristol, Nov. 22,		
1848, by Rev. R. H. Seeley	3	45
Luanna, d. Amos, b. Aug. 28, 1785	TR1	516
Lucinda, d. Amos, b. Mar. 14, 1791	TR1	516
STOCKING, Adelia A., of Plymouth, m. Orlando F. **YALE**, of		
Bristol, Jan. 12, 1845, by Rev. J. S. Covill	3	21
STONE, Abigail, d. James, b. Apr. 30, 1782	TR1	516
Elisha, s. James, b. Jan. 30, 1784	TR1	516
Elisa, m. Thadeus **BRISTOL**, Nov. 8, 1848, by Rev. Charles		
Chittenden	3	41
James, m. Molly **ROBERTS**, Apr. 27, 1780	TR1	494
Mary L., of Terryville, m. David W. **GOODRICH**, of		
Millbury, Dec. 29, 1844phg2Rev. Henry F. Roberts.		
Witnesses: Elijah Stone, Elvira Stone, [ ] Foster	3	20
Molly, d. James, b. Sept. 20, 1785	TR1	516
Phene, d. William, of Harwinton, m. Gad **BARTHOLOMEW,**		

	Vol.	Page

STONE, (cont.)

May 23, 1804 — TR1 534

Roswell, of Warren, O., m. Caroline N. I. **MERRIMAN**, of
Bristol, [Sept.] 16, 1822, by Rev. Jonathan Cone — 1 16

Susannah, of Litchfield, m. Edward **NOON**, of Bristol,
Jan. 2, 1853, by Rev. Lester Lewis — 3 63

Willis S., of Burlington, m. Caroline M. **PERKINS**, of
Bristol, Nov. 17, 1852, by Rev. Stephen Rushmore — 3 65

STOUGHTON, Andrew, of Plymouth, m. Julia E. **HOOKER**, of
Bristol, Sept. 30, 1824, by Rev. Jonathan Cone — 1 24

STRICKLAND, Jacob, of New Britain, m. Helen A. **HILL**, of
Bristol, Jan. 19, 1848, by Rev. R. H. Seeley — 3 37

STRONG, Ebenezer W., m. Merina A. **PARSONS**, Dec. 22, 1841,
by Merrill Richardson — 3 4

Jane R., of New Hartford, m. George F. **SADD**, of
Austinburgh, O., May 31, 1847, by Rev. R. H. Seely — 3 33

STUNDLEY, Laura, m. John **WINSTON**, b. of Bristol, Dec. 12,
1816, by Rev. Jonathan Cone — TR4 529

SUHER, Louis, m. Augusta **GREINER**, b. of Germany, Oct. 15,
1854, by Rev. L. C. Cheeney — 3 71

SUTLIFF, Nancy, of Wolcott, m. Jared **ALLEN**, of Plymouth,
Nov. 28, 1821, by Rev. Orra Martin — 1 11

SWAN, John, of Hebron, m. Mrs. Nancy H. **GLOVER**, of Coventry,
Feb. 23, 1847, by Rev. R. H. Seely — 3 30

SWEET, Simon C., of Farmington, m. Genet **SMITH**, of
Southington, Sept. 20, 1829, by Charles G. Ives, J. P. — 1 56

TAYLOR, Ruth, Mrs., m. Thomas **JEROME**, b. of Bristol, Feb. 18,
1823, by Rev. Jonathan Cone — 1 20

TERRY, Hannah M., m. Samuel B. **SMITH**, b. of Bristol, May 5,
1830, by Rev. Abner J. Leavenworth — 1 61

Milo, m. Mrs. Abigail **MURPHY**, Sept. 20, 1838, by Rev.
David L. Parmelee — 1 123

Ralph E., m. Ruth L. **HUBBELL**, Oct. 9, 1844, by R. H. Seely — 3 20

Theodore, m. Juliaett **PIERCE**, b. of Bristol, Mar. 24,
1830, by Rev. A. J. Leavenworth — 1 60

THOMAS, Eron N., of Rose Wayne Cty., N. Y., m. Rachel M.
GAYLORD, of Bristol, Sept. 15, 1844, by Rev. Henry F.
Roberts — 3 19

Jane, m. Charles R. **HAYES**, of New Haven, Feb. 11, 1849,
by Rev. Charles Chittenden — 3 42

John M., m. Catharine R. **NORTON**, Jan. 31, 1844, by R. H.
Seely. Int. Pub. Jan. 28, 1844 — 3 15

THOMPSON, THOMSON, Christiana R., m. Edgar **SKINNER**,
May 2, 1838, by Rev. David L. Parmelee — 1 119

Elinor, m. Samuel **LEWIS**, Jan. 17, 1770 — TR1 494

Elisha J., of Southington, m. Adine **PECK**, of Bristol,
Apr. 30, 1843, by Irenus Atkins — 3 11

Harriet, of Bristol, m. Stephen **THOMPSON**, of Watertown,

	Vol.	Page
THOMPSON, THOMSON, (cont.)		
Dec. 26, 1847, by Rev. Harvey Husted	3	36
Henrietta L., m. Edward N. **PIERCE**, Oct. 23, 1837, by		
Rev. David L. Parmelee	1	117
Henry R., m. Georgiana E. **WILLIAMS**, b. of Bristol, June		
2, 1851, by Rev. Henry H. Fitch	3	53
Hiram P., m. Sarah A. **RICHARDS**, b. of Bristol, Feb. 14,		
1851, by Rev. William H. Goodrich	3	52
Jerusha A., Mrs. of Bristol, m. Elihu **KILLPATRICK**, of		
Washington Cty., Miss., Aug. 11, 1848, by Rev. Lester		
Lewis	3	40
Stephen, of Watertown, m. Harriet **THOMPSON**, of Bristol,		
Dec. 26, 1847, by Rev. Harvey Husted	3	36
THORP, Katharine, Mrs., m. Dr. Titus **MERRIMAN**, May 3, 1827,		
by Jonathan Cone, V. D. M.	1	39
Rachel S., of North Haven, m. Albert J. **PARKER**, of		
Wallingford, Sept. 20, 1846, by Edward Savage	3	29
Thankfull, of Bristol, m. Asa **HITCHCOCK**, of Chesire,		
Feb. 20, 1828, by Jonathan Cone, V. D. M.	1	44
William, of Bristol, m. Harriet **GILBERT**, of [ ], Nov. 10,		
1831, by Rev. H. Stanwood	1	67
TODD, Almera A., m. Luther **PRITCHARD**, Sept. 8, 1833, by Rev.		
David L. Parmelee	1	89
Emily, m. Lyman F. **WARNER**, b. of Bristol, Apr. 30, 1854,		
by Irenus Atkins	3	69
Esther Ann, of Plymouth, m. Levi N. **PECK**, of Cheshire,		
Nov. 6, 1836, by Rev. Joseph S. Covill	1	110
Mary, m. Porter A. **NORTON**, b. of Bristol, Sept. 18, 1828,		
by Rev. Henry Stanwood	1	46
TOLBERT, Ann Eliza, of Burlington, m. Monroe **BARNES**, of		
Bristol, Nov. 27, 1847, by Irenus Atkins	3	36
TOLLES, Curtiss, of Bethany, m. Julianna **WELTON**, of Wolcott,		
Feb. 11, 1844, by Rev. Joseph S. Covell	3	15
TOMPKINS, George W., of Waterbury, m. Alice **RADCLIFFE**, of		
Bristol, July 22, 1852, by Tracy Peck, J. P.	3	61
[TRACY], **TRASCY**, Rachel, m. Lement **PECK**, Sept. 23, 1782	TR1	534
TRAGANOWAN, William, m. Faith **WARD**, b. of Bristol, May 9,		
1849, by Rev. C. Chittenden	3	43
TREADWELL, Charles H., m. Jane A. **ELKEY**, Mar. 3, 1853, by		
Rev. William H. Goodrich	3	66
Mary, m. Epaphroditus **HARRISON**, Mar. 17, 1853, by Rev.		
William H. Goodrich	3	66
TREAT, Nancy, m. Augustus **NORTON**, Nov. 20, 1839, by Rev.		
Orsamus Allen	1	138
Orrin R., m. Mary A. **ATWATER**, b. of Bristol, July 22,		
1839, by Rev. Orsamus Allen	1	130
TUBBS, John E., m. Clarissa **PARMELEE**, b. of New Britain,		
Jan. 11, 1852, by Rev. Henry Fitch	3	58

	Vol.	Page
TUTTLE, Abner, m. Hannah A. **PARKER**, May 27, 1838, by Rev. David L. Parmelee	1	120
Chloe, of Bristol, m. Smith **DART**, of Vernon, Jan. 12, 1843, by Edward Savage	3	12
Daniel, m. Sally **HILLS**, b. of Bristol, Nov. 26, 1822, by Rev. Jonathan Cone	1	17
Hannah, of Bristol, m. Pinney **KELSEY**, of Bloomfield, June 1, 1843, by Edward Savage	3	13
Harriet N., m. Wilford H. **NETTLETON**, b. of Bristol, June 9, 1847, by Rev. R. H. Seeley	3	33
Jane E., of Bristol, m. Stephen **ATWATER**, of Plymouth, Oct. 27, 1851, by Rev. Lewis Gunn	3	58
Leanora, of Bristol, m. John **IVES**, of Chesire, Oct. 27, 1842, by Rev. Joseph S. Covell	3	9
Lockwood, of Burlington, m. Louisa A. **HUNGERFORD**, of Bristol, Feb. 1, 1846, by Rev. A. S. Francis	3	27
Mary A., m. Edwin S. **LEWIS**, Nov. 4, 1830, by Rev. Abner J. Leavenworth	1	63
Mary A., of Bristol, m. John C. **WHITING**, of New Hartford, Oct. 16, 1853, by Rev. Samuel G. Matthewson	3	68
Philemon, of Prospect, m. Jane E. **ROYCE**, of Bristol, Mar. 27, 1842, by Rev. Joseph S. Covell	3	5
Salome, of Plymouth, m. Julius A. **OLMSTED**, of Canton, Nov. 17, 1843, by Edward Savage	3	14
Samuel B., m. Eveline S. **IVES**, Apr. 7, 1835, by Rev. David L. Parmelee	1	99
TWITCHELL, TWITCHEL, Edward, m. Selina D. **CARTER**, Sept. 3, 1835, by Rev. David L. Parmelee	1	102
Sheldon W., m. Mary **ATWATER**, Mar. 22, 1826, by Rev. Daniel Wildman	1	32
UPSON, Betsey, m. Austin **WILCOX**, b. of Bristol, Nov. 28, 1822, by Rev. Jonathan Cone	1	18
Eleanor R., m. Hezekiah M. **BURNHAM**, b. of Bristol, Sept. 24, 1845, by Rev. A. S. Francis	3	25
Emma, of Bristol, m. Curtis **PORTER**, of Farmington, Dec. 21, 1828, by Rev. Irenus Atkins, of Southington	1	47
George R., m. Emily **BARTHOLOMEW**, Nov. 25, 1824, by Luther Hart	1	25
Marshall, of Wolcott, m. Esther J. **BARKER**, of Bristol, Sept. 28, 1848, by Rev. R. H. Seeley	3	45
Polly Chena, d. Fremend, m. John **BENTON**, Oct. 13, 1802	TR1	534
USHER, Josiah C., m. Ruth **FRISBIE**, Sept. 9, 1828, by Jonathan Cone, V. D. M.	1	46
Statira H., of Hartford, m. Gen. Stephen F. **PALMER**, of Ashford, June 18, 1827, by Jonathan Cone, V. D. M.	1	40
VORSE, Caroline, of New Haven, m. Smith **BENNET**, of New Hartford, Jan. 21, 1852, by Rev. Lester Lewis	3	58
WADSWORTH, William R., of East Hartford, m. Phidelia **YALE**,		

	Vol.	Page
WADSWORTH, (cont.)		
of Bristol, Apr. 2, 1850, by Rev. Lester Lewis	3	48
WARD, Faith, m. William **TRAGANOWAN**, b. of Bristol, May 9,		
1849, by Rev. C. Chittenden	3	43
WARFIELD, Sarah, Mrs. of Springfield, m. Calvin **MILLARD**, of		
Bristol, Sept. 1, 1841, by Charles G. Ives, J. P.	3	3
WARNER, Asahel, of Waterbury, m. Abagail **DAYTON**, of Bristol,		
Dec. 4, 1842, by Rev. Joseph S. Covel	3	10
Garret P., of Bristol, m. Hannah **BENHAM**, of Waterbury,		
Dec. 28, 1845, by Rev. Joseph S. Covill	3	26
Hannah, of Bristol, m. Levi **HALL**, of Wolcott, May 1, 1844,		
by Rev. Joseph S. Covill	3	16
Horace H., m. Sally S. **YALE**, b. of Bristol, Apr. 2,		
1850, by Rev. Lester Lewis	3	48
Lydia M., of Southington, m. George W. **CURTISS**, of		
Burlington, Aug. 2, 1826, by Jonathan Cone, V. D. M.	1	34
Lyman F., m. Emily **TODD**, b. of Bristol, Apr. 30, 1854,		
by Irenus Atkins	3	69
WATERS, Seraphina, of Bristol, m. James R. **SMITH**, of		
Southington, Sept. 18, 1851, by Rev. Lester Lewis	3	56
WATTON, Jason, of South Coventry, m. Julia Ann **LARKIN**, of		
Bristol, Jan. 5, 1834, by Rev. H. Stanwood	1	93
WAY, Alfred, m. Esther J. **HUBBARD**, Jan. 13, 1829, by Jonathan		
Cone, V. D. M.	1	48
WEBSTER, Sarah, m. Daniel **BARNES**, Nov. 23, 1785	TR1	489
WELCH, Drucilla, m. Julius R. **MITCHELL**, Jan. 21, 1845, by		
Rev. Edward Savage	3	21
George, m. Thalia **WILDMAN**, b. of Bristol, Feb. 22, 1829,		
by Rev. Henry Stanwood	1	50
Helen Maria, m. Andrew Fuller **ATKINS**, b. of Bristol,		
May 6, 1849, by Rev. Lester Lewis	3	47
Henry L., of Bristol, m. Antoinette S. **HALL**, of Southington,		
June 24, 1840, by Rev. Simon Shailor	1	137
Hiram J., m. Sophronia **ATWATER**, b. of Bristol, May 3,		
1837, by Rev. Orsamus Allen	1	112
Zelinda, of Bristol, m. Ely **HILL**, of Hanover, Mass.,		
Jan. 1, 1840, by Rev. Simon Shailer	1	133
WELLS, Joseph A., m. Sarah C. **BOARDMAN**, Nov. 22, 1832, by		
Rev. David L. Parmelee	1	80
WELTON, Edward, of Bristol, m. Polly **SMITH**, of Waterbury,		
July 4, 1844, by Edward Savage	3	18
Julianna, of Wolcott, m. Curtiss **TOLLES**, of Bethany,		
Feb. 11, 1844, by Rev. Joseph S. Covell	3	15
Leicester C., of Harwinton, m. Orra **MATTHEWS**, of Bristol,		
Oct. 28, 1845, by Rev. Joseph S. Covill	3	25
WEST, Alonso, of Stafford, m. Julia A. **BALDWIN**, of New		
Hartford, Aug. 8, 1849, by Rev. Lester Lewis	3	44
Alvah, of Stafford, m. Mary Ann **HILLS**, of Bristol,		

	Vol.	Page
WEST, (cont.)		
[ ], by Rev. Lester Lewis	3	50
WESTON, William, m. Caroline **PICKET**, b. of Bristol, Jan. 29,		
1853, by Rev. Stephen Rushmore	3	65
WETTON, Noah E., m. Mahitable J. **BUCKLEY**, July 12, 1832, by		
Rev. David L. Parmelee	1	73
WHEATON, Roswell B., m. Levia **ANDREWS**, Sept. 29, 1838, by		
Rev. David L. Parmelee	1	124
WHEELER, Eunice, m. Randal A. **CASTLE**, Sept. 12, 1838, by		
Rev. E. S. Stout	1	125
Ransley H., of Levonia, N. Y., m. Sally M. **WOODEN**, of		
Bristol, Oct. 19, 1836, by Rev. Harvey Husted	1	108
WHITE, Heman, of Montgomery, Ala., m. Catharine **MALLORY**,		
of Bristol, Oct. 17, 1842, by Rev. Joseph S. Covell	3	8
WHITING, John C., of New Hartford, m. Mary A. **TUTTLE**, of		
Bristol, Oct. 16, 1853, by Rev. Samuel G. Matthewson	3	68
WHITMAN, Abbe, of Southington, m. Nelson **LEE**, of Bristol,		
Oct. 5, 1820, by Rev. Jonathan Coe	1	1
WHITMORE, Elizabeth H., m. Hiram **BOTSFORD**, Jan. 16, 1839,		
by Rev. David L. Parmelee	1	127
WHITNEY, Boylston, of Bristol, m. Orffy **CLARK**, of Farmington,		
Oct. 11, 1845, by Rev. A. S. Francis	3	25
WIERD, Rhoda, d. Seth, m. Marcus **HART**, Jan. 17, 1786	TR1	494
WIGHTMAN, Charles G., of Philadelphia, m. Jane A. **PARKER**, of		
Bristol, Apr. 10, 1854, by Irenus Atkins	3	68
Elbridge, m. Ursula **PERKIINS**, b. of Bristol, June 17,		
1829, by Rev. Henry Stanwood	1	52
Jennet, of Southington, m. Edward **LEWIS**, of Wolcott,		
Nov. 24, 1828, by Rev. Irenus Atkins, of Southington	1	47
John, of Southington, m. Orrilla **ANDREWS**, of Bristol,		
Oct. 9, 1821, by Rev. Orra Martin	1	11
Mary Ann, of Southington, m. Albert B. **WILCOX**, of Bristol,		
Sept. 13, 1821, by Rev. Orra Martin	1	9
Voluntine, m. Esther **NEAL**, b. of Southington, May 2,		
1842, by Rev. James Squire	3	7
WILCOX, WILLCOX, Adeline E., m. James A. **BEACH**, Jan. 10,		
1841, by Rev. David L. Parmelee	3	1
Albert B., of Bristol, m. Mary Ann **WIGHTMAN**, of		
Southington, Sept. 13, 1821, by Rev. Orra Martin	1	9
Alburt Bushnel, s. Elias [& Phebe], b. Jan. 15, 1799	TR1	537
Austin, m. Betsey **UPSON**, b. of Bristol, Nov. 28, 1822,		
by Rev. Jonathan Cone	1	18
Austin, m. Charolotte Louisa **BARTHOLOMEW**, of Bristol,		
Mar. 30, 1847, by Rev. R. H. Seely	3	31
Austin, m. Sarah **FULLER**, of Simsbury, Jan. 18, 1851,		
by Rev. William H. Goodrich	3	59
Elias, m. Phebe **SMITH**, of Southington, Mar. 4, 1798	TR1	537
Elias Monson, s. Elias & Phebe, b. Mar. 20, 1810	TR1	529

	Vol.	Page

WILCOX, WILLCOX, (cont.)

Linus, m. Emeline **HART**, Feb. 13, 1825, by Rev. Jonathan
Cone — 1 — 26

Munson, m. Mrs. Harriet E. **NORTON**, b. of Bristol, Apr. 18,
1847, by Rev. Lester Lewis — 3 — 34

Nancy, m. David **STEELE**, b. of Bristol, Nov. 28, 1822,
by Rev. Jonathan Cone — 1 — 18

Phebe Hurmele, d. Elias [& Phebe], b. Aug. 22, 1802 — TR1 — 537

Sally Mariah, d. Elias [& Phebe], b. June 30, 1806 — TR1 — 537

Sarah Maria, of Bristol, m. Samuel **BARNES**, of Burlington,
Jan. 15, 1829, by Rev. Aaron Pearce — 1 — 49

William, m. Sarah Ann **YALE**, Sept. 11, 1839, by Rev. David
L. Parmelee — 1 — 131

WILDMAN, Charles B., of Danbury, m. Mrs. Amanda
HITCHCOCK, of Bristol, Aug. 30, 1835, by Rev.
Orsamus Allen — 1 — 102

Thalia, m. George **WELCH**, b. of Bristol, Feb. 22, 1829,
by Rev. Henry Stanwood — 1 — 50

Thomas, of Danbury, m. Sarah **NORTON**, of Bristol, Oct. 8,
1821, by Rev. Daniel Wildman — 1 — 10

WILLIAMS, Cornelius R., of Wethersfield, m. Caroline **HOOKER**,
of Bristol, Sept. 4, 1831, by Rev. Abner J. Leavenworth — 1 — 66

Georgiana E., m. Henry R. **THOMPSON**, b. of Bristol, June
2, 1851, by Rev. Henry H. Fitch — 3 — 53

Timothy S., of Middletown, m. Kiziah **HUNGERFORD**, of
Bristol, Dec. 24, 1826, by Jonathan Cone, V. D. M. — 1 — 36

WILMOT, Lucius, of Burlington, m. Lavina **HOTCHKISS**, of
Norfolk, Jan. 4, 1829, by Rev. Henry Stanwood — 1 — 48

Rhoda, wid. of Burlington, m. Ambrose **BARNS**, of Plymouth,
Nov. 27, 1821, by Rev. Jonathan Cone — 1 — 12

WILSON, Eliza, of Hartford, m. John **PORTCH**, of Bristol, Apr.
2, 1847, by Rev. R. H. Seely — 3 — 32

WINCHELL, Seth, of Bristol, m. Jane **LEWIS**, of Southington,
Apr. 14, 1850, by Rev. Harvey Camp — 3 — 49

WINSTON, WINSTONE, Alanson, m. Nancy M.
BARTHOLOMEW, May 9, 1839, by Rev. David L.
Parmelee — 1 — 129

Annis, m. John G. **COWLES**, Nov. [ ], 1838, by Rev. David
L. Parmelee — 1 — 126

Eunice*, m. Thomas Franklin **FULLER**, [Aug.] 29, 1821, by
Rev. Jonathan Cone *(Written in Pencil "Lucy"?) — 1 — 9

Eunice, of Bristol, m. Benjamin **DEALLING**, of Middletown,
Oct. 30, 1822, by Rev. Jonathan Cone — 1 — 17

Granvill, of Lynchburg, Va., m. Helen M. **WINSTON**, of
Bristol, Sept. 4, 1850, by Rev. William H. Goodrich — 3 — 50

Helen M., of Bristol, m. Granvill **WINSTON**, of Lynchburg,
Va., Sept. 4, 1850, by Rev. William H. Goodrich — 3 — 50

John, m. Laura **STUNDLEY**, b. of Bristol, Dec. 12, 1816,

	Vol.	Page
WINSTON, WINSTONE, (cont.)		
by Rev. Jonathan Cone	TR4	529
Wellington, m. Jane C. **BARTHOLOMEW,** b. of Bristol, Sept.		
14, 1842, by Rev. Joseph S. Covell	3	8
WINTHERBURY, Jane, of Ohio, m. Martin **JUDD,** of Avon, Dec.		
2, 1849, by Rev. Lester Lewis	3	46
WOOD, Mary Ann, m. Edwin A. **BASSETT,** Nov. 30, 1836, by		
Rev. David L. Parmelee	1	109
WOODFORD, Asahel, of Farmington, m. Flora **HUMPHREY,** of		
Bristol, Sept. 12, 1827, by Charles G. Ives, J. P.	1	41
WOODIN, WOODEN, Austin, m. Mariette **MITCHELL,** b. of		
Bristol, Dec. 6, 1829, by Rev. Henry Stanwood	1	58
Calvin, 2nd, of Harwinton, m. Mary **GRIGGS,** of Plymouth,		
Feb. 28, 1827, by Charles G. Ives, J. P.	1	37
Sally M., of Bristol, m. Ransley H. **WHEELER,** of Levonia,		
N. Y., Oct. 19, 1836, by Rev. Harvey Husted	1	108
WOODRUFF, Albert P., of Bristol, m. Marilla N. **CRANE,** of		
Winsted, Sept. 15, 1853, by Rev. Lester Lewis	3	63
Henry I., of Farmington, m. Elizabeth P. **CARRIER,** of		
Glastonbury, May 20, 1851, by Rev. Lester Lewis	3	54
Joel, of Southington, m. Lucy M. **FORBES,** of Bristol,		
Sept. 1, 1845, by Rev. Edward Savage	3	24
John M., m. Annah I. **CADY,** June 4, 1837, by Rev. David		
L. Parmelee	1	114
WOOLWORTH, Chester A., of Bristol, m. Malenna **FARRELL,** of		
Waterbury, May 19, 1841, by Rev. James Squier	3	2
Franklin, m. Sarah E. **CURTISS,** b. of Bristol, Apr. 6, 1853,		
by E. C. Jones	3	68
WRIGHT, Angeline E., of Waterbury, m. Henry **ALLEN,** of		
Bristol, June 1, 1852, by Rev. Henry Fitch	3	60
Cornelia E., of Bristol, m. Adison **SPENCER,** of New		
Hartford, Oct. 24, 1843, by Edward Savage	3	14
YALE, Abel, m. Mrs. Lorene **BROWN,** b. of Bristol, June 28, 1821,		
by Rev. Jonathan Cone	1	7
Elmore, m. Lucy A. **HART,** b. of Bristol, Apr. 16, 1843,		
by S. W. Smith, Elder	3	11
Flora, m. Hiram **NORTON,** b. of Bristol, Nov. 24, 1831,		
by Charles G. Ives, J. P.	1	68
Lorena S., of Bristol, m. Burritt E. **BARKER,** of Plymouth,		
Apr. 8, 1845, by Rev. Edward Savage	3	22
Lydia, m. Edward **ROOT,** Oct. 17, 1838, by Rev. David L.		
Parmelee	1	124
Mary J., of Bristol, m. Avaristo **PECK,** of Burlington,		
Mar. 26, 1846, by Edward Savage	3	30
Orlando F., of Bristol, m. Adelia A. **STOCKING,** of Plymouth,		
Jan. 12, 1845, by Rev. J. S. Covill	3	21
Phidelia, of Bristol, m. William R. **WADSWORTH,** of East		
Hartford, Apr. 2, 1850, by Rev. Lester Lewis	3	48

	Vol.	Page
YALE, (cont.)		
Rosey Anne, of Bristol, m. Adna **HART**, of Burlington, Feb. 5, 1821, by Rev. Jonathan Cone	1	4
Sally S., m. Horace H. **WARNER**, b. of Bristol, Apr. 2, 1850, by Rev. Lester Lewis	3	48
Sarah Ann, m. William **WILCOX**, Sept. 11, 1839, by Rev. David L. Parmelee	1	131
William H., of Bristol, m. Mary D. **BUNNELL**, of Southington, Nov. 25, 1841, by Rev. Joseph S. Covill	3	4
YOUNG, Sarah Ann, m. John **PHELPS**, Jr., July 8, 1832, by Rev. David L. Parmelee	1	72

BROOKFIELD VITAL RECORDS
1788 - 1852

67

Page

BANKS, John O., of Patterson, N. Y., m. Thirsy **BENNIT**, of Brookfield,
    Oct. 12, 1826, by W[illia]m Meeker, J. P.   22

Joseph A., of Bridgeport, m. Suson **SHERMAN**, of Brookfield, Dec. 24,
    1851, by Rev. H. D. Noble   67

BARLOW, Betsey, of Brookfield, m. Rubin **WOOD**, of Danbury, Nov. 5,
    1820, by Benjamin Benham   12

Betsey M., m. Horrace **WILDMAN**, b. of Brookfield, Sept. 4, 1850,
    by Rev. Isaac Sanford   68

Daniel, d. July 18, 1823   110

E[ ]*, m. John **PORTER**, b. of Brookfield, Sept. 10, 1826, by
    Abner Brundage *(Possibly "Elizabeth")   22

Hiram, m. Phebe **HATCH**, Dec. 15, 1839, by Rev. Z. Cook, of Danbury   47

Jerusha, d. Mar. 9, 1823   110

Rachel, wid., d. [ ]   111

Sarah, of Brookfield, m. Nirum **WHEELER**, of Roxbury, Jan. 22, 1835,
    by Rev. Joseph S. Covell   38

BARNES, BARNS, Daniel F., of Danbury, m. Flora E. **STURDEVANT**, of
    Brookfield, June 26, 1849, by Rev. D. C. Curtis   63

Eli H., of Danbury, m. Margaret **HAWLEY**, of Brookfield, Oct. 11,
    1835, by Rev. Lemuel B. Hull   40

Ezra R., of Danbury, m. Caroline **STARR**, of Brookfield, Oct. 23,
    1844, by Rev. H. D. Noble   57

Geradus, of Waterbury, m. Orpha **OAKLEY**, of Brookfield, Oct. 12,
    1830, by Joseph S. Covell   30

BARNUM, Garry, m. Emma **COLE**, Mar. 11, 1849, by Rev. William Biddle   62

Isaac, of Bethel, m. Lavina **BABBIT**, of Brookfield, May 26, 1841,
    by Rev. Edward C. Bull   51

Isaac C., of Danbury, m. Jane **FOOT**, of Brookfield, Sept. 14, 1834,
    by Rev. Charles G. Selleck, of Ridgefield   37

Isaac C., m. Luana **WILDMAN**, b. of Brookfield, Mar. 4, 1849, by
    Rev. H. D. Noble   66

BARTRAM, Horace B., m. Easter M. **PECK**, June 15, 1828, by Benjamin
    Benham   23

BARDSLEY, Philo, of Newtown, m. Dorcas J. **RATHBONE**(?), of Brookfield,
    Sept. 8, 1823, by Rev. Benjamin Benham   17

BEEBE, Amanda, of Brookfield, m. Isaac B. **WALKER**, of Bridgeport, Dec.
    31, 1844, by Rev. H. D. Noble   58

Huldah, w. Joseph B., d. Oct. 22, 1827   112

Laura, m. Charles **HURD**, Mar. 24, 1824, by Abner Brundage   18

Lary A*., of Brookfield, m. Harry **GLOVER**, of Newtown, Jan. 16, 1822,
    by Rev. Daniel Burhans *("A" nearly erased; possible "Lucy")   15

Serputia L., of Danbury, m. Phebe **SMITH**, of Brookfield, Oct. 15,
    1823, by Abner Brneda   17

BEERS, Chancey A., of Bridgewater, m. Laura **DUNNING**, of Brookfield,
    Apr. 4, 1841, by Rev. Edward C. Bull   50

David, of Newtown, m. Margaret **PRAY**, of Brookfield, Apr. 12, 1835,
    by Rev. Joseph S. Covell   39

Harriett F*., m. John G. **FOSTER**, b. of Brookfield, May 31, 1846,

Page

BEERS, (cont.)
    by Rev. H. D. Noble *(Possibly "Harriet F. **BURR**,") 57
    Rebecca, m. Benjamin **JONES**, b. of Brookfield, Nov. 4, 1835, by
      Rev. Joseph S. Covell 41
    Sophia H., of Brookfield, m. Edwin S. **HOYT**, of Winsted, May 14, 1851,
      by Rev. H. D. Noble 67
BENEDICT, Charles, of New Milford, m. Permelia **KULLER***, of Brookfield,
    Oct. 8, 1831, by Rev. Joseph S. Covell *(**KEELER?**) 33
    Charles S., of Danbury, m. Harriet **KEELER**, of Brookfield, Apr. 14,
      1841, by Rev. Edward C. Bull 50
    E. Sanford, of Danbury, m. Eleaner M. **WARNER**, of West Troy, May 6,
      1845, by Rev. Dan C. Curtis 54
    Elisur, m. Fanny **MERWIN**, Jan. 1, 1824, by Abner Brundage 18
    Henry W., of Newtown, m. Cloe **TURRELL**, of Brookfield,
      [, 1850 (?)], by Rev. William Biddle 64
    John D., of Danbury, m. Angeline **LACY**, of Brookfield, Nov. 18,
      1828, by Rev. Benjamin Benham 24
    Martin, see under Martin **BURDICK**
    Nelson, of Brookfield, m. Janett **BUCKINGHAM**, Oct. 1, 1848, by
      Rev. William Riddle 62
    Nirum, m. Lucy **SMITH**, Apr. 26, 1821, by Benjamin Benham 13
    Orilla M., m. Burr B. **NORTHROP**, b. of Brookfield, Oct. 5, 1834,
      by Rev. N. M. Urmston, of Newton 37
BENHAM, Benjamin, of New Milford, m. Sally Minerva **SHERMAN**, of
    Brookfield, Oct. 1, 1827, by Rev. Lemuel B. Hull 23
    Candace V. B.. of Brookfield, m. Augustus C. **BOORAM**, M. D., of
      New York, Oct. 14, 1851, by Rev. H. D. Noble 67
BENNETT, BENNET, BENNIT, Almira, m. Elizur **ELWOOD**, b. of
    Brookfield, Jan. 6, 1841, by A. Brundage 49
    Caleb, d. Jan. 31, 1832 112
    Henriet, m. Elizur **ELWOOD**, b. of Brookfield, Nov. 1, [1821], by
      Abner Brundage 14
    John F., m. Sally M. **DOBBS**, b. of Brookfield, Apr. 20, 1834, by
      Abner Brundage 36
    Sarah Ann, m. Philo **SHERMAN**, Oct. 21, 1832, by Rev. Joseph S.
      Covell 34
    Thirsy, of Brookfield, m. John O. **BANKS**, of Patterson, N. Y.,
      Oct. 12, 1826, by W[illia]m Meeker, J. P. 22
BETTS, David, d. [ ], 1825 111
BIDDLE, Sarah Lydia, of Brookfield, m. Andrew **ABRAHAM**, of New York,
    Feb. 6, 1849, by Rev. William Biddle 62
BIRCH, Alfred H., [s. Heman & Lydia], b. Nov. 10*, 1812; d. Aug. 27, 1816
    *(Possibly "17") 7
    Catharine, [d. Heman & Lydia], b. Dec. 6, 1815 7
    Mary, d. [Heman & Lydia], b. May 27, 1822 7
    Susan Elizabeth, [d. Heman & Lydia], b. Dec. 23, 1819 7
BISHOP, Naomi, m. Drake **NORTHRUP**, Dec. 11, 1783, by Rev. Thomons
    Brooks 1

Page

CAMP, Amos, m. Sally Ann MERWIN, b. of Brookfield, Jan. 1, 1827, by
    Rev. David Bennet | 22
    Annis, w. David P., d. Sept. 3, 1822 | 110
    Asa W., m. Maranda WARNER, b. of Brookfield, Oct. 6, 1822, by
    Rev. Benjamin Benham | 16
    Asa W., b. Feb. 18, 1825 | 11
    Asa W., s. Asa W., b. Feb. 18, 1825 | 20
    Eliza Maria, d. Daniel, b. Apr. 24, 1822 | 4
    Heppe, m. Amiel PECK, Jan. 8, 1764 | 5
    Jane, m. Jedediah WELLMAN, May 16, 1824, by Rev. Benjamin
    Benham | 18
    Lucy, w. David P., d. Dec. 19, 1815 | 110
    Mary A., b. Aug. 21, 1823 | 11
    Mary A., d. Asa W., b. Aug. 21, 1823 | 20
    Polly M., m. Alva BABBIT, b. of Brookfield, Apr. 16, 1826, by A.
    Brundage | 21
    Selies*, of Newtown, m. Mabel SMITH, Sept. 11, 1822, by Daniel
    Blackman, J. P. *(Silas?) | 16
    Silas, m. Betsey Ann WELMAN, b. of Brookfield, Nov. 3, [1822],
    by Rev. Benjamin Benham | 16
CAMPBELL, Elizabeth, [d. wid. Mary], was on Jan. 19, [1811], 9 yrs. of age | 9
    Imogeni, [d. wid. Mary], was on Sept. 21, [1811], 12 yrs. of age | 9
    John M., of Roxbury, m. Mary BLACKMAN, of Brookfield, Jan. 5, 1851,
    by Rev. William Biddle | 64
    Rodereh Ouris, [s. wid. Mary], was on Apr. 2, [1811] 6 yrs. of age | 9
CANFIELD, Arza, m. Harriet CHAMBERLAIN, b. of Brookfield, Aug. 24,
    1823, by Abner Brundage | 17
    Arza, Dr., d. Nov. 17, 1826 | 27
    Egbert B., of Bridgewater, m. Eliza Ann BROWN, of Brookfield,
    Dec. 7, 1840, by Abner Brundage | 49
    Harriet, wid. Dr. A., d. Jan. 11, 1827 | 27
    Joseph Harvey, of Bridgewater, m. Mary ANDREWS, of Brookfield,
    Nov. 25, 1841, by Abner Brundage | 49
CARPENTER, Austin, of Derby, m. Mary WHITLOCK, of Brookfield, Dec.
    24, 1826, by Eli Ruggles, J. P. | 22
CARTER, Mary E., of Ridgefield Summit Cty., O., m. James A. (?) PECK,
    of Brookfield, Apr. 9, 1848, by Rev. William Biddle | 61
CHAMBERLAIN, Harriet, m. Arza CANFIELD, b. of Brookfield, Aug. 24,
    1823, by Abner Brundage | 17
CLARK, James Starr, s. Everit & Anna, b. Dec. 3, 1822 | 8
    Sally, m. Daniel B. COOK, Mar. 24, 1791 | 8
COGSWELL, Amelia, of Monroe, m. Michael C. DONNALLY, of New York,
    Oct. 16, 1849, by Rev. D. C. Curtis | 63
    John G., of Monroe, m. Abigail J. MOREHOUSE, of Brookfield, Dec.
    25, 1851, by Rev. H. D. Noble | 67
COLE, Emma, m. Garry BARNUM, Mar. 11, 1849, by Rev. William Biddle | 62
    Henry W., m. Mary Ann MERWIN, b. of Brookfield, Apr. 12, 1829,
    by Abner Brundage | 25

Page

COLQUHOUN, [see also CALHOUN], Rufus, m. Eliza STEVENS, Apr. 25,
    1847, by Rev. William Biddle   59
CONGER, Harriot, m. Albert JUDSON, Mar. 14, 1826, by Abner Brundage   21
COOK, COOKE, Daniel B., m. Sally CLARK, Mar. 24, 1791   8
    Daniel B., m. Sally CURTIS, Feb. 2, 1794   7
    Daniel B., m. 2nd w. Sally CURTIS, Feb. 2, 1794   8
    Daniel B., m. Lucy PRATT, Oct. 8, 1795   7
    Daniel B., m. 3rd w. Lucy PRATT, Oct. 8, 1795   8
    Joseph Pratt, s. [Daniel B. & Lucy], b. Dec. 6, 1800   8
    Sally, w. [Daniel B.], d. Apr. 25, 1793   8
    Sally, 2nd w. [Daniel B.], d. Dec. 12, 1794   8
    Tames Clark, s. [Daniel B. & Sally], b. June 25, 1792   8
CORNING, William, m. Hannah LOBDELL, b. of Brookfield, Dec. 24, 1827,
    by Abner Brundage   23
CORNWALL, George Clapp, m. Mary Amarilus NORTHROP, b. of
    Brookfield, Sept. 17, 1844, by Rev. Dan C. Curtis   53
    John, m. Sophia A. PECK, b. of Brookfield, Nov. 7, 1841, by Rev.
    Edward C. Bull   51
CRANE, Csear F. W., m. Hannah A. JENNINGS, b. of Brookfield, Aug. 28,
    1836, by Joel Sherman, J. P.   43
CROFT, Samuel S., of Patterson, m. Lucretia FOOT, of Brookfield, Aug.
    12, 1821, by Rev. Benjamin Benham   14
CURTIS, Sally, m. Daniel B. COOKE, Feb. 2, 1794   7
    Sally, m. Daniel B. COOKE, Feb. 2, 1794; d. Dec. 12, 1794   8
CUTLIN, Henry, m. Scyntha STARR, Nov. 19, 1840, by Rev. Luceiss Atwater   48
DAVIS, Olive E., of Brookfield, m. Joseph F. BROTHERTON, of Wilton,
    Apr. 28, 1850, by Rev. D. C. Curtis   64
DAYTON, Mary J., of Mesuod (?), m, Charles SHEPHERD, of Newtown,
    Mar. 28, 1847, by Rev. D. C. Curtis   58
DeFOREST, Lockwood, of Bridgeport, m. Mary TOMLINSON, of Brookfield,
    Sept. 11, 1831, by Rev. Joseph S. Covell   32
DIBBLE, David B., m. Mary C. STEPHENS, b. of Brookfield, Sept. 6, 1847,
    by Rev. E. D. Noble   59
    David Botsford, [s. Ethel], b. Oct. 24, 1822   20
    Edwin Smith, [s. Ethel], b. May 4, 1820   20
    Ethel, b. July 21, 1786; m. [ ], Oct. 22, 1812   20
    Ezra B., of Bridgeport, m. Sarah E. ANDREWS, of Brookfield, Oct.
    1, 1850, by Rev. D. C. Curtis   65
    Ezra Bennit, [s. Ethel], b. Oct. 25, 1824   20
    Hoyt, m. Julia SMITH, b. of Danbury, Nov. 22, 1830, by Abner
    Brundgage   30
    Lorry Sophia, [d. Ethel], b. Feb. 2, 1818   20
    Lucy Delia, [d. Ethel], b. Oct. 8, 1815   20
    William Fairman, s. Ethel, b. Oct. 31, 1813   20
    Zenus L., m. Harriet C. GRAY, b. of Brookfield, Mar. 28, 1847, by Rev.
    H. D. Noble   58
DICKERMAN, DEKIMAN, Ira, of Newtown, m. Betsey HURD, of
    Brookfield, Feb. 10, 1822, by Rev. Daniel Burhans   15

Page

FAIRCHILD, (cont.)
    June 19, 1850, by Rev. D. C. Curtis   65
    Mary, of Brookfield, m. Joseph **NEWMAN**, of Newburyport, Mass.,
      Dec. 7, 1829, by Joseph S. Covell   28
    Mary, of Newtown, m. Charles W. **STEVENS**, of Brookfield, Nov. 27,
      1834, by Abner Brundage   37
FARNUM, Daniel H., of Litchfield, m. Lucy M. **KNAP**, of Brookfield,
    Sept. 19, 1838, by Abner Brundage   46
    Henry L., of South Farms, m. Eliza **MERWIN**, of Brookfield, Jan. 29,
      1840, by Abner Brundage   47
FENNER, Samuel, of Danbury, m. Phebe **HALL**, of Brookfield, Apr. 8, 1835,
    by Rev. Joseph S. Covell   39
FOOT, Abel, his w.[ ], d. Oct. [ ], 1825   111
    Ann Genette, m. Daniel **WILDMAN**, b. of Brookfield, Feb. 8, 1829,
      by Rev. Benjamin Benham   24
    Beers, m. Permelia A. **MERWIN**, b. of Brookfield, Apr. 5, 1829, by
      Abner Brundage   25
    Jane, of Brookfield, m. Isaac C. **BARNUM**, of Danbury, Sept. 14, 1834,
      by Rev. Charles G. Selleck, of Ridgefield   37
    John L., m. Hannah Clarrissa **BLACKMAN**, Apr. 18, 1841, by Rev.
      Nathan Rice   49
    Lucretia, of Brookfield, m. Samuel S. **CROFT**, of Patterson, Aug. 12,
      1821, by Rev. Benjamin Benham   14
    Sherman, m. Clarine **PECK**, Oct. 11, 1835, by Abner Brundage   41
FOSTER, John G., m. Harriett F. **BEERS***, b. of Brookfield, May 31, 1846,
    by Rev. H. D. Noble *(Possibly "BURR")   57
    John Noble, s. David A., b. Dec. 16, 1822   8
FULLER, William G., of New Milford, m. Mary Diana **TONGUE**, of
    Brookfield, Nov. 21, 1838, by Bryant Smith, J. P.   45
GEDNEY, David, of New York, m. Caroline **QUINTARD**, of Brookfield, Mar.
    25, 1823, by Abner Brundage   16
GILBERT, Wanzer S., of Newtown, m. Lovina **SEELEY**, of Brookfield, Aug.
    22, 1830, by Joseph S. Covell   29
GILLMAN, GILMON, Elisha, of East Hartford, d. Feb. 19, 1826, at the
    house of Levi Bostwick, ae 29 y.   112
    ----, of East Hartford, d. Feb. 19, 1826, ae 29 y. at the house
      of Levi Bostwick   20
    ----, from Hartford, d. Feb. 19, 1826   112
GLOVER, Benjamin N., of Newtown, m. Harriet A. **LAKE**, of Brookfield,
    Feb. 12, 1845, by Rev. H. D. Noble   58
    Harry, of Newtown, m. Lary A*. **BEEBE**, of Brookfield, Jan. 16,
      1822, by Rev. Daniel Burhans *(Possibly "Lucy A.")   15
    Julia, m. Botsford **TERRELL**, b. of Newtown, Sept. 22, 1822, by
      Rev. Benjamin Benham   16
    William B., of Newtown, m. Harriet A. **PECK**, of Brookfield, Nov.
      7, 1832, by Rev. Joseph S. Covell   34
GOODSELL, Lucy G., m. Homer C. **BRUSH**, b. of Brookfield, Sept. 12,
    1830, by Joseph S. Covell   29

Page

GOODSELL, (cont.)

Sturges, his child d. [ ], 1823* *(Possibly "1829")   110

GRAHAM, George, of Waterbury, m. Nancy A. **IVES**, of Roxbury, Jan. 14,
1851, by Rev. William Biddle   65

GRAVES, John S., of New Haven, m. Polly **MERWIN**, of Brookfield, July 23,
1837, by Abner Brundage   45

GRAY, Abel H., m. Tamore **HUBBELL**, b. of Brookfield, Dec. 18, 1825,
by Rev. Benjamin Benham   20

Abigail, of Brookfield, m. Henry **MAY**, of Newtown, June 29, 1836,
by Rev. T. Hitchcock, of Newtown   43

Buel, of Columbia, N. Y., m. wid. Darmaras **JACKSON**, of Brookfield,
June 29, 1823, by Eli Ruggles, J. P.   17

Harriet C., m. Zenus L. **DIBBLE**, b. of Brookfield, Mar. 28, 1847,
by Rev. H. D. Noble   58

Mabel, m. George **KEELER**, b. of Brookfield, Nov. 25, 1827, by
Abner Brundage   23

Rheuel, d. Feb. 18, 1824   110

Sally A., see Sally A. **GREEY**   17

GREEY*, Sally A., m. Benjamin **KEELER**, b. of Brookfield, Oct. 5, 1823,
by Abner Brundage *(Probably "GRAY")   17

GREGORY, David S., s. Stevens, b. May 25, 1823   9

Elisa, m. Horace R. **NORTHROP**, b. of Brookfield, Nov. 28, 1832,
by Abner Brundage   33

Emma A., of Brookfield, m. Alfred **PUGSLEY**, of Patterson, N. Y.,
Nov. 5, 1829, by Abner Brundage   26

Mary, d. Nov. 14, 1825   111

Stephen, of Danbury, m. Electa **HAWLEY**, of Brookfield, Oct. 21,
1821, at the house of wid. Hannah **HAWLEY**, by Daniel Tomlinson,
J. P.   14

Stephen, his child d. Jan. 3, 1826   112

Steven, his child d. [ ], 1823* *(Possibly "1829")   110

GUIER, John, d. [ ], 1825   111

GURLEY, Jason, of Hartford, m. Selina **STURDEVANT**, of Brookfield, Jan.
11, 1830, by Rev. Benjamin Benham   26

HABBELL, [see under HUBBELL]

HALL, [see also HULL], Allen, of Newtown, m. Huldah A. **TAYLOR**, of
Brookfield, Dec. 21, 1831, by Bryant Smith, J. P.   32

Louisa*, m. Homer **STURDEVANT**, b. of Brookfield, Feb. 10, 1848,
by Rev. D. C. Curtis *(Possibly "Allen HULL")   60

Phebe, of Brookfield, m. Samuel **FENNER**, of Danbury, Apr. 8, 1835,
by Rev. Joseph S. Covell   39

HALLAWAY, Sarah E., of Pawlings, N. Y., m. Ira **SHERMAN**, of Newtown,
Dec. 24, 1840, by Hubbell Wildman, J. P.   48

HALLOCK, Jessee H., of New Milford, m. Polly **WHITLOCK**, of Brookfield,
Mar. 16, 1843, by Z. Davenport   53

HAMLIN, Hester, m. Elizur **ELWOOD**, Jan. 8, 1843, by Z. Davenport   52

Ira, his child d. [ ], 1823* *(Possibly "1829")   110

Joseph, m. Amy **RUGGLES**, b. of Brookfield, Nov. 28, 1833, by Rev.

Page

HAMLIN, (cont.)

Joseph S. Covell   36

Susan Harriet, m. Nathan W. **KEELER,** Dec. 24, 1843, by Rev.
Dan C. Curtis   52

HANSON, Stephen N., of Brookfield, m. Lucinda **STEWART,** of Bridgewater,
May 17, 1849, by Rev. D. C. Curtis   63

HATCH, Phebe, m. Hiram **BARLOW,** Dec. 15, 1839, by Rev. Z. Cook, of
Danbury   47

HAWLEY*, Benjamin, m. Besy **PECK,** b. of Brookfield, Oct. 21, 1821, by
Abner Brundage *(Word crossed out)   14

Betsey, m. Zopher **BROWN,** Nov. 2, 1825, by Abner Brundage   19

Charles, [s. Daniel], b. Feb. 6, 1804   8

Charles, m. Anna **NORTHROP,** b. of Brookfield, Apr. 13, 1826, by
A. Brundage   21

Charles, m. Anna **MERWIN,** b. of Brookfield, Dec. 28, 1834, by
Abner Brundage   38

Daniel, d. Feb. 9, 1826, in the 60th y. of his age   112

Eleazar D., [s. Daniel], b. Feb. 5, 1788   8

Electa, of Brookfield, m. Stephen **GREGORY,** of Danbury, Oct. 21, 1821,
at the house of wid. Hannah Hawley, by Daniel Tomlinson, J. P.   14

Fanny M., of South Britain, m. Jesse L. **JACKSON,** of Brookfield,
Apr. 6, 1851, by Rev. H. D. Noble   67

Lucy, [d. Daniel], b. June 3, 1801   8

Lucy, m. Elmore B. **NORTHROP,** b. of Brookfield, Dec. 4, 1821, by
Abner Brundage   14

Margaret, of Brookfield, m. Eli H. **BARNS,** of Danbury, Oct. 11,
1835, by Rev. Lemuel B. Hull   40

Munson, of New Fairfield, m. Sarah **McLEAN,** of Danbury, Apr. 28,
1850, by Rev. D. C. Curtis   64

Sidney, [s. Daniel], b. Apr. 3, 1807   8

HEPBORN, Mary, wid., d. Jan. 13, 1826   112

HICKOK, Ebenezer Lauren, of Bethel, m. Sarah Juliette **HUBBELL,** of
Brookfield, June 4, 1851, by Rev. D. C. Curtis   69

HOLEMAN, HOLIMAN, Lucia, m. Daniel **TOMLINSON,** b. of Brookfield,
Sept. 18*, 1835, by Rev. Joseph S. Covell *(Fig. 8 uncertain)   41

Lucia M., m. Hiram B. **NOBLE,** of New Milford, Jan. 23, 1839, by
Abner Brundage   46

HOLLY, Harriet G., of Brookfield, m. Alvah S. **BUTLER,** of Skeneatetes,
N. Y., Aug. 29*, 1852, by Rev. Dan C. Curtis *(Possibly "24th")   69

Juliett S., m. Dr. Amos L. **WILLIAMS,** b. of Brookfield, Oct. 16,
1833, by Abner Brundage   35

HOYER, Augustus, of Germany, m. Jane **McCURDEY,** of Ireland, Mar. 4,
1850, by Rev. D. C. Curtis   63

HOYT, Edwin S., of Winsted, m. Sophia H. **BEERS,** of Brookfield, May 14,
1851, by Rev. H. D. Noble   67

HUBBELL, HABBELL, Amos, d. [ ], 1825   111

Amos, of Sherman, m. Lucy **LOCKWOOD,** of Brookfield, Oct. 28, 1840,
by Abner Brundage   48

Page

HUBBELL, HABBELL, (cont.)

Sarah Juliette, of Brookfield, m. Ebenezer Lauren **HICKOK**, of
Bethel, June 4, 1851, by Rev. D. C. Curtis   69

Tamore, m. Abel H. **GRAY**, b. of Brookfield, Dec. 18, 1825, by Rev.
Benjamin Benham   20

HULL, [see also **HALL**], Amilia, d. Aug. 21, 1825   111

Henerita, d. Sept. 29, 1825   111

HURD, Betsy, of Brookfield, m. Ira **DECKIMAN**, of Newtown, Feb. 10, 1822,
by Rev. Daniel Burhans   15

Charles, m. Laura **BEEBE**, Mar. 24, 1824, by Abner Brundage   18

Philo, m. Malinda **TOMLINSON**, Oct. 5, 1823, by Rev. Benjamin
Benham   17

Samuel F., of Bridgeport, m. Julia **TOMLINSON**, of Brookfield, Dec.
24, 1824, by Rev. Benjamin Benham   19

HURLBUT, HURLBERT, HURLBUTT, [E]unis Sophiah, d. Foster, b. July
30, 1822   8

Foster, his child d. [ ]   111

George, of Roxbury, m. Thalia A. **MERWIN**, of Brookfield, Jan. 7,
1833, by Abner Brundage   35

Marinda, m. Hiram **LAKE**, b. of Brookfield, Nov. 29, 1822, by
Benjamin Benham   16

Orrilla, of Brookfield, m. Israel **PERKINS**, of Waterbury, Sept.
7, 1830, by Joseph S. Covell   29

Samuel Evets, s. Foster, d. Oct. 30, 1825   20

Sard, his child d. [ ], 1824   110

IVES, Nancy A., of Roxbury, m. George **GRAHAM**, of Waterbury, Jan. 14,
1851, by Rev. William Biddle   65

JACKSON, Damaras, wid., of Brookfield, m. Buel **GRAY**, of Columbia,
N. Y., June 29, 1823, by Eli Ruggles, J. P.   17

Jesse L., of Brookfield, m. Fanny M. **HAWLEY**, of South Britain,
Apr. 6, 1851, by Rev. H. D. Noble   67

Joel, m. Mathea **ELWOOD**, Nov. 1, 1821, by Abner Brundage   14

Mary M., of Brookfield, m. Truman **MALLERY**, of Roxbury, Apr. 7,
1847, by Rev. D. C. Curtis   59

Niram, of Danbury, m. Lucy **KEELER**, of Brookfield, Apr. 18, 1841,
by Ebner Brundage   49

JENNINGS*, David Pay, of New Milford, m. Martha **MEAD**, of Brookfield,
Nov. 3, 1853, by Rev. Richard D. Higby *(Or "GENNINGS")   69

Edson Sherman, s. David, b. Aug. 10*, 1822 *(Possibly "15" or "18")   4

Elizabeth, of Brookfield, m. George **MATHEWS**, of Waterbury, Nov.
30, 1848, by Rev. H. D. Noble   66

Hannah A., m. Csear F. W. **CRANE**, b. of Brookfield, Aug. 28, 1836,
by Joel Sherman, J. P.   43

JOHNSON, Emeline, of Brookfield, m. Barzillai B. **KELLOGG**, of New
Fairfield, Sept. 8, 1845, by Rev. H. D. Noble   56

Henry M., of Bridgeport, m. Lois **JONES**, of Brookfield, Nov. 15,
1848, by Rev. D. C. Curtis   63

JONES, Benjamin, m. Rebecca **BEERS**, b. of Brookfield, Nov. 4, 1835,

Page

JONES, (cont.)
　　by Rev. Joseph S. Covell　41
　　Charles, b. May 5, 1823　9
　　Lois, of Brookfield, m. Henry M. JOHNSON, of Bridgeport, Nov. 15,
　　　　1848, by Rev. D. C. Curtis　63
JUDSON, Adeline, of Brookfield, m. Nelson C. BROCKINGTON, of
　　　　Danbury, May 21, 1846, by Rev. H. D. Noble　57
　　Albert, m. Harriot CONGER, Mar. 14, 1826, by Abner Brundage　21
KEELER, Amy, m. Daniel N. WARNER, b. of Brookfield, Apr. 21, 1842, by
　　　　Abner Brundage　50
　　Benjamin, m. Sally A. GREEY*, b. of Brookfield, Oct. 5, 1823, by
　　　　Abner Brundage　*(Probably "GRAY")　17
　　Ezra, d. July [ ], 1825　111
　　Frederick, m. Hellen WARNER, b. of Brookfield, Aug. 31, 1846,
　　　　by Rev. D. C. Curtis　55
　　George, m. Mabel GRAY, b. of Brookfield, Nov. 25, 1827, by Abner
　　　　Brundage　23
　　George, m. Jane* TOMLINSON, b. of Brookfield, Nov. 22, 1835, by
　　　　Rev. Joseph S. Covell　*(Probably "June")　42
　　Hannah, m. John MERWIN, b. of Brookfield, Jan. 31, 1822, by Abner
　　　　Brundage　15
　　Harriet, of Brookfield, m. Charles S. BENEDICT, of Danbury, Apr.
　　　　14, 1841, by Rev. Edward C. Bull　50
　　Hulda, w. Benj[amin], d. July 28, 1823　110
　　Julia, of Brookfield, m. Martin BURDICK*, of New York, Jan. 1,
　　　　1845, by Rev. Dan C. Curtis　*(Or "BENDICK")　54
　　Lucy, of Brookfield, m. Niram JACKSON, of Danbury, Apr. 18, 1841,
　　　　by Abner Brundage　49
　　Nathan W., m. Susan Harriet HAMLIN, Dec. 24, 1843, by Rev. Dan C.
　　　　Curtis　52
　　Permelia *, of Brookfield, m. Charles BENEDICT, of New Milford,
　　　　Oct. 8, 1831, by Rev. Joseph S. Covell　*("Permelia KULLER")　33
　　Sarah, of Brookfield, m. George B. SANFORD, of Putney, Vt., Nov.
　　　　8, 1836, by A. Brundage　44
　　Zeruah, m. Darius BRISTOLL, b. of Brookfield, Jan. 24, 1821, by
　　　　Robert B. Ruggles, J. P.　12
KELLOGG, Barzillai B., of New Fairfield, m. Emeline JOHNSON, of
　　　　Brookfield, Sept. 8, 1845, by Rev. H. D. Noble　55
　　Medad Rogers, of New Fairfield, m. Evalina A. PECK, of Brookfield,
　　　　Nov. 7, 1836, by A. Brundage　44
　　Polly Ann, m. Solomon W. STEVENS, b. of Brookfield, Oct. 8, 1826,
　　　　by Abner Brundage　22
KNAPP, Barzillai, of Danbury, m. A. M. REID, of Brookfield, Sept. 17,
　　　　1848, by Rev. William Biddle　62
　　Hannah, m. Roswell T. PARKER, b. of Brookfield, June 19, 1831, by
　　　　Joseph S. Covell　31
　　Lucy M., of Brookfield, m. Daniel H. FARNUM, of Litchfield, Sept.
　　　　19, 1838, by Abner Brundage　46

Page

KULLER*, Permelia, of Brookfield, m. Charles BENEDICT, of New Milford,
    Oct. 8, 1831, by Rev. Joseph S. Covell *(KEELER?)   33
LACY, LACEY, Angeline, of Brookfield, m. John D. BINEDICT, of Danbury,
    Nov. 18, 1828, by Rev. Benjamin Benham   24
  Emeline, of Brookfield, m. Herman THORP, of Newtown, Jan. 30, 1831,
    by Joseph S. Covell   31
  Rachel, m. Salmon R. STARR, Dec. 1, 1824, by Rev. Benjamin Benjam   18
LAKE, Betsey, of Brookfield, m. Glover SANFORD, of Sallesbury, Feb. 4,
    1822, by Rev. Benjamin Benham   15
  Harriet A., of Brookfield, m. Benjamin N. GLOVER, of Newtown, Feb.
    12, 1845, by Rev. H. D. Noble   58
  Hiram, m. Marinda HURLBUT, b. of Brookfield, Nov. 20, 1822, by Rev.
    Benjamin Benham   16
  Joseph S., of Newtown, m. Hannah R. SMITH, of Brookfield, Apr. 25,
    1849, by Rev. H. D. Noble   66
  Polly, m. Henry* RUGGLES, b. of Brookfield, Nov. 2, 1823, by Rev.
    Benjamin Benham *("Harry")   18
LAMPSON, Harriet, of New Milford, m. Canfield S.* WILDMAN, of
    Brookfield, Oct. 11, 1838, by Joel C. Sherman, J. P.
    *("S." doubtful, possibly "I")   45
LATTIN, Sarah E., of Brookfield, m. George T. PATCHIN, of New Milford,
    Feb. 8, 1852, by Rev. Isaac Sanford   68
LAWRENCE, Mary, m. Thomas TAYLOR, b. of Brookfield, Nov. 10, 1841,
    by Rev. Edward C. Bull   52
LEACH, Ephraim, of Sherman, m. Mary MEEKER, of Brookfield, Feb. 4,
    1830, by Joseph S. Covell   28
LEE, Robert G., m. Ruth Ann BRISTOLL, b. of Brookfield, Feb. 6, 1848,
    by Rev. H. D. Noble   61
LENT, Lucinda, m. David N. PECK, b. of Brookfield, Oct. 31, 1847, by
    Rev. D. C. Curtis   60
LEWIS, Ann, m. Adoniram F. NORTHROP, b. of Newtown, Aug. 22, 1841,
    by Rev. Edward C. Bull   51
LOBDELL, Betsey, m. Levi BOSTWICK, Jr., Dec. 30, 1810   10
  Dennis B., his child, d. [ ]   111
  Hannah, m. William CORNING, b. of Brookfield, Dec. 24, 1827, by
    Abner Brundage   23
  John, m. Laura Ann WHEELER, b. of New Milford, Aug. 11, 1845, by
    Rev. D. C. Curtiss   54
  Lewis, of Brookfield, m. Janett ADKINS, of Danbury, June 6, 1847,
    by Rev. William Biddle   56
  Sally, m. Byram B. BUCKENHAM, Dec. 7, 1825, by Rev. Benjamin
    Benham   20
  Susan M., m. Sidney SMITH, b. of Brookfield, Nov. 27, 1834, by
    Rev. Joseph S. Cornell   38
LOCKWOOD, Isaac, Jr., m. Olivet DUNNING, b. of Brookfield, Nov. 12,
    1826, by A. Brundage   21
  Lucy, of Brookfield, m. Amos HUBBELL, of Sherman, Oct. 28, 1840,
    by Abner Brundage   48

Page

LONG, William, see William **TONG**   39
LOVELACE, George E., m. Ann Jennett **EDGET**, Feb. 23, 1851, by Rev.
    William Biddle   65
McCURDEY, Jane, of Ireland, m. Augustus **HOYER**, of Germany, Mar. 4,
    1850, by Rev. D. C. Curtis   63
McLANE, McLAIN, McLEAN, Alexander, of Danbury, m. Sally **MEEKER**,
    of Brookfield, Nov. 15, 1831, by Rev. Joseph S. Covell   34
    Mary, of Danbury, m. Nathan **SMITH**, of Brookfield, Jan. 30, 1831,
       by Joseph S. Covell   31
    Sarah, of Danbury, m. Munson **HAWLEY**, of New Fairfield, Apr. 28,
       1850, by Rev. D. C. Curtis   64
MALLERY, Truman, of Roxbury, m. Mary M. **JACKSON**, of Brookfield,
    Apr. 7, 1847, by Rev. D. C. Curtis   59
MATHEWS, George, of Waterbury, m. Elizabeth **JENNINGS**, of Brookfield,
    Nov. 30, 1848, by Rev. H. D. Noble   66
MAY, Henry, of Newtown, m. Abigail **GRAY**, of Brookfield, June 29, 1836,
    by Rev. T. Hitchcock, of Newtown   43
MEAD, Martha, of Brookfield, m. David Pay **JENNINGS***,of New Milford,
    Nov. 3, 1853, by Rev. Richard D. Higby *(Or "**GENNINGS**")   69
MEEKER, Mary, of Brookfield, m. Ephraim **LEACH**, of Sherman, Feb. 4,
    1830, by Joseph S. Covell   28
    Sally, of Brookfield, m. Alexander **McLANE**, of Danbury, Nov. 15,
       1831, by Rev. Joseph S. Covell   34
MERCHANT, Orson, of Redding, m. Polly Ann **WHEELER**, of Brookfield,
    Nov. 27, 1846, by Rev. H. D. Noble   67
MERWIN, MURWIN, Andrew, m. wid. Rhoda **STARR**, b. of Brookfield, Feb.
    23, 1830, by Abner Brundage   26
    Anna, m. Charles **HAWLEY**, b. of Brookfield, Dec. 28, 1834, by
       Abner Brundage   38
    Caroline, m. Ralph B. **PECK**, b. of Brookfield, Mar. 13, 1836,
       by Abner Brundage   43
    Eliza, of Brookfield, m. Henry L. **FARNUM**, of South Farms, Jan.
       29, 1840, by Abner Brundage   47
    Fanny, m. Elizur **BENEDICT**, Jan. 1, 1824, by Abner Burndage   18
    John, m. Hannah **KEELER**, b. of Brookfield, Jan. 31, 1822, by
       Abner Brundage   15
    Laura, m. Sherman **SMITH**, b. of Brookfield, Mar. 6, 1825, by
       Abner Brundage   19
    Loes, d. May 15, 1822   110
    Mary Ann, m. Henry W. **COLE**, b. of Brookfield, Apr. 12, 1829,
       by Abner Brundage   25
    Minarva, m. Isaac T. **WISE**, Jan. 31, 1821, by Rev. William Andrews   12
    Nancy C., m. John **STEWART**, Sept. 29, 1835, by Abner Brundage   40
    Patty, m. John H. **NORTHROP**, Nov. 5, 1822, by Abner Brundage   16
    Permelia A., m. Beers **FOOT**, b. of Brookfield, Apr. 5, 1829, by
       Abner Brundage   25
    Polly, of Brookfield, m. John S. **GRAVES**, of New Haven, July 23,
       1837, by Abner Brundage   45

MERWIN, MURWIN, (cont.)

Salina, of Brookfield, m. Rufus **PARKER**, of Woodbury, Apr. 28,
1839, by Abner Brundage ... 46

Sally Ann, m. Amos **CAMP**, b. of Brookfield, Jan. 1, 1827, by Rev.
David Bennet ... 22

Samuel E., m. Rubey **NEARING**, b. of Brookfield, Dec. 20, 1829,
by A. Brundage ... 26

Thalis A., of Brookfield, m. George **HURLBUT**, of Roxbury, Jan. 7,
1833, by Abner Brundage ... 35

Urana, m. Ransby* **SOMERS**, Mar. 8, 1830, by Abner Brundage
(*Possibly "Ransley") ... 26

Urania, wid., d. Dea. Ashbill **DUNNING**, Mar. 28, 1838, by Abner
Brundage ... 46

MORE, John, m. Ann Mariah **STARR**, Oct. 7, 1830, by Joseph S. Covell ... 30

MOREHOUSE, Abigail J., of Brookfield, m. John G. **COGSWELL**, of
Monroe, Dec. 25, 1851, by Rev. H. D. Noble ... 67

Phebe, m. Rufus **CALHOUN**, b. of Brookfield, Feb. 14, 1849, by
Rev. William Biddle ... 62

William, m. Polly **OSBURN**, b. of Brookfield, Jan. 16, 1825, by
Eli Ruggles, J. P. ... 19

MORGAN, Peter, of Danbury, m. Susan **MORRIS**, of Brookfield, Sept. 3,
1844, by Rev. Shaler J. Hillyer ... 53

MORRIS, MORICE, Alfred, of Danbury, m. Hannah **STARR**, of Brookfield,
Apr. 7, 1824, by Reuben Booth, J. P. ... 18

Catharine A., m. Andrew **NORTHROP**, b. of Brookfield, Apr. 22, 1845,
by Rev. H. D. Noble ... 56

Samuel, of Danbury, m. Phebe **STARR**, of Brookfield, Jan. 17, 1821,
by William Cooke, J. P. ... 13

Susan, of Brookfield, m. Peter **MORGAN**, of Danbury, Sept. 3, 1844,
by Rev. Shaler J. Hillyer ... 53

NEARING, John H., m. Elizabeth **THORP**, b. of Brookfield, Nov. 10, 1830,
by Joseph S. Covell ... 30

Rubey, m. Samuel E. **MERWIN**, b. of Brookfield, Dec. 20, 1829, by
A. Brundage ... 26

NEWMAN, Joseph, of Newburyport, Mass., m. Mary **FAIRCHILD**, of
Brookfield, Dec. 7, 1829, by Joseph S. Covell ... 28

NOBLE, Hiram B., of New Milford, m. Lucia M. **HOLEMAN**, Jan. 23, 1839,
by Abner Brundage ... 46

NORTHROP, NORTHRUP, Adoniram F., m. Ann **LEWIS**, b. of Newtown,
Aug. 22, 1841, by Rev. Edward C. Bull ... 51

Albart, s. Drake & Naomi, b. Jan. 29, 1788 ... 1

Andrew, d. Aug. 15, 1825 ... 111

Andrew, d. Aug. 15, 1825 ... 112

Andrew, m. Catharine A. **MORRIS**, b. of Brookfield, Apr. 22, 1845,
by Rev. H. D. Noble ... 56

Anna, m. Charles **HAWLEY**, b. of Brookfield, Apr. 13, 1826, by A.
Brundage ... 21

Burr B., m. Orilla M. **BENEDICT**, b. of Brookfield, Oct. 5, 1834,

Page

NORTHROP, NORTHRUP, (cont.)
    by Rev. N. M. Urmston, of Newtown   37
    Clara, m. Martin W. **SOMERS,** Apr. 21, 1821, by Noah A. Lacy, J. P.   13
    David W., m. Mariah **BLACKMAN,** b. of Brookfield, May 31, 1821,
      by Rev. Benjamin Benham   13
    Drake, m. Naomi **BISHOP,** Dec. 11, 1783, by Rev. Thomons Brooks   1
    Elizabeth, m. Ashbill W. **DUNNING,** b. of Brookfield, Oct. 5, 1834,
      by Abner Brundage   37
    Elmore B., m. Lucy **HAWLEY,** b. of Brookfield, Dec. 4, 1821, by
      Abner Brundage   14
    Ezra, d. Dec. 4, 1822   110
    Flora, m. Sherman **DUNNING,** b. of Brookfield, Nov. 13, 1821, by
      Abner Brundage   14
    Hannah, of Brookfield, m. Lyman **NORTHROP,** of Cornwall, Sept. 11,
      1825, by Abner Brundage   19
    Harriet, m. Ira **WILDMAN,** b. of Brookfield, Feb. 14, 1830, by
      Joseph S. Covell   28
    Horace R., m. Elisa **GREGORY,** b. of Brookfield, Nov. 28, 1832,
      by Abner Brundage   33
    John H., m. Patty **MERWIN,** Nov. 5, 1822, by Abner Brundage   16
    John H., d. June 12, 1825   111
    Lucius* C., m. Caroline S. **TOMLINSON,** b. of Brookfield, Feb. 27,
      1842, by Rev. Edward C. Bull *(Possibly "Lewis")   52
    Lyman, s. Drake & Naomi, b. Mar. 28, 1785   1
    Lyman, of Cornwall, m. Hannah **NORTHROP,** of Brookfield, Sept. 11,
      1825, by Abner Brundage   19
    Maria, of Brookfield, m. Almon W. **THORP,** of New Milford, Sept. 8,
      1822, by Rev. Benjamin Benham   15
    Mary Amarilus, m. George Clapp **CORNWALL,** b. of Brookfield, Sept.
      17, 1844, by Rev. Dan C. Curtiss   53
    Minerva C., of Brookfield, m. Almon C. **RANDALL,** of Bridgewater,
      Jan. 26, 1845, by Rev. H. D. Noble   58
    Sarah, of Brookfield, m. Hirum **FAIRCHILD,** of Newtown, Jan. 20,
      1824, by Abner Brundage   18
    Susannah, wid. d. [   ]   111
    Wait, d. Dec. 6, 1824   110
OAKLEY, Orpha, of Brookfield, m. Geradus **BARNES,** of Waterbury, Oct.
    12, 1830, by Joseph S. Covell   30
    Polly, of Brookfield, m. John **EDMUNDS,** of Southbury, Nov. 10,
      1831, by Rev. Joseph S. Covell   33
    Sarah B., m. Sherman B. **RUGGLES,** Jan. 8, 1833, by Rev. Joseph S.
      Covell   34
ODELL, Almon, of Brookfield, m. Elizabeth **TURRELL,** of Redding, Apr.
    12, 1840, by Rev. Edward C. Bull   47
OSBORN, OSBORNE, OSBURN, Clarinda, of Brookfield, m. Levi
    DISBROW, of Sherman, Sept. 9, 1846, by Rev. H. D. Noble   57
    Elias, d. [   ]   111
    Elizabeth, Mrs., m. Calvin **WARD,** b. of Brookfield, Mar. 16, 1851, by

Page

OSBORN, OSBORNE, OSBURN, (cont.)

    Rev. William Biddle   65

    Ezra Burton, s. Ezra, b. Dec. 9*, 1822   *("7th"?)   9

    Hannah, of Brookfield, m. Ira **WHEELER**, of New Fairfield, Feb. 2,
      1834, by Rev. Joseph S. Covell   36

    James M., m. Elisabeth Ann **WILEMAN**, b. of Brookfield, Jan. 25,
      1825, by Rev. Benjamin Benham   19

    Jenett, of Brookfield, m. Benjamin **PAYNE**, of Danbury, Jan. 15,
      1851, by Rev. Isaac Sanford   68

    John, m. Mary Ann **EDGET**, Oct. 28, 1849, by Ebenezer Blackman, J. P.   61

    Lewis, d. [ ], 1825   111

    Phebe, m. Robert B. R. **BRISTOLL**, b. of Brookfield, Jan. 5, 1845,
      by Bryant Smith, J. P.   53

    Polly, m. William **MOREHOUSE**, b. of Brookfield, Jan. 16, 1825, by
      Eli Ruggles, J. P.   19

OTIS, Harriet, of Brookfield, m. Homer **BRIGGS**, of New Milford, Apr. 2,
    1849, by Rev. H. D. Noble   66

PARKER, Lucy, m. Alfred M. **BRUNDAGE**, b. of Brookfield, Aug. 11, 1833,
    by Abner Brundage   35

    Roswell T., m. Hannah **KNAPP**, b. of Brookfield, June 19, 1831, by
      Joseph S. Covell   31

    Rufus, of Woodbury, m. Salina **MERWIN**, of Brookfield, Apr. 28, 1839,
      by Abner Brundage   46

PATCHIN, George T., of New Milford, m. Sarah E. **LATTIN**, of Brookfield,
    Feb. 8, 1852, by Rev. Isaac Sanford   68

PAYNE, Benjamin, of Danbury, m. Jenett **OSBORNE**, of Brookfield, Jan.
    15, 1851, by Rev. Isaac Sanford   68

PEASE, Abigail, of Newtown, m. Thomas **SHERMAN**, of Brookfield,
    (colored), July 5, 1844, by Rev. Dan C. Curtis   54

PECK, Alice, [d. Amiel & Heppe], b. Jan. 2, 1774   5

    Amiel, m. Heppe **CAMP**, Jan. 8, 1764   5

    Amiel & w. Heppe, had d. [ ], b. July 6, 1784   5

    Arza Canfield, s. John A., b. June 8, 1822   4

    Besy, m. Benjamin **HAWLEY***, b. of Brookfield, Oct. 21, 1821, by
      Abner Brundage *(Word crossed out)   14

    Clarine, m. Sherman **FOOT**, Oct. 11, 1835, by Abner Brundage   41

    Cyrenus, of Brookfield, m. Abigail **BLAKE**, of New Preston, Apr. 19,
      1841, by Rev. Edward C. Bull   51

    David N., m. Lucinda **LENT**, b. of Brookfield, Oct. 31, 1847, by
      Rev. D. C. Curtis   60

    Easter M., m. Horace B. **BARTRAM**, June 15, 1828, by Benjamin
      Benham   23

    Evalina A., of Brookfield, m. Medad Rogers **KELLOGG**, of New
      Fairfield, Nov. 7, 1836, by A. Brundage   44

    Garry, of Burningham, m. Sarah E. **RUGGLES**, of Brookfield, Oct. 4,
      1847, by Rev. D. C. Curtis   60

    George W., m. Mary A. **ANDREWS**, b. of Brookfield, Nov. 6, 1836, by
      Abner Brundage   44

Page

PECK, (cont.)

Hannah, d. Amiel & Heppe, b. Oct. 17*, 1766 *(Possibly 7th")   5

Hannah, [d. Amiel & Heppe], d. Aug. 17, 1775   5

Hannah, 2nd, d. [Amiel & Heppe], b. Mar. 11, 1781   5

Harriet A., of Brookfield, m. William B. **GLOVER**, of Newtown, Nov.
7, 1832, by Rev. Joseph S. Covell   34

Harriet E., m. Reuben B. **BAILEY**, of South East, N. Y., Feb. 21,
1847, at the house of her father, by W[illia]m Long   56

Henrietta, m. Benjamin M. **STARR**, b. of Brookfield, Sept. 9, 1832,
by Abner Brundage   33

Henry L., m. Eliza **SMITH**, b. of Brookfield, Oct. 19, 1828, by
Abner Brundage   25

James A., (?), of Brookfield, m. Mary E. **CARTER**, of Bridgefield,
Summit Cty., O., Apr. 9, 1848, by Rev. William Biddle   61

Julius, s. Amiel & Heppe, b. Apr. 9, 1765   5

Lemuel, s. Amiel & Heppe, b. Dec. 23, 1768   5

Lemuel, [s. Amiel & Heppe], d. July 23, 1775   5

Lemuel, 2nd, s. [Amiel & Heppe], b. Sept. 25, 1777   5

Louisa, of Newtown, m. Harley **SANFORD**, of New Milford, Nov. 25,
1829, by Joseph S. Covell   28

Lucy Ann, m. Edwin C. **SMITH**, b. of Brookfield, Oct. 21, 1846,
by Rev. D. C. Curtis   55

Mary, d. [Amiel & Heppe], b. Dec. 15, [   ]   5

Ralph B., m. Caroline **MERWIN**, b. of Brookfield, Mar. 13, 1836,
by Abner Brundage   43

Sally Ann, m. Justis **PERRY**, b. of Brookfield, Oct. 16, 1825, by
Benjamin Banham   19

Sophia A., m. John **CORNWALL**, b. of Brookfield, Nov. 7, 1841, by
Rev. Edward C. Bull   51

PERKINS, Israel, of Waterbury, m. Orrilla **HURLBERT**, of Brookfield, Sept.
7, 1830, by Joseph S. Covell   29

Sarah Ann, of Brookfield, m. Joseph S. **ELWOOD**, of Danbury, Jan.
16, 1836, by John Hawley, J. P.   42

PERRY, Justis, m. Sally Ann **PECK**, b. of Brookfield, Oct. 16, 1825,
by Benjamin Benham   19

Sophia A., m. Horace C. **CABLES**, b. of Brookfield, Oct. 1, 1846,
by Rev. D. C. Curtis   55

PHELPS, Betsey Ann, of Brookfield, m. Henry **SWIFT**, of Bridgewater,
Dec. 16, 1849, by Rev. William Biddle   62

PLATT, Mary, formerly from Bridgewater, d. Feb. 16, 1825   110

POMROY, Orool, d. [   ], 1825   111

PORTER, George, of Stratford, m. Betty Mary **BALDWIN**, of Brookfield,
Nov. 26, 1830, by Joseph S. Covell   30

John, m. E[   ]* **BARLOW**, b. of Brookfield, Sept. 10, 1826, by
Abner Brundage *(Possibly "Elizabeth")   22

PRATT, Lucy, m. Daniel B. **COOKE**, Oct. 8, 1795   7

Lucy, m. Daniel B. **COOKE**, Oct. 8, 1795   8

PRAY, Margaret, of Brookfield, m. David **BEERS**, of Newtown, Apr. 12,

Page

PRAY, (cont.)

    1835, by Rev. Joseph S. Covell   39

PRINDLE, Mary Ann, of Newtown, m. William **TONG***, of Brookfield, May

    24, 1835, by Rev. Joseph S. Covell *(Possibly "**LONG**")   39

PUGSLEY, Alfred, of Patterson, N. Y., m. Emma A. **GREGORY**, of

    Brookfield, Nov. 5, 1829, by Abner Brundage   26

QUIGLY, John G., of Bethel, m. Harriet **STURDEVANT**, of Brookfield, June

    27, 1830, by Rev. James Kant, of Trumbull   29

QUINTARD, Caroline, of Brookfield, m. David **GEDNEY**, of New York,

    Mar. 25, 1823, by Abner Brundage   16

RANDALL, RANDAL, Almon C., of Bridgewater, m. Minerva C.

    NORTHROP, of Brookfield, Jan. 26, 1845, by Rev. H. D. Noble   58

    William A., of Brookfield, m. Phebe M. **BRISTOLL**, of Brookfield,

    Oct. 7, 1827, by Rev. Amos Bassett   23

RATHBONE, ROTHBONE, Betsey Ann, of Brookfield, m. Stephen G.

    STURGES, of Danbury, Apr. 27, 1831, by Joseph S. Covell   31

    Dorcas J*., of Brookfield, m. Philo **BARDSLEY**, of Newtown, Sept.

    8, 1823, by Rev. Benjamin Benham   17

    Louisa, d. Sept. 2, 1822   110

REED, REID, A. M., of Brookfield, m. Barzillai **KNAPP**, of Danbury, Sept.

    17, 1848, by Rev. William Biddle   62

    Asa, his w. [   ], d. [   ]   111

    Jonathan H., d. Feb. 13, 1826   112

REYTER(?), John P., of Newtown, m. Lucy **STEPHENS**, of Brookfield,

    Dec. 21, 1845, by Rev. H. D. Noble   56

ROBBINS, Edwin, m. Elisabeth N. **DUNNING**, b. of Brookfield, Apr. 17,

    1848, by Rev. D. C. Curtis   63

ROE, Harvey, of Northeast Dutchess Cty., N. Y., m. Mary Elizabeth

    BLACKMAN, of Brookfield, Oct. 8, 1844, by Abner Brundage   53

ROSE, Mary Francis, m. Stephen **EDGETT**, b. of Brookfield, Nov. 30, 1848,

    by Bryant Smith, J. P.   61

RUGGLES, Amy, m. Joseph **HAMLIN**, b. of Brookfield, Nov. 28, 1833, by

    Rev. Joseph S. Covell   36

    Betsey, of Brookfield, m. Benjamin **TREAT**, of Bridgewater, New

    Milford, Dec. 11, 1850, by Rev. H. D. Noble   66

    Harry, see Henry **RUGGLES**   18

    Henry*, m. Polly **LAKE**, b. of Brookfield, Nov. 2, 1823, by Rev.

    Benjamin Benham *(Or "Harry")   18

    Henry, his child d. [   ], 1825   111

    Huldah, of Brookfield, m. Peter **STEVENS**, of Montrose, Pa., Dec.

    31, 1851, by Rev. D. C. Curtis   68

    Lucia, m. Samuel **WHITLOCK**, b. of Brookfield, Dec. 21, 1837, by

    Abner Brundage   45

    Robert B., d. May 13, 1823   110

    Rosanni, m. Lemuel **WAKLEE**, Dec. 13, 1781   5

    Salina, of Brookfield, m. Elisha A. **BREWER**, of Mt. Morris, N. Y.,

    Nov. 1, 1847, by Rev. H. D. Noble   59

    Sally, of Brookfield, m. Daniel O. **WHEELER**, of Bridgeport, June 16,

Page

RUGGLES, (cont.)

    1822, by Rev. Benjamin Benham   15

    Sarah E., of Brookfield, m. Garry **PECK**, of Burmingham, Oct. 4,

        1847, by Rev. D. C. Curtis   60

    Sherman B., m. Sarah B. **OAKLEY**, Jan. 8, 1833, by Rev. Joseph S.

        Covell   34

    Sibel, w. Timothy, d. Jan. 3, 1789, in the 46th y. of her age   2

SANFORD, George B., of Putney, Vt., m. Sarah **KEELER**, of Brookfield,

        Nov. 8, 1836, by A. Brundage   44

    Glover, of Sallesbury, m. Betsey **LAKE**, of Brookfield, Feb. 4,

        1822, by Rev. Benjamin Benham   15

    Harley, of New Milford, m. Louisa **PECK**, of Newtown, Nov. 25,

        1829, by Joseph S. Covell   28

    Sarah C., of Brookfield, m. Sam[ue]l W. **WADSWORTH**, of New Haven,

        Sept. 18, 1844, by Rev. H. D. Noble   57

SCOTT, George, of Fishkill, N. Y., m. Almira **STEVENS**, of Brookfield,

        Nov. 14, 1836, by A. Brundage   44

SCUDDER, Isaac B., m. Betsey A. **SKIDMORE**, Oct. 28, 1832, by Joseph S.

        Covell   34

SEELEY, Lovina, of Brookfield, m. Wanzer S. **GILBERT**, of Newtown,

        Aug. 22, 1830, by Joseph S. Covell   29

SHEPHERD, Charles, of Newtown, m. Mary J. **DAYTON**, Mesuod(?), Mar.

        28, 1847, by Rev. D. C. Curtis   58

SHERMAN, Abel, m. Sarah **BRADLEY**, b. of Brookfield, Nov. 24, 1825,

        by Rev. Benjamin Benham   19

    Betty, w. Samuel, d. Jan. 22, 1825   110

    Charles, of Brookfield, m. Eliza Ann **WEED**, of Danbury, Apr. 25,

        1847, by Rev. H. D. Noble   59

    Eliza Ann, m. Ammen Booth **BLACKMAN**, b. of Brookfield, Mar. 30,

        1851, by Rev. H. D. Noble   67

    Flora, m. Ira **STEVENS**, b. of Brookfield, Dec. 20, 1821, by

        Benjamin Benham   14

    Grace, m. Albert **WEEKS**, b. of Brookfield, Feb. 3, 1841,

        by Rev. Edward C. Bull   50

    Ira, of Newtown, m. Sarah E. **HALLAWAY**, of Pawlings, N. Y., Dec.

        24, 1840, by Hubbel Wildman, J. P.   48

    Joel C., m. Sally **WELCH**, b. of Brookfield, Dec. 19, 1820, by

        Eli Ruggles, J. P.   12

    Matthew, d. Apr. 1, 1825   110

    Philo, m. Sarah Ann **BENNETT**, Oct. 21, 1832, by Rev. Joseph S. Covell   34

    Rufus, d. Mar. 22, 1822   110

    Sally Minerva, of Brookfield, m. Benjamin **BENHAM**, of New Milford,

        Oct. 1, 1827, by Rev. Lemuel B. Hull   23

    Samuel, d. Apr. 19, 1825   110

    Suson, of Brookfield, m. Joseph A. **BANKS**, of Bridgeport, Dec. 24,

        1851, by Rev. H. D. Noble   67

    Thomas, of Brookfield, m. Abigail **PEASE**, of Newtown, (colored),

        July 5, 1844, by Rev. Dan C. Curtis   54

SHERMAN, (cont.)

William, m. Betsey **BRISTOLL**, b. of Brookfield, Oct. 9, 1826, by
Rev. Benjamin Benham   22

SKIDMORE, Betsey A., m. Isaac B. **SCUDDER**, Oct. 28, 1832, by Joseph
S. Covell   34

SMITH, Edwin C., m. Lucy Ann **PECK**, b. of Brookfield, Oct. 21, 1846,
by Rev. D. C. Curtis   55

Eli, m. Lydia T. **WANGER**, b. of Brookfield, Jan. 21, 1821, by
Medad Rogers   12

Eliza, m. Henry L. **PECK**, b. of Brookfield, Oct. 19, 1828, by
Abner Brundage   25

Faithful, m. Elizabeth **BROWNELL**, May 7, 1794   6

Hannah R., of Brookfield, m. Joseph S. **LAKE**, of Newtown, Apr. 25,
1849, by Rev. H. D. Noble   66

Julia, m. Hoyt **DIBBLE**, b. of Danbury, Nov. 22, 1830, by Abner
Brundage   30

Lois, d. Faithful & Elizabeth, b. Mar. 16, 1798   6

Lucy, m. Nirum **BENEDICT**, Apr. 26, 1821, by Benjamin Benham   13

Lydia, of Brookfield, m. David B. **STURGES**, of Danbury, Oct. 1,
1826, by Rev. Benjamin Benham   21

Mabel, m. Selies* **CAMP**, of Newtown, Sept. 11, 1822, by Daniel
Blackman, J. P. *(Silas?)   16

Mary, m. Elijah **STARR**, Nov. 26, 1772, by Rev. Thomas Brooks   4

Nathan, of Brookfield, m. Mary **McLAIN**, of Danbury, Jan. 30, 1831,
by Joseph S. Covell   31

Phebe, of Brookfield, m. Serputia L. **BEEBE**, of Danbury, Oct. 15,
1823, by Abner Brneda   17

Rebecca, w. Joseph, d. Jan. 14, 1827   27

Sherman, m. Laura **MERWIN**, b. of Brookfield, Mar. 6, 1825, by
Abner Brundage   19

Sidney, m. Susan M. **LOBDELL**, b. of Brookfield, Nov. 27, 1834,
by Rev. Joseph S. Cornell   38

Sylva, m. Nathan **TURNER**, b. of Brookfield, June 19, 1831, by
Joseph S. Covell   32

SOMERS, Martin W., m. Clara **NORTHROP**, Apr. 21, 1821, by Noah A.
Lacy, J. P.   13

Ransby*, m. Urana **MURWIN**, Mar. 8, 1830, by Abner Brundage
*(Possibly "Ransley")   26

Susan R., m. Alfred S. **CAMMEYERS**, b. of Brookfield, Feb. 10,
1848, by Rev. H. D. Noble   61

SPENCER, Lydia, of Sherman, m. Herman **BRUNSON**, of New Milford, May
31, 1834, by Henry Ruggles, J. P.   36

STARR, Ann Mariah, m. John **MORE**, Oct. 7, 1830, by Joseph S. Covell   30

Anna, d. Elijah & Mary, b. July 30, 177[5]   4

Benjamin M., m. Henrietta **PECK**, b. of Brookfield, Sept. 9, 1832,
by Abner Brundage   33

Caroline, of Brookfield, m. Ezra R. **BARNS**, of Danbury, Oct. 23,
1844, by Rev. H. D. Noble   57

Page

STARR, (cont.)

Scyntha, m. Henry **CUTLIN**, Nov. 19, 1840, by Rev. Luceiss Atwater   48

Elijah, m. Mary **SMITH**, Nov. 26, 1772, by Rev. Thomas Brooks   4

Elijah, Jr., [s. Elijah & Mary], b. Jan. 16, 1787   4

Eluid, d. July 27, 1825   111

Hannah, of Brookfield, m. Alfred **MORRIS**, of Danbury, Apr. 7, 1824,
    by Reuben Booth, J. P.   18

Hannah, wid., d. Feb. 13, 1826   112

Lodeme, d. [Elijah & Mary], b. Feb. 7, 1778   4

Phebe, of Brookfield, m. Samuel **MORICE**, of Danbury, Jan. 17, 1821,
    by William Cooke, J. P.   13

Polly, d. Elijah & Mary, b. May 14, 1773   4

Polly Ann, d. Zar, Jr., d. May 23, 1824   110

Rachel, [d. Elijah & Mary], b. Apr. 30, 1784   4

Rebecah, [d. Elijah & Mary], b. June 15, 1789   4

Rhoda, wid., d. Andrew **MURWIN**, b. of Brookfield, Feb. 23, 1830,
    by Abner Brundage   26

Salmon R., m. Rachel **LACY**, Dec. 1, 1824, by Rev. Benjamin Benham   18

Tryphene, [d. Elijah & Mary], b. June 2, 1793   4

STEVENS, STEPHENS, Almira, of Brookfield, m. George **SCOTT**, of
    Fishkill, N. Y., Nov. 14, 1836, by A. Brundage   44

Amos, m. Flora **WARNER**, Apr. 6, 1824, by Abner Brundage   18

Charles W., of Brookfield, m. Mary **FAIRCHILD**, of Newtown, Nov. 27,
    1834, by Abner Brundage   37

Edwin, s. Zalmon, b. Feb. 11, 1822   6

Eliza, m. Rufus **COLQUHOUN**, Apr. 25, 1847, by Rev. William Biddle   59

Ezra, of New Fairfield, m. Mary **TAYLOR**, of Brookfield, Feb. 17,
    1847, by Rev. D. C. Curtis   55

Ira, m. Flora **SHERMAN**, b. of Brookfield, Dec. 20, 1821, by
    Benjamin Benham   14

Ira, his child d. Jan. 14, 1826   112

John, his wid., [   ], d. Jan. 16, 1826   112

Lucy, of Brookfield, m. John P. **REYTER**(?), of Newtown, Dec. 21,
    1845, by Rev. H. D. Noble   56

Margaret, d. Clark, b. Apr. 24, 1827   4

Mary, d. Clerk, b. July 14, 1822   4

Mary C., m. David B. **DIBBLE**, b. of Brookfield, Sept. 6, 1847, by
    Rev. H. D. Noble   59

Peter, of Montrose, Pa., m. Huldah **RUGGLES**, of Brookfield, Dec.
    31, 1851, by Rev. D. C. Curtis   68

Solomon W., m. Polly Ann **KELLOGG**, b. of Brookfield, Oct. 8, 1826,
    by Abner Brundage   22

STEWART, Albert, d. [   ]   111

John, m. Nancy C. **MERWIN**, Sept. 29, 1835, by Abner Brundage   40

Lucinda, of Bridgewater, m. Stephen N. **HANSON**, of Brookfield,
    May 17, 1849, by Rev. D. C. Curtis   63

Philander, Dr. of Roxbury, m. Anna M. **DUNNING**, of Brookfield,
    Sept. 13, 1835, by Erastus Cole   40

Page

STRINGHAM, Henry, of Newrochel, N. Y., m. Eliza **TOMLINSON**, of New
    Fairfield, Mar. 7, 1823, by Daniel Tomlinson, J. P.   16

STURDEVANT, STURDAVANT, Flora E., of Brookfield, m. Daniel F.
    BARNES, of Danbury, June 26, 1849, by Rev. D. C. Curtis   63

    Harriet, of Brookfield, m. John G. **QUIGLY**, of Bethel, June 27,
    1830, by Rev. James Kant, of Trumbull   29

    Homer, m. Louisa **HALL***, b. of Brookfield, Feb. 10, 1848, by Rev.
    D. C. Curtis *(Possibly "HULL")   60

    John, of New Milford, m. Comfort Mary **BUCKENHAM**, of Brookfield,
    Mar. 2, 1824, by Daniel Tomlinson, J. P.   18

    Selina, of Brookfield, m. Jason **GURLEY**, of Hartford, Jan. 11,
    1830, by Rev. Benjamin Benham   26

STURGES, David B., of Danbury, m. Lydia **SMITH**, of Brookfield, Oct.
    1, 1826, by Rev. Benjamin Benham   21

    Stephen G., of Danbury, m. Betsey Ann **RATHBONE**, of Brookfield,
    Apr. 27, 1831, by Joseph S. Covell   31

SWIFT, Henry, of Bridgewater, m. Betsey Ann **PHELPS**, of Brookfield,
    Dec. 16, 1849, by Rev. William Biddle   62

TALMAGE, Warren, of New Canaan, m. [, Aug.] 5, [1821],
    by R. B. Ruggles, J. P.   13

TAYLOR, Daniel G., of Washington, m. Lucy A. **BRISTOLL**, of Brookfield,
    Dec. 25, 1844, by Rev. H. D. Noble   58

    Huldah A., of Brookfield, m. Allen **HALL**, of Newtown, Dec. 21, 1831,
    by Bryant Smith, J. P.   32

    Mary, of Brookfield, m. Ezra **STEVENS**, of New Fairfield, Feb. 17, 1847,
    by Rev. D. C. Curtis   55

    Thomas, m. Mary **LAWRENCE**, b. of Brookfield, Nov. 10, 1841, by
    Rev. Edward C. Bull   52

TERRELL, TERREL, Angeline, of Norwalk, m. Benedict P. **WOOD**, of
    Brookfield, Sept. 11, 1831, by B. F. Northrop   32

    Botsford, m. Julia **GLOVER**, b. of Newtown, Sept. 22, 1822, by Rev.
    Benjamin Benham   16

    Cloe, of Brookfield, m. Henry W. **BENEDICT**, of Newtown,
    [, 1850(?)], by Rev. William Biddle   64

    Elizabeth, of Redding, m. Almon **ODELL**, of Brookfield, Apr. 12,
    1840, by Rev. Edward C. Bull   47

THAYNE, Augustus, of New Milford, m. Electa **FAIRCHILD**, of Newtown,
    Feb. 17, 1829, by Abner Brundage   25

THOMAS, James, d. Sept. 12, 1824   110

THORP, Almon W., of New Milford, m. Maria **NORTHROP**, of Brookfield,
    Sept. 8, 1822, by Rev. Benjamin Benham   15

    Edward, m. Cornelia **TOMLINSON**, b. of Brookfield, Sept. 29, 1839,
    by Rev. Edward C. Bull   47

    Elizabeth, m. John H. **NEARING**, b. of Brookfield, Nov. 10, 1830,
    by Joseph S. Covell   30

    Herman, of Newtown, m. Emeline **LACEY**, of Brookfield, Jan. 30,
    1831, by Joseph S. Covell   31

TISHENER, Elihu, of Orange, N. J., m. Maria **WALEY**, of Brookfield, May

Page

TISHENER, (cont.)

    27, 1821, by Daniel Tomlinson, J. P.   12

TOMLINSON, Caroline S., m. Lucius* C. **NORTHROP,** b. of Brookfield

    Feb. 27, 1842, by Rev. Edward C. Bull *(Possibly "Lewis")   52

    Cornelia, m. Edward **THORP,** b. of Brookfield, Sept. 29, 1839, by

    Rev. Edward C. Bull   47

    Daniel, m. Lucia **HOLDMAN,** b. of Brookfield, Sept. 18*, 1835, by

    Rev. Joseph S. Covell *(Fig. 8 uncertain)   41

    Eliza, of New Fairfield, m. Henry **STRINGHAM,** of Newrochel, N. Y.,

    Mar. 7, 1823, by Daniel Tomlinson, J. P.   16

    Jane *, m. George **KEELER,** b. of Brookfield, Nov. 22, 1835, by Rev.

    Joseph S. Covell *(Possibley "June")   42

    Julia, of Brookfield, m. Samuel F. **HURD,** of Bridgeport, Dec. 24,

    1824, by Rev. Benjamin Benham   19

    June, see Jane **TOMLINSON**   42

    Malinda, m. Philo **HURD,** Oct. 5, 1823, by Rev. Benjamin Benham   17

    Mary, of Brookfield, m. Lockwood **DeFOREST,** of Bridgeport, Sept.

    11, 1831, by Rev. Joseph S. Covell   32

TONGUE, TONG, Mary Diana, of Brookfield, m. William G. **FULLER,** of

    New Milford, Nov. 21, 1838, by Bryant Smith, J. P.   45

    William*, of Brookfield, m. Mary Ann **PRINDLE,** of Newtown, May 24,

    1835, by Rev. Joseph S. Covell *(Possibly "William **LONG**")   39

TREAT, Benjamin, of Bridgewater, m. Betsey **RUGGLES,** of Brookfield,

    Dec. 11, 1850, by Rev. H. D. Noble   66

TREDWAY, George, of Litchfield, m. Minerva M. **WISE,** Mar. 8, 1829, by

    A. Brundage   25

TRYON, Anor, w. William, d. Dec. 28, 1823   110

    Daniel, s. W[illia]m, d. Oct. 2, 1823   110

TURNER, Nathan, m. Sylva **SMITH,** b. of Brookfield, June 19, 1831,

    by Joseph S. Covell   32

    William, of New Milford, m. Deborah **CAMERON,** of Brookfield,

    Nov. 29, 1829, by Joseph S. Covell   28

TURRELL, see under **TERRELL**

WADSWORTH, Sam[ue]l W., of New Haven, m. Sarah C. **SANFORD,** of

    Brookfield, Sept. 18, 1844, by Rev.H. D. Noble   57

WAKLEE, Annis, d. Lemuel & Rosanni, b. Oct. 9, 1782   5

    Hannah, d. Lemuel & Rosanni, b. Sept. 30, 1794   5

    Lemuel, m. Rosanni **RUGGLES,** Dec. 13, 1781   5

    Lodeme, d. Lemuel & Rosanne, b. July 17, 1785   5

WALEY, Maria, of Brookfield, m. Elihu **TISHENER,** of Orange, N. J., May

    27, 1821, by Daniel Tomlinson, J. P.   13

WALKER, Charles J., of Newtown, m. Catharine C. **ARNOLD,** of Brookfield,

    Feb. 26, 1851, by Rev. D. C. Curtis   69

    Isaac B., of Bridgeport, m. Amanda **BEEBE,** of Brookfield, Dec. 31,

    1844, by Rev. H. D. Noble   58

WANGER, [see also **WANZER**], Lydia T., m. Eli **SMITH,** b. of Brookfield,

    Jan. 21, 1821, by Medad Rogers   12

WANZER, [see also **WANGER**], Eliza, m. Nelson **WARNER***, June 8, 1826,

Page

WANZER, (cont.)
    by Rev. Benjamin Benham *(Possibly "WARREN")   21
WARD, Calvin, m. Mrs. Elizabeth OSBORN, b. of Brookfield, Mar. 16,
    1851, by Rev. William Biddle   65
WARNER, Alva W., m. Fanny BABBIT, b. of Brookfield, Aug. 20, 1828, by
    Rev. John Lovejoy   24
    Daniel N., m. Amy KEELER, b. of Brookfield, Apr. 21, 1842, by
        Abner Brundage   50
    Eleaner M., of West Troy, m. E. Sanford BENEDICT, of Danbury,
        May 6, 1845, by Rev. Dan C. Curtis   54
    Flora, m. Amos STEVENS, Apr. 6, 1824, by Abner Brundage   18
    Hellen, m. Frederick KEELER, b. of Brookfield, Aug. 31, 1846, by
        Rev. D. C. Curtis   55
    Maranda, m. Asa W. CAMP, b. of Brookfield, Oct. 6, 1822, by Rev.
        Benjamin Benham   16
    Nelson*, m. Eliza WANZER, June 8, 1826, by Rev. Benjamin Benham
        *(Possibly "Nelson WARREN")   21
    Polly M., of Brookfield, m. Edmund BOSTWICK, of Ohio, Sept. 5,
        1833, by Abner Brundage   35
WARREN, Nelson, see Nelson WARNER   21
WEED, Eliza Ann, of Danbury, m. Charles SHERMAN, of Brookfield, Apr.
    25, 1847, by Rev. H. D. Noble   59
WEEKS, Albert, m. Grace SHERMAN, b. of Brookfield, Feb. 3, 1841, by
    Rev. Edward C. Bull   50
WELCH, Sally, m. Joel C. SHERMAN, b. of Brookfield, Dec. 19, 1820, by
    Eli Ruggles, J. P.   12
WELLMAN, WELMAN, Betsey Ann, m. Silas CAMP, b. of Brookfield, Nov.
    3, [1822], by Rev. Benjamin Benham   16
    Caroline, d. [ ]   111
    Jedediah, m. Jane CAMP, May 16, 1824, by Rev. Benjamin Benham   18
WHEELER, Daniel O., of Bridgeport, m. Sally RUGGLES, of Brookfield,
    June 16, 1822, by Rev. Benjamin Benjam   15
    Ira, of New Fairfield, m. Hannah OSBORNE, of Brookfield, Feb. 2,
        1834, by Rev. Joseph S. Covell   36
    Laura Ann, m. John LOBDELL, b. of New Milford, Aug. 11, 1845, by
        Rev. D. C. Curtiss   54
    Nirum, of Roxbury, m. Sarah BARLOW, of Brookfield, Jan. 22, 1835,
        by Rev. Joseph S. Covell   38
    Polly Ann, of Brookfield, m. Orson MERCHANT, of Redding, Nov. 27,
        1846, by Rev. H. D. Noble   57
    Reed, d. [ ], 1825   111
WHITLOCK, Mary, of Brookfield, m. Austin CARPENTER, of Derby, Dec.
    24, 1826, by Eli Ruggles, J. P.   22
    Polly, of Brookfield, m. Jessee H. HALLOCK, of New Milford, Mar.
        16, 1843, by Z. Davenport   53
    Samuel, m. Lucia RUGGLES, b. of Brookfield, Dec. 21, 1837, by
        Abner Brundage   45
WILDMAN, [see also WILEMAN], Canfield S*., of Brookfield, m. Harriet

BROOKLYN VITAL RECORDS
1786 - 1850

	Vol.	Page
ABBOTT, ABBOT, Orinda, m. Asaph ADAMS, Oct. 20, 1785	1	60
Warren W., of Hampton, m. Maria E. FRANKLIN, of		
Brooklyn, Feb. 23, 1823, by Rev. Samuel J. May	4	12
ADAMS, Aaron, m. Huldah COGSWELL, Apr. 19, 1793	1	60
Abijah, m. Dorcas FASSETT, Nov. 1, 1787	1	60
Albigence, s. Asaph & Orinda, b. May 2, 1786	1	1
Amanda, d. Elisha, Jr. & Mary, b. Oct. 11, 1820	1	231
Amanda, m. Edwin B. CARTOR, b. of Brooklyn, Dec. 25,		
1839, by Rev. G. J. Tillotson	4	71
Arba, s. Elisha & Eleanor, b. May 21, 1798	1	1
Arba, s. Elisha & Eleanor, b. May 21, 1798; d. July 5, 1798	2	1
Arba, s. Elisha & Eleanor, d. July 5, 1798	1	40
Asaph, m. Orinda ABBOTT, Oct. 20, 1785	1	60
Augustus, s. Aaron & Huldah, b. May 5, 1794	1	1
Charles, s. Willard & Abigail, b. June 10, 1793	1	231
Charles R., s. William P. & Abby, b. Sept. 29, 1846, in		
Brooklyn	2	2
Charles R., d. Sept. 4, 1847, ae 11 m.	2	80
Cynthia, of Brooklyn, m. Horace DAY of Killingly, Feb. 5,		
1838, by Edward Spalding. J. P.	4	65
David, s. Philemon & Sarah, b. Sept. 8, 1789	1	231
David, s. Philemon & Sarah, d. Dec. 18, 1817, ae 21 y.		
3 m. 20 d.	1	40
Deborah, d. Shubael & Anne, b. July [ ], 178[ ]	1	1
Edwin, s. Willard & Abigail, b. Mar. 7, 1799	1	231
Eleanor, w. Elisha, d. Sept. 23, 1825, in the 52d y. of her age	1	40
Elisha, m. Eleanor AUSTIN, Dec. 6, 1795	1	60
Elisha, s. Elisha & Eleanor, b. Feb. 9, 1797	1	1
Elisha, s. Elisha & Eleanor, b. Feb. 9, 1797	2	1
Elisha, Jr., m. Mary CADY, Jan. 3, 1819	1	60
Elisha, s. Elisha & Eleanor, d. Aug. 11, 1825, in the 29th		
y. of his age	1	40
Elisha, of Brooklyn, m. Sarah KINGSLEY, of Sterling, May 4,		
1828, by Nathaniel Cole, Elder, in Plainfield	4	32
Emily, d. Elisha, Jr. & Mary, b. Oct. 21, 1819	1	231
Emily, m. Edmund H. BARD, b. of Brooklyn, Mar. 11, 1841,		
by Rev. Geo[rge] J. Tillotson	4	73
Experience, w. Willard, d. Jan. 10, 1790	1	40
Experience, d. Willard & Abigail, b. Feb. 3, 1801	1	231
Flora, d. Elisha & Eleanor, b. Dec. 8, 1804	2	1
Hannah, m. Denison CADY, Nov. 30, 1802	1	62

	Vol.	Page
ADAMS, (cont.)		
Harvey, of Killingly, m. Eunice **COPELAND**, of Thompson, Dec. 7, 1820, by Daniel Dow, V. D. M.	4	2
Joab F., m. Lucretia **HERRICK**, b. of Brooklyn, Nov. 29, [1827], by Rev. Samuel J. May	4	31
John, s. Willard & Abigail, b. July 23, 1797	1	231
John, Capt., m. Hannah **FASSETT**, Nov. 2, 1802, by John Parrish, J. P.	3	1
John C., s. William P. & Abby, b. Oct. 1, 1845, in Brooklyn	2	2
John Marvin, s. Titus & Betsey, d. June 18, 1823, ae 16 y.	1	40
Lois, d. Elisha & Eleanor, b. Jan. 18, 1801	2	1
Lucy, d. Willard, d. Feb. 19, 1794	1	40
Lucy, d. Willard, d. Feb. 19, 1794	1	42
Lucy, d. Willard & Experience, b. Dec. 21, 17[ ]	1	1
Margaret, m. Jedidiah **ASHCRAFT**, Jr., Aug. 10, 1769	1	60
Mary E., m. Henry D. **BINGHAM**, b. of Canterbury, Oct. 23, 1837, by Rev. G. J. Tillotson	4	64
Miranda, d. Elisha & Eleanor, b. Feb. 28, 1803	2	1
Miranda, m. Levi **ROSS**, b. of Brooklyn, Mar. 2, 1830, by Rev. John O. Birdsall, at the house of Elisha Adams	4	39
Moses, s. Willard & Abigail, b. Apr. 28, 1795	1	231
Philemon, m. Sarah **DAY**, Dec. 13, 1774	1	60
Prescilla, wid., Peter, d. July 15, 1826, in the 96th y. of her age	1	40
Robert, s. Shubael & Anne, b. Aug. [ ], 178[ ]	1	1
Royal, s. Asaph & Orinda, b. Oct. 24, 1787	1	1
Rufus, s. Philemon & Sarah, b. Oct. 1, 1779	1	231
Rufus, m. Susannah **HOPKINS**, Dec. 29, 1805	1	60
Rufus, s. Philemon & Sarah, d. Oct. 20, 1814, ae 35 y.	1	40
Sally, d. Philemon & Sarah, b. Jan. 27, 1782	1	231
Sally, m. Colonel **TARBOX**, Feb. 3, 1799	1	77
Sally, m. Benjamin **TANNER**, Jan. 23, 1807	1	77
Titus, s. Philemon & Sarah, b. Aug. 5, 1777	1	231
Titus, m. Betsey **O'BRIEN**, June 23, 1805	1	60
Titus, m. Betsey **O'BRIAN**, b. of Brooklyn, June 23, 1805, by John Parrish, J. P.	3	6
Titus, s. Philemon & Sarah, d. Jan. 26, 1824, ae 46 y.	1	40
Welcome, s. Philemon & Sarah, b. Aug. 13, 1791	1	231
Welcome, s. Philemon & Sarah, d. June 7, 1818,ae 26 y. 10 m.	1	40
Willard, m. Experience **CADY**, Nov. 24, 1786	1	60
Willard, m. abigail **MARRY** (?), Dec. 28, 1790	1	60
Willard, s. Willard & Abigail, b. Oct. 19, 17[ ]	1	1
-----, d. William P., stone cutter, ae 34, & Abby, ae 31, b. Apr. 4, 1850	2	107
AKINS, Hannah, m. Pascal **CADY**, Feb. 18, 1805	1	62
ALLEN, [see also **ALLYN,**], Arba Adams, s. John, Jr. & Alice W., b. Mar. 6, 1827	2	2
Elizabeth, m. Andrew **JOHNSON**, b. of Brooklyn, Jan. 21,		

	Vol.	Page
ALLEN, (cont.)		
1846, by Rev. G. J. Tillotson	4	84
Eunice, d. Oct. 26, 1847, ae 55	2	90
Frances Wilmarth, d. John, Jr. & Alice W., b. Apr. 29, 1842	2	2
James, of New Lisbon, N. Y., m. Nancy **PARKER**, of		
Brooklyn, Oct. 24, 1821, by Vine Robinson, J. P.	4	4
John, farmer, d. July 22, [1850], ae 84	2	127
John Edward, s. John, Jr. & Alice W., b. Oct. 20, 1837	2	2
Ludovice, m. Pardon **BENNETT**, b. of Brooklyn, Sept. 24,		
1820, by Rev. Roswell Whitmore, Killingly	4	1
Mary Ann, of Brooklyn, m. Marvin A. **DEXTER**, of Killingly,		
Nov. 25, 1829, by Rev. Roswell Whitmore	4	38
William Colwell, s. John, Jr. & Alice, b. May 28, 1830	2	2
----, s. Ezra W., merchant, ae 31, & Lucinda, ae 26, b.		
July 18, 1850	2	119
ALLERTON, Abby, twin with Jane, d. John R. & Adeline, b. Oct.		
12, 1845	2	3
Adeline, m. John **ALLERTON**, b. of Brooklyn, Sept. 25,		
1842, by Rev. R. Camp	4	77
Frances A., d. John R. & Adeline, b. Aug. 6, 1843	2	3
George, s. John & Molly, b. June 17, 1813; d. Apr. 6, 1842	2	3
George, d. Apr. 6, 1842, ae 29 y.	1	40
Henry, s. John R., farmer, ae 37, & Adeline, ae 33, b.		
Jan. 29, 1848	2	83
Jane, twin with Abby, d. John R. & Adeline, b. Oct. 12, 1845	2	3
John, m. Molly **BARRETT**, Apr. 10, 1810	2	3
John, d. Jan. 3, 1839, ae 74 y.	1	40
John, m. Adeline **ALLERTON**, b. of Brooklyn, Sept. 25, 1842,		
by Rev. R. Camp	4	77
John Russell, s. John & Molly, b. Apr. 12, 1811	2	3
Mary Ann, d. John & Molly, b. Dec. 2, 1818; d. Nov. 26, 1836	2	3
Mary Ann, d. Nov. 26, 1836, ae 18 y.	1	40
Molly, w. John, d. July 4, 1838, ae 60 y.	1	40
William, s. John & Molly, b. May 9, 1816; d. Apr. 16, 1834	2	3
William, d. Apr. 16, 1834, ae 18 y.	1	40
ALLYN, [see also **ALLEN**], Albigence, s. Jabez & Mary, b. May		
23, 1765	1	1
Albegence, m. Prescilla **DAVIS**, May 17, 1800	1	60
Anna, d. Jabez & Mary, b. July 18, 1760	1	1
Anne, m. Ignatius **WILSON**, Nov. 30, 1780	1	78
Azubah, d. Jabez & Mary, b. June 15, 1771	1	1
Azuba, m. Eddy **WINSLOW**, July 5, 1795	1	78
Betsey, d. Jabez & Mary, b. Mar. 20, 1781	1	1
Betsey, m. Stevens **TYLER**, b. of Brooklyn, Aug. 6, 1809,		
by John Parrish, J. P.	3	5
Dan[i]el, s. Jabez & Mary, b. Oct. 23, 1758	1	1
Daniel, d. Apr. 14, 1776	1	40
Elizabeth Nason, d. John, Jr. & Alice Wilmarth, b. Apr.	2	2

	Vol.	Page
ALLYN, (cont.)		
22, 1822	2	2
Esther, d. Jabez & Mary, b. June 2, 1776	1	1
Esther, d. Dec. 31, 1778	1	40
Eunice, d. Parker & Lois, b. July 7, 17[ ]	1	1
George Chandler, s. John, Jr. & Alice Wilmarth, b. Apr. 8, 1824	2	2
Jabez Albigence, s. Albigence & Priscilla, b. Nov. 18, 1804	1	231
John, m. Anna **HAVEN**, Nov. 9, 1794	2	2
John, s. John & Anna, b. Feb. 6, 1797	2	2
Katharine, d. Jabez & Mary, b. Apr. 22, 1777	1	1
Lucy, d. Jabez & Mary, b. Sept. 14, 1773	1	1
Ludovice, d. Albigence & Priscilla, b. May 15, 1801	1	231
Mary, d. Jabez & Mary, b. May 10, 1767	1	1
Mary, m. John **RICE**, Nov. 21, 1793	1	75
Mary Ann, d. John & Anna, b. Feb. 23, 1807	2	2
Nancy, d. John & Anna, b. Oct. 19, 1798	2	2
Nancy, m. Uriah C. **PRINCE**, Sept. 16, 1821, by Rev. Joseph Chicering	4	5
Nathan, s. Parker & Louis, b. Apr. 3, 1781	1	1
Susannah, d. Parker & Lois, b. June 13, 1791	1	1
Sybel, d. Jabez & Mary, b. Aug. [ ], [1763]	1	1
Sybel, d. Apr. 5, 1773	1	40
Tamison, d. Jabez & Mary, b. Mar. 10, 178[ ]	1	1
ALMY, Obadiah, of Canterbury, m. Excy **PROFFET**, Mar. 4, 1816, by John Parish, J. P.	3	8
Phebe, of Smithfield, R. I., m. Russell **MARBLE**, of Mendon, Mass., July 21, 1839, by Rev. William Coe	4	70
ALWORTH, [see also **AYLESWORTH**], James, d. Oct. 12, 1797	1	40
AMES, Amelia, d. Miller & Hannah Augusta, b. July 9, 1795	1	231
Catharine, m. Philip F. **RUSS**, of Willimantic, Oct. 18, 1846, by Rev. Herman Snow	4	84
Dyar, Jr., of Seneca Falls, N. Y., m. Charlotte **BAKER**, of Brooklyn, [July] 8, [1832], by Rev. Samuel J. May	4	47
Hannah Augusta, m. John Wilkes **GILBERT**, Nov. 27, 1799	1	66
ANGELL, **ANGEL**, George, of Pomfret, m. Louisa **CADY**, of Brooklyn, Jan. 27, 1840, by Rev. William Coe	4	71
Stephen, of Scituate, R. I., m. Mary Emily **AUSTIN**, of Foster, R. I., July 2, 1839, by Rev. William Coe	4	69
----, s. Horatio N., farmer, ae 43, & Abby S., ae 39, b. Aug. 14, 1849	2	109
ANTHONY, Henry, of Providence, R. I., m. Charlotte **BENSON**, of Brooklyn, Oct. 22, 1826, by Rev. Samuel J. May	4	25
ARNOLD, Charles Moulton, s. Esben & Sophia, b. June 27, 1824	2	1
Daniel, s. Daniel & Lora, b. Oct. 2, 1824	2	1
Daniel, Jr., of Brooklyn, m. Eliza L. **HOLT**, of Abington Soc. in Pomfret, Apr. 23, 1848, by Rev. Ebenezer Loomis	2	79
Daniel, Jr., of Brooklyn, m. Eliza L. **HOLT**, of Abington,		

	Vol.	Page
ARNOLD, (cont.)		
Apr. 23, 1848, by Rev. E. Loomis	4	99
Esbon, of Thompson, m. Sophia **STOWELL**, of Brooklyn,		
Mar. 17, 1822, by Rev. John Paine, of Hampton	4	9
Gurdon, s. Augustus & Lydia, b. July 16, 1824	2	1
ASHCRAFT, Alfred, m. Hannah **YOUNG**, Dec. 29, 1803	1	60
Alfred, m. Ann **BURROUGHS**, Sept. 22, 1816	1	60
Asenath, d. Jedediah, Jr. & Margaret, b. [ ]	1	1
Betsey, twin with Sally, d. Jedidiah, Jr. & Margaret,		
b. July 3, 1780	1	1
Bridget, w. John, d. Dec. 3, 1826	1	40
Desire, d. Jedediah, Jr. & Margaret, b. Mar. 7, 1770	1	1
Ebenezer, m. Catharine **BURROWS**, May 8, 1800	1	60
Hannah, w. Alfred, d. Jan. 16, 1806	1	40
Hannah, d. Alfred & Ann, b. May 1, 1817	2	1
Hannah, d. Alfred & Ann, d. Sept. 4, 1825, in the 9th y. of		
her age	1	40
Harriet, d. Alfred & Hannah, b. Aug. 5, 1805	2	1
Harriet, of Brooklyn, m. Eleazer **BARTLETT**, of Killingly,		
Dec. 17, 1826, by Rev. Roswell Whitmore, of Killingly	4	26
James, twin with Jared, s. Jedidiah, Jr. & Margaret, b.		
Oct. 15, 1785	1	1
Jared, twin with James, s. Jedidiah, Jr. & Margaret, b.		
Oct. 15, 1785	1	1
Jedidiah, Jr., m. Margaret **ADAMS**, Aug. 10, 1769	1	60
John, d. Mar. 4, 1826, in the 78th y. of his age	1	40
John Burroughs, s. Alfred & Ann, b. Dec. 9, 1818	2	1
Jonathan, s. Jedidiah, Jr. & Margaret, b. Jan. 24, 1772	1	1
Joseph, s. Jedidiah, Jr. & Margaret, b. Sept. 30, 1774	1	1
Lucy, m. James **HYDE**, Nov. 7, 1797	1	67
Polly, d. Jedidiah, Jr. & Margaret, b. Mar. 22, 1778	1	1
Sally, twin with Betsey, d. Jedidiah, Jr. & Margaret,		
b. July 3, 1780	1	1
ASHLEY, Love, m. Daniel **DAVISON**, July 6, 1809	1	63
William S., of Hampton, m. Maria A. **CHURCH**, of		
Willimantic, May 4, 1853, by Rev. Geo[rge] J. Tillotson	4	111
AUSTIN, Eleanor, m. Elisha **ADAMS**, Dec. 6, 1795	1	60
Emily Wait, d. Joseph & Abigail, b. Feb. 1, 1816	1	231
Isaac Gallup, s. Joseph & Abigail, b. July 18, 1820	1	231
Jeremiah, s. John & Content, b. Nov. 29, 1781	1	1
Joseph, m. Abigail **WOODWARD**, Jan. 5, 1815	1	60
Mary Emily, of Foster, R. I., m. Stephen **ANGEL**, of Scituate,		
R. I., July 2, 1839, by Rev. William Coe	4	69
Mary Gallup, d. Joseph & Abigail, b. June 19, 1817	1	231
Mary Woodward, d. Joseph & Abigail, b. Oct. 21, 1818	1	231
AVERELL, Lucretia, of Pomfret, m. Godfrey **BROWN**, of		
Brooklyn, Mar. 13, 1823	2	7
AYLESWORTH, AYELSWORTH, ALESWORTH, Emily, of		

	Vol.	Page

AYLESWORTH, AYELSWORTH, ALESWORTH, (cont.)

Brooklyn, m. James **ROTHWELL,** of Killingly, May 6,
1846, by Rev. Benjamin C. Phelps, of West Killingly — 4 — 84

Emor A., d. July 25, [1848], ae 12 m. 23 d. — 2 — 91

Stephen, m. Sarah **FROST,** Jr., Apr. 17, 1796 — 1 — 60

BABCOCK, Charles, m. Eliza **LATHROP,** b. of Willimantic, Aug.
22, 1853, by Rev. C. Y. DeNormandie — 4 — 109

BACKUS, Olive, m. Eben **SHEPARD,** Oct. 18, 1807 — 1 — 76

Stephen, m. Eunice **WHITNEY,** Sept. 2, 1798 — 1 — 61

Susan, d. Thomas, Jr. & Almira, b. Sept. 1, 1824 — 2 — 5

Thomas, s. Thomas, Jr. & Almira, b. Oct. 9, 1822 — 2 — 5

BACON, Betsey, m. Bela P. **SPAULDING,** Mar. 26, 1806 — 1 — 76

Cha[rle]s, m. Anne **PUTNAM,** Oct. 20, 1852, by Rev. R.
Camp — 4 — 108

BADGER, Sally, m. Rufus **PARRISH,** Sept. 26, 1799, by John
Parrish, J. P. — 3 — 1

BAGGS, Samuel, m. Margaret **BARR,** b. of Brooklyn, Nov. 26,
1854, by Rev. Sylvester Barrows — 4 — 115

BAILEY, Almira, d. Sylvanus & Mira, b. Dec. 7, 1816 — 1 — 233

Almira Elizabeth, m. Ralph **WEBB,** [Jan.] 4, [1835], by
Rev. Samuel J. May — 4 — 57

Charles Henry, s. Sylvanus & Mira, b. Apr. 1, 1831 — 2 — 5

Samuel Peck, s. Sylvanus & Mara, b. Mar. 9, 1827 — 2 — 5

Sylvanus, m. Mira **INGRAHAM,** Jan. 18, 1816 — 1 — 61

Sylvanus, m. Mira **LYON,** Jan. 18, 1816, by John Parish, J. P. — 3 — 9

BAKER, Abby, m. Ebenezer **BARRETT,** b. of Brooklyn, Mar. 3,
1825, by Rev. James Porter, of Pomfret — 4 — 19

Almond, s. John & Mary, b. Dec. 27, 1771 — 2 — 5

Almond, m. Hannah **TUCKER,** May 19, 1807 — 1 — 61

Almond, clothier, d. Jan. 9, 1850, ae 77 — 2 — 122

Charlotte, of Brooklyn, m. Dyar **AMES,** Jr., of Seneca Falls,
N. Y., [July] 8, [1832], by Rev. Samuel J. May — 4 — 47

David, s. Erastus & Lois, b. Aug. 16, 1788 — 1 — 2

David, farmer, b. Pomfret, res. Brooklyn, m. Harriet E.
A. **HARRIS,** Feb. 23, [1851], by Uriel Fuller — 2 — 130

David, m. Harriet Eleanor **HARRIS,** b. of Brooklyn, Feb.
23, 1851, by Uriel Fuller, J. P. — 4 — 103

Deborah, m. John **SEARLES,** Nov. 28, 1807 — 1 — 76

Ebenezer, s. Joseph & Lucy, b. July 22, 1783 — 1 — 2

Ebenezer, Dr., m. Betsey **WILLIAMS,** Feb. 17, 1805 — 1 — 61

Ebenezer, Dr., d. Dec. 11, 1820 — 1 — 41

Ebenezer, m. Caroline **CADY,** b. of Brooklyn, Nov. 10,
1822, by David C. Bolles, J. P. — 4 — 11

Elizabeth, d. Joseph & Lucy, b. Feb. 19, 1780 — 1 — 2

Elizabeth, m. Pascal Paoli **TYLER,** Sept. 17, 1797 — 1 — 77

Ellen L., of Brooklyn, m. William G. **HOWARD,** of
Newburyport, Apr. 19, 1836, by Rev. G. J. Tillotson — 4 — 61

Emily Margaret, m. Lieut. William Williams **MATHER,**

	Vol.	Page
BAKER, (cont.)		
June 21, 1830, by Rev. Samuel J. May	4	43
Erastus, m. Lois **WITHEY**, Nov. 4, 1787	1	61
Frank Ebenezer, s. Ebenezer & Caroline, b. Jan. 26, 1823	2	6
George, s. Erastus & Lois, b. July 15, 1790	1	2
James s. Jos[eph] & Lucy, b. Sept. 11, 1788	1	2
John, d. July 19, 1806, in the 66th y. of his age	1	41
John, s. Almond & Hannah, b. Oct. 5, 1812	2	5
John F., s. John M., wagon maker, ae 36, & Sarah, ae 30, b. Sept. 14, 1849	2	121
Joseph, m. Lucy **DEVOTION**, Feb. 11, 1779	1	61
Joseph, s. Joseph & Lucy, d. June 8, 1797, ae 10 m. 22 d.	1	41
Joseph, Jr., m. Artametia **SKINNER**, May 18, 1801, by John Parrish, J. P.	3	1
Joseph, d. May 16, 1804, ae 55	1	41
Julia A., of Brooklyn, m. Roderick **DAVISON**, of Willimantic, Apr. 3, 1849, by Rev. G. J. Tillotson	4	100
Julia Ann, d. Ebenezer & Caroline, b. Dec. 5, 1825	2	6
Julia Ann, ae 24, b. Brooklyn, m. Roderick **DAVISON**, cabinet maker, ae 25, b. Munson, Mass., res. Willimantic, Apr. 3, 1849, by Rev. George J. Tillotson	2	105
Lucy Maria, d. Joseph & Lucy, b. Mar. 23, 1793	1	2
Martha, d. Joseph & Lucy, b. June 7, 1786	1	2
Mary, d. Almond & Hannah, b. Dec. 10, 1809	2	5
Mary, wid., John, d. July 16, 1818	1	41
Mary, of Brooklyn, m. Henry **RUSSELL**, of Grafton, Mass., Oct. 14, 1844, by Rev. Geo[rge] J. Tillotson	4	80
Rufus Lathrop, s. Jos[eph] & Lucy, b. Dec. 6, 1790	1	2
Sarah, d. Joseph & Lucy, b. Sept. 23, 1781	1	2
Sophia Maria, d. Erastus & Lois, b. Jan. 23, 1792	1	2
Sophronia, m. James **NYE**, b. of Brooklyn, July 4, 1841, by Rev. Geo[rge] J. Tillotson	4	74
William, m. Sarah Ann **HARVEY**, b. of Brooklyn, Feb. 21, 1842, by Daniel P. Tyler, J. P.	4	75
BALDWIN, Benjamin B., of West Springfield, Mass., m. Emily **GALLUP**, of Brooklyn, [Nov.] 27, [1827], by Rev. Ambrose Edson	4	30
Sarah, m. Hiram **CHACE**, b. of Brooklyn, Oct. 25, 1836, by Rev. G. J. Tillotson	4	62
Seth P., m. Lydia S. **KEECH**, b. of Brooklyn, Nov. 16, 1835, by Joseph Tyler, J. P.	4	60
Seth P., m. Celinda **FARNHAM**, Nov. 30, 1837, by Rev. Mr. Bullard	4	116
BARD, Edmund H., m. Emily **ADAMS**, b. of Brooklyn, Mar. 11, 1841, by Rev. Geo[rge] J. Tillotson	4	73
James D., of Boston, m. Caroline P. **MAIN**, of Brooklyn, May 12, 1840, by Rev. G. J. Tillotson	4	72
Sophronia, m. Samuel **ROBBINS**, b. of Brooklyn, Nov. 26,		

	Vol.	Page
BARD, (cont.)		
1837, by Rev. G. J. Tillotson	4	65
BARNETT, Caroline Christiana, of Boston, m. Alfred **STILLE**, M. D., of Philadelphia, Pa., Nov. 4, 1841, by Rev. R. Camp	4	75
BARR, Margaret, m. Samuel **BAGGS**, b. of Brooklyn, Nov. 26, 1854, by Rev. Sylvester Barrows	4	115
BARRETT, Adaline, d. Capt. Joseph P. & Nancy L. W., b. Feb. 25, 1823	2	5
Adeline B., of Brooklyn, m. Charles W. **FISK**, of Worcester, Mass., Apr. 21, 1846, by Rev. G. J. Tillotson	4	84
Alphonso, s. Capt. Jos[eph] P. & Nancy L. W., d. July 15, 1833, in the 8th y. of his age	1	44
Ebenezer, m. Abby **BAKER**, b. of Brooklyn, Mar. 3, 1825, by Rev. James Porter, of Pomfret	4	19
Elizabeth, d. July 19, 1787	1	41
Harvey, s. William & Lucy, b. Apr. 13, 1796	1	232
Harvey, s. William & Lucy, d. Jan. 2, 1817, in the 21st y. of his age	1	44
Henry Martin, s. Capt. Joseph P. & Nancy L. W., b. Jan. 4, 1828; d. Sept. 11, 1832	2	5
Henry Martin, 2d, s. Capt. Joseph P. & Nancy L. W., b. June 26, 1832	2	5
Henry Martyn, s. Capt. Jos[eph] P. & Nancy L. W., d. Sept. 11, 1832	1	44
James, s. W[illia]m & Lucy, d. Sept. 20, 1799	1	41
James Harvey, s. Capt. Joseph Phelps & Nancy Laura Whipple, b. June 21, 1821	1	233
James Harvey, s. Capt. Joseph P. & Nancy L. W., b. June 20, 1821	2	5
Joseph Phelps, m. Nancy Laura Whipple **CONVERSE**, June 11, 1820, by Rev. Daniel Dow, of Thompson	4	1
Lucy, w. William, d. Apr. 5, 1834, in the 81st y. of her age	1	44
Molly, m. John **ALLERTON**, Apr. 10, 1810	2	3
Philena, d. W[illia]m & Lucy, d. Feb. 28, 1799	1	41
Thomas Erksine, s. Capt. Joseph P. & Nancy L. W., b. Mar. 28, 1830	2	5
BARROWS, James M., m. Louisa G. **GILBERT**, Apr. 14, 1831, by Rev. Roswell Whitmore	4	45
BARTLETT, Eleazer, of Killingly, m. Harriet **ASHCRAFT**, of Brooklyn, Dec. 17, 1826, by Rev. Roswell Whitmore, of Killingly	4	26
BASSETT, BASSET, Clarrissey, of Killingly, d. Mar. 19, 1848, ae 71	2	84
Joseph, clothier, b. Killingly, d. June 10, 1851, ae 54	2	134
Margaret, m. Charles **FOSTER**, b. of Brooklyn, Sept. 12, 1822, by Vine Robinson, J. P.	4	10
BATTEY, Abbey E., m. Abel **WEEKS**, of Canterbury, Nov. 3, 1850, by Rev. G. J. Tillotson	4	103

	Vol.	Page

BATTEY, (cont.)

Mercy, of Brooklyn, m. Silas **BURGESS**, of Providence, R.
I., Nov. 24, 1844, by Rev. Geo[rge] J. Tillotson | 4 | 81

BENNETT, BENNET, Alice, m. Daniel **DAVIS**, Nov. 24, 1803 | 1 | 63

Antoinette Allen, d. Pardon & Ludovice Davis Allen, b.
Jan. 8, 1823 | 2 | 5

Asa D., m. Sarah [   ] **WILLIAMS**, Nov. 6, 1853, by Rev.
R. Camp | 4 | 110

Ebenezer S., of Canterbury, m. Mary Ann **WILLSON**, of
Brooklyn, May 5, 1850, by Cha[rle]s Adams, J. P. | 4 | 102

John, of Plainfield, m. Maria **BUTTS**, of Canterbury, Mar.
14, 1826, by John Parish, J. P. | 3 | 10

Ludovice Davis **ALLEN**, w. Pardon, d. Feb. 1, 1823, in the
22d y. of her age | 1 | 41

Matilda, m. Luther **YOUNG**, b. of Brooklyn, Mar. 31, [1831],
by Rev. Roswell Whitmore | 4 | 44

Olive of Brooklyn, m. Lewis **HIG[G]INBOTHAM,** of
Pomfret, Aug. 9, 1846, by Rev. Benjamin C. Phelps, of
West Killingly | 4 | 85

Pardon, m. Ludovice **ALLEN**, b. of Brooklyn, Sept. 24,
1820, by Rev. Roswell Whitmore, Killingly | 4 | 1

Ruhamah, m. Benjamin **WOOD**, Nov. 23, 1786 | 1 | 78

BENSON, Charlotte, of Brooklyn, m. Henry **ANTHONY**, of
Providence, R. I., Oct. 22, 1826, by Rev. Samuel J. May | 4 | 25

Eliza Davis, d. George W., & Catharine, b. Feb. 24, 1841 | 2 | 6

Francis, d. Oct. 31, 1832, ae 38 y. | 1 | 44

George, d. Dec. 11, 1836, in the 85th y. of his age | 1 | 44

George, s. George W. & Catharine, b. Jan. 7, 1839 | 2 | 6

Henry Egbert, s. George W. & Catharine, b. Oct. 7, 1837 | 2 | 6

Helen Eliza, of Brooklyn, m. William Lloyd **GARRISON**, of
Boston, Sept. 4, 1834, by Rev. Samuel J. May | 4 | 55

BERIAND, Lucy had d. Eunice Lucinda **FRASIER** & great
granddaughter of Lucy **SHAWONE**, b. Mar. 28, 1813 | 1 | 238

BERNE, Michael, s. John, farmer, ae 23, & Frederica, ae 27,
b. Apr. 2, 1849 | 2 | 95

BICKFORD, Phebe, m. Ira **WHEELER**, Apr. 2, 1815 | 1 | 78

BICKNELL, BIGNAL, Edwin, of Killingly, m. Mariette
STEDMAN, of Brooklyn, Feb. 2, 1851, by Rev. S. W.
Coggeshall | 4 | 103

Edwin M., moulder, ae 28, of E. Brooklyn, m. Mariaette
STEDMAN, ae 26, b. Brooklyn, Feb. 2, 1851, by Rev.
Sam[ue]l Coggeshall (His 2d marriage) | 2 | 132

BIGELOW, John D., of Brookfield, Mass., m. Emily
SCARBOROUGH, of Brooklyn, Oct. 27, 1840, by Rev.
G. J. Tillotson | 4 | 73

Lucy, of Leicester, Mass., m. Herbert **WILLIAMS**, Aug. 19,
1822 | 1 | 78

Lucy, of Leicester, Mass., m. Herbert **WILLIAMS**, Aug. 19,

	Vol.	Page
BIGELOW, (cont.)		
1822	2	65
BIGNAL, [see under **BICKNELL**]		
BINGHAM, Henry D., m. Mary E. **ADAMS**, b. of Canterbury, Oct.		
23, 1837, by Rev. G. J. Tillotson	4	64
BISHOP, Phebe, m. Charles W. **JENKINS**, b. of Brooklyn, Apr.		
14, 1835, by Rev. G. J. Tillotson	4	58
BISSELL, Anne, d. Sept. 18, 1847, ae 97	2	88
BLAISDELL, Christiana M., of Franklin, Me., m. Harvey		
SPALDING, of Plainfield, Feb. 8, 1847, by Rev. Samuel		
May	4	86
BLANCHARD, David, s. Elias & Lucy, d. May 2, 1813	1	41
Elias, s. Elias & Lucy, d. Sept. 17, 1792	1	41
Elias, d. June 19, 1835, in the 78th y. of his age	1	44
Joseph, of Foster, R. I., m. Nancy **HARRIS**, of Brooklyn,		
Dec. 9, 1821, by David C. Bolles, J. P.	4	7
Lucy, m. William **HEBBARD**, Dec. 19, 1813	1	67
Lucy, w. Elias, d. Oct. 15, 1827	1	41
Martha, d. Elias & Lucy, d. Sept. 24, 1823	1	41
Sally, d. Elias & Lucy, b. July 4, 1798	1	232
Sanford, s. Elias & Lucy, d. Jan. 20, 1789	1	41
Sarah, m. Lucius **CADY**, b. of Brooklyn, June 5, [1828],		
by Rev. A. Edson	4	33
BOARDMAN, William D., Dr., of Cattskill, N. Y., m. Marcia Ann		
MORGAN, of Brooklyn, Apr. 16, 1832, by Rev.		
Geo[rge] J. Tillotson	4	47
BOLLES, Armin, m. Alice **SEARLS**, b. of Brooklyn, Apr. 8, 1839,		
by Rev. Thomas Huntington	4	68
David C., m. Fanny **MATHER**, Nov. 5, 1821, by Joseph		
Chickering	4	5
David Charles, s. David C. & Fanny, b. Apr. 11, 1825	2	6
Frances Mather, d. Rev. David C. & Fanny, b. Jan. 19, 1831	2	6
George A., s. Armin, farmer, ae 54, & Alice, ae 40, b.		
Apr. 7, 1850	2	121
Julia Ann, d. David C. & Fanny, b. Feb. 22, 1823	2	6
Susan M., ae 20, of Brooklyn, m. Emanuel **SPAULDING**,		
merchant, of Eastford, Mar. [ ], 1851, by Nicholas		
Branch	2	133
William Mather, s. David C. & Fanny, b. Feb. 28, 1827	2	6
BOND, Sarah Ann, of Brooklyn, m. Alteria **HARVEY**, of Windham,		
Aug. 26, 1838, by George Sharpe, J. P.	4	66
BORDEN, Betsey, d. Dr. Ebenezer & Betsey, b. Sept. 14, 1805	1	232
Ebenezer, Dr., m. Betsey **DAVIS**, Nov. 6, 1803	1	61
BOWEN, Catharine S., of Brooklyn, m. Edmond **BURNHAM**, of		
Hampton, [Nov.] 9, [1851], by Geo[rge] G. Channing.		
Intention published	4	105
BOWMAN, Betsey, d. Elisha & Elizabeth, b. July 27, 1785	1	2
Elisha, s. Elisha & Elizabeth, b. Mar. 31, 1788	1	2

	Vol.	Page
BOWMAN, (cont.)		
Thomas, s. Elisha & Elizabth, b. Aug. 23, 1790	1	2
BOWNES, James H., s. Ira M., farmer, ae 25, of Hampton, &		
Caroline, ae 23, b. Nov. 25, 1847	2	83
BOYDEN, Abigail, m. Hazel **WITHEY**, Nov. 24, 1799	1	78
BRAMAN, Charlotte Tyler, d. Thomas & Cornelia, b. Oct. 23,		
1839	2	4
Helen Elizabeth, d. Thomas & Cornelia, b. Nov. 12, 1845	2	4
Isabella Graham, d. Thomas, silversmith, ae 38, & Cornelia		
T., ae 32, b. Jan. 26, 1848	2	93
Louisa Cornelia, d. Thomas & Cornelia, b. Nov. 2, 1842	2	4
Thomas, m. Cornelia J. **TYLER**, b. of Brooklyn, Apr. 7,		
1836, by Rev. G. J. Tillotson	4	60
BRANCH, Kezia, m. Nathan **WITTER**, Dec. 15, 1753	1	78
BRAND, Jane, d. Gardner, manufacturer, ae 21, & Harriet, ae		
19, b. Jan. 2, 1850	2	119
Jane E., of E. Brooklyn, d. June 29, [1851], ae 18 m.	2	132
BRIGGS, Joseph W., of Voluntown, m. Mary **MOFFITT**, of		
Killingly, Oct. 19, 1845, by Rev. G. J. Tillotson	4	82
BROOKS, Charles, Rev., of Hingham, Mass., m. Cecilia		
WILLIAMS, of Brooklyn, [June] 27, [1827], by Rev.		
Samuel J. May	4	28
John, of Western in Co. of Worcester, m. [ ] **JOHNSON**,		
of Brooklyn, Oct. 9, 1816, by John Parish, J. P.	3	9
BROUGHTON, Nathan, m. Lydia **CADY**, Mar. 28, 1802	1	61
BROWN, Abigail, m. Isaac **CLEVELAND**, Jan. 18, 1808	1	62
Alethea, d. Alpheas & Sarah, b. Apr. 11, 1785	1	2
Alathia, m. Phinehas **SEARLES**, Mar. 21, 1802	1	76
Alpheas, s. Alpheas & Sarah, b. Apr. 24, 1791	1	2
Alpheas, d. Feb. 5, 1794	1	41
Amma Tufts, s. Rufus & Mary, b. Nov. 22, 1799	1	232
Andrew Dixon, s. Godfrey & Lucretia, b. July 19, 1824,		
at Brooklyn	2	7
Andrew Murdock, s. Shubael & Nancy, b. May 19, 1807	1	232
Anne Putnam, d. James & Emily, b. July 25, 1829	2	7
Artemus, s. Shubael & Nancy, b. May 17, 1788	1	232
Artemus, m. Amanda **FISK**, Dec. 13, 1818	1	61
Benjamin, s. Benjamin & Susannah, b. May 25, 1807	1	233
Catharine, d. James & Emily, b. Jan. 11, 1823	2	7
Catharin[e], m. Willard **DAY**, Sept. 20, 1841, by Rev. R. Camp	4	74
Charles Joseph, s. Benj[amin], farmer, ae 43, & Emeline		
E., ae 37, b. Aug. 2, 1850	2	125
Daniel, s. Alpheas & Sarah, b. Mar. 4, 1778	1	2
Daniel Putnam, s. James & Emily, b. Jan. 25, 1825;		
d. Aug. 19, 1828	2	7
Ebenezer Eliakim, s. Rufus & Mary, b. Mar. 6, 1798	1	232
Eliza Joann, d. Godfrey & Lucretia, b. Apr. 22, 1828,		
at Brooklyn; d. Sept. 14, 1830, at Pomfret	2	7

	Vol.	Page

\ **BROWN**, (cont.)

Elliot, of Brooklyn, m. Phebe M. **WESCOTT**, of Coventry,
R. I., Aug. 26, 1849, by Rev. J. Ferris. Intention pub.
Aug. 26, 1849 — 4 — 102

Emilyne, d. Benjamin & Susannah, b. Jan. 1, 1809 — 1 — 233

Emeline, m. Samuel W. **STEVENS**, b. of Brooklyn, Sept. 5,
1836, by Rev. G. J. Tillotson — 4 — 62

Emily, d. James & Emily, b. Sept. 20, 1827 — 2 — 7

George, s. Shubael & Nancy, b. Apr. 14, 1801 — 1 — 232

George, s. James & Emily, b. July 30, 1832 — 2 — 7

George Sumner, s. James & Emily, b. Mar. 19, 1821;
d. Apr. 12, 1824 — 2 — 5

George Sumner, s. James & Emily, b. Mar. 19, 1821;
d. Apr. 12, 1824 — 2 — 7

George Throop, s. Benjamin & Susannah, b. Dec. 20, 1810 — 1 — 233

Godfrey, s. Shubael & Nancy, b. Dec. 27, 1792 — 1 — 232

Godfrey, of Brooklyn, m. Lucretia **AVERELL**, of Pomfret,
Mar. 13, 1823 — 2 — 7

Gurdon, s. Shubael & Nancy, b. May 2, 1797 — 1 — 232

Gurdon, s. Capt. Shubael & Nancy, d. Mar. 20, 1823, ae 25 y. — 1 — 41

Harriet G., ae 20, b. Glastonbury, res. Brooklyn, m. Elisha
CARPENTER, lawyer, ae 25, b. Ashford, res. Eastford,
Ct., Mar. 30, 1848, by George J. Tillotson — 2 — 93

Harriet G., of Brooklyn, m. Elisha **CARPENTER**, of Eastford,
Mar. 31, 1848, by Rev. G. J. Tillotson — 4 — 99

Henry, of Pomfret, m. Prudy Ann **PRATT**, of Brooklyn, Aug.
28, 1842, by Rev. Thomas Huntington — 4 — 77

Henry, carpenter, of Pomfret, d. Feb. 24, 1848, ae 55 — 2 — 80

James, s. Shubael & Nancy, b. May 5, 1795 — 1 — 232

James, m. Emily **PUTNAM**, Apr. 9, 1820 — 1 — 61

James Dixon, s. James & Emily, b. Oct. 20, 1834 — 2 — 7

Jesse, s. Shubael & Nancy, b. Aug. 1, 1790 — 1 — 232

John, s. Alpheas & Sarah, b. Nov. 24, 1781 — 1 — 2

John, s. Shubael & Nancy, b. July 4, 1786 — 1 — 232

Joseph, [twin with Mary], s. Alpheas* & Sarah, b. July
17, 1796 (*Arnold Copy has "Joseph". Corrected by L.
B. B.) — 1 — 2

Joseph Williams, s. Rufus & Mary, b. Jan. 7, 1804 — 1 — 232

Juliette, m. George L. **HOPKINS**, b. of Scituate, R. I.,
Nov. 30, 1852, by Rev. Geo[rge] J. Tillotson — 4 — 107

Laura, d. Shubael & Nancy, b. July 18, 1805 — 1 — 232

Laura, d. Capt. Shubael & Nancy, d. Aug. 29, 1820, ae 15 y. — 1 — 41

Lucretia Waldo, d. Godfrey & Lucretia, b. Feb. 4, 1831,
at Pomfret — 2 — 7

Lucy, w. Jedidiah, d. Feb. 14, 1789 — 1 — 41

Mary, [twin with Joseph], d. Alpheas* & Sarah, b. July 17,
1796 (*Arnold Copy has Joseph". Corrected by L. B. B.
— 1 — 2

	Vol.	Page
BROWN, (cont.)		
Mary E., d. Samuel J., farmer, ae 31, & Arthusa, ae 26,		
b. Jan. 28, 1848	2	86
Mary Elizabeth, d. Rufus & Mary, b. May 18, 1813	1	233
Nancy, d. Shubael & Nancy, b. Mar. 31, 1803	1	232
Nancy, d. Artemus & Amanda, b. Oct. 8, 1819	1	233
Nancy, Mrs., b. Sterling, res. Brooklyn, d. Oct. 30,[1848], ae 87	2	98
Nathan, s. Alpheas & Sarah, b. Aug. 2, 1783	1	2
Nathan, s. Alpheas & Sarah, d. Sept. 16, 1787	1	41
Nathan, s. Alpheas & Sarah, b. Mar. 28, 1789	1	2
Olive, m. Jacob B. **WITTER**, Nov. 23, 1794	1	78
Polly L., m. Clark **PARKER**, Nov. 11, 1816	2	46
Polly Litchfield, d. Alpheas & Sarah, b. Apr. 26, 1793	1	2
Prudence, housekeeper, d. Aug. 30, 1847, ae 60	2	80
Rufus, m. Mary **WILLIAMS**, May 16, 1797	1	61
Russell M., of Jewett City, m. Mercy A. **REED**, Feb. 15,		
1852, by Rev. G. J. Tillotson	4	107
Sarah, d. Alpheas & Sarah, b. May 16, 1787	1	2
Shubael, m. Nancy **DIXON**, Dec. 15, 1785	1	61
Shubael, s. Shubael & Nancy, b. Apr. 10, 1799	1	232
Stephen, of Pomfret, m. Lydia **SPALDING**, of Brooklyn,		
Jan. 14, 1827, by Jona[than] A. Welch, J. P.	4	27
Susan, d. Benjamin & Susannah, b. Feb. 9, 1806	1	232
Susan C., d. Benjamin, Jr., farmer, ae 41, & Emeline G.,		
ae 36, b. June 20, 1848	2	81
Thomas, s. Alpheas & Sarah, b. Dec. 10, 1779	1	2
Waty, m. Wyllys **DEAOLPH**, Mar. 31, 1805	1	63
William Averell, s. Godfrey & Lucretia, b. Aug. 8, 1826,		
at Brooklyn	2	7
William Rufus, s. Rufus & Mary, b. July 29, 1805	1	233
BROWNELL, W[illia]m, of Smithfield, R. I., m. Nancy **GRAVES**,		
of Brooklyn, Aug. 9, 1846, by Rev. Benjamin C. Phelps,		
of West Killingly	4	85
BROWNING, Joseph Boardman, s. Beriah H. & Sarah E., b. Nov.		
18, 1843	2	4
BUCHEE, James L., m. Patience B. **HARRINGTON**, b. of Scituate,		
R. I., May 17, 1836, by Rev. G. J. Tillotson	4	61
BUNN, Sophia M., m. Daniel **HAWKINS**, b. of Brooklyn, Sept. 17,		
1844, by Rev. G. J. Tillotson	4	80
BURGESS, Alden, Jr., of Brooklyn, m. Abby **KINGSBURY**, of		
Killingly, Oct. 7, 1839, by Rev. William Coe	4	71
Harriet Louisa, d. Alden & Abby, b. Dec. 25, 1841, in		
Brooklyn	2	4
Horace, physician, ae 25, of Plainfield, m. Ruby **GALLUP**,		
ae 28, b. Sterling, Sept. 3, [1850], by Rev. George J.		
Tillotson	2	124
Horace, M. D., of Plainfield, m. Ruby **GALLUP**, of Brooklyn,		
Sept. 5, 1850, by Rev. George J. Tillotson	4	104

	Vol.	Page

BURGESS, (cont.)

Ira, s. Alden & Abby, b. Jan. 18, 1840, in Killingly 2 4

Silas, of Providence, R. I., m. Mercy **BATTY**, of Brooklyn,
Nov. 24, 1844, by Rev. Geo[rge] J. Tillotson 4 81

BURLINGHAM, Ellen M., d. Benjamin, dresser tender, ae 33, &
Calista, ae 30, b. July 27, 1849 2 103

BURN, John, s. John, farmer, ae 25, & Bridget, ae 28, b.
Dec. 15, 1850 2 123

BURNET, Lester, of Hampton, m. Olive **CLEAVELAND**, of
Brooklyn, Jan. 1, 1828, by Rev. Ambrose Edson 4 30

BURNHAM, **BURNAM**, Alba, of Homer, N. Y., m. Celia
MARTIN, of Brooklyn, Sept. 13, 1830, by Rev. Samuel
J. May 4 43

Ebenezer, m. Sally **CHENEY**, Mar. 6, 1825, by Rev. Samuel
J. May 4 19

Edmund, of Hampton, m. Hannah **ROBBINS**, of Brooklyn,
Aug. 13, 1838, by Rev. William Coe 4 66

Edmond, of Hampton, m. Catharine S. **BOWEN**, of Brooklyn,
[Nov.] 9, [1851], by Geo[rge] G. Channing. Int. Pub. 4 105

John L., of Hampton, m. Elizabeth **PHILLIPS**, of Brooklyn,
Nov. 15, 1846, by Rev. Benjamin C. Phelps, of West
Killingly 4 87

BURROUGHS, [see also **BURROWS**], Ann, m. Alfred
ASHCRAFT, Sept. 22, 1816 1 60

Joseph, d. Nov. 26, 1830, in the 89th y. of his age 1 44

BURROWS, [see also **BURROUGHS**], Catharine, m. Ebenezer
ASHCRAFT, May 8, 1800 1 60

Eunice, d. of Esther **GALLUP**, m. Edwin E. **KNAPPING**, July
23, 1838, by Daniel P. Tyler, J. P. "Married with the
consent of Esther **GALLUP**, the mother of said Eunice a
minor." 4 66

BURTON, Charles, m. Elizabeth **HUTCHINS**, Oct. 10, 1839, by
Rev. R. Camp 4 72

Chester C., s. Lewis G. & Caroline E., b. Apr. 20, 1834 2 6

Lewis G., m. Caroline E. **KIES**, Apr. 24, 1831, by Samuel
J. May 4 45

BUSWELL, Ann Maria, d. Jabez & Orvilla, b. Oct. 6, 1822 2 5

BUTLER, Samuel W., of Ashford, m. Lavina M. **UTLEY**, of
Brooklyn, May 28, 1823, by Rev. James Porter, of
Pomfret 4 13

BUTTS, Amos, s. Henry, laborer, ae 51, & Rebecca, ae 28, b.
Jan. 3, [1851] 2 131

Anna, m. Joel **DAVISON**, Apr. 17, 1821, by Rev. Hutchins
Taylor 4 3

Asaph, s. Simeon & Betsey, b. Mar. 15, 1802 1 232

Benjamin Burnham, s. Simeon & Betsey, b. Aug. 26, 1805 1 232

Betsey, m. Benj[amin] **WEAVER**, Dec. 8, 1797 1 78

Erastus, s. Simeon & Betsey, b. Sept. 8, 1812 1 233

	Vol.	Page
BUTTS, (cont.)		
Erastus, s. Simeon & Betsey, d. July 31, 1814, in the 2d y. of		
his age	1	41
Esther, d. Simeon & Betsey, b. Nov. 13, 1797	1	232
Esther, m. Gordon **JEFFERY**, b. of Brooklyn, Jan. 11, 1818,		
by John Parish, J. P.	3	9
Eunice, w. Dea. Samuel, d. Mar. 26, 1806, in the 65th		
y. of her age	1	41
Eunice, d. Henry, agriculturist, & Rebecca, b. Jan. 9, 1850	2	117
Eunice, d. Feb. 15, 1850	2	118
Hannah, m. James **RUDE**, Oct. 10, 1801	1	75
Harriet L., ae 17, of Brooklyn, m. Theodore F. **ROBBINS**,		
silversmith, ae 23, of Brooklyn, Nov. 23, 1847, by Rev.		
T. Huntington	2	79
Harriet L., m. Theodore F. **ROBBINS**, b. of Brooklyn,		
[Nov.] 25, [1847], by Rev. Tho[ma]s Huntington	4	99
Lewis E., s. Frank, laborer, ae 45, & Lydia, ae 43, b.		
Jan. 11, 1850	2	123
Lucy, d. Simeon & Betsey, b. Sept. 4, 1799	1	232
Luther, m. Polly **WEAVER**, Apr. 15, 1798	1	61
Maria, of Canterbury, m. John **BENNET**, of Plainfield,		
Mar. 14, 1826, by John Parish, J. P.	3	10
Mary, m. Ebenezer **CADY**, Dec. 1, 1791	1	62
Mary E.,, m. Edwin G. **MAINE**, b. of Brooklyn, [Nov.] 26,		
[1843], by Rev. Thomas Huntington	4	79
Nan, d. Luther & Polly, b. Oct. 2, 1798	1	232
Samuel, Dea., m. Loderna **FULLER**, Apr. 16, 1807	1	61
Sarah, m. John **LITCHFIELD**, Jan. 30, 1800	1	70
Simeon, m. Betsey **PATTENGALL**, Jan. 17, 1797	1	61
William, s. Simeon & Betsey, b. Feb. 10, 1808	1	232
CADY, Abial, wid. Gideon, d. Feb. 5, 1828, in the 90th y.		
of her age	1	44
Adeline J., m. William W. **COVELL**, b. of Providence, R.		
I., Mar. 6, 1843, by Rev. George J. Tillotson	4	78
Almira, d. Pascal & Hannah, b. Mar. 11, 1806	1	236
Amanda, m. William **SPAULDING**, Oct. 7, 1792	1	76
Amos, s. Dan[ie]l & Mary, b. Dec. 28, 1768	1	235
Anna, m. Elijah **THAYER**, Dec. 30, 1773	1	77
Annis, d. Dan[ie]l & Mary, b. Oct. 18, 1783	1	235
Asahel, m. Ruth **INGRAHAM**, Mar. 13, 1783	1	62
Barker, s. Asahel & Ruth, b. June 11, 1784	1	3
Betsey, d. Jonath[a]n & Christian, b. Apr. 20, 1795	1	234
Billa, s. Jonathan & Christian, b. Apr. 22, 1790	1	234
Calista, d. Ezra & Prescilla, b. Jan. 26, 1794	1	234
Calista, m. Havilah **TAYLOR**, Dec. 22, 1816	1	77
Caroline, d. Eliakim & Jerusha, b. Sept. 30, 1794	1	244
Caroline, m. Ebenezer **BAKER**, b. of Brooklyn, Nov. 10,		
1822, by David C. Bolles, J. P.	4	11

	Vol.	Page
CADY, (cont.)		
Charles, s. Denison & Hannah, b. Apr. 21, 1814	1	243
Charles, s. Denison & Hannah, d. May 20, 1814	1	42
Charles, s. Elisha & Betsey, b. Jan. 1, 1825	2	10
Charles, s. Edwin & Lydia, b. Sept. 23, 1829	2	10
Charles, m. Lucy CLEVELAND, b. of Brooklyn, Aug. 4, 1845, by Rev. G. J. Tillotson	4	81
Charles Lemuel, s. Lemuel & Lydia, b. Aug. 10, 1831; d. Dec. 8, 1832	2	12
Chester, of Pomfret, m. Harriet KEYES, of Brooklyn, Mar. 20, 1826, by Rev. Samuel J. May	4	23
Cynthia, d. Uriah & Joanna, b. Feb. 14, 1775	1	3
Dan[ie]l, m. Mary SPAULDING, Oct. 6, 1762	1	62
Denison, m. Hannah ADAMS, Nov. 30, 1802	1	62
Denison, d. June 3, 1844, ae 65	1	44
Dille Melora, d. Lemuel & Lydia, b. July 25, 1825	2	12
Ebenezer, m. Mary BUTTS, Dec. 1, 1791	1	62
Ebenezer, s. Edwin & Lydia, b. Dec. 26, 1831	2	10
Edith, d. Ezra & Priscilla, b. Oct. 16, 1800	1	236
Edith, m. Thomas GREENE, Jan. 1, 1821, by John Parish, J. P.	3	2
Edith, m. Thomas GREEN, b. of Brooklyn, Jan. 1, 1821, by John Parish, J. P.	4	13
Edwin, s. Eben[eze]r & Mary, b. Apr. 18, 1799	1	234
Edwin Constant, s. Edwin & Lydia, b. Nov. 1, 1833	2	10
Eleazer, s. Jonathan & Christian, b. May 27, 1788	1	234
Eleazer, s. Jonathan & Christian, d. Dec. 27, 1788	1	42
Eliakim, s. Daniel & Mary, b. June 24, 1763	1	235
Eliakim, s. Daniel & Mary, b. June 27, 1763	1	243
Eliakim, m. Jerusha SPAULDING, June 8, 1784	1	62
Eliakim, m. Mrs. Fanny DARBY, [Apr.] 3, [1833], by Rev. Samuel J. May	4	50
Elisha, s. Eliakim & Jerusha, b. Apr. 23, 1792	1	244
Elisha, m. Betsey DARBE, May 9, 1819	2	10
Eliza, d. Samuel & Alice, b. May 22, 1821	1	236
Eliza, d. Samuel & Alice, b. May 22, 1821	2	8
Elizabeth, twin with Mary, d. Denison & Hannah, b. Oct. 4, 1806	1	243
Elizabeth, of Brooklyn, m. Archibald FRY, of Griswold, Dec. 27, 1829, by Rev. John O. Birdsall, at the house of Denison Cady	4	38
Emily, d. Eben[eze]r & Mary, b. Apr. 6, 1803	1	235
Emily L., d. Lucius, farmer, ae 52, & Fidelia, ae 42, b. July 5, 1848	2	86
Emily Luthera, d. Lucius & Lucy, b. July 5, 1848, at Brooklyn, Ct.	2	10
Eunice, d. Uriah & Joanna, b. Jan. 28, 1763	1	3
Experience, m. Willard ADAMS, Nov. 24, 1786	1	60

	Vol.	Page
CADY, (cont.)		
Ezra, m. Prescilla **DOWNING,** June 13, 1782	1	62
Fidelia, d. Elisha & Betsey, b. May 27, 1827	2	10
George, s. Edwin & Lydia, b. Jan. 22, 1828	2	10
George Hawkins, s. Elisha & Betsey, b. Oct. 10, 1834	2	10
George Hewell, s. Lemuel & Lydia, b. Aug. 5, 1824;		
d. Mar. 18, 1825	2	12
Gideon, m. Abiah **WEBBER,** Mar. 28, 1777	1	62
Gideon, s. Ezra & Prescilla, b. Feb. 8, 1790	1	234
Gideon, d. May 12, 1800	1	44
Gordon, s. Eliakim & Jerusha, b. Jan. 12, 1790	1	243
Gurdon, s. Elisha & Betsey, b. Aug. 15, 1822	2	10
Hannah, d. Dan[ie]l & Mary, b. July 27, 1776	1	235
Hannah, d. Eben[eze]r & Hannah, b. Dec. 6, 1790	1	3
Hannah, m. Erastus **PIERCE,** Feb. 9, 1800	1	74
Harriet Searles, d. Elisha & Betsey, b. Dec. 7, 1838	2	10
Jerusha, w. of Eliakim & d. of Caleb & Jerusha **SPAULDING,**		
b. Apr. 24, 1760	1	243
Joanna, d. Denison & Hannah, b. Mar. 9, 1812	1	243
Joanna, d. Denison & Hannah, d. May 6, 1812	1	42
Joel, s. Ezra & Prescilla, b. Aug. 22, 1787	1	234
Joseph Gurdon, s. Lemuel & Lydia, b. Oct. 25, 1819;		
d. Nov. 4, 1824	2	12
Lemuel, s. Gideon & Abiel, b. May 8, 1781	1	3
Lemuel, m. Lydia **TAYLOR,** Apr. 27, 1819, by John Parish, J.P.	3	2
Lemuel, m. Lydia **TAYLOR,** Apr. 29, 1819	2	12
Lorin, s. Elisha & Betsey, b. May 9, 1820	2	10
Louisa, of Brooklyn, m. George **ANGELL,** of Pomfret, Jan. 27, 1840, by Rev. William Coe	4	71
Lovel, s. Eliakim & Jerusha, b. Sept. 15, 1784	1	243
Lucina, d. Eliakim & Jerusha, b. Feb. 1, 1786	1	243
Lucynda, d. May 13, 1790	1	42
Lucius, s. Eliakim & Jerusha, b. Aug. 27, 1797	1	244
Lucius, m. Sarah **BLANCHARD,** b. of Brooklyn, June 5, [1828], by Rev. A. Edson	4	33
Lucy, d. Uriah & Joanna, b. Apr. 8, 1765	1	3
Lucy, m. Joshua **MILES,** May 25, 1779	1	71
Lucy, m. Daniel **KIES,** Dec. 29, 1801	1	69
Lucy, m. Daniel **KIES,** Dec. 29, 1801	2	31
Lucy Ann, d. Uriah & Joanna, b. May 8, 1768	1	3
Luther, s. Dan[ie]l & Mary, b. Apr. 30, 1781	1	235
Lydia, d. Dan[ie]l & Mary, b. Feb. 23, 1771	1	235
Lydia, d. Timothy & Lois, b. Nov. 14, 1780, at Stephentown, N. Y.	1	234
Lydia, d. Eben[eze]r & Mary, b. Jan. 17, 1795	1	234
Lydia, m. Nathan **BROUGHTON,** Mar. 28, 1802	1	61
Lydia M., of Brooklyn, m. Henry **JOHNSON,** of Coventry, R.		

	Vol.	Page
CADY, (cont.)		
May 23, 1830, by Uriel Fuller, J. P.	4	42
Sarah F., d. Lucius & Lucy, b. Oct. 3, 1835, at Canterbury	2	10
Seth, of Pomfret, m. Catharine K. **DORRAN[CE]**, of Brooklyn,		
Apr. 13, 1842, by Rev. George J. Tillotson	4	76
Sophronia, d. Ezra & Prescilla, b. June 14, 1797	1	234
Stephen Pardee, s. Eben[eze]r & Hannah, b. July 25, 1786	1	3
Uriah, 2d, m. Joanna **HEWIT[T]**, Apr. 8, 1762	1	62
Wealthy, d. Uriah & Joanna, b. May 18, 1771	1	3
William, of Brooklyn, m. Deborah **DEAN**, of Chaplin, Aug.		
6, 1843, by Daniel Bennett, J. P.	4	78
William Akins, s. Pascal & Hannah, b. Mar. 12, 1808	1	236
William Augustus, s. Eliakim & Jerusha, b. Apr. 16, 1803	1	244
Willys, s. Eben[eze]r & Hannah, b. Mar. 29, 1784	1	3
CARD, ----, s. Silas, wagon maker, of Plainfield, & Cintha,		
of Plainfield, b. Feb. 22, 1850	2	121
CARDER, Lysander, m. Mary **SCARBOROUGH**, b. of Brooklyn,		
Oct. 16, 1837, by Rev. G. J. Tillotson	4	64
CARPENTER, Elisha, lawyer, ae 25, b. Ashford, res. Eastford,		
Ct., m. Harriet G. **BROWN**, ae 20, b. Glastonbury, res.		
Brooklyn, Ct., Mar. 30, 1848, by George J. Tillotson	2	93
Elisha, of Eastford, m. Harriet G. **BROWN**, of Brooklyn,		
Mar. 31, 1848, by Rev. G. J. Tillotson	4	99
CARTER, Asa Ebenezer, s. Adin & Maria, b. July 17, 1822	1	244
Curtis, m. Mary **WADE**, b. of Brooklyn, Nov. 24, 1836, by		
Rev. G. J. Tillotson	4	63
Edwin B., m. Amanda **ADAMS**, b. of Brooklyn, Dec. 25, 1839,		
by Rev. G. J. Tillotson	4	71
Edwin Bradford, s. Adin & Maria, b. Feb. 20, 1817	1	243
Eliza Niles, d. Adin & Eliza, b. Nov. 2, 1837	1	244
Emily Permelia, d. Adin & Maria, b. Sept. 5, 1830	1	244
Lucy Ann, d. Adin & Maria, b. Mar. 25, 1819	1	243
Lucy Ann, m. George **HICKS**, b. of Broolklyn, Nov. 13,		
1842, by Rev. G. J. Tillotson	4	77
Marcia Maria, d. Adin & Maria, b. Aug. 15, 1825	1	244
Marcia Maria, m. George **HICKS**, b. of Brooklyn, Oct. 8,		
1843, by Rev. G. J. Tillotson	4	79
Mary Jane, d. Curtis M. & Mary, b. May 13, 1837	2	12
Sarah Eliza, d. Adin & Maria, b. Mar. 28, 1828	1	244
Stephen Butts, s. Adin & Polly, b. Sept. 2, 1839	1	244
CARVER, William H., m. Hannah **TAYLOR**, b. of Brooklyn, [Jan.]		
18, [1835], by Rev. Samuel J. May	4	57
CASHMAN, Betsey, d. Isaac & Susan, b. July 3, 17[ ]	1	3
James, s. W[illia]m & Ruth, b. Dec. 23, 1776	1	3
John, s. W[illia]m & Ruth, b. Sept. 7, 1781	1	3
Peter, s. W[illia]m & Ruth, b. May 14, 1779	1	3
Robert Waterman, s. W[illia]m & Ruth, b. Oct. 29, 17[ ]	1	3
CHACE, [see under **CHASE**]		

	Vol.	Page
CHAFFEE, CHAFEE, CHAFEY, Cyriel S., of Woodstock, m.		
Zipporah A. **WEBB,** of Brooklyn, May 4, 1848, by Rev.		
G. J. Tillotson	4	99
Israel D., m. Mary **FRANKLIN,** b. of Brooklyn, [Dec.] 25,		
[1828], by Rev. Ambrose Edson	4	34
James Dwight, s. Israel D. & Ann, b. Dec. 15, 1823, in		
Willington	2	11
Lucius Dimmock, s. Israel D. & Ann, b. Mar. 10, 1825,		
in Willington	2	11
Serel S., farmer, ae 32, of Woodstock, m. Zippera A. **WEBB,**		
ae 26, b. Windham, res. Woodstock, May 4, 1848, by		
Rev. Geo[rge] J. Tillotson	2	87
CHAMBERLAIN, CHAMBERLIN, Adaline, d. John & Sally, b.		
Aug. 16, 1804	1	236
Asa, of Woodstock, m. Betsey **DARBE,** of Brooklyn, Feb. 7,		
1810, by John Parrish, J. P.	3	8
Betsey, d. John & Sally, b. Oct. 7, 1799	1	235
Betsey, d. John & Sally, d. Apr. 19, 1806, in the 7th y.		
of her age	1	42
Caroline J., of Killingly, m. Joseph **COGSWELL,** of Brooklyn,		
Oct. 5, 1846, by Rev. Benj[ami]n C. Phelps, of West		
Killingly	4	87
Hannah, d. John & Sally, b. Nov. 29, 1797	1	235
John, m. Sally **WEAVER,** Dec. 11, 1796	1	62
John Pierpoint, s. John & Sally, b. Dec. 31, 1806	1	236
Mary Ann, d. John & Sally, b. Sept. 9, 1801	1	235
Sally, w. John, d. Dec. 31, 1806, in the 29th y. of her age	1	42
CHANNING, Martha, m. Dr. Erastus **ROBINSON,** Apr. 23, 1809	1	75
CHAPIN, Benjamin, m. Susan **SOULE,** Oct. 7, 1815	1	62
Geo[rge] H., b. Plainfield, d. June 23, 1851, ae 7	2	134
CHAPLIN, Sally, m. Daniel **TYLER,** 2d, June 10, 1790	1	77
CHAPMAN, Benjamin S., farmer, d. Apr. 8, 1850, ae 22	2	118
Charles, s. Samuel & Polly, b. June 25, 1806	1	235
Esther, w. of Amaziah, b. May 25, 1740; d. May 31, 1790	1	42
Esther, d. Sam[ue]l & Polly, b. Nov. 27, 1800	1	235
Frederick William, s. Sam[ue]l & Polly, b. Feb. 20, 1804	1	235
Harriet, d. Samuel & Polly, b. May 29, 1808	1	235
Harriet S., d. Sanford B., farmer, ae 28, & Laura H.,		
ae 25, b. Jan. 16, 1851	2	127
Jared, s. Sam[ue]l & Polly, b. Aug. 16, 1796	1	234
Joseph, s. Samuel & Polly, b. Jan. 13, 1811	1	236
Maria, d. Sam[ue]l & Polly, b. May 22, 1802	1	235
Martha, d. Sam[ue]l & Polly, b. Feb. 19, 1799	1	234
Samuel, m. Polly **SEARLE,** Sept. 28, 1794	1	62
Sanford W., b. Norwich, res. Brooklyn, d. Nov. 2, [1849],		
ae 2 m. 8 d.	2	112
CHASE, CHACE, Hiram, m. Sarah **BALDWIN,** b. of Brooklyn,		
Oct. 25, 1836, by Rev. G. J. Tillotson	4	62

	Vol.	Page
CHASE, CHACE, (cont.)		
----, s. Edwin S., cashier in bank, ae 26, & Abby S., ae 20, b. July 10, 1850	2	107
CHENEY, George, m. Susan **FASSETT**, b. of Brooklyn, Jan. 27, 1833, by Uriel Fuller, J. P.	4	49
Nancy Jane, d. George & Susan, b. Dec. 25, 1835	2	11
Sally, m. Ebenezer **BURNHAM**, Mar. 6, 1825, by Rev. Samuel J. May	4	19
William Russell, s. George & Susan, b. Oct. 2, 1833	2	11
[CHESEBOROUGH], CHEESBOROUGH, Mary E., Mrs., m. Samuel H. **GREEN**, b. of Brooklyn, Dec. 28, 1851, by Rev. Thomas Huntington, of Abington	4	105
CHILD, Elisha, of Pomfret, m. Lora **DAVISON**, of Brooklyn, Mar. 31, [1828], by Rev. Sam[ue]l Jos[ia]h May	4	31
CHILSON, Olive, m. William **FOSTER**, Jan. 1, 1815	1	65
CHURCH, Maria A., of Willimantic, m. William S. **ASHLEY**, of Hampton, May 4, 1853, by Rev. Geo[rge] J. Tillotson	4	111
CLARK, CLARKE, Aete, d. Moses & Melicent, b. Feb. 20, 1794	1	235
Amelia, d. Moses & Melicent, b. Aug. 24, 1791	1	234
Betsey, d. Dan[ie]l & Lydia, b. Oct. 3, 1782	1	234
Betsey, d. Moses & Melicent, b. Feb. 13, 1800	1	235
Betsey, of Brooklyn, m. Samuel **NAURSE***, of Pomfret, May 11, 1824, by Rev. James Porter, of Pomfret (***NOURSE?**)	4	17
Charles, s. Moses & Melecent, b. Dec. 11, 1808	2	8
Charles, of Norwich, m. Ann Elizabeth **HUNTINGTON**, Oct. 22, 1838, by Rev. Thomas Huntington	4	68
Daniel, m. Lydia **DAVISON**, Jan. 29, 1780	1	62
Daniel, twin with [ ], s. Dan[ie]l & Lydia, b. Mar. 17, 1791. "His brother and twin lived about two hours, not having any Christian name"	1	234
Daniel, s. Dea. Daniel & Lydia, d. Mar. 18, 1791	1	42
Daniel, s. Dan[ie]l & Lydia, b. Apr. 9, 1792	1	234
David, s. Moses & Melecent, b. Apr. 7, 1803	2	8
David, m. Emily **HYDE**, b. of Brooklyn, [Apr.] 28, [1829], by Rev. Ambrose Edson	4	35
Deborah L., m. Robert **KINNE**, b. of Plainfield, Oct. 2, 1831, by Rev. David C. Bolles. Int. pub.	4	46
Elizabeth, of Brooklyn, m. Benjamin **LEWIS**, of Java, Genesee Co., N. Y., Nov. 23, 1836, by Rev. G. J. Tillotson	4	63
Emily, d. Moses & Melecent, b. June 11, 1811	2	8
Emily, of Brooklyn, m. Elihu **GALLUP**, of Norwich, June 11, 1833, by Rev. G. J. Tillotson	4	51
Esther, d. Dan[ie]l & Lydia, b. Mar. 15, 1786	1	234
George, s. Moses & Melecent, b. Aug. 14, 1805	2	8
George W., d. Dec. 14, 1847, ae 10 m.	2	87
Henry, s. Moses & Melicent, b. Oct. 17, 1795	1	235

	Vol.	Page
CLARK, CLARKE, (cont.)		
James, m. Lucy A. **POTTER**, b. of Hampton, Sept. 21, 1846, by Rev. Benjamin C. Phelps, of West Killingly	4	87
James, m. Agnes **LOWRY**, b. of Brooklyn, Mar. 2, 1852, by Rev. G. J. Tillotson	4	107
John, s. Dan[ie]l & Lydia, b. Sept. 21, 1794	1	234
John, s. Moses & Melecent, b. June 11, 1814	2	8
John H., of Providence, m. Charlotte S. **HUNTINGTON**, of Brooklyn, Apr. 16, 1846, by Rev. Tho[ma]s Huntington	4	83
Julius, s. Moses & Melicent, b. Aug. 22, 1789	1	234
Lucy, d. Dan[ie]l & Lydia, b. Apr. 7, 1788	1	234
Lydia, d. Dan[ie]l & Lydia, b. Feb. 14, 1781	1	234
Pallina, d. Moses & Melecent, b. July 12, 1798	1	235
Paulina, m. Dr. Thomas **HUNTINGTON**, Apr. 18, 1831, by Dan[ie]l G. Sprague, Hampton	4	45
Sarah E., d. Frances, tanner & currier, ae 35, & Sarah M., ae 27, b. May 12, [1849]	2	100
Sophia, m. Eben **WITTER**, Sept. 21, 1848, by Daniel P. Tyler, J. P.	4	100
CLEVELAND, Aaron Augustus, s. John & Polly, b. Jan. 21, 1797	1	234
Alice, d. Charles, silversmith, ae 25, & Juliaette, ae 23, b. Apr. 4, 1851	2	123
Clarrissa, m. Whitmore **SHEPARD**, Mar. 10, 1784	1	76
Colbe C., m. Flora **FARNHAM**, Sept. 19, 1825, by Vine Robinson, J. P.	4	20
Eva Orphelia, twin with Rosette, d. Charles, farmer, ae 22, & Juliaette ae 20, b. Oct. 21, 1847	2	93
Harriet, d. John & Polly, b. Mar. 10, 1799	1	234
Henry P., laborer, ae 19, of Brooklyn, m. Mary M. **ROGERS**, ae 18, of Pomfret, Jan. 9, 1848, by Rev. T. Huntington	2	79
Henry P., m. Mary Maria **ROGERS**, b. of Brooklyn, [Jan.] 9, [1848], by Rev. Thomas Huntington	4	88
Isaac, m. Abigail **BROWN**, Jan. 18, 1808	1	62
James Hervey, s. Isaac & Abigail, b. Jan. 3, 1816	1	243
Jane F., m. Lewis **SEARLS**, b. of Brooklyn, Dec. 12, 1853, by Rev. C. Y. DeNormandie	4	111
Joseph, Capt., d. Feb. 9, 1795	1	42
Lucina, m. Amos **PALMER**, Mar. 3, 1816	1	74
Lucius, of Brooklyn, m. Sarah **CADY**, of Tolland, May 23, 1830, by Uriel Fuller, J. P.	4	42
Lucy, m. Charles **CADY**, b. of Brooklyn, Aug. 4, 1845, by Rev. G. J. Tillotson	4	81
Molly, m. Joseph **GILBERT**, Dec. 4, 1791	1	66
Nancy Juliet, d. Isaac & Abigail, b. Aug. 17, 1813	1	243
Olive, wid. of Capt. Jos[eph], d. Mar. 20, 1820	1	42
Olive, of Brooklyn, m. Lester **BURNET**, of Hampton, Jan. 1, 1828, by Rev. Ambrose Edson	4	30
Olive Brown, d. Isaac & Abigail, b. Oct. 13, 1809	1	236

CLEVELAND, (cont.)

	Vol.	Page
Rosette, twin with Eva Orphelia, d. Charles, farmer, ae 22, & Juliaette, ae 20, b. Oct. 21, 1847	2	93
Samuel, of Brooklyn, , m. Lucy JONES, of Lisbon, Apr. 17, 1820, by Vine Robinson, J. P.	4	36
Serviah, m. Joel C. SEARLES, Nov. 29, 1805	1	76
CLOUD, Eli, s. Daniel & Mary, b. Sept. 2, 1771	1	235
COGGESHAL, William A., of New London, m. Harriet HUNTINGTON, of Brooklyn, [Mar.] 10, [1846], by Rev. Thomas Huntington	4	82
COGSWELL, Calista, d. William & Polly, b. Apr. 5, 1821	2	8
Caroline, d. William & Polly, b. Jan. 30, 1830	2	8
Eliza, d. William & Polly, b. Jan. 15, 1815	2	8
Eliza, m. Charles P. LITCHFIELD, b. of Brooklyn, "last evening", by Rev. Geo[rge] J. Tillotson. Dated Dec. 15, 1834	4	57
Hannah, w. Capt. Nathaniel, d. July 24, 1790, in the 43rd y. of her age	1	42
Huldah, m. Aaron ADAMS, Apr. 19, 1793	1	60
James W., s. Joseph, farmer, & Caroline, b. Oct. 17, 1847	2	85
James W., s. William & Polly, b. Sept. 2, 1816	2	8
Jane, d. William & Polly, b. May 18, 1832	2	8
Joseph, s. William & Polly, b. Jan. 19, 1825	2	8
Joseph, of Brooklyn, m. Caroline J. CHAMBERLIN, of Killingly, Oct. 5, 1846, by Rev. Benj[ami]n C. Phelps, of West Killingly	4	87
Lucretia, d. William & Polly, b. Feb. 28, 1819	2	8
Lucretia, of Brooklyn, m. Erastus DANIELSON, of Killingly, Oct. 1, 1838, by Rev. G. J. Tillotson	4	67
Mary Ann, d. William & Polly, b. June 1, 1823	2	8
Molly, m. Stephen FROST, June 26, 1789	1	65
Nancy Amelia, d. William & Polly, b. Apr. 17, 1835	2	8
Nathaniel, Capt., m. Freelove WILLIAMS, May 12, 1791	1	62
Nathaniel, Capt., d. Nov. 16, 1821, in the 80th y. of his age	1	42
Sally, d. William & Polly, b. Feb. 16, 1827	2	8
Susan E., d. Mar. 5, [1849], ae 5 d.	2	112
Susan E., d. Joseph, farmer, ae 25, & Caroline, ae 23, b. Oct. 10, 1849	2	112
William, s. Nathaniel & Freelove, b. Nov. 11, 1793	1	235
William, m. Polly DOWNING, Mar. 7, 1814	1	62
William, m. Polly DOWNING, Mar. 7, 1814	2	8
COLBURN, Sarah, housekeeper, d. Nov. 12, 1849, ae 42	2	118
COLE, Albert H., of Killingly, m. Hannah R. WORDEN, of Brooklyn, June 21, 1846, by Rev. Herman Snow	4	83
Betsey, weaver on looms, ae 19, b. R. I., res. Brooklyn, m. Jabez MILLER, harness maker, ae 23, b. Utica, res. Brooklyn, Aug. 27, 1848, by Rev. J. Livsey	2	104
Lydia E., m. Archibald GORDON, b. of Brooklyn, Oct. 24,		

	Vol.	Page
COLE, (cont.)		
1852, by Rev. Sidney Dean	4	106
COLLAR, Jonathan, d. Feb. 25, 1794	1	42
Sarah, d. Apr. 3, 1820, in the 78th y. of her age	1	44
COLLINS, Joshua, of Brooklyn, m. Sabry **HOSMER**, of		
Woodstock, Apr. 10, [1840], by Rev. Benj[amin] N.		
Harris	4	72
Melora Ann, d. Charles, stone workman, ae 39, & Betsey,		
ae 40, b. Jan. 17, 1850	2	119
Olive Frances, d. Charles, laborer, ae 37, & Betsey Ann,		
ae 38, b. Jan. 23, 1848	2	91
Philip, d. Feb. 11, 1850, ae 5	2	120
COLWELL, William, m. Martha M. **WILLIAMS**, b. of Brooklyn,		
Jan. 5, 1839, by Rev. William Coe	4	68
CONANT, Albert, of Bridgewater, Mass., m. Catharine		
SCARBOROUGH, of Brooklyn, Dec. 27, 1848, by Rev.		
J. Ferris. Int. Pub. Dec. 24, 1848	4	101
Albert, "draughtsman", ae 27, b. Vermont, res. N. Y.,		
m. Catharine **SCARBOROUGH** ae 25, b. Brooklyn, Ct.,		
res. N. Y., Dec. 29, 1848, by Jacob Ferris	2	97
Theordore Scarborough, s. Albert, "draughtsman", ae 28,		
of Boston, & Catharine, ae 26, b. July 9, 1850	2	109
CONVERSE, Nancy Laura Whipple, m. Joseph Phelps **BARRETT**,		
June 11, 1820, by Rev. Daniel Dow, of Thompson	4	1
COON, Desire, m. Clarke **EGGLESTON**, b. of Hampton, Apr. 18,		
1824, by Rev. Samuel J. May	4	16
Emily Brown, d. Frank, farmer, ae 48, & Susan A. 36, b.		
Mar. 6, 1850	2	111
Frank, m. Susanna **HALE**, Aug. 7, 1831, by E. B. Kellogg	4	46
Harriet Ann, d. Asa, farmer, ae 28, & Ruby, ae 23, b.		
Oct. 5, 1847	2	89
COOPER, Hannah, m. Nathaniel **HUNT**, Jan. 25, 1807	1	67
Martha, m. Marvil **JOSLIN**, June 23, 1822, by Vine		
Robinson, J. P.	4	9
COPELAND, Daniel, m. Mary **STEVENS**, Feb. 5, 1807	1	62
Daniel, m. Eunice **STEVENS**, Nov. 18, 1813	1	62
David, s. Jonathan & Esther, b. Sept. 8, 1788	1	3
Elisha, s. Samuel & Polly, b. [ ]	1	3
Eliza, w. Royal, d. May 3, 1820	1	42
Esther, d. Jonathan & Esther, b. Apr. 11, 1785	1	3
Eunice, d. Jonathan & Esther, b. Mar. 8, 1791	1	3
Eunice, of Thompson, m. Harvey **ADAMS**, of Killingly,		
Dec. 7, 1820, by Daniel Dow, V. D. M.	4	2
Harriet, d. Daniel & Eunice, b. June 21, 1816	1	236
Jonathan, s. Jonathan & Esther, b. Oct. 16, 1786	1	3
Mary, w. Daniel, d. Oct. 15, 1812, in the 27th y. of her age	1	42
Mary, d. Daniel & Eunice, b. Aug. 29, 1814	1	236
Olive, d. Daniel & Mary, b. Jan. 4, 1808	1	236

	Vol.	Page
COPELAND, (cont.)		
Ordela, d. Daniel & Mary, b. Apr. 8, 1810	1	236
Royal, s. Jonathan & Esther, b. Mar. 20, 1793	1	3
Royal, m. Eliza **HIDE**, Mar. 19, 1820	1	62
Royal, m. Harriot **HYDE**, b. of Brooklyn, Apr. 3, 1821,		
by Rev. Hutchins Taylor	4	2
CORBIN, Julia A., of Brooklyn, m. Henry H. **SHIPPEE**, of		
Brooklyn, Sept. 15, 1846, by Rev. Benjamin C. Phelps, of		
West Killingly	4	86
COSTELLO, Thomas, s. Patrick & Ann, b. Apr. 26, 1852	2	11
COTTON, Simon L., farmer, ae 27, of Pomfret, m. Martha Ann		
MATHER, ae 22, of Brooklyn, May 29, 1848, by Rev.		
John Stone	2	79
COULSON, Elizabeth, d. W[illia]m & Sarah, b. Feb. 4, 1737	1	3
COVELL, William W., m. Adeline J. **CADY**, b. of Providence, R.		
I., Mar. 6, 1843, by Rev. George J. Tillotson	4	78
COWPERTHWA[ITE], Hulings, of Philadelphia, m. Caroline		
Elizabeth **TYLER**, [Nov.] 24, 1824, by A. Edson	4	18
CRAIN, Charles, of Providence, R. I., m. Susan P. **PHILLIPS**,		
of Plainfield, Apr. 5, 1836, by Rev. G. J. Tillotson	4	60
CRANALL, Prudence, of Canterbury, m. Rev. Calvin **PHILLEO**,		
of Ithica, N. Y., Aug. 12, 1834, by Rev. Geo[rge] J.		
Tillotson	4	55
CUMMINGS, Jane, of Killingly, m. Samuel L. **TITUS**, of		
Brooklyn, Dec. 12, 1837, by Rev. G. J. Tillotson	4	65
CURTISS, CURTIS, Charles Henry, s. Chauncey & Polly, b. Jan.		
31, 1833	2	9
Charlotte Ann, d. Chauncey & Polly, b. May 24, 1830	2	9
George Searles, s. Chauncey & Polly, b. Sept. 12, 1827	2	9
James Alexander, s. Chauncey & Polly, b. Feb. 5, 1842	2	9
Jane, d. Chauncey & Polly, b. Oct. 13, 1838	2	9
John Lovell, s. Chauncey & Polly, b. Aug. 7, 1835	2	9
Maryett, d. Chauncey & Polly, b. Aug. 1, 1825	2	9
Phebe, m. Dyer **DOWNING**, Dec. 31, 1807	1	63
Phebe, m. Jedediah **DOWNING**, b. of Brooklyn, Dec. 31,		
1807, by John Parrish, J. P.	3	4
Rufus D., of Killingly, m. Lydia A. **PHILLIPS**, of Killingly,		
Mar. 6, 1848, by Rev. Ebenezer Loomis	2	79
Rufus D., m. Lydia A. **PHILLIPS**, b. of Killingly, Mar.		
6, 1848, by Rev. E. Loomis	4	88
Sarah, d. Chauncey & Polly, b. July 17, 1844	2	9
Thomas Adams, s. Chauncey & Polly, b. May 7, 1823	2	9
CUSHMAN, Daniel Tyler, s. Lathrop & Catharine, b. May 8, 1816	1	236
Julia Esther, d. Lathrop & Catharine, b. Mar. 11, 1808	1	236
Mary Ann, d. Lathrop & Caty, b. Mar. 13, 1799	1	235
Rebeckah, d. Nov. 2, 1847, ae 87	2	90
CUTLER, Simon, of Plainfield, m. Mrs. Lucy **GORDON**, of		
Canterbury, [Apr] 18, [1830], by Rev. Ambrose Edson	4	41

	Vol.	Page
DABNEY, Charles, d. July 10, 1825, in the 55th y. of his age	1	43
Charles Henry, m. Ellen Maria JONES, b. of Providence,		
R. I., [Apr] 27, [1830], by Rev. Ambrose Edson	4	41
Charles P., s. Charles & Dorcas, b. Jan. 10, 1801, at Killingly	2	14
Frances, d. John G. & Hannah F., b. Sept. 2, 1830	2	17
Francis Henry, s. Charles & Dorcas, b. Apr. 27, 1813	2	14
George W., s. Charles & Dorcas, b. July 7, 1805, at K[illingly];		
d. Apr. 22, 1806, at Killingly	2	14
Harriet, d. Charles & Dorcas, b. Apr. 5, 1807, at Killingly;		
d. Oct. 4, 1814, at Brooklyn	2	14
John Dickinson, d. [sic] John G. & Hannah Frances, b.		
Sept. 20, 1828	2	17
John G., s. Charles & Dorcas, b. Aug. 14, 1797	2	14
John Platt, s. John G. & Hannah Frances, b. Apr. 12, 1824	2	17
Lucia D., d. Charles & Dorcas, b. Nov. 10, 1803; d. Sept.		
17, 1804, at Killingly	2	14
Lucinda, d. Charles & Dorcas, b. Nov. 26, 1810, at B[rooklyn]	2	14
Lucinda, of Brooklyn, m. Jasper TUCKER, of West		
Brookfield, Mass., Sept. 5, 1837, by Rev. G. J. Tillotson	4	64
Martha Ann, d. John G. & Hannah F., b. Apr. 16, 1822	2	17
Mary, d. Charles & Dorcas, b. Nov. 6, 1793	2	14
Mary, m. Ebenezer SCARBOROUGH, Apr. 10, 1814	2	53
Mira, d. Charles & Dorcas, b. Apr. 4, 1799; d. Apr. 2, 1809	2	14
Roxa Ann, d. Charles & Dorcas, b. June 25, 1817	2	14
Roxa Ann, of Brooklyn, m. W[illia]m L. WARNER, of New		
London, Sept. 30, 1839, by Rev. G. J. Tillotson	4	69
William, s. Charles & Dorcas, b. Dec. 3, 1795	2	14
William Henry, s. John G. & Hannah, b. Oct. 20, 1832	2	17
DAINS, [see also DEAN], Abigail, d. Mar. 19, 1826, ae 79, y. 6 m.	1	43
Alice, w. Daniel, d. Mar. 14, 1824, in the 53rd y. of her age	1	43
C[h]loe, d. Daniel & Allice, b. Sept. 18, 1811	1	237
Mary, d. Daniel & Alice, b. Aug. 12, 1806	1	237
Samuel, d. May 10, 1822, in the 78th y. of his age	1	43
Samuel, d. May 10, 1822, ae 78 y. 10 m.	1	43
DANIELS, Martha M., of Brooklyn, m. Edward PRICHARD, of		
Derby, Conn., Sept. 8, 1851, by Rev. G. J. Tillotson	4	104
DANIELSON, Erastus, of Killingly, m. Lucretia COGSWELL, of		
Brooklyn, Oct. 1, 1838, by Rev. G. J. Tillotson	4	67
Hezekiah L., of Killingly, m. Laura S. WEAVER, of Brooklyn,		
Jan. 18, 1826, by Rev. Roswell Whitmore	4	23
Jacob W., of Killingly, m. Lucy M. PRINCE, of Brooklyn,		
Sept. 11, 1827, by Rev. Ambrose Edson	4	29
DARBY, DARBE, Abigail, m. Joel LAMB, Mar. 16, 1794	1	70
Alpheas, s. W[illia]m & Huldah, b. Dec. 18, 1781	1	4
Alpheas, m. Betsey DUNHAM, Nov. 22, 1803	1	63
Ardelia, d. Bela & Susannah, b. Feb. 22, 1832	2	14
Asahel, m. Jerusha GRANT, Nov. 25, 1792	1	63
Bela, s. W[illia]m & Huldah, b. Oct. 19, 1777	1	4

	Vol.	Page
DARBY, DARBE, (cont.)		
Bela, m. Susannah **YOUNG**, Feb. 26, 1807	2	14
Betsey, d. W[illia]m & Huldah, b. Feb. 6, 1794	1	4
Betsey, w. Alpheas, d. Jan. 18, 1806	1	43
Betsey, of Brooklyn, m. Asa **CHAMBERLIN**, of Woodstock,		
Feb. 7, 1810, by John Parrish, J. P.	3	8
Betsey, m. Elisha **CADY**, May 9, 1819	2	10
Betsey, of Brooklyn, m. W[illia]m **WHEELER**, of Canterbury,		
[Sept.] 11, [1836], by Rev. Thomas Huntingon	4	61
Charles, s. Alpheas & Betsey, b. Sept. 6, 1805	1	237
Daniel, s. W[illia]m & Huldah, b. July 17, 1790	1	4
David, s. Asahel & Jerusha, b. Nov. 10, 1796	1	4
David Pierce, s. Bela & Susannah, b. Feb. 27, 1816	2	14
Elisha, s. W[illia]m & Huldah, b. Nov. 19, 1775	1	4
Fanny, Mrs., m. Eliakim **CADY**, [Apr.] 3, [1833], by Rev.		
Samuel J. May	4	50
Huldah, w. William, d. May 6, 1813, in the 59th y. of her age	1	43
Jedediah, s. W[illia]m & Huldah, b. July 20, 1783	1	4
Lemuel Edmonds, s. Bela & Susannah, b. Oct. 12, 1808	2	14
Maria, d. Asahel & Jerusha, b. Mar. [ ]	1	4
Molly, d. Asahel & Jerusha, b. June 4, 1793	1	4
Nathan, s. W[illia]m & Huldah, b. Sept. 22, 1787	1	4
Sarah, m. Calvin **HUBBARD**, Nov. 10, 1778	1	67
Sarah, m. Lewis **WORDEN**, b. of Brooklyn, Sept. 17, 1844,		
by Rev. G. J. Tillotson	4	80
DAVIS, Betsey, m. Dr. Ebenezer **BORDEN**, Nov. 6, 1803	1	61
Daniel, m. Alice **BENNET**, Nov. 24, 1803	1	63
Pamela, m. Samuel **KIES**, Apr. 26, 1807	1	69
Prescilla, m. Albegence **ALLYN**, Mar. 17, 1800	1	60
Samuel,, of Pomfret, m. Polly **PIKE**, of Brooklyn, Nov.		
16, 1826, by Rev. Samuel J. May	4	26
DAVISON, Aaron, m. Lodicy **MARTIN**, Oct. 28, 1792	1	63
Abigail, w. Peter, d. Mar. 28, 1781	1	43
Alpheas, s. Peter & Abigail, b. May 20, 1781	1	4
Benjamin Weaver, s. Ephraim & Anna, b. Jan. 9, 1798	1	4
Beriah, m. Mary **UTLEY**, Apr. 2, 1807	1	63
Caroline A., of Brooklyn, m. John P. **PRENTICE**, of Pomfret,		
Nov. 27, 1845, by Rev. G. J. Tillotson	4	82
Caroline Asenath, d. Beriah & Mary, b. Mar. 21, 1810	1	237
Catharine, w. Daniel, d. Dec. 9, 1807	1	43
Chloe Permelia, d. Joel & Anna, b. May 4, 1825	2	13
Clarrissa, d. Aaron & Lodicy, b. Oct. 11, 1795	1	237
Daniel, s. Daniel & Catharine, b. Jan. 15, 1784	1	4
Daniel, m. Love **ASHLEY**, July 6, 1809	1	63
Deborah, d. Joseph & Lydia, b. July 20, 1792; d. June 17, 1804	2	13
Deborah, d. Joseph & Lydia, d. June 17, 1804	1	43
Delia J., d. Oct. 3, 1849, ae 9	2	118
Delia Jane, d. George & Ardelia, b. Nov. 20, 1839	2	13

	Vol.	Page

DAVISON, (cont.)

Edward Henry, s. George L. & Lydia Maria, b. Aug. 3, 1841 — 2 — 18

Edwin, s. Beriah & Mary, b. Sept. 24, 1824 — 2 — 14

Eliza, twin with Mary, d. Beriah & Mary, b. Mar. 4, 1808 — 1 — 237

Eliza, d. Aug. 24, 1850, ae 42 — 2 — 128

Elizabeth Williams, d. John & Elizabeth, b. July 7, 1800 — 1 — 237

Ephraim, m. Anna **WEAVER,** Mar. 12, 1795 — 1 — 63

Eunice, d. Joseph & Lydia, b. Sept. 1, 1799 — 2 — 13

Frances M., d. Septimus & Margaret, b. Aug. 23, 1828 — 2 — 18

Frances M., ae 23, m. John **PALMER,** merchant, ae 31, b.
Ashford, res. Brooklyn, Sept. 16, 1850, by Rev. R. Camp — 2 — 126

Frances M., m. John **PALMER,** Sept. 16, 1850, by Rev. R.
Camp — 4 — 102

George, s. Joseph & Lydia, b. Jan. 26, 1804 — 2 — 13

George Luther, s. Beriah & Mary, b. Nov. 27, 1811 — 1 — 237

George Warren, s. George L. & Lydia Maria, b. Feb. 12, 1838 — 2 — 18

Hannah, d. Dan[ie]ll & Catharine, b. June 23, 1787 — 1 — 4

Henry H., s. Septimus & Margaret, b. Dec. 19, 1835, at
Coventry, Conn. — 2 — 18

Herbert, s. Beriah & Mary, b. Apr. 23, 1821 — 1 — 237

Herbert, s. Beriah & Mary, b. Apr. 23, 1821 — 2 — 14

Hezekiah, s. Dan[ie]ll & Catharine, b. June 13, 1780 — 1 — 4

Hezekiah, s. Daniel & Catharine, d. Jan. 30, 1799, at sea — 1 — 43

Joel, s. Daniel & Catharine, b. Nov. 13, 1790 — 1 — 4

Joel, m. Anna **BUTTS,** Apr. 17, 1821, by Rev. Hutchins Taylor — 4 — 3

John, s. John & Elizabeth, b. Dec. 1, 1798 — 1 — 237

John C., s. Joseph & Lydia, b. Aug. 15, 1794 — 2 — 13

Joseph, s. Joseph & Lydia, b. Feb. 23, 1788 — 2 — 13

Joseph, d. June 24, 1841, ae 83 y. — 1 — 44

Lora, of Brooklyn, m. Elisha **CHILD,** of Pomfret, Mar. 31,
[1828], by Rev. Sam[ue]l Jos[ia]h May — 4 — 31

Lucy, d. Joseph & Lydia, b. Mar. 12, 1790 — 2 — 13

Lucy, d. Septimus & Margaret, b. June 3, 1830 — 2 — 18

Lydia, m. Daniel **CLARK,** Jan. 29, 1780 — 1 — 62

Lydia, wid. Joseph, d. Feb. 8, 1846, ae 82 — 1 — 44

Lydia Maria, d. George & Ardelia, b. Aug. 17, 1837 — 2 — 13

Malinda, d. Daniel & Catharine, b. Mar. 30, 1793 — 1 — 4

Mary, twin with Eliza, d. Beriah & Mary, b. Mar. 4, 1808 — 1 — 237

Mary, d. Beriah & Mary, d. Apr. 3, 1808, ae 1 m. — 1 — 43

Nathan, s. Joseph & Lydia, b. Dec. 20, 1796 — 2 — 13

Peter, m. Susannah **WEAVER,** Nov. 6, 1781 — 1 — 63

Philena, d. Joseph & Lydia, b. Apr. 7, 1786 — 2 — 13

Polly, d. Dan[ie]ll & Catharine, b. Sept. 11, 1785 — 1 — 4

Ralph Utley, s. Beriah & Mary, b. Nov. 11, 1814 — 1 — 237

Roderick, cabinet maker, ae 25, b. Munson, Mass., res.
Willimantic, m. Julia Ann **BAKER,** ae 24, b. Brooklyn,
Apr. 3, 1849, by Rev. George J. Tillotson — 2 — 105

Roderick, of Willimantic, m. Julia A. **BAKER,** of Brooklyn,

	Vol.	Page
DEAN, (cont.)		
6, 1843, by Daniel Bennett, J. P.	4	78
Leonard, of Eastford, m. Elizabeth R. **POTTER,** of Sterling,		
Jan. 1, 1852, by Rev. George J. Tilotson	4	108
DEAOLPH, Amasa, s. Charles & Elizabeth, b. June 11, 1780, at		
Hartland, Conn.	1	4
Betsey, d. Charles & Elizabeth, b. Nov. 7, 1775	1	4
Betsey, d. Charles & Elizabeth, d. Feb. 17, 1823, in the		
48th y. of her age	1	43
Charles, s. Charles & Elizabeth, b. Sept. 18, 1773, at Norwich	1	4
Clement, s. Charles & Elizabeth, b. Apr. 30, 1790	1	4
Elisha, s. Charles & Elizabeth, b. Oct. 1, 1786	1	4
Erastus, s. Charles & Elizabeth, b. Feb. 11, 1779	1	4
Erastus, s. Charles & Elizabeth, d. Jan. 16, 1794, in		
the 15th y. of his age	1	43
Erastus, s. Ulysses & Waty, b. Mar. 31, 1807	1	237
Gilese Meigs, s. Charles & Elizabeth, b. Nov. 7, 1782	1	4
Polly, d. Charles & Elizabeth, b. Jan. 20, 1792	1	4
Polly, d. Charles & Elizabeth, d. Nov. 29, 1800, in the		
9th y. of her age	1	43
Wyllys, s. Charles & Elizabeth, b. May 22, 1777	1	4
Wyllys, m. Waty **BROWN,** Mar. 31, 1805	1	63
DENISON, David, m. Anne **PAINE,** Dec. 3, 1789	1	63
Patience, Mrs., late of Newport, R. I., m. Ebenezer		
SPALDING, of Brooklyn, Oct. 1, 1823, by Rev. Samuel		
J. May	4	15
William, of Lancaster, N. H., m. Polly **PRINCE,** of Brooklyn,		
[Sept.] 3, [1827], by Rev. Samuel J. May	4	30
DeNORMANDIE, Courtland Y., m. Almira B. **STETSON,** b. of		
Brooklyn, May 22, 1853, by Rev. I. H. Coe. Int. pub.		
[May 22, 1853]	4	109
DEVOTION, Lucy, m. Joseph **BAKER,** Feb. 11, 1779	1	61
DEXTER, Marvin A., of Killingly, m. Mary Ann **ALLEN,** of		
Brooklyn, Nov. 25, 1829, by Rev. Roswell Whitmore	4	38
DICKINSON, Martha, m. James **GRIFFIN,** b. of Brooklyn, Jan. 1,		
1828, by Rev. Ambrose Edson	4	30
DIXON, Nancy, m. Shubael **BROWN,** Dec. 15, 1785	1	61
DONAHOE, Christopher, s. Thomas, agriculturist, & Ann, b.		
June 17, 1850	2	117
DORRANCE, DORRAN, Alla Mary, d. John G. & Hannah, b.		
Dec. 3, 1820	2	15
Andrew Murdock, s. John G. & Hannah, b. Jan. 14, 1819	2	15
Caroline, d. Samuel & Amey, b. Nov. 19, 1806	2	15
Caroline E., of Brooklyn, m. Henry **PALMER,** of Plainfield,		
[Mar.] 4, [1830], by Rev. Ambrose Edson	4	40
Catharine K., of Brooklyn, m. Seth **CADY,** of Pomfret,		
Apr. 13, 1842, by Rev. George J. Tillotson	4	76
Elizabeth, d. Samuel & Amey, b. Dec. 19, 1808	2	15

	Vol.	Page
DOWNING, (cont.)		
Lucy, d. Joseph & Abigail, d. Aug. 10, 1799	1	43
Martha, d. Joseph & Abigail, b. Oct. 21, 1785	1	237
Nathaniel Filton, s. Joseph & Abigail, b. Oct. 13, 1800	1	237
Polly, m. William **COGSWELL**, Mar. 7, 1814	1	62
Polly, m. William **COGSWELL**, Mar. 7, 1814	2	8
Prescilla, m. Ezra **CADY**, June 13, 1782	1	62
Sarah, d. Joseph & Abigail, b. Nov. 23, 1781	1	237
Theoda, d. Joseph & Abigail, b. Apr. 29, 1779	1	237
William, s. Joseph & Abigail, b. June 16, 1788	1	237
DRESSER, Henry, of Pomfret, m. Phebe Ann **STONE**, of		
Thompson, Dec. 18, 1836, by Rev. G. J. Tillotson	4	63
DUNHAM, Betsey, m. Alpheas **DARBE**, Nov. 22, 1803	1	63
DUNLAP, Tamson, wid., d. Nov. 14, 1813	1	43
DURFEY, Benjamin, of Greenville, Norwich, m. Harmony		
KINGSLEY, of Brooklyn, Feb. 16, 1836, by Rev. G. J.		
Tillotson	4	59
DURHAM, Ellen M., d. John, laborer, ae 27, & Ann, ae 29, b.		
June 20, 1850	2	119
DYER, Alfred, s. Henry & Martha W., b. Oct. 15, 1847	2	17
Alfred Sidney, s. Henry **AUGUSTUS**, farmer, ae 29, & Martha,		
ae 24, b. Oct. 15, 1847	2	89
Arthur, s. Henry A., nurseryman, & Martha, b. Dec. 12, 1849	2	117
Henry A., m. Martha **WHITE**, b. of Brooklyn, Oct. 26, 1846,		
by Rev. Riverius Camp	4	86
EASTON, Albert A., of Bristol, R. I., m. Clarissa **GROVER**, of		
Killingly, Nov. 8, 1846, by Rev. Benja[min] C. Phelps, of		
West Killingly	4	87
EATON, Esther, housekeeper, d. Aug. 5, 1849, ae 70	2	122
EDDY, Hannah C., m. William **FOSTER**, b. of Brooklyn, Mar. 29,		
1846, by Rev. Herman Snow	4	82
EDWARDS, Alla Mary, m. Edwin **TYLER**, Sept. 4, 1821, by Rev.		
Joseph Chickering	4	5
Perry, manufacturer, ae 22, b. Plainfield, res. Plainfield,		
m. Maria **HAWKINS**, Housekeeper, ae 22, b. Killingly,		
res. Plainfield, Mar. 24, [1850], by Reverius Camp	2	114
Perry, of Plainfield, m. Maria **HAWKINS**, of Plainfield,		
Mar. 24, 1850, by Rev. R. Camp	4	102
Richard C., merchant, ae 30, b. Hunter, N. Y., res. N.		
Y. City, m. Mary E. **WILLIAMS**, ae 23, b. Newburyport,		
Mass., June 6, 1849, by Prof. Edwards A. Parke	2	105
Richard Cunningham, of New York, m. Mary E. **WILLIAMS**,		
of Brooklyn, June 6, 1849, by Rev. Edwards A. Park, of		
Andover Theological Seminary	4	101
EGGLESTON, Clarke, m. Desire **COON**, b. of Hampton, Apr. 18,		
1824, by Rev. Samuel J. May	4	16
ELDREDGE, Charles, s. James & Lucy, b. July 31, 1784	1	5
Edward, s. James & Lucy, b. Oct. 18, 1794	1	5

	Page	Page
ELDREDGE, (cont.)		
Frances May, d. James & Lucy b. Feb. 28, 1791	1	5
Frank, s. James & Lucy, b. Aug. 3, 1787	1	5
Giles R., m. Deborah **SCARBOROUGH**, Jan. 2, 1806	1	64
James, Capt., had negro Jack, b. July 30, 1787; Venus,		
b. Oct. 17, 1788; Jennie, b. Apr. 2, 1790	1	15
James, Capt., had negro Primus, s. of Venus, b.		
Jan. 15, 1808, in Brooklyn. "Both mother & child are by		
law entitled to their freedom when they arrive at the age		
of 25 y."	1	15
Mary, [d. James & Lucy], b. Oct. 11, 1780, at Groton, Conn.	1	5
Mary, m. Joseph W. **RICE**, Aug. 5, 1804	1	75
Nancy, m. James McCLELLAN,, Dec. 8, 1805	1	71
Oliver, s. James & Lucy, b. Mar. 14, 1789	1	5
ELLISON, George W., of Uxbridge, Mass., m. Mrs. Harriet		
WARREN, of Brooklyn, Sept. 3, 1851, by Rev. George J.		
Tillotson	4	104
ELLSWORTH, ELSWORTH, [see also **ALWORTH**], Nancy, m.		
Luther **SCARBOROUGH**, Nov. 15, 1808	1	76
Sophia, m. David **PRINCE**, Apr. 18, 1815	1	74
ELY, Edwin, of Killingly, m. Betsey H. **WEAVER**, of Brooklyn,		
Nov. 13, 1836, by Rev. G. J. Tillotson	4	63
ESTABROOK, Simon R., of Holden, Mass., m. Frances A.		
SCARBOROUGH, of Brooklyn, Mar. 30, 1830, by Rev.		
Samuel J. May	4	42
FARNHAM, FARNAM, Caroline E., d. Thomas A. & Caroline E.,		
b. May 3, 1842	2	19
Caroline E., 1st w. Thomas A., d. May 7, 1842	1	45
Celinda, m. Seth P. **BALDWIN**, Nov. 30, 1837, by Rev. Mr.		
Bullard	4	116
Dolly Amada, m. Martin Herrick **WILLIAMS**, Mar. 2, [1834],		
by Samuel J. May	4	54
Edwin, s. Thomas A. & Eliza, b. May 17, 1846	2	19
Flora, m. Colbe C. **CLEVELAND**, Sept. 19, 1825, by Vine		
Robinson, J. P.	4	20
Harriet, d. Thomas A. & Eliza, b. Nov. 11, 1843	2	19
Roy, s. Thomas A. & Caroline E., b. Dec. 12, 1829;		
d. Apr. 28, 1842	2	19
----, s. Thomas A., mule driver, ae 34, & Eliza, ae 25,		
b. July 17, 1850	2	121
FARRINGTON, Sukey, m. John **WILLIAMS**, 2d, Dec. 25, 1793	1	78
FASSETT, Dorcas, m. Abijah **ADAMS**, Nov. 1, 1787	1	60
Hannah, m. Capt. John **ADAMS**, Nov. 2, 1802, by John		
Parrish, J. P.	3	1
Joab, m. Lite **HERRICK**, Jan. 5, 1792	1	65
Josiah, m. Abigail **STEVENS**, Apr. 16, 1789 (Corrected		
to read "Josiah **FROST**". L. B. B.)	1	65
Lucia, pauper, d. May 30, 1849, ae 50	2	102

	Vol.	Page
FASSETT, (cont.)		
Maria, of Winchester, N. H., m. William **LITCHFIELD**, of		
Brooklyn, Dec. 1, 1839, by Rev. William Coe	4	70
Mary, d. June 30, 1835, in the 70th y. of her age	1	45
Phebe A., d. Apr. 10, 1836, ae 44 y. 7 d.	1	45
Susan, m. George **CHENEY**, b. of Brooklyn, Jan. 27, 1833,		
by Uriel Fuller, J. P.	4	49
William, m. Susannah **LITCHFIELD**, July 28, 1791		
(Corrected by L. B. B. to read "William **FROST**")	1	65
Zerviah, w. William, d. Nov. 12, 1790	1	45
FAULKNER, Lucy, of Brooklyn, m. Randal **THOMPSON**, of		
North Stonington, July [27], 1823, by John Parish, J. P.	3	3
Sally, m. John **INGRAHAM**, Dec. 31, 1815	1	68
FERRIS, Mary E. B., d. Jacob, clergyman, ae 28, & Lou[i]sa,		
ae 28, b. Sept. 29, 1848	2	95
FILLMORE, Charles, s. William & Theody, b. July 5, 1807	1	6
William, s. William & Theody, b. July 8, 1792	1	6
FISHER, Cynthia E., d. Charles, shoemaker, ae 39, & Elizabeth,		
ae 25, b. Oct. 20, 1848	2	103
Elinor, d. Charles M., shoemaker, ae 27, & Elizabeth,		
ae 26, b. Feb. 20, 1850	2	119
W[illia]m H., laborer, b. Thompson, res. Brooklyn, d. Sept. 27,		
[1848], ae 9	2	91
FISK, Amanda, m. Artemus **BROWN**, Dec. 13, 1818	1	61
Charles W., of Worcester, Mass., m. Adeline B. **BARRETT**,		
of Brooklyn, Apr. 21, 1846, by Rev. G. J. Tillotson	4	84
Lodicea Ann, m. Elmer **WILLIAMS**, Mar. 29, 1829, by Rev.		
Orrin Catlin, at Sanywait Village, N. Y.	2	62
FITCH, Charles, Rev., of Abington, m. Zerviah **ROATH**, of		
Brooklyn, May 19, [1828], by Rev. Ambrose Edson	4	32
James E., s. Theophilus Stanton, farmer, ae 31, of East		
Brooklyn, & Lydia, ae 34, b. Mar. 14, 1851	2	132
FOGG, Edward, m. Caroline Mary **PUTNAM**, Jan. 6, 1834, by Rev.		
E. B. Kellogg	4	53
Edward, s. Edward & Caroline M., b. Oct. 14, 1840;		
d. Dec. 16, 1842	2	20
Elizabeth, d. Edward & Caroline M., b. Dec. 8, 1838	2	20
Mary, d. Edward & Caroline M., b. Jan. 25, 1837;		
d. July 31, 1840	2	20
Mary Putnam, d. Edward & Caroline M. b. Oct. 11, 1843	2	20
Thomas Brinley, s. Edward & Caroline M., b. Oct. 28, 1834	2	20
FORTUNE, Lucy, m. Prince **KNOWLS**, Dec. 27, 1818, by John		
Parish, J. P.	3	2
FOSTER, Albert, s. Samuel P. & Lorinda, b. June 13, 1825,		
in Canterbury	1	238
Caroline Elizabeth, d. Charles & Margaret, b. Feb. 23, 1826	2	19
Charles, m. Margaret **BASSET**, b. of Brooklyn, Sept. 12,		
1822, by Vine Robinson, J. P.	4	10

	Vol.	Page
FOSTER, (cont.)		
Charles Henry, s. Charles & Margaret, b. July 22, 1823	2	19
Edwin, s. Samuel P. & Lorinda, b. Nov. 30, 1832	1	238
Eliza, d. Samuel P. & Lorinda, b. Sept. 13, 1818	1	238
Frances Harriet, d. Charles & Margaret, b. Nov. 11, 1824,		
at Ashford	2	19
Frank M., s. W[illia]m, ae 30, teacher, & Mary S., ae 30,		
b. Jan. 1, 1850	2	107
George Washington, s. Samuel P. & Lorinda, b. Oct. 4, 1830	1	238
Henry, s. Samuel P. & Lorinda, b. Nov. 24, 1822	1	238
Herbert, s. Samuel P. & Lorinda, b. Sept. 1, 1820	1	238
James Anthony, s. William, Jr. & Mary S., b. May 10, 1846	2	19
Jane, d. Samuel P. & Lorinda, b. Dec. 19, 1835, in Brooklyn	1	238
Marion, d. Samuel P. & Lorinda, b. May 15, 1828, in Brooklyn	1	238
Nancy E., of Brooklyn, m. Isaac **HENDLY**, of Abington,		
Sept. 28, 1853, by Rev. Thomas Huntington	4	112
Samuel P., m. Lorinda **MATHER**, Apr. 22, 1817	1	65
William, m. Olive **CHILSON**, Jan. 1, 1815	1	65
William, s. William & Olive, b. Apr. 5, 1817	1	238
William, m. Hannah C. **EDDY**, b. of Brooklyn, Mar. 29, 1846,		
by Rev. Herman Snow	4	82
FOX, Anson, of Hampton, m. Lucy M. **LITCHFIELD**, Oct. 10,		
1825, by Rev. A. Edson	4	22
Mary, of Hampton, m. Chester **SHEPARD**, of Brooklyn, [Feb.]		
18, [1827], by Rev. A. Edson	4	27
FRANKLIN, Andrew Murdock, s. Henry T. & Dorcas, b. Jan. 16,		
1823	1	238
Anna, w. James, d. Dec. 15, 1822	1	45
Charles Lucien, s. Henry T. & Dorcas, b. Sept. 1, 1809	1	6
Dorcas, w. Henry T., d. Aug. 30, 1832, in the 48th y. of		
her age at Brooklyn, N. Y.	1	45
Emeline, d. Henry Tolman & Dorcas, b. Apr. 23, 1805	1	6
Emily Tryphenia, d. Henry T. & Dorcas, b. Oct. 9, 1820;		
d. Nov. 6, 1823	1	238
Emily Tryphenia, d. Henry T. & Dorcas, d. Nov. 6, 1823	1	45
George Henry, s. Henry T. & Dorcas, b. Oct. 4, 1814	1	6
Harriet, d. James & Clarrissa, his 2d w., b. Apr. 10, 1824	2	20
Henry Chaffee, s. Henry T. & Dorcas, b. Oct. 6, 1826	1	238
Henry Tolman, s. Henry & Dorothy, b. Feb. 6, 1778,		
at Woodstock	1	6
Henry Tolman, m. Dorcas **MURDOCK**, Dec. 27, 1801	1	65
Jared Durkee, s. James & Anna, b. Nov. 20, 1814	2	20
Laura Ann, d. James & Anna. b. Dec. 13, 1811	2	20
Maria, d. Henry Tolman & Dorcas, b. Mar. 26, 1803	1	6
Maria E., of Brooklyn, m. Warren W. **ABBOT**, of Hampton,		
Feb. 23, 1823, by Rev. Samuel J. May	4	12
Mary, m. Israel D. **CHAFFEE**, b. of Brooklyn, [Dec.] 25,		
[1828], by Rev. Ambrose Edson	4	34

	Vol.	Page

FRANKLIN, (cont.)

Mary W., of Brooklyn, m. Stephen C. **WESTON**, of
Willington, [Dec] 25, [1828], by Rev. Ambrose Edson — 4 — 34

Nancy Elizabeth, d. Henry T. & Dorcas, b. June 17, 1817 — 1 — 238

Olive, d. Henry T. & Dorcas, b. Mar. 19, 1812 — 1 — 6

Orrin Utley, s. James & Anna, b. Apr. 21, 1817 — 2 — 20

Vine Robinson, s. John & Laurie P., b. Jan. 2, 1843, at
Hampton — 2 — 20

William Hammond, s. John, farmer, ae 30, & Laura P., ae
29, b. July 19, [1849] — 2 — 95

William Robert, s. Henry T. & Dorcas, b. July 3, 1807 — 1 — 6

FRASIER, Eunice Lucinda, d. Lucy **BERIAND**, gt. gd. dau. of
Lucy **SHAWONE**, b. Mar. 28, 1813 — 1 — 238

FRINK, Lucy, m. Peter Schuyler **PUTNAM**, July 9, 1785 — 1 — 74

FROST, Daniel, s. Capt. Stephen & Molly, b. June 10, 1795 — 1 — 6

John, s. Josiah & Abigail, b. Sept. 16, 1794 — 1 — 6

John Marvin, s. Capt. Stephen & Molly, b. Dec. 19, 1801 — 1 — 6

Jonas, d. Mar. 3, 1805, in the 80th y. of his age — 1 — 45

Josiah, m. Abigail **STEVENS**, Apr. 16, 1789 (Arnold Copy
had "Josiah **FASSETT**". Corrected by L. B. B.) — 1 — 65

Jossier, s. Josiah & Abigail, b. Jan. 8, 1790 — 1 — 6

Lucia, d. Capt. Stephen & Molly, b. May 20, 1792 — 1 — 6

Nathaniel Cogswell, s. Stephen & Molly, b. May 28, 1790 — 1 — 6

Phebe Alvin, d. W[illia]m & Susannah, b. Apr. 3, 1792 — 1 — 6

Sally, d. Josiah & Abigail, b. [ ] 27, 1792 — 1 — 6

Sarah, Jr., m. Stephen **ALESWORTH**, Apr. 17, 1796 — 1 — 60

Stephen, m. Molly **COGSWELL**, June 26, 1789 — 1 — 65

Susannah, w. Jonas, d. May 16, 1792, in the 62nd y. of her age — 1 — 45

Susannah, d. W[illia]m & Susannah, b. July 29, 1794 — 1 — 6

William, m. Susannah **LITCHFIELD**, July 28, 1791 (Arnold
Copy has "William **FASSETT**". Corrected by L. B. B.) — 1 — 65

FRY, Archibald, of Griswold, m. Elizabeth **CADY**, of Brooklyn,
Dec. 27, 1829, by Rev. John O. Birdsall, at the house of
Denison Cady — 4 — 38

Nathaniel, of Griswold, m. Emily **WOODWORTH**, of
Brooklyn, Mar. 1, 1835, by Rev. Thomas Huntington — 4 — 60

FULLER, Ellen Amelia, d. Uriel & Amelia, b. Nov. 15, 1821 — 1 — 238

Helen A., of Brooklyn, m. Frederick P. **GROW**, of
Millardsville, Pa., Sept. 28, 1842, by Rev. G. J. Tillotson — 4 — 77

Loderna, m. Dea. Samuel **BUTTS**, Apr. 16, 1807 — 1 — 61

Mary, m. Nathan **WITTER**, 2d, Mar. 18, 1784 — 1 — 78

GALLUP, Charles Albert, s. John & Lucy, b. Feb. 27, 1814 — 1 — 239

Daniel P., farmer, d. June 1, 1851, ae 21 — 2 — 126

Edward, s. John & Lucy, b. Sept. 1, 1807 — 1 — 239

Edward, s. John & Lydia*, d. Nov. 4, 1807 (*Should be
"Lucy". Corrected by L. B. B.) — 1 — 46

Edward, s. John, 3rd, & Maria C., b. Aug. 24, 1842 — 2 — 22

Edward Clark, s. John & Lucy, b. Aug. 14, 1808 — 1 — 239

	Vol.	Page
GALLUP, (cont.)		
Edward L., s. Nathan L., teacher, ae 35, & Lucy A., ae		
25, b. Apr. 23, 1851	2	123
Edward L., d. June 22, [1851], ae 2 m.	2	124
Elihu, of Norwich, m. Emily **CLARK**, of Brooklyn, June 11,		
1833, by Rev. G. J. Tillotson	4	51
Eliza, of Brooklyn, m. Obadiah T. **WALDO**, of Westminster		
Soc., Canterbury, [Mar.] 31, [1826], by Rev. A. Edson	4	24
Ellen Maria, d. John, 3rd, & Maria C., b. May 4, 1838	2	22
Emila, d. John & Lucy, b. Jan. 26, 1806	1	239
Emily, of Brooklyn, m. Benjamin B. **BALDWIN**, of West		
Springfield, Mass., [Nov.] 27, [1827], by Rev. Ambrose		
Edson	4	30
Esther, d. John & Lucy, b. Apr. 11, 1818	1	239
Esther, m. William P. **POTTER**, b. of Brooklyn, May 19,		
1842, by Rev. G. J. Tillotson	4	76
Harriet, d. John & Lucy, b. July 14, 1825; d. Jan. 31, 1841	1	239
Harriet, d. John & Lucy, d. Jan. 31, 1841, in the 61st		
y. of her age	1	46
Henry Tyler, s. John 3rd, & Maria C., b. Dec. 11, 1834	2	22
James, s. John & Lucy, b. May 25, 1820	1	239
John, 3rd, m. Maria C. **TYLER**, b. of Brooklyn, [Sept.]		
11, [1832], by Rev. George J. Tillotson	4	48
John, farmer, b. Groton, Ct., res. Brooklyn, d. Jan. 25,		
1850, ae 73	2	108
John Chester, s. John & Lucy, b. Feb. 25, 1812	1	239
Joseph Henry, of Preston, m. Sarah Maria **PARISH**, of		
Brooklyn, Nov. 21, 1834, by Rev. Samuel J. May	4	56
Lodowick, m. Nancy **WHITE**, b. of Pomfret, Sept. 22, 1834,		
by Rev. G. J. Tillotson	4	56
Lucy, d. John & Lucy, b. Aug. 3, 1810	1	239
Lucy, of Brooklyn, m. James L. **SIKES**, of Suffield, Mass.,		
Nov. 14, [1832], by Rev. C. J. Tillotson	4	48
Nathan Lester, s. John & Lucy, b. Mar. 29, 1816	1	239
Ruby, ae 28, b. Sterling, m. Horace **BURGESS**, physician,		
ae 25, of Plainfield, Sept. 3, [1850], by Rev. George J.		
Tillotson	2	124
Ruby, of Brooklyn, m. Horace **BURGESS**, M. D., of Plainfield,		
Sept. 5, 1850, by Rev. George J. Tillotson	4	104
Thomas Palmer, s. John & Lucy, b. July 5, 1823	1	239
GARDINER, Hannah, m. Samuel **WILLIAMS**, 3rd, June 12, 1781	1	78
GARRISON, George Thompson, s. William Lloyd & Helen Eliza,		
of Boston, b. Feb. 13, 1836	2	21
William Lloyd, of Boston, m. Helen Eliza **BENSON**, of		
Brooklyn, Sept. 4, 1834, by Rev. Samuel J. May	4	55
GEER, Levi, s. John & Jerusha, b. Nov. 22, 1775	1	7
Rufus, s. John & Jerusha, b. Nov. 25, 1777	1	7
Zerviah, d. John & Jerusha, b. Oct. 3, 1779	1	7

	Vol.	Page
GILBERT, Abigail, d. Joseph & Molly, b. Dec. 22, 1792	1	7
Benjamin, m. Betsey **PIERCE**, Nov. 20, 1791	1	66
Betsey, d. Benjamin & Betsey, b. June 5, 1794	1	7
Deborah, d. John Wilks & Hannah Augusta, b. Mar. 30, 1802	1	7
Deborah, of Brooklyn, m. Chauncey **SUMNER**, of Spencer, Mass., June 1, 1854, by Rev. G. J. Tillotson	4	113
Delight, twin with Dorcas, d. John & Rachel, b. Oct. 23, 1772	1	7
Dorcas, twin with Delight, d. John & Rachel, b. Oct. 23, 1772	1	7
Ebenezer, s. Eleazer & Sarah, b. July 13, 1789	1	7
Edward, s. John Wilks & Hannah Augusta, b. Sept. 8, 1800	1	7
Eliza, d. John & Lucy, b. July 10, 1804	1	7
Emila Frances, d. Benjamin & Betsey, b. Nov. 22, 1812	1	239
Esther, d. John & Rachel, b. Feb. 20, 1779	1	7
Euripta, twin with Septimus, s. John & Rachel, b. Oct. 2, 1783	1	7
George Godfrey, s. John W. & Hannah Augusta, b. Oct. 20, 1814	2	21
George Henry, s. Capt. Benjamin & Betsey, b. Feb. 15, 1806	1	239
Hannah, d. John & Rachel, b. Oct. 27, 1774	1	7
Harriet, d. John W. & Hannah Augusta, b. June 17, 1808	2	21
Harriet S., m. Earl **WARNER**, b. of Brooklyn, June 5, 1833, by Rev. G. J. Tillotson	4	50
Henry, s. Benjamin & Betsey, b. Aug. 25, 179[ ]	1	7
Henry, s. Capt. Benjamin & Betsey, d. Mar. 28, 1804, in the 12th y. of his age	1	46
Horace, s. Capt. Benjamin & Betsey, b. July 30, 1802	1	239
Jasper, s. John & Rachel, b. Nov. 14, 178[ ]	1	7
John, Jr., d. Sept. 30, 1785	1	46
John, s. Eleazer & Sarah, b. Aug. 11, 1786	1	7
John G., of Mendon, Mass., m. Sarah **WEBB**, of Brooklyn, May 29, 1844, by Rev. G. J. Tillotson	4	80
John Paine, s. Benjamin & Betsey, b. Nov. 15, 1797	1	7
John W., d. Dec. 25, 1843, 72 y.	1	46
John Wilks, s. John, Jr. & Rachel, b. Oct. 11, 1770	1	7
John Wilkes, m. Hannah Augusta **AMES**, Nov. 27, 1799	1	66
Joseph, m. Molly **CLEVELAND**, Dec. 4, 1791	1	66
Joseph, s. Benj[ami]n & Betsey, b. May 20, 1800	1	7
Joseph, d. Sept. 13, 1801, ae 36 y.	1	46
Joseph Cleveland, s. Joseph & Molly, b. Dec. 28, 1796	1	239
Louisa G., d. John W. & Hannah Augusta, b. July 4, 1810	2	21
Louisa G., m. James M. **BARROWS**, Apr. 14, 1831, by Rev. Roswell Whitmore	4	45
Lucy M., m. Timothy H. **MORSE**, b. of Brooklyn, [June] 24, [1826], by Rev. A. Edson	4	24
Lucy Maria, d. John Wilks & Hannah Augusta, b. Feb. 21, 1804	1	7
Mary A., m. Nathaniel **WILLIAMS**, b. of Brooklyn, [1852], by Rev. Sylvester Barrows	4	108
Mary Augusta, d. John W. & Hannah Augusta, b. Apr. 21,		

	Vol.	Page
GILBERT, (cont.)		
1806	2	21
Molly, d. Joseph & Molly, b. Oct. 4, 1795	1	7
Molly, m. Samuel **SCARBOROUGH**, Jr., Oct. 7, 1803	1	76
Molly, d. Joseph & Molly, d. Aug. 12, 1815, in the 20th		
y. of her age	1	46
Nabby, d. Joseph & Molly, d. Oct. 6, 1801, ae 9 y.	1	46
Olive, d. Joseph & Molly, b. Aug. 6, 1801	1	239
Perrygreen, s. John & Rachel, b. Jan. 4, 1777	1	7
Septimus, twin with Euripta, s. John & Rachel, b. Oct. 2, 1783	1	7
Wyllys, s. John & Rachel, b. Apr. 2, 1781	1	7
GILLMUR, David, of Munson, Mass., m. Hannah P. **TYLER**, of		
Brooklyn, [July] 14, [1840], by Rev. Thomas Huntington	4	73
GOODELL, Richard, Jr., m. Hitty **TYLER**, Dec. 26, 1803	1	66
GORDON, Archibald, m. Lydia E. **COLE**, b. of Brooklyn, Oct. 24,		
1852, by Rev. Sidney Dean	4	106
Lucy, Mrs., of Canterbury, m. Simon **CUTLER**, of Plainfield,		
[Apr] 18, [1830], by Rev. Ambrose Edson	4	41
GOULD, Nathan H., b. Pomfret, res. Brooklyn, d. Dec. 15, 1849		
ae 14	2	120
GRANT, Jerusha, m. Asahel **DARBY**, Nov. 25, 1792	1	63
Margaret, of Brooklyn, m. Bradley **GREEN**, of Burrelville,		
R. I., Aug. 17, 1822, by Vine Robinson, J. P.	4	10
Sarah A., of Cumberland, R. I., m. James **McCANN**, of		
Smithfield, R. I., July 10, 1834, by Rev. G. J.		
Tillotson	4	55
GRAVES, Artemus, operative in mill, b. Killingly, res.		
E. Brooklyn, d. Apr. 6, [1851], ae 66	2	132
Nancy, of Brooklyn, m. W[illia]m **BROWNELL**, of		
Smithfield, R. I., Aug. 9, 1846, by Rev. Benjamin C.		
Phelps, of West Killingly	4	85
Reuben, m. Polly **SWEET**, Nov. 6, 1804	1	66
GRAY, John, Jr., m. Sarah S. **PAINE**, Mar. 4, [1833], by Rev.		
Samuel J. May	4	49
Susan Elizabeth, d. John, Jr. & Sarah S., b. May 22, 1834	2	22
GREEN, GREENE, Bradley, of Burrelville, R. I., m. Margaret		
GRANT, of Brooklyn, Aug. 17, 1822, by Vine Robinson,		
J. P.	4	10
Emeline, m. James A. **PRATT**, b. of Killingly, Dec. 11,		
1853, by Jona[than] A. Welch, J. P.	4	110
Hannah, m. Solomon **OLIN**, Sept. 8, 1843, by Sam[ue]l		
Webb, J. P.	4	78
Joseph K., m. Lucy **KELLEY**, b. of Brooklyn, Apr. 19,		
1835, by Rev. Roswell Whitmore	4	58
Samuel H., m. Mrs. Mary E. **CHEESBOROUGH**, b. of		
Brooklyn, Dec. 28, 1851, by Rev. Thomas Huntington, of		
Abington	4	105
Sarah M., of Brooklyn, m. John D. **STRAIT**, of Canterbury,		

	Vol.	Page
GREEN, GREENE, (cont.)		
Dec. 31, 1843, by Sam Webb, J. P.	4	79
Thomas, m. Edith **CADY**, Jan. 1, 1821, by John Parish, J. P.	3	2
Thomas, m. Edith **CADY**, b. of Brooklyn, Jan. 1, 1821, by		
John Parish, J. P.	4	13
GREENSLIT, David, m. Betsey **SEARLS**, May 26, 1840, by Rev.		
Tho[ma]s Huntington	4	73
William F., of Hampton, m. Esther **DORRANCE**, of Brooklyn,		
Apr. 13, 1842, by Rev. George J. Tillotson	4	76
GRIFFIN, James, m. Martha **DICKINSON**, b. of Brooklyn, Jan. 1,		
1828, by Rev. Ambrose Edson	4	30
GRIFFITH, GRIFFITHS, Adeline E., d. Eben, manufacturer, ae		
27, Olive, ae 24, b. Feb. 8, 1850	2	119
Ebin, of Killingly, m. Olive **HANDELL**, of Brooklyn, Feb.		
28, 1847, by Rev. Benja[min] C. Phelps, of West		
Killingly	4	88
GRIMES, Catharine, d. Charles, farmer, ae 25, & Ann, ae 27,		
b. Apr. 28, 1850	2	109
GROSVENOR, Elizabeth, m. Timeus **PIERCE**, May 4, 1779	1	74
Mason, Rev., of Ashfield, Mass., m. Esther D.		
SCARBOROUGH, of Brooklyn, June 19, 1833, by Rev.		
Geo[rge] J. Tillotson	4	51
GROVER, Clarissa, of Killingly, m. Albert A. **EASTON**, of		
Bristol, R. I., Nov. 8, 1846, by Rev. Benja[min] C.		
Phelps, of West Killingly	4	87
GROW, Frederick P., of Millardsville, Pa., m. Helen A. **FULLER**,		
of Brooklyn, Sept. 28, 1842, by Rev. G. J. Tillotson	4	77
Helen E., d. Frederick P., merchant, ae 31, of Carbendale,		
Pa., & Helen A., ae 27, b. Aug. 25, 1848	2	95
GURLEY, Lydia, m. Benjamin **PIERCE**, Dec. 24, 1786	1	74
HAKES, Billings, of Stonington, m. Lucy Maria **PIERCE**, of		
Brooklyn, [Aug.] 30, [1829], by Rev. Ambrose Edson	4	36
HALE, HAILE, Attia H., d. Daniel M., physician, ae 41, & Genette,		
ae 35, b. Sept. 18, 1849	2	107
Bethiah, d. Nathan & Lydia, b. Mar. 28, 1805, at Foster,		
m. Samuel **ROBBINS**, [ ]; d. Mar. 28, 1835, at		
Brooklyn	2	51
Bethiah, m. Samuel **ROBBINS**, Jan. 4, 1824	2	51
Jane L., d. Daniel M. & Genette, b. Oct. 31, 1846	2	24
Susanna, m. Frank **COON**, Aug. 7, 1831, by E. B. Kellogg	4	46
HALL, Henry, farmer, ae 30, b. Canterbury, res. Griswold, m.		
2d w. Emeline **HARRIS**, housekeeper, ae 35, b.		
Brooklyn, res. Lisbon, July 7, 1850, by Rev. Coggeshall	2	118
Henry, of Canterbury, m. Mrs. Emelin **HARRIS**, of Brooklyn,		
July 7, 1850, by Rev. S. W. Coggeshall, Killingly	4	102
Joab, of Middletown, m. Mary **RICH**, of Middletown, late		
residents of Brooklyn, Nov. 20, 1825, by David C. Bolles,		
J. P.	4	21

	Vol.	Page
HALL, (cont.)		
Josiah, s. Vine & Susannah, b. Nov. 20, 1794	1	8
Mary Sheffield, d. Vine & Susannah, b. Feb. 27, 1797	1	8
HAMMOND, Henry, of Pomfret, m. Emma **DORRANCE**, of		
Brooklyn, Apr. 8, 1840, by Rev. G. J. Tillotson	4	72
HANDELL, Olive, of Brooklyn, m. Ebin **GRIFFITH**, of Killingly,		
Feb. 28, 1847, by Rev. Benja[min] C. Phelps, of West		
Killingly	4	88
HARDING, Francis Dwight, s. Eddy & Louisa P., b. June 10, 1837	2	25
HARRINGTON, Patience B., m. James L. **BUCHEE**, b. of Scituate,		
R. I., May 17, 1836, by Rev. G. J. Tillotson	4	61
HARRIS, Abby Ann, d. Daniel & Mehitable, b. Jan. 22, 1821	2	23
Bela, s. Sam[ue]l & Elizabth, b. Apr. 1, 1781	1	8
Bethiah, d. Reuben & Lydia*, d. Feb. 19, 1792 (*Should		
be "Lucy". Corrected by L. B. B.	1	47
Betsey, d. Sam[ue]l & Elizabeth, b. May 18, 1793	1	8
Cynthia, d. Sam[ue] & Elizabeth, b. Aug. 12, 1791	1	8
Daniel, s. Samuel & Elizabeth, b. Aug. 30, 1779	1	8
Daniel, s. Reuben & Lucy, b. July 3, 1794	1	8
David, s. Heber & Polly, b. May 3, 1802	1	8
Edward, s. Sam[ue]l & Elizabeth, b. Dec. 29, 1782	1	8
Edwin, s. Hosea & Eunice, b. Feb. 12, 1808	2	23
Elihu, s. Reuben & Lucy, b. Mar. 22, 1790	1	8
Elisha, s. Sam[ue]l & Elizabeth, b. June 5, 1786	1	8
Emeline, housekeeper, ae 35, b. Brooklyn, res. Lisbon,		
m. 2d h. Henry **HALL**, farmer, ae 30, b. Canterbury, res.		
Griswold, July 7, 1850, by Rev. Coggeshall	2	118
Emelin[e], Mrs., of Brooklyn, m. Henry **HALL**, of Canterbury,		
July 7, 1850, by Rev. S. W. Coggeshall, Killingly	4	102
Erastus P., s. Hosea & Eunice, b. Mar. 24, 1815	2	23
Erastus P., m. Amy **HERRICK**, b. of Brooklyn, Feb. 9, 1840,		
by Rev. William Coe	4	71
Franklin, s. Hosea & Eunice, b. Aug. 24, 1801	2	23
Franklin, m. Abigail **MILLET**, b. of Brooklyn, Dec. 9, 1821,		
by David C. Bolles, J. P.	4	6
George Washington, s. Hosea & Eunice, b. Oct. 24, 1812	2	23
Hannah, ae 16, of Brooklyn, m. Thomas **RILEY**, sailor,		
ae 25, of Brooklyn, May 21, 1848, by Rev. Tillotson	2	79
Hannah, of Brooklyn, m. Thomas **RILEY**, of Mass., May 21,		
1848, by Rev. G. J. Tillotson	4	99
Harriet E. A., m. David **BAKER**, farmer, b. Pomfret, res.		
Brooklyn, Feb. 23, [1851], by Uriel Fuller	2	130
Harriet Eleanor, m. David **BAKER**, b. of Brooklyn, Feb. 23,		
1851, by Uriel Fuller, J. P.	4	103
Heber, m. Polly **PHILLIPS**, Dec. 8, 1799	1	67
Henry Webb, s. Hosea & Eunice, b. Jan. 24, 1806	2	23
Hieram, s. Heber & Polly, b. Nov. 20, 1800	1	8
Hosea, m. Eunice **PELLETT**, Jan. 8, 1792	1	67

	Vol.	Page
HARRIS, (cont.)		
Jeremiah, s. Reuben & Lucy, b. Sept. 30, 1792	1	8
Joanna, d. Hosea & Eunice, b. Feb. 16, 1810	2	23
Joel, of Foster, R. I., m. Loiza **HARRIS**, of Brooklyn,		
Dec. 30, 1821, by David C. Bolles, J. P.	4	8
John, s. Sam[ue]l & Elizabeth, b. Dec. 6, 1787	1	8
Jonathan, d. Jan. 14, 1847, ae 42 y.	1	47
Joseph, s. Reuben & Lucy, b. Oct. 17, 1783	1	8
Loiza, of Brooklyn, m. Joel **HARRIS**, of Foster, R. I.,		
Dec. 30, 1821, by David C. Bolles, J. P.	4	8
Louisa, d. Hosea & Eunice, b. Feb. 9, 1799	2	23
Lucretia, d. Reuben & Lucy, b. May 23, 1797	1	8
Luther, s. Reuben & Lucy, b. Sept. 24, 1787	1	8
Lydia had illeg. child James **WILLIAMS**, b. Dec. 2, 1795	1	9
Martin, s. Hosea & Eunice, b. Aug. 29, 1794	2	23
Mary Eliza, d. Daniel & Mehitable, b. Jan. 11, 1820	2	23
Mehetable, w. Daniel, d. Mar. 5, 1822, ae 38 y. 8 m. 18 d.	1	47
Mela, d. Sam[ue]l & Elizabeth, b. July 18, 1789	1	8
Nancy, d. Hosea & Eunice, b. Jan. 27, 1804	2	23
Nancy, of Brooklyn, m. Joseph **BLANCHARD**, of Foster,		
R. I., Dec. 9, 1821, by David C. Bolles, J. P.	4	7
Nathan, s. Sam[ue]l & Elizabeth, b. Sept. 11, 1784	1	8
Shuebael, s. Heber & Polly, b. Sept. 13, 1803	1	8
Solomon, s. Hosea & Eunice, b. Dec. 25, 1796	2	23
Thomas, s. Hosea & Eunice, b. Sept. 22, 1792	2	23
Timothy Herrick, s. Erastus P. & Amy, b. Sept. 27, 1842	2	26
HARVEY, Alteria, of Windham, m. Sarah Ann **BOND**, of Brooklyn,		
Aug. 26, 1838, by George Sharpe, J. P.	4	66
Mary J., d. John, mason, ae 30, & Julia L, ae 22, of		
East Brooklyn, b. Dec. 29, 1851	2	132
Sarah Ann, m. William **BAKER**, b. of Brooklyn, Feb. 21,		
1842, by Daniel P. Tyler, J. P.	4	75
HATCH, Lydia, m. Darius **SHELDON**, Nov. 4, 1804	1	76
HAUGHTON, Anne Maria, of Boston, m. Alexander Hamilton		
DAY, of Georgia, Aug. 9, 1830, by E. B. Kellogg	4	43
HAVEN, Anna, m. John **ALLYN**, Nov. 9, 1794	2	2
HAWKINS, Arnold, d. July 9, 1847, ae 60 y.	1	47
Daniel, m. Sophia M. **BUNN**, b. of Brooklyn, Sept. 17, 1844,		
by Rev. F. J. Tillotson	4	80
Harriet, m. Nathan P. **WITTER**, b. of Brooklyn, Mar. 8,		
1846, by Rev. Herman Snow	4	82
Maria, housekeeper, ae 22, b. Killingly, res. Plainfield,		
m. Perry **EDWARDS**, manufacturer, ae 22, b. Plainfield,		
res. Plainfield, Mar. 24, [1850], by Reverius Camp	2	114
Maria, m. Perry **EDWARDS**, b. of Plainfield, Mar. 24, 1850,		
by Rev. R. Camp	4	102
Matilda, ae 20, b. Killingly, res. Killingly, m. George		
H. **ROOD**, carpenter, ae 29, b. N. Y. State, res. Killingly,	2	100

	Vol.	Page
HAWKINS, (cont.)		
May 16, 1849, by Jacob Ferris	2	100
Millia, of Brooklyn, m. G. H. **ROOD**, of Killingly,		
May 16, 1849, by Rev. J. Ferris. Int. pub. May 13, 1849	4	100
HAYWARD, Augustus, s. Charles & Rebeckah, b. Feb. 23, 1791	1	8
Hannah T., housekeeper, b. Bridgewater, Mass., res.		
Brooklyn, d. July 31, [1850], ae 59 (Perhaps 1851?)	2	124
Thomas Cotton, m. Eliza **SUMNER**, Apr. 30, 1801	1	67
HEAD, Josephine Ann Smith, m. Bernard **PENROSE**, of Phila.,		
Apr. 28, 1842, by Rev. R. Camp	4	76
HEBBARD, Elizabeth, d. William & Lucy, b. Aug. 29, 1815	1	240
Harriet, d. William & Lucy, b. Aug. 23, 1817	1	240
Lucy Maria, d. William & Lucy, b. Sept. 3, 1820	1	240
William, m. Lucy **BLANCHARD**, Dec. 19, 1813	1	67
HENDLY, Isaac, of Abington, m. Nancy E. **FOSTER**, of Brooklyn,		
Sept. 28, 1853, by Rev. Thomas Huntington	4	112
HENRY, George William, s. William & Ann Maria, b. Dec. 8, 1840	2	24
HERRICK, HERICK, HRRICK, Ama, w. Benjamin, d. June 9,		
1790	1	47
Amey, d. Timothy & Rebe, b. Sept. 16, 1819	1	240
Amy, m . Erastus P. **HARRIS**, b. of Brooklyn, Feb. 9, 1840,		
by Rev. William Coe	4	71
Amy Church, d. Benj[amin] & Sarah, b. Jan. 2, 1793	1	8
Benj[amin], s. Benjamin & Ama, b. Sept. 11, 1779	1	8
Benj[amin], s. Benj[amin], d. Dec. 10, 1779, ae 93 d.	1	47
Benjamin, m. Sarah **PIERCE**, Dec. 30, 1790	1	67
Betsey, d. Timothy & Rebe, b. July 5, 1810	1	240
Betsey, m. Jacob **KIMBALL**, b. of Brooklyn, June 8, 1834,		
by Uriel Fuller, J. P.	4	55
Emily Maria, d. Timothy & Rebe, b. Feb. 28, 1831;		
d. May 22, 1832	2	23
Emily Maria, d. Timothy & Rebe, d. May 22, 1832	1	47
Hannah, m. Reuben **KAMP**, Dec. 28, 1800	1	69
Harvey, s. Martin & Hannah, b. Dec. 14, 1814	1	240
James, m. Eunice **PARKE**, Dec. 23, 1804	1	67
James Phillips, s. Benjamin & Ama, b. Nov. 5, 1774	1	8
Lite, m. Joab **FASSETT**, Jan. 5, 1792	1	65
Lucretia, d. Timothy & Rebe, b. June 18, 1807	1	240
Lucretia, m. Joab F. **ADAMS**, b. of Brooklyn, Nov. 29,		
[1827], by Rev. Samuel J. May	4	31
Marcia, d. Timothy & Rebe, b. June 22, 1814	1	240
Marcia, of Brooklyn, m. Amos W. **SNOW**, of Chaplin, Nov.		
30, 1837, by Rev. G. J. Tillotson	4	65
Patty, d. Rufus & Prudence, b. Apr. 22, 1781	1	8
Sally, m. Palmer **WILLIAMS**, May 31, 1795	1	78
Septimus Pooler, s. Martin & Hannah, b. Jan. 31, 1807	1	240
Thomas, s. Martin & Hannah, b. June 16, 1808	1	240
Timothy, s. Benjamin & Ama, b. Oct. 21, 1776	1	8

HERRICK, HERICK, HRRICK, (cont.)	Vol.	Page
Timothy, m. Rebe **WHEELER**, Sept. 19, 1805	1	67
Timothy, s. Timothy & Rebe, b. Apr. 1, 1822	1	240
William, s. Martin & Hannah, b. Nov. 18, 1809	1	240

HEWITT, HEWIT, HEWETT, Alice, d. Stephen & Alice, b. Sept. 3, 1784 — 1 — 8

Elisha, s. Stephen & Alice, b. Aug. 15, 1781 — 1 — 8

Eliza, d. Joseph & Jerusha, b. Sept. 5, 1803 — 1 — 240

Joanna, m. Uriah **CADY**, 2d, Apr. 8, 1762 — 1 — 62

Joseph, m. Jerusha **MORSE**, Feb. 19, 1802 — 1 — 67

Joseph Denison, s. Stephen & Alice, b. Aug. 14, 1782 — 1 — 8

Lucy, d. Stephen & Alice, b. Sept. 2, 1786 — 1 — 8

Russell, s. Joseph & Jerusha, b. Jan. 25, 1805 — 1 — 240

[HIBBARD], [see under HEBBARD]

HICKS, George, m. Lucy Ann **CARTER**, b. of Brooklyn, Nov. 13, 1842, by Rev. G. J. Tillotson — 4 — 77

George, m. Marcia Maria **CARTER**, b. of Brooklyn, Oct. 8, 1843, by Rev. G. J. Tillotson — 4 — 79

HIDE, [see under HYDE]

HIG[G]INBOTHOM, Lewis, of Pomfret, m. Olive **BENNETT**, of Brooklyn, Aug. 9, 1846, by Rev. Benjamin C. Phelps, of West Killingly — 4 — 85

HILL, Elbridge G., of Plainfield, m. Mary Ann **LITCHFIELD**, of Brooklyn, Dec. 8, 1839, by Rev. William Coe — 4 — 70

John W., of Plainfield, m. Susan **SHEURMAN**, of Brooklyn, Oct. 25, 1835, by Rev. Ziba Loveland, of Plainfield — 4 — 59

HOLBROOK, Corinne Tyler, d. James, U. S. Post Office Agent, ae 39, & Mary B., ae 37, b. May 17, 1850 — 2 — 107

James, m. Mary Baker **TYLER**, b. of Brooklyn, June 9, 1833, by Rev. Geo[rge] J. Tillotson — 4 — 51

Margaret, of Abbington, m. Septimus **DAVISON**, of Brooklyn, Oct. 16, 1826, by Rev. Sam[ue]l J. May — 4 — 25

HOLT, Eliza L., of Abington Soc. in Pomfret, m. Daniel **ARNOLD**, Jr., of Brooklyn, Apr. 23, 1848, by Rev. Ebenezer Loomis — 2 — 79

Eliza L., of Abington, m. Daniel **ARNOLD**, Jr., of Brooklyn, Apr. 23, 1848, by Rev. E. Loomis — 4 — 99

Vine, m. Susannah **KNOWLES**, Oct. 28, 1793 — 1 — 67

HOPKINS, George L., m. Juliette **BROWN**, b. of Scituate, R. I., Nov. 30, 1852, by Rev. Geo[rge] J. Tillotson — 4 — 107

Susannah, m. Rufus **ADAMS**, Dec. 29, 1805 — 1 — 60

HORTON, Patience, m. William **LEVALLY**, b. of Canterbury, Apr. 27, 1823, by Rev. Thomas J. Murdock — 4 — 12

HOSMER, Sabry, of Woodstock, m. Joshua **COLLINS**, of Brooklyn, Apr. 10, [1840], by Rev. Benj[amin] N. Harris — 4 — 72

HOWARD, Ann Chapin, m. Waldo **HUTCHINS**, Feb. 9, 1819 — 1 — 67

Ellen Lydia, d. William G. & Ellen Law, b. Jan. 28, 1837 — 2 — 24

William G., of Newburyport, m. Ellen L. **BAKER**, of Brooklyn, Apr. 19, 1836, by Rev. G. J. Tillotson — 4 — 61

HOWE, Benjamin, of Topsfield, Mass., m. Waty W. **TYLER**, of

	Vol.	Page
HOWE, (cont.)		
Brooklyn, May 31, 1842, by Rev. G. J. Tillotson	4	76
Edmund G., of Hartford, Conn., m. Frances **KIES**, of		
Brooklyn, June 15, 1836, by Rev. G. J. Tillotson	4	61
HOWEY (?), Lucina, d. Feb. 20, 1849, ae 50	2	104
HOWLAND, Julia A., d. Peter, farmer, ae 44, & Elizabeth,		
ae 44, b. Aug. 11, 1847	2	86
Julia Ann, d. Jan. 24, 1849, ae 1 y. 5 m. 13 d.	2	100
HUBBARD, [see also **HEBBARD**], Calvin, m. Sarah **DARBY**, Nov.		
10, 1778	1	67
Calvin, d. Aug. 18, 1781	1	47
Calvin, s. Calvin & Sarah, b. Dec. 24, 1781	1	8
Ebenezer, s. Eben[eze]r & Mollie, b. July 5, 1789	1	8
Filene, d. Calvin & Sarah, b. Jan. 6, 1780	1	8
Lydia, d. Eben[eze]r & Mollie, b. June 26, 1786	1	8
Mary, of Brooklyn, m. Fre[e]born **YOUNG**, of Killingly,		
Oct. 21, 1804, by John Parrish, J. P.	3	6
Polly, d. Eben[eze]r & Molly, b. Aug. 30, 1793	1	8
Reuben, s. Eben[eze]r & Mollie, b. Dec. 10, 1784	1	8
William, s. Eben[eze]r & Mollie, b. June 4, 1791	1	8
HUMES, Hannah, m. Benjamin **WEAVER**, May 28, 1806	1	78
HUNT, Nathaniel, m. Hannah **COOPER**, Jan. 25, 1807	1	67
Sarah, of Smithfield, R. I., m. Joseph H. **LOVEJOY**, Aug.		
9, 1846, by Rev. Benjamin C. Phelps, of West Killingly	4	85
HUNTINGTON, Ann Elizabeth, m. Charles **CLARK**, of Norwich,		
Oct. 22, 1838, by Rev. Thomas Huntington	4	68
Charlotte S., of Brooklyn, m. John H. **CLARK**, of Providence,		
Apr. 16, 1846, by Rev. Tho[ma]s Huntington	4	83
Charlotte Stoddard, d. Thomas & Elizabeth, b. May 21, 1825	2	24
Elizabeth, w. Dr. Thomas, d. Apr. 1, 1830	1	47
Emily Clark, d. Thomas & Paulina, b. Oct. 22, 1833	2	24
George, s. Thomas & Paulina, b. Nov. 5, 1835	2	24
Harriet, d. Thomas & Elizabeth, b. Jan. 10, 1823	2	24
Harriet, of Brooklyn, m. William A. **COGGESHAL**, of New		
London, [Mar.] 10, [1846], by Rev. Thomas Huntington	4	82
Henry, s. Thomas & Elizabeth, b. Feb. 4, 1827	2	24
Louisa, d. Thomas & Paulina, b. Feb. 5, 1832	2	24
Lucy Ann, m. Stephen **WHEELER**, Aug. 4, [1833], by Rev.		
Samuel J. May	4	52
Mary W., d. Jan. 2, 1824	1	47
Thomas, Dr., m. Paulina **CLARK**, Apr. 18, 1831, by Dan[ie]l		
G. Sprague, Hampton	4	45
Thomas, s. Thomas & Paulina, b. May 25, 1838	2	24
HUTCHINS, Ann Kezia, d. Waldo & Ann C., b. Jan. 21, 1821	1	240
Ann Kezia, d. Waldo & Ann C., b. Jan. 21, 1821	2	23
Ann Kezia, d. Waldo & Ann C., d. Mar. 16, 1825	1	47
Elizabeth, m. Charles **BURTON**, Oct. 10, 1839, by Rev. R.		
Camp	4	72

	Vol.	Page

HUTCHINS, (cont.)

George H., laborer, ae 21, b. Pomfret, res. Brooklyn,
m. Harriet **PARRISH**, ae 16, of Brooklyn, Aug. 17, 1847,
by Abiel Converse, J. P.   2   81

Mary Thompson, d. Waldo & Ann C., b. Jan. 8, 1825   2   24

Waldo, m. Ann Chapin **HOWARD**, Feb. 9, 1819   1   67

Waldo, s. Waldo & Ann C., b. Sept. 30, 1822   2   24

Waldo, d. Mar. 14, 1826, in the 36th y. of his age   1   47

HUZZY, Amos T., of Townsend, Vt., m. Lucy Maria **SMALL**, of
Brooklyn, both persons of color, July 1, 1832, by Rev.
George J. Tillotson   4   47

HYDE, HIDE, Adeline, ae 25, b. Brooklyn, m. Warren **MILLS**,
carpenter, ae 25, of Springfield, Dec. 18, 1849, by George
J. Tillotson   2   122

Adeline L., of Brooklyn, m. Warren W. **MILLS**, of Springfield,
Mass., Dec. 19, 1849, by Rev. G. J. Tillotson   4   103

Caroline, d. Lucina, b. Apr. 13, 1825   2   25

Celia Ann, m. James E. **MAIN**, Mar. 12, 1834, by Rev.
Geo[rge] J. Tillotson   4   53

Charles, s. Edmund, farmer, ae 43, & Mary Ann, ae 36, b.
Mar. 6, 1849   2   99

Charlotte, d. Samuel & Ann, b. Apr. 23, 1825   2   25

Edmund, of Brooklyn, m. Mary A. **KNIGHT**, of Charlton,
Mass., Apr. 7, 1841, by Rev. Geo[rge] J. Tillotson   4   74

Eliza, m. Royal **COPELAND**, Mar. 19, 1820   1   62

Elizabeth, d. Samuel & Ann, b. July 30,1803   2   25

Elizabeth, of Brooklyn, m. Harry **HYDE**, of Canterbury,
Sept. 15, 1822, by Rev. Roswell Whitmore   4   11

Elizabeth, w. Jabez, d. Nov. 6, 1829, in the 84th y. of her age   1   47

Emily, m. David **CLARK**, b. of Brooklyn, [Apr] 28,[1829],
by Rev. Ambrose Edson   4   35

Harriot, m. Royal **COPELAND**, b. of Brooklyn, Apr. 3, 1821,
by Rev. Hutchins Taylor   4   2

Harry, of Canterbury, m. Elizabeth **HYDE**, of Brooklyn, Sept.
15, 1822, by Rev. Roswell Whitmore   4   11

Henry William, s. Samuel & Ann, b. Mar. 26, 1811   2   25

James, s. Samuel & Ann, b. Sept. 8, 1818   2   25

James, m. Lucy **ASHCRAFT**, Nov. 7, 1797   1   67

Lucina, d. James & Lucy, b. Nov. 19, 1798   1   240

Lucina had d. Caroline, b. Apr. 13, 1825   2   25

Lucina, of Brooklyn, m. Benjan **YOUNG**, of Killingly, Mar.
9, 1834, by Daniel Williams, Clerk, at Killingly   4   53

Lucinda, d. Samuel & Ann, b. Feb. 17, 1806, at Killingly   2   25

Lucy, d. Feb. 1, 1849, ae 70   2   104

Marcia, m. Joseph N. **SOLLACE**, b. of Brooklyn, Apr. 2,
1833, by Rev. Geo[rge] J. Tillotson   4   50

Philury, d. Samuel & Ann, b. Dec. 13, 1804, at Killingly   2   25

Philury, of Brooklyn, m. Giles **WOODWORTH**, of Killingly,

	Vol.	Page

HYDE, HIDE, (cont.)

Nov. 27, 1823, by Rev. Roswell Whitmore — 4 — 16

Sarah J., d. Edmund, farmer, ae 45, & Mary Ann, ae 38,
b. Sept. 5, 1850 — 2 — 127

INGRAHAM, John, m. Sally **FAULKNER,** Dec. 31, 1815 — 1 — 68

Mary, d. John & Sally, b. May 19, 1830 — 2 — 29

Mira, m. Sylvanus **BAILEY,** Jan. 18, 1816 — 1 — 61

Ruth, m. Asahel **CADY,** Mar. 13, 1783 — 1 — 62

William Hutchins, s. John & Sally, b. Oct. 10, 1827 — 2 — 29

JACOBS, Ida Ardelia, d. Albert, mason, ae 26, of Willimantic,
& Dolly C., ae 25, b. Aug. 3, 1850 — 2 — 129

JAMES, Lucy Maria, m. Edwin **NEWBURY,** b. of Brooklyn,
[Apr.] 25, 1824, by Ambrose Edson — 4 — 17

Mary H., m. Carlton B. **NEWBURY,** Oct. 2, [1831], by
Geo[rge] J. Tillotson — 4 — 46

JEFFERS, Lydia H., of Woonsocket, R. I., m. Edwin G. **POTTER,**
of Sterling, [Feb.] 3, [1852], by Geo[rge] G. Channing — 4 — 106

JEFFERY, Gordon, m. Esther **BUTTS,** b. of Brooklyn, Jan. 11,
1818, by John Parish, J. P. — 3 — 9

JEFFORDS, Anna, d. Apr. 17, 1823, in the 85th y. of her age — 1 — 48

Hannah, w. John, d. Feb. 21, 1805, in the 80th y. of her age — 1 — 48

John, d. Apr. 14, 1807 — 1 — 48

JENKINS, Charles W., m. Phebe **BISHOP,** b. of Brooklyn, Apr. 14,
1835, by Rev. G. J. Tillotson — 4 — 58

JENKS, Minerva, m. Joseph **PARKS,** b. of Brooklyn, Dec. 16,
1824, by John Parish, J. P. — 3 — 10

Minerva, m. Joseph **PARKES,** b. of Brooklyn, Dec. 16, 1824,
by John Parish, J. P. — 4 — 18

JOHNSON, Abner, m. Sarah A. **REED,** b. of Brooklyn, Mar. 13,
1845, by Rev. G. J. Tillotson — 4 — 81

Alice, d. Oct. 10, [1848], ae 3 — 2 — 98

Andrew, m. Elizabeth **ALLEN,** b. of Brooklyn, Jan. 21, 1846,
by Rev. G. J. Tillotson — 4 — 84

Andrew, m. Jane M. **TAYLOR,** b. of Brooklyn, Jan. 25, 1852,
by Rev. Geo[rge] J. Tillotson — 4 — 108

Elizabeth A., domestic, b. Brooklyn, res. East Brooklyn,
d. Oct. 14, 1848, ae 26 — 2 — 104

George H., s. Hammon, farmer, ae 28, & Eliza, ae 26, b.
Oct. 16, 1849 — 2 — 119

Henry, of Conventry, R. I., m. Lydia M. **CADY,** of Brooklyn,
Nov. 23, 1834, by Rev. Samuel J. May — 4 — 56

Mary Eliza, d. Henry, brick maker, ae 39, & Lydia Minerva,
ae 35, b. Apr. 1, 1850 — 2 — 111

Mary Elizabeth, d. David & Elizabeth, b. Sept. 6, 1836 — 2 — 29

----, of Brooklyn, m. John **BROOKS,** of Western in county of
Worcester, Oct. 9, 1816, by John Parish, J. P. — 3 — 9

----, s. Andrew, farmer, ae 39, & Elizabeth P., ae 26,
b. Oct. 7, 1848 — 2 — 103

	Vol.	Page
JONES, Ellen Maria, m. Charles Henry **DABNEY**, b. of Providence, R. I., [Apr.] 27, [1830], by Rev. Ambrose Edson	4	41
Lucy, of Lisbon, m. Samuel **CLEVELAND**, of Brooklyn, Apr. 17, 1820, by Vine Robinson, J. P.	4	36
JOSLIN, JOSSELYN, Charles, of Burrelville, m. Sarah **UTLEY**, of Douglass, [Jan.] 11, [1835], by Rev. Samuel J. May	4	57
Marvil, m. Martha **COOPER**, June 23, 1822, by Vine Robinson, J. P.	4	9
JUSTIN, Jehiel, m. Caroline **TAYLOR**, Dec. 27, 1828, by John Parish, J. P.	3	10
Jehiel, m. Caroline **TAYLOR**, Dec. 27, 1828, by John Parish, J. P.	4	34
KAMP, [see under **KEMP**]		
KEACH, KEECH, Betsey, m. Samuel **TRIPP**, [b. of Brooklyn], June 24, 1849, by Rev. S. W. Coggeshall	4	100
Betsey, weaver on looms, ae 26, of Brooklyn, m. Samuel **TRIPP**, shoemaker, ae 29, b. Canterbury, res. Brooklyn, July 8, 1849, by Rev. Coggeshall	2	104
Ezekiel, manufacturer, b. R. I., res. Brooklyn, d. Sept. 9, 1849, ae 65	2	120
Horace, farm laborer, b. R. I., res. Brooklyn, d. Oct. 7, [1848], ae 34	2	98
Lydia S., m. Seth P. **BALDWIN**, b. of Brooklyn, Nov. 16, 1835, by Joseph Tyler, J. P.	4	60
KELLEY, Lucy, m. Joseph K. **GREENE**, b. of Brooklyn, Apr. 19, 1835, by Rev. Roswell Whitmore	4	58
Rebecca S., of Brooklyn, m. Albert **SPENCER**, of Windham, Oct. 1, 1845, by Rev. Benjamin C. Phelps, of West Killingly	4	81
KEMP, KAMP, Charles Ames, s. Henry, laborer, ae 43, & Betsey, ae 43, b. Oct. 5, 1850	2	129
Eliza, of Brooklyn, m. William H. **LOCKE**, of Foster, R. I., July 27, 1845, by Uriel Fuller, J. P.	4	86
Hannah, housekeeper, d. Apr. 11, 1850, ae 87	2	120
Harriet, twin with Henry, d. Reuben & Hannah, b. July 28, 1808	1	10
Henry, twin with Harriet, s. Reuben & Hannah, b. July 28, 1808	1	10
Henry, m. Betsey **SHOALS**, b. of Brooklyn, [July] 1, [1827], by Rev. Samuel J. May	4	28
Jerusha, d. Reuben & Hannah, b. June 22, 1801	1	10
Jerusha, of Brooklyn, m. Sylvanus **MOFFIT**, of Killingly, Feb. 24, [1828], by Rev. Samuel J. May	4	31
Lucinda, d. Reuben & Hannah, b. Nov. 11, 1803	1	10
Martha, m. Olney **TANNER**, Jan. 18, 1830, by Rev. Sam[uel] J. May	4	39
Patty, d. Reuben & Hannah, b. May 19, 1806	1	10
Reuben, m. Hannah **HERRICK**, Dec. 28, 1800	1	69

	Vol.	Page
KEMP, KAMP, (cont.)		
Ursula, of Brooklyn, m. Ebenezer S. **SNOW**, of Hampton,		
Oct. 16, 1853, by Rev. C. Y. DeNormandie	4	110
KENDALL, KENDAL, KINDALL, Alice, d. John & Lois, b. Feb.		
8, 1784	1	10
Annice, d. John & Lois, b. Oct. 3, 1786	1	10
Annis, m. Joseph **TYLER**, b. of Brooklyn, [Sept.] 17,		
[1827], by Rev. Sam[uel] J. May	4	29
Chauncey, twin with Nancy, s. John & Lois, b. Oct. 22, 1792	1	10
Deliverance, b. Killingly, res. Brooklyn, d. Oct. 17, [1849], ae		
82	2	115
John, m. Lois **PALMER**, Mar. 8, 1781	1	69
John, s. John & Lois, b. Nov. 15, 1790	1	10
John T., s. John W., farmer, ae 30, of Canterbury, & Harriet A.		
W., ae 28, of Canterbury, b. Mar. 27, 1850	2	113
Lois, d. John & Lois, b. Oct. 20, 1781	1	10
Nancy, twin with Chauncey, d. John & Lois, b. Oct. 22, 1792	1	10
Nathan, s. John & Lois, b. Nov. 12, 1797	1	10
KENT, Alfred, s. Joseph & Hannah, b. June 6, 1792	1	10
Ezra, s. Joseph & Hannah, b. Oct. 23, 1795	1	10
Ira, s. Joseph & Hannah, b. Oct. 28, 1793	1	10
KENYON, KINYON, Amy, m. Samuel **DORRANCE**, Dec. 19,		
1805	1	63
Emily, of Sterling, m. Henry **PARKS**, of Providence,		
Feb. 4, 1838, by Rev. G. J. Tillotson	4	66
KEYES, [see also **KIES**], Harriet, of Brooklyn, m. Chester		
CADY, of Pomfret, Mar. 20, 1826, by Rev. Samuel J.		
May	4	23
KIBBEE, Israel N., m. Phebe **MATHEWSON**, b. of Brooklyn, Aug.		
3, 1854, by Rev. Sylvester Barrows	4	113
KIES, [see also **KEYES**], Caroline d. Daniel & Lucy, b. Oct.		
28, 1805	2	31
Caroline E., m. Lewis G. **BURTON**, Apr. 24, 1831, by		
Samuel J. May	4	45
Charles, s. Daniel & Lucy, b. Nov. 29, 1803	1	10
Charles, s. Daniel & Lucy, b. Nov. 29, 1803; d. Mar. 15, 1806	2	31
Charles, s. Daniel & Lucy, d. Mar. 15, 1806, in the		
3rd y. of his age	1	49
Charles Harvey, s. Daniel & Lucy, b. Aug. 11, 1813	2	31
Daniel, m. Lucy **CADY**, Dec. 29, 1801	1	69
Daniel, m. Lucy **CADY**, Dec. 29, 1801	2	31
Delia, d. Daniel & Lucy, b. Nov. 30, 1809	2	31
Delia Scarborough, of Brooklyn, m. Daniel Allen **TAYLOR**,		
of Providence, Mar. 2, [1834], by Samuel J. May	4	54
Frances, of Brooklyn, m. Edmund G. **HOWE**, of Hartford,		
Conn., June 15, 1836, by Rev. G. J. Tillotson	4	61
Harriet, d. Daniel & Lucy, b. Mar. 12, 1807	2	31
Lucy Ann, d. Daniel & Lucy, b. Sept. 28, 1811;		

	Vol.	Page
KIES, (cont.)		
d. Feb. 25, 1815	2	31
Lucy Ann, d. Daniel & Lucy, d. Feb. 25, 1815, in the 4th y. of her age	1	49
Nathan Cady, s. Daniel & Lucy, b. Sept. 6, 1820	2	31
Pamelia, m. Daniel C. **ROBINSON**, [Sept] 22, [1828], by Rev. Ambrose Edson	4	33
Samuel, m. Pamela **DAVIS**, Apr. 26, 1807	1	69
KIMBALL, KYMBAL, Andrew Johnson, s. Jacob & Betsey, b. Sept. 25, 1836	2	30
Charlotte Ann, d. Jacob & Betsey, b. Mar. 12, 1847	2	30
Gurdon P., s. Jacob, farmer, ae 41, & Betsey, ae 38, b. June 20, 1848	2	86
Gurdon Parker, s. Jacob & Betsey, b. June 20, 1848	2	30
Jacob, m. Betsey **HERRICK**, b. of Brooklyn, June 8, 1834, by Uriel Fuller, J. P.	4	55
James Whitcomb, s. Jacob & Betsey, b. Nov. 24, 1841	2	30
Lewis Fossett, s. Jacob & Betsey, b. Mar. 24, 1851	2	30
Lewis Fassett, s. Jacob, farmer, ae 44, & Betsey, ae 41, b. Mar. 29, 1851	2	129
Nathan, d. Jan. 3, 1787	1	49
Sarah Jane, d. Jacob & Betsey, b. Oct. 9, 1838	2	30
KING, Ann Eliza, d. Richard & Celia Ann, b. Nov. 29, 1842	2	31
Charles Dexter, s. Richard & Celia Ann, b. Nov. 5, 1840	2	31
Jane Spaulding, d. Richard & Celia Ann, b. Jan. 27, 1846	2	31
Julius Cleow, s. Richard & Celia Ann, b. June 2, 1848	2	31
Julius Cleow(?), s. Richard, silversmith, ae 31, & Celia Ann, ae 28, b. June 2, 1848	2	78
Richard, of Brooklyn, m. Celia A. **SPALDING**, of Killingly, Oct. 16, 1839, by Rev. Benj[ami]n N. Harris	4	69
KINGSBURY, Abby, of Killingly, m. Alden **BURGESS**, Jr., of Brooklyn, Oct. 7, 1839, by Rev. William Coe	4	71
Deliverance, m. Joseph **SCARBOROUGH**, Feb. 24, 1780	1	76
Joseph, m. Rahumah **CADY**, b. of Brooklyn, June 30, 1805, by John Parrish, J. P.	3	7
KINGSLEY, Harmony, of Brooklyn, m. Benjamin **DURFEY**, of Greenville, Norwich, Feb. 16, 1836, by Rev. G. J. Tillotson	4	59
Sarah, of Sterling, m. Elisha **ADAMS**, of Brooklyn, May 4, 1828, by Nathaniel Cole, Elder, in Plainfield	4	32
KINNE, KINNEY, Martin, m. Mary K, **LATHROP**, b. of Lisbon, Mar. 23, 1840, by Rev. William Coe	4	71
Robert, m. Deborah L. **CLARK**, b. of Plainfield, Oct. 2, 1831, by Rev. David C. Bolles. Int. pub.	4	46
Robert, m. Louisa **WALLS**, b. of Plainfield, Aug. 19, 1832, by Uriel Fuller, J. P.	4	48
KINYON, [see under **KENYON**]		
KNAPPING, Edwin E., m. Eunice **BURROWS**, d. of Esther		

	Vol.	Page
LEVALLY, (cont.)		
Apr. 27, 1823, by Rev. Thomas J. Murdock	4	12
LEWIS, Benjamin, m. Cynthia **MERRET,** Mar. 22, 1798	1	70
Benjamin, of Java, Genesee Co., N. Y., m. Elizabeth		
CLARK, of Brooklyn, Nov. 23, 1836, by Rev. G. J.		
Tillotson	4	63
Cynthia, see under Zinthia		.
John, s. Benj[amin] & Gynthia, b. Apr. 25, 1807	1	11
Seth, s. Benjamin & Cynthia, b. Apr. 24, 1802	1	11
Zinthia, d. Benjamin & Zinthia, b. Aug. 11, 1804	1	11
LINCOLN, Sarah, ae 24, b. Hampton, m. Elkanah **LATHROP,**		
carpenter, ae 24, b. Plainfield, res. Brooklyn, Sept.		
17, 1849, by Rev. Jacob Ferris	2	105
Sarah, of Hampton, m. Elkanah **LATHROP,** of Brooklyn, Sept.		
17, 1848, by Rev. J. Ferris. Int. pub. Sept. 17, 1848	4	101
LITCHFIELD, Abigail, d. Daniel & Olive, b. Apr. 13, 1797	1	11
Alathea, d. Daniel & Olive, b. Aug. 6, 1809	1	241
Alva Preston, s. Edward & Amanda, b. Oct. 1, 1824	2	33
Andrew Murdock, s. Uriah & Sally, b. Oct. 28, 1807	1	11
Asa Spaulding, s. Uriah & Sally, b. Nov. 8, 1795	1	11
Betsey, d. John & Sarah, b. Aug. 14, 1803	1	11
Betsey, d. John & Sarah, d. Oct. 8, 1805	1	50
Charles P., s. John & Sally, b. July 19, 1810	1	241
Charles P., m. Eliza **COGSWELL,** b. of Brooklyn, Dec. 15,		
1834, by Rev. Geo[rge] J. Tillotson	4	57
Daniel, s. Uriah & Sally, b. June 21, 1793	1	11
Daniel, m. Olive **PIERCE,** Sept. 22, 1796	1	70
Dewitt Clinton, s. Asa S. & Lucy, b. Aug. 18, 1825	1	241
Edward, s. Dan[i]el & Olive, b. Mar. 13, 1799	1	11
Eleazer, Jr., s. Eleazer & Kezia, b. Mar. 26, 1787	1	11
Eleazer, s. Uriah & Sally, b. July 16, 1805	1	11
Elias, s. Daniel & Olive, b. Sept. 16, 1816	1	241
Elmina, d. John & Sarah, b. Jan. 27, 1805	1	11
Esther, m. Remington **WEAVER,** Feb. 16, 1812, by John		
Parish, J. P.	3	8
Eunice, d. John & Sarah, b. Jan. 13, 1807	1	11
Eunice, d. John & Sarah, d. Aug. 24, 1825, in the 19th		
y. of her age	1	50
Fanny, d. John & Sarah, b. May 27, 1808	1	11
Foster, twin with Francis, s. John & Sarah, b. Sept. 15, 1815	1	241
Francis, twin with Foster, s. John & Sarah, b. Sept. 15, 1815	1	241
Francis, farmer, ae 36, of Brooklyn, s. John, m. Alice		
SPENCER, ae 28, of Warwick, b. in East Greenwich, d.		
Capt. John, Mar. 29, 1852, at Warwick, R. I., by Rev.		
Thomas Tillinghast	4	112
Frederick, s. John & Sarah, b. Jan. 30, 1801	1	11
George, s. John & Sarah, b. June 29, 1813	1	241
James, s. Daniel & Olive, b. Jan. 25, 1812	1	241

	Vol.	Page

LITCHFIELD, (cont.)

James, m. Susan **THORNTON**, b. of Brooklyn, Sept. 4, 1836,
  by Rev. G. J. Tillotson — 4 — 62
John, s. Eleazer & Kezia, b. May 23, 1791 — 1 — 11
John, s. Uriah & Sally, b. Nov. 18, 1798 — 1 — 11
John, m. Sarah **BUTTS**, Jan. 30, 1800 — 1 — 70
John, d. Apr. 15, 1828, in the 68th y. of his age — 1 — 50
John Gordon, s. Daniel & Olive, b. June 1, 1803 — 1 — 241
Lucy, d. Uriah & Sally, b. Aug. 22, 1791 — 1 — 11
Lucy, d. John & Lucy, d. Dec. 18, 1791 — 1 — 50
Lucy, d. Uriah & Sally, d. Mar. 11, 1793 — 1 — 50
Lucy, d. Nov. 9, 1803, ae 74 y. — 1 — 50
Lucy, d. John & Sarah, b. Oct. 5, 1820 — 1 — 241
Lucy M., m. Anson **FOX**, of Hampton, Oct. 10, 1825, by
  Rev. A. Edson — 4 — 22
Lucy Mary, d. Daniel & Olive, b. May 18, 1805 — 1 — 241
Mary, d. Uriah & Sally, b. Sept. 17, 1789 — 1 — 11
Mary, d. Uriah & Sally, d. Mar. 4, 1793 — 1 — 50
Mary, d. Charles P. & Eliza, b. Mar. 10, 1841 — 2 — 33
Mary Ann, d. John & Sally, b. Aug. 23, 1808 — 1 — 241
Mary Ann, of Brooklyn, m. Elbridge G. **HILL**, of Plainfield,
  Dec. 8, 1839, by Rev. William Coe — 4 — 70
Olive, d. Daniel & Olive, b. Sept. 16, 1807 — 1 — 241
Olive, of Brooklyn, m. Alva **PRESTON**, of Hampton, Aug.
  18, 1830, by Rev. Ambrose Edson — 4 — 42
Olive, w. Daniel, d. Apr. 1, 1835, ae 59 — 1 — 50
Sarah, d. Charles P. & Eliza, b. Mar. 1, 1837; d. Jan. 22, 1838 — 2 — 33
Susannah, m. William **FASSETT***, July 28, 1791 (*Should
  be **FROST"**. Corrected by L. B. B.) — 1 — 65
Thomas Jefferson, s. Daniel & Olive, b. Jan. 27, 1801 — 1 — 11
Uriah, m. Sarah **WITTER**, Nov. 27, 1788 — 1 — 70
Uriah, s. Daniel & Olive, b. Jan. 22, 1814 — 1 — 241
William, of Brooklyn, m. Maria **FASS[ ]**, of Winchester,
  N. H., Dec.1, 1839, by Rev. William Coe — 4 — 70
William Foster, s. Charles P. & Eliza, b. Oct. 12, 1835 — 2 — 33
William Riley, s. Edward & Amanda, b. July 22, 1822 — 2 — 33

LITTLEHALE, Nancy, weaver, ae 35, b. Mass., m. 2d h. David
  WOODWARD, ae 49, of Brooklyn, Jan. 28, 1849, by
  Rev. Ferris — 2 — 104
Nancy W., Mrs., of Northbridge, Mass., m. David
  WOODWARD, Jan. 14, 1849, by Rev. J. Ferris.
  Intention pub. Jan. 14, 1849 — 4 — 101

LOCKE, William H., of Foster, R. I., m. Eliza **KEMP**, of Brooklyn,
  July 27, 1845, by Uriel Fuller, J. P. — 4 — 86

LONG, Lucy, m. Richard **MOFFITT**, Aug. 27, 185[4], by Uriel
  Fuller, J. P. — 4 — 114
Lucy D., of Hampton, m. Richard **MOFFITT**, of Brooklyn,
  Aug. 27, 1854, by Uriel Fuller, J. P. — 4 — 116

	Vol.	Page
[LOOMIS], LOOMICE, LUMMIS, Eunice, m. Anthony		
TARBOX, b. of Coventry, R. I., Jan. 1, 1844, by Rev.		
Geo[rge] J. Tillotson	4	79
William, worker in factory, b. Canterbury, res. Brooklyn,		
d. July 24, 1849, ae 16	2	104
LORD, Elisha, m. Sophia **WHITNEY**, Nov. 28, 1799	1	70
Lucy, w. Elisha, d. Apr. 22, 1796	1	50
Lucy, d. Elisha & Lucy, b. Oct. 12, 1800	1	11
Lucy, d. Elisha & Sophia, d. Nov. 4, 1800	1	50
W[illia]m Danielson, s. Elisha & Lucy, b. Apr. 20, 1796	1	11
William Danielson, s. Elisha & Lucy, d. July 6, 1801	1	50
LOVE, Sarah A., of Coventry, R. I., m. Isaac **TILLINGHAST**, of		
Killingly, Conn., Mar. 21, 1853, by Rev. Courtland Y.		
DeNormandie	4	109
LOVEJOY, Joseph H., m. Sarah **HUNT**, of Smithfield, R. I., Aug.		
9, 1846, by Rev. Benjamin C. Phelps, of West Killingly	4	85
LOWRY, LOWREY, Agnes, m. James **CLARK**, b. of Brooklyn,		
Mar. 2, 1852, by Rev. G. J. Tillotson	4	107
Eliza A., d. James, agriculturist, & Mary, b. July 11, 1850	2	117
James, m. Mary **LOWREY**, b. of Brooklyn, Apr. 4, 1853, by		
Rev. Geo[rge] J. Tillotson	4	111
Mary, m. James **LOWREY**, b. of Brooklyn, Apr. 4, 1853, by		
Rev. Geo[rge] J. Tillotson	4	111
LUMMIS, [see under **LOOMIS**]		
LUTHER, Flavel S., s. Flavel S., cabinet maker, ae 25, of		
Killingly, CT., & Jane J., ae 26, b. Mar. 26, 1850	2	107
LYON, Mira, m. Sylvanus **BAILEY**, Jan. 18, 1816, by John Parish.		
J. P.	3	9
MAHAN, John B., of New York, m. Nancy Ann **SPALDING**, of		
Brooklyn, Sept. 27, 1835, by Daniel T. Tyler, J. P.	4	58
MAIN, MAINE, Caroline P., of Brooklyn, m. James D. **BARD**, of		
Boston, May 12, 1840, by Rev. G. J. Tillotson	4	72
Charles G., farmer, d. Dec. 17, [1850], ae 39	2	127
Daniel, s. Daniel, farmer, ae 34, of W. Killingly, & Lucy		
E., ae 29, b. Aug. 19, 1850	2	132
Edwin G., m. Mary E. **BUTTS**, b. of Brooklyn, [Nov.] 26,		
[1843], by Rev. Thomas Huntington	4	79
Elias H., m. Sarah S. **DORRANCE**, b. of Brooklyn, Dec. 1,		
1835, by Rev. Geo[rge] J. Tillotson	4	59
Elizabeth, m. Joshua **WEBB**, May 4, 1830, by E. B. Kellogg	4	41
George J., s. Charles G., farmer, ae 39, & Frances M.,		
ae 30, b. Aug. 9, 1849	2	112
Hannah, m. Ira **WHEELER**, b. of Brooklyn, Apr. 10, 1845,		
by Rev. Herman Snow	4	81
Henry W., s. William W., butcher, ae 35, & Mary L., ae 30,		
b. Sept. 27, 1847	2	93
James E., m. Celia Ann **HYDE**, Mar. 12, 1834, by Rev.		
Geo[rge] J. Tillotson	4	53

	Vol.	Page
MALBONE, George R., m. Rheuama **SAMPSON**, June [ ], 1824,		
by John Paine	4	17
MARBLE, Russell, of Mendon, Mass., m. Phebe **ALMY**, of		
Smithfield, R. I., July 21, 1839, by Rev. William Coe	4	70
MARRY(?), Abigail, m. Willard **ADAMS**, Dec. 28, 1790	1	60
MARTIN, Anson, s. Nathaniel & Sarepta, b. Feb. 12, 1817	2	35
Anson, farmer, d. July 14, 1848, ae 31	2	90
Celia, d. Nathaniel & Sarepta, b. June 17, 1812	2	35
Celia, of Brooklyn, m. Alba **BURNAM**, of Homer, N. Y.,		
Sept. 13, 1830, by Rev. Samuel J. May	4	43
Cornelia, d. Nathaniel & Sarepta, b. Jan. 10, 1815	2	35
Elizabeth, d. Nathaniel & Sarepta, b. Oct. 9, 1824	2	35
Jane E., d. Jasper, farmer, ae 37, & Emeline T., ae 28,		
b. Oct. 29, 1847	2	89
Jasper, s. Nathaniel & Sarepta, b. Oct. 11, 1810	2	35
Jasper, m. Emeline S. **TAYLOR**, b. of Brooklyn, Nov. 19,		
1838, by Rev. William Coe	4	68
Lincoln, s. Nathaniel & Sarepta, b. Aug. 29, 1826	2	35
Lodicy, m. Aaron **DAVISON**, Oct. 28, 1792	1	63
Nathaniel, b. Mar. 9, 1788; m. Sarepta **WILLIAMS**, Feb. 4,		
1810	2	35
Nathaniel, m. Sarepta **WILLIAMS**, Feb. 4, 1810	1	71
Nathaniel, s. Nathaniel & Sarepta, b. Dec. 14, 1819	2	35
Nathaniel, farmer, b. Hampton, res. Brooklyn, d. June		
3, 1848, ae 60	2	90
Sarepta, d. Nathaniel & Sarepta, b. Feb. 8, 1822	2	35
MASCRAFT, Addison, m. Emily E. **WITTER**, Feb. 12, 1854, by		
Rev. C. Y. DeNormandie	4	113
MATHER, Eleazer, m. Fanny **WILLIAMS**, Oct. 24, 1802	1	71
Fanny, m. David C. **BOLLES**, Nov. 5, 1821, by Joseph		
Chickering	4	5
Lorinda, m. Samuel P. **FOSTER**, Apr. 22, 1817	1	65
Martha Ann, ae 22, of Brooklyn, m. Simon L. **COTTON**,		
farmer, ae 27, of Pomfret, May 29, 1848, by Rev. John		
Stone	2	79
William Williams, s. Eleazer & Fanny, b. May 24, 1804	1	12
William Williams, Lieut., m. Emily Margaret **BAKER**, June		
21, 1830, by Rev. Samuel J. May	4	43
MATHEWSON, Albert, twin with Arthur, s. Rufus S. & Faith W.,		
b. Sept. 11, 1837	1	242
Arthur, twin with Albert, s. Rufus S. & Faith W.,		
b. Sept. 11, 1837	1	242
Charles, s. Darius & Mary, b. Mar. 24, 1812	1	242
Cordelia, d. Darius & Mary, b. Mar. 17, 1808	1	242
Darius, m. Mary **SMITH**, Dec. 2, 1800	1	71
George Bowen, s. Darius & Mary, b. Apr. 19, 1804	1	12
Harriet, d. Darius & Mary, b. May 26, 1810	1	242
Harriet Cordelia, d. Rufus S. & Faith W., b. Jan. 14, 1831	1	242

	Vol.	Page
MATHEWSON, (cont.)		
Huldah, d. Darius & Mary, b. Apr. 8, 1806	1	242
John McClellan, s. Rufus S. & Faith W., b. Oct. 3, 1834	1	242
Mary Trumbull, d. Rufus S. & Faith W., b. Oct. 3, 1832	1	242
Nancy, d. Darius & Mary, b. Sept. 10, 1814	1	242
Phebe, m. Israel N. **KIBBEE,** b. of Brooklyn, Aug. 3, 1854,		
by Rev. Sylvester Barrows	4	113
Rufus Smith, s. Darius & Mary, b. Sept. 14, 1802	1	12
William Williams, s. Rufus S. & Faith W., b. Feb. 9, 1829	1	242
MAY, Charlotte Coffin, d. Rev. Samuel J. & Lucretia F., b.		
Apr. 24, 1833	2	36
John Edward, s. Rev. Samuel J. & Lucretia F., b. Oct. 7, 1829	2	36
Joseph, s. Rev. Samuel Joseph & Lucretia F., b. June 27, 1827;		
d. Dec. 1828	2	36
McCANN, James, of Smithfield, R. I., m. Sarah A. **GRANT,** of		
Cumberland, R. I., July 10, 1834, by Rev. G. J. Tillotson	4	55
McCLELLAN, James, m. Nancy **ELDREDGE,** Dec. 8, 1805	1	71
MEACH, Daniel, of Canterbury, m. Ruhamah **CADY,** of Brooklyn,		
Feb. 23, 1809, by John Parrish, J. P.	3	5
MERRET, MERET, MERIT, Cynthia, m. Benjamin **LEWIS,** Mar.		
22, 1798	1	70
Elizabeth, d. Nathan & Elizabeth, b. Apr. 2, 1797	1	12
Eunice, m. Joseph **NOTT*,** Dec. 16, 1799 (* Should be		
"SCOTT". Corrected by L. B. B.)	1	76
Larry, d. Nathan & Elizabeth, b. Oct. 26, 1803	1	12
Lucinda, d. Nathan & Elizabeth, b. Dec. 5, 1806	1	13
Mary Vaun, d. Nathan & Elizabeth, b. Oct. 7, 1800	1	12
Nathan, m. Elizabeth **WHEAT,** Dec. 24, 1795	1	71
MILES, David, s. Joshua & Lucy, b. Jan. 24, 1791	1	12
David, s. Joshua & Lucy, d. Feb. 10, 1801	1	51
Eben[eze]r, s. Joshua & Lucy, b. July 14, 1788	1	12
Jonathan, s. Joshua & Lucy, b. Apr. 16, 1793	1	12
Joshua, m. Lucy **CADY,** May 25, 1779	1	71
Joshua, 2d, s. Joshua & Lucy, b. Mar. 21, 1780	1	12
Lucy, d. Joshua & Lucy, b. Mar. 8, 1782	1	12
Mary, d. Joshua & Lucy, b. Apr. 15, 1785	1	12
Parker, s. Jesse & Alice, b. Oct. 28, 1787	1	12
Sarah, d. Joshua & Lucy, b. [ ] 18, 1795	1	12
MILLER, Jabez, harness maker, ae 23, b. Utica, res. Brooklyn,		
m. Betsey **COLE,** weaver on looms, ae 19, b. R. I., res.		
Brooklyn, Aug. 27, 1848, by Rev. J. Livesey	2	104
MILLET, Abigail, m. Franklin **HARRIS,** b. of Brooklyn, Dec. 9,		
1821, by David C. Bolles, J. P.	4	6
MILLS, Warren, carpenter, ae 25, of Springfield, m. Adeline		
HYDE, ae 25, b. Brooklyn, Dec. 18, 1849, by George J.		
Tillotson	2	122
Warren W., of Springfield, Mass., m. Adeline L. **HYDE,**		
of Brooklyn, Dec. 19, 1849, by Rev. G. J. Tillotson	4	103

	Vol.	Page
MOFFITT, MOFFIT, Isaac, m. Sophia C. **PALMER**, b. of		
Killingly, Mar. 29, 1835, by Daniel Williams, Elder	4	58
Mary, of Killingly, m. Joseph W. **BRIGGS**, of Voluntown,		
Oct. 19, 1845, by Rev. G. J. Tillotson	4	82
Richard, m. Lucy **LONG**, Aug. 27, 185[4], by Uriel Fuller,		
J. P.	4	114
Richard, of Brooklyn, m. Lucy D. **LONG**, of Hampton, Aug.		
27, 1854, by Uriel Fuller, J. P.	4	116
Sylvanus, of Killingly, m. Jerusha **KEMP**, of Brooklyn,		
Feb. 24, [1828], by Rev. Samuel J. May	4	31
MORGAN, Ebenezer, s. Roswell & Cynthia, b. Feb. 26, 1794	1	12
Elijah, s. Roswell & Cynthia, b. Oct. 18, 1787	1	12
Gurdon, s. Roswell & Cynthia, b. Oct. 7, 1798	1	12
Jasper, s. Roswell & Cynthia, b. Apr. 22, 1796	1	12
John, s. Roswell & Cynthia, b. Jan. 31, 1801	1	12
John, s. Roswell & Cynthia, d. June 18, 1801	1	51
Lucy, d. Roswell & Cynthia, b. Sept. 10, 1789	1	12
Marcia Ann, of Brooklyn, m. Dr. William D. **BOARDMAN**, of		
Cattskill, N. Y., Apr. 16, 1832, by Rev. Geo[rge] J.		
Tillotson	4	47
Nathan, s. Roswell & Cynthia, b. Oct. 17, 1791	1	12
Nathan, s. Roswell & Cynthia, d. Feb. 26, 1793	1	51
Roswell, m. Cynthia **WITTER**, Nov. 22, 1786	1	71
Thomas Branch, s. Roswell & Cynthia, b. July 30, 1802	1	12
MORSE, Elihu, s. Elihu & Lucy, b. July 3, 1793	1	12
Elisha, m. Lucy **PALMER**, Sept. 23, 1792	1	71
Jerusha, m. Joseph **HEWITT**, Feb. 19, 1802	1	67
Pitt, s. Elihu & Lucy, b. Feb. 21, 1796	1	12
Timothy H., m. Lucy M. **GILBERT**, b. of Brooklyn, [June]		
24, [1826], by Rev. A. Edson	4	24
MURDOCK, Andrew, Capt., d. Jan. 1, 1805	1	51
Dorcas, d. Zerah & Dorcas, b. Jan. 9, 1785, at Amena,		
Dutchess County, State of New York	1	13
Dorcas, m. Henry Tolman **FRANKLIN**, Dec. 27, 1801	1	65
MURR[A]Y, James Henry, s. James, jeweler, ae 21, & Bridget,		
ae 20, b. Apr. 10, 1849	2	100
NAURSE, Samuel, of Pomfret, m. Betsey **CLARK**, of Brooklyn,		
May 11, 1824, by Rev. James Porter, of Pomfret	4	17
NEWBURY, Carlton B., m. Mary H. **JAMES**, Oct. 2, [1831], by		
Geo[rge] J. Tillotson	4	46
Charlotte E., d. Edwin, manufacturer, ae 50, & Lucy, ae		
46, b. Feb. 6, 1850	2	121
Charlotte E., d. May 29, 1850, an infant	2	122
Charlotte Elizabeth, d. Edwin & Lucy Maria, b. June 4, 1834	2	40
Edwin, m. Lucy Maria **JAMES**, b. of Brooklyn, [Apr.] 25,		
1824, by Ambrose Edson	4	17
Edwin James, s. Edwin & Lucy Maria, b. Feb. 19, 1826	2	40
Frances Elizabeth, d. Edwin & Lucy Maria, b. Feb. 8 1840	2	40

	Vol.	Page

NEWBURY, (cont.)

Helen Maria, d. Edwin & Lucy Maria, b. Apr. 19, 1825 — 2 — 40

Henry, s. Edwin & Lucy Maria, b. Mar. 11, 1829;
d. May 23, 1834 — 2 — 40

Henry Dwight, s. Edwin & Lucy Maria, b. Aug. 28, 1836 — 2 — 40

Mary Jane, d. Edwin & Lucy Maria, b. Jan. 19, 1831 — 2 — 40

NEWLAND, Joseph Priestly, Dr., of Utica, N. Y., m. Mary Ann
SEARLES, of Brooklyn, Sept. 9, 1838, by Rev. William
Coe — 4 — 67

NEY, [see also NYE], Drusilla, m. Abner **DOWNING,** Feb. 10,
1820 — 2 — 17

Esther, m. John **POOLER,** Dec. 15, 1814 — 1 — 74

NILES, Charlotte Hyde, d. George A. & Dolly, b. Apr. 15, 1829 — 2 — 41

Daniel Bennett, s. George A. & Dolly, b. Oct. 18, 1831 — 2 — 41

Lydia, of Pomfret, m. Stephen **WHEELER,** of Brooklyn,
Mar. 11, 1821, by John Parish, J. P. — 3 — 3

Lydia, of Pomfret, m. Stephen **WHEELER,** of Brooklyn, Mar.
11, 1821, by John Parish, J. P. — 4 — 14

William, m. Roxanna **RUSSELL,** b. of Brooklyn, Nov. 16,
1826, by Rev. Samuel J. May — 4 — 26

NORTON, Abijah, m. Eunice **ZEBEDEE,** Nov. 14, 1820, by John
Parish, J. P. — 4 — 13

Abijah, m. Eunice **ZEBEDEE,** Dec. 15, 1820, by John Parish,
J. P. — 3 — 2

NOTT*, Joseph, m. Eunice **MERRET,** Dec. 16, 1799 (*Should be
"SCOTT". Corrected by L. B. B.) — 1 — 76

NOURSE, [see under NAURSE]

NYE, [see also NEY], James, m. Sophronia **BAKER,** b. of
Brooklyn, July 4, 1841, by Rev. Geo[rge] J. Tillotson — 4 — 74

Samuel G., m. Amelia M. W. **SYMONDS,** b. of Danielsonville,
Dec. 25, 1854, by Rev. C. Y. DeNormandie — 4 — 115

O'BRIEN, O'BRIAN, Betsey, m. Titus **ADAMS,** June 23, 1805 — 1 — 60

Betsey, m. Titus **ADAMS,** b. of Brooklyn, June 23, 1805,
by John Parrish, J. P. — 3 — 6

OLIN, Solomon, m. Hannah **GREEN,** Sept. 8, 1843, by Sam[ue]l
Webb, J. P. — 4 — 78

OLNEY, Frances Harriet, of Pomfret, m. Barnabus **PHINNEY,** of
Lee, Mass., [Sept.] 21, [1828], by Rev. Ambrose Edson — 4 — 33

PAINE, Anne, m. David **DENISON,** Dec. 3, 1789 — 1 — 63

Daniel, m. Mehetable **LESTER,** Dec. 2, 1790 — 1 — 74

Lydia, d. Seth, Jr. & Lydia, b. Apr. 27, 1786 — 1 — 1

Lydia, d. Seth, Jr. & Lydia, b. Apr. 27, 1786 — 1 — 14

Mabel, w. Seth, d. Feb. 21, 1792 — 1 — 54

Mary, d. Seth, Jr. & Lydia, b. Dec. 17, 1788 — 1 — 14

Mary, Mrs. m. Phinehas **SEARLS,** b. of Brooklyn, Aug. 28,
1825, by Rev. Samuel J. May — 4 — 22

Nathan, of Pomfret, m. Mary **WITTER,** of Brooklyn, Feb.
26, 1807, by John Parish, J. P. — 3 — 4

	Vol.	Page
PAINE, (cont.)		
Rebeckah, d. Seth & Lydia, b. Oct. 27, 1790	1	14
Sarah S., m. John **GRAY**, Jr., Mar. 4, [1833], by Rev.		
Samuel J. May	4	49
Seth, d. Feb. 24, 1792	1	54
PALMER, Alfred, of Windham, m. Abigail **PARKHURST**, of		
Brooklyn, Oct. 16, 1839, by Rev. Benj[ami]n N. Harris	4	69
Alfred, of Windham, m. Caroline **PARKHURST**, of Brooklyn,		
[Feb.] 21 [1843], by Rev. Tho[ma]s Huntington	4	78
Amos, m. Lucina **CLEVELAND**, Mar. 3, 1816	1	74
Avery G., m. Lucy **STANBURY**, b. of Brooklyn, Jan. 30,		
1823, by John Parish, J. P.	3	3
Avery G., m. Lucy **STANBURY**, b. of Brooklyn, Jan. 30,		
1823, by John Parish, J. P.	4	14
Benjamin E., m. Susan **SPAULDING**, Nov. 24, 1812	1	74
Cordelia, d. Amos & Lucina, b. Sept. 9, 1819	1	247
Ernest Greenwood, s. Francis S., merchant, ae 28, of		
Mobile, Ala., & Mary A., ae 27, b. June 3, [1849]	2	95
Frank Spaulding, s. Benjamin E. & Susan, b. July 21, 1820	1	247
Henry, of Plainfield, m. Caroline E. **DORRANCE**, of		
Brooklyn, [Mar.] 4, [1830], by Rev. Ambrose Edson	4	40
John, merchant, ae 31, b. Ashford, res. Brooklyn, m.		
Frances M. **DAVISON**, ae 23, Sept. 16, 1850, by Rev. R.		
Camp	2	126
John, m. Frances M. **DAVISON**, Sept. 16, 1850, by Rev. R.		
Camp	4	102
John Gray, s. Amos & Lucina, b. Apr. 17, 1817	1	247
Joseph, merchant's clerk, d. Mar. 24, 1850, ae 24	2	108
Joseph Henry, s. Benjamin E. & Susan, b. Mar. 12, 1826	2	45
Lois, m. John **KENDALL**, Mar. 8, 1781	1	69
Lucretia Maria, d. Benjamin E. & Susan, b. Sept. 20, 1815	1	247
Lucretia Maria, m. Henry **WASHBURN**, Jr., of Taunton,		
Mass., Nov. 20, [1833], by E. B. Kellogg	4	52
Lucy, m. Elisha **MORSE**, Sept. 23, 1792	1	71
Lydia, d. Thaddeus & Thankful, b. May 23, 1790	1	14
Nathaniel M., s. Orrin T., tailor, ae 33, & Eliza P.,		
ae 31, b. Oct. 21, 1849	2	107
Sophia C., m. Isaac **MOFFITT**, b. of Killingly, Mar. 29,		
1835, by Daniel Williams, Elder	4	58
Thaddeus, s. Thaddeus & Thankful, b. Apr. 2, 1788	1	14
William Scott, s. Orrin T., tailor, ae 31, & Elizabeth		
B., ae 29, b. Aug. 21, 1847	2	78
PARK, PARKE, PARKS, PARKES, Eunice, m. James **HERRICK**,		
Dec. 23, 1804	1	67
Henry, of Providence, m. Emily **KINYON**, of Sterling, Feb. 4,		
1838, by Rev. G. J. Tillotson	4	66
Joseph, m. Minerva **JENKS**, b. of Brooklyn, Dec. 16, 1824,		
by John Parrish, J. P.	3	10

	Vol.	Page
PARK, PARKE, PARKS, PARKES, (cont.)		
Joseph, m. Minerva **JENKS**, b. of Brooklyn, Dec. 16, 1824,		
by John Parish, J. P.	4	18
Joseph, s. Joseph & Minerva, b. Feb. 11, 1829	2	44
Sarah A., of Brooklyn, m. Francis P. **DOWNING**, of Pomfret,		
Apr. 26, 1849, by Rev. E. Loomis	4	100
Sarah Ann, d. Joseph & Minerva, b. May 29, 1825	2	44
William, s. Joseph & Minerva, b. Aug. 19, 1831	2	44
PARKER, Alithea, d. Clark & Polly L., b. Aug. 3, 1825	2	46
Alithea, d. May 14, [1849], ae 23	2	106
Alpheas Brown, s. Clark & Polly L., b. Mar. 25, 1827	2	46
Anna, m. Amasa **POOLER**, Oct. 10, 1819	1	74
Charles Clark, s. Clark & Polly L., b. Oct. 18, 1823	2	46
Clark, m. Polly L. **BROWN**, Nov. 11, 1816	2	46
Gurdon, s. Clark & Polly L., b. Sept. 20, 1818	2	46
Lucius Prior, s. Ephraim & Lucy, b. Aug. 31, 1795	1	15
Nancy, of Brooklyn, m. James **ALLEN**, of New Lisbon, N. Y.,		
Oct. 24, 1821, by Vine Robinson, J. P.	4	4
PARKHURST, Abigail, d. Jonathan & Lois, b. Feb. 21, 1812, at		
Plainfield	1	247
Abigail, of Brooklyn, m. Alfred **PALMER**, of Windham, Oct.		
16, 1839, by Rev. Benj[ami]n N. Harris	4	69
Caroline, d. Jonathan & Lois, b. Oct. 18, 1818	1	247
Caroline, of Brooklyn, m. Alfred **PALMER**, of Windham,		
[Feb.] 21, [1843], by Rev. Tho[ma]s Huntington	4	78
Charles Spaulding, s. Jonathan & Lois, b. Nov. 8, 1814,		
at Plainfield	1	247
Harriet, d. Jonathan & Lois, b. Aug. 9, 1816, at Plainfield	1	247
Harriet, of Brooklyn, m. Jacob C. **WARREN**, of Killingly,		
Mar. 29, 1842, by Rev. Thomas Huntington	4	75
Jonathan, m. Lois **PIERCE**, Nov. 13, 1809	1	74
Lucretia, d. Jonathan & Lois, b. Dec. 8, 1820	1	247
Lucretia, of Brooklyn, m. Edmund L. **WARREN**, of Killingly,		
[Mar.] 13, [1844], by Rev. Thomas Huntington	4	79
PARKS, [see under **PARK**]		
PARRISH, PARISH, Elizabeth, w. John, d. Jan. 6, 1802	1	54
George L., carpenter, b. Pomfret, res. Brooklyn, d. Aug.		
7, [1850] or 1851], ae 25	2	131
Harriet, ae 16, of Brooklyn, m. George H. **HUTCHINS**,		
laborer, ae 21, b. Pomfret, res. Brooklyn, Aug. 17, 1847,		
by Abiel Converse, J. P.	2	81
John, m. Elizabeth **WHITNEY**, May 30, 1790	1	74
Lucretia A., of Pomfret, m. Hollis **PERRIN**, of Brooklyn,		
Apr. 13, 1846, by Rev. G. J. Tillotson	4	84
Rufus, m. Sally **BADGER**, Sept. 26, 1799, by John Parrish,		
J. P.	3	1
Sarah Maria, of Brooklyn, m. Joseph Henry **GALLUP**, of		
Preston, Nov. 21, 1834, by Rev. Samuel J. May	4	56

	Vol.	Page

PARRISH, PARISH , (cont.)

Sybbel, m. Lemuel (?) **WEEKS**, b. of Pomfret, Mar. 6, 1809,
by John Parrish, J. P. — 3 — 5

PATRICK, Eliza F., d. William, farmer, & Margaret, b. Mar.
14, 1850 — 2 — 117

PATTENGALL, Betsey, m. Simeon **BUTTS**, Jan. 17, 1797 — 1 — 61

PECK, James W., m. Caroline M. **LADD**, b. of Boston, Nov. 29,
1846, by Rev. Herman Snow — 4 — 85

PECKHAM, Mary Adalaide, d. Robert C., Jr., butcher, ae 37, &
Sarah A., ae 35, b. Mar. 31, 1848 — 2 — 91

PELLET, Betsey, d. Jonathan & Hannah, b. Mar. 7, 1787 — 1 — 14

Eunice, m. Hosea **HARRIS**, Jan. 8, 1792 — 1 — 67

Gurdon, s. Jonathan & Hannah, b. Dec. 25, 1790 — 1 — 15

Palmer, of Canterbury, m. Mary E. **PLACE**, of Canterbury,
July 4, 1848, by Rev. G. J. Tillotson — 2 — 79

Polly, d. Jon[atha]n & Hannah, b. Feb. 20, 1789 — 1 — 14

PENFIELD, Evolin, m. Sophronia **TITUS**, b. of Brooklyn, Nov.
28, [1839], by Rev. William Coe — 4 — 70

PENNIMAN, Caroline M., m. Lucius **SPENCER**, of Pomfret,
[Mar.] 4, [1830], by Rev. Ambrose Edson — 4 — 40

PENROSE, Bernard, of Phila., m. Josephine Ann Smith **HEAD**,
Apr. 28, 1842, by Rev. R. Camp — 4 — 76

PERRIN, PERREN, Cynthia Ann, d. William & Maryetta, b. Apr.
22, 1844 — 2 — 44

Hollis, of Brooklyn, m. Lucretia A. **PARRISH**, of Pomfret,
Apr. 13, 1846, by Rev. G. J. Tillotson — 4 — 84

James Henry, s. William & Maryetta, b. Mar. 14, 1847 — 2 — 44

Jonathan H., s. Hollis, carpenter & Lucretia A., b. Aug.
13, 1849 — 2 — 117

Jonathan H., d. Mar. 15, 1850 — 2 — 118

Polly Lucretia, d. William & Maryetta, b. Aug. 11, 1845 — 2 — 44

PETT, Elizabeth Van, of Brunswick, N. Y., m. William K.
ROBBINS, of Brooklyn, Sept. 20, 1829, by Rev. Samuel
J. May — 4 — 37

PHILLEO, Calvin, Rev., of Ithica, N. Y., m. Prudence **CRANALL**,
of Canterbury, Aug. 12, 1834, by Rev. Geo[rge] J.
Tillotson — 4 — 55

PHILLIPS, Calvin D., s. Pardon, farmer, ae 49, & Mary K.,
ae 33, b. Apr. 28, 1848 — 2 — 88

Catherine M., Mrs., farmer's wife, b. Foster, R. I.,
res. Pomfret, d. Sept. 12, [1848], ae 34 — 2 — 98

Elizabeth, of Brooklyn, m. John L. **BURNHAM**, of Hampton,
Nov. 15, 1846, by Rev. Benja[min] C. Phelps, of West
Killingly — 4 — 87

Lydia A., of Killingly, m. Rufus D. **CURTIS**, of Killingly,
Mar. 6, 1848, by Rev. Ebenezer Loomis — 2 — 79

Lydia A., m. Rufus D. **CURTIS**, b. of Killingly, Mar. 6,
1848, by Rev. E. Loomis — 4 — 88

	Vol.	Page
PHILLIPS, (cont.)		
Polly, m. Heber **HARRIS**, Dec. 8, 1799	1	67
Susan P., of Plainfield, m. Charles **CRAIN**, of Providence,		
R. I., Apr. 5, 1836, by Rev. G. J. Tollotson	4	60
PHINNEY, Barnabus, of Lee, Mass., m. Frances Harriet **OLNEY**,		
of Pomfret, [Sept.] 21, [1828], by Rev. Ambrose Edson	4	33
PIDGE, Abby L, ae 20, of Brooklyn, m. Stephen H. **TRIP[P]**,		
farmer, of Brooklyn, Jan. 11, 1848, by Rev. Ebenezer		
Loomis	2	79
Abby L., m. Stephen H. **TRIPP**, b. of Brooklyn, Jan. 11,		
184[8], by Rev. E. Loomis	4	88
Josiah, m. Mira **WHEELER**, Nov. 27, 1823, by Rev. Samuel		
J. May. Int. pub.	4	15
PIERCE, Abby Mary, of Brooklyn, m. George **TOWNSEND**, of		
Exeter, R. I., Aug. 5, 1827, by Uriel Fuller, J. P.	4	29
Abigail, d. Capt. Delano & Abigail, d. Mar. 10, 1795	1	54
Abigail Mary, d. Erastus & Hannah, b. Mar. 17, 1806	1	246
Amos, s. Thom[as] & Lucy, b. May 14, 1788	1	14
Asa Sapulding, s. Erastus & Hannah, b. June 1, 1808	1	247
Benjamin, m. Lydia **GURLEY**, Dec. 24, 1786	1	74
Betsey, m. Benjamin **GILBERT**, Nov. 20, 1791	1	66
Betsey, d. Timeus & Elizabeth, d. Apr. 2, 1792	1	54
Betsey, d. Timeus & Elizabeth, b. Feb. 20, 1799	1	14
Charles Pinckney, twin with George Frderick, s. Benjamin		
& Lydia, b. Apr. 14, 1802	1	15
Dave, s. Benjamin & Lydia, b. Nov. 5, 1787	1	14
Delano, s. Delano & Abigail, b. July 19, 1786	1	14
Deidama, d. Erastus & Hannah, b. Dec. 9, 1801	1	246
Diadama, of Brooklyn, m. W[illia]m A. **SCARBOROUGH**, of		
Pomfret, [Feb.] 28, [1826], by Rev. A. Edson	4	23
Edward Allen, s. David & Elizabeth, b. Jan. 12, 1841	2	47
Emily, d. Erastus & Hannah, b. Apr. 24, 1804	1	246
Erastus, m. Hannah **CADY**, Feb. 9, 1800	1	74
George Frederick, twin with Charles Pinckney, s. Benjamin		
& Lydia, b. Apr. 14, 1802	1	15
George Gurley, s. David & Elizabeth, b. Nov. 2, 1834	2	47
Henry, s. Benjamin & Lydia, b. Apr. 14, [ ]	1	14
John Hammond, s. Erastus & Hannah, b. Aug. 27, 1800	1	246
Lite, d. Sept. 21, 1804, in the 59th y. of her age	1	54
Lois, d. Delano & Abigail, b. Oct. 6, 1790	1	14
Lois, m. Jonathan **PARKHURST**, Nov. 13, 1809	1	74
Lucy, d. Benjamin & Lydia, b. June 16, 1793	1	15
Lucy, d. Benjamin & Lydia, d. Jan. 2, 1794, in the 1st		
y. of her age	1	54
Lucy, d. Benjamin & Lydia, b. Jan. 23, 1798	1	15
Lucy Maria, of Brooklyn, m. Billings **HAKES**, of Stonington,		
[Aug.] 30, [1829], by Rev. Ambrose Edson	4	36
Maria, d. Benj[amin] & Lydia, b. [ ]	1	14

	Vol.	Page
PIERCE, (cont.)		
Olive, m. Daniel **LITCHFIELD**, Sept. 22, 1796	1	70
Oliver, s. Timeus & Elizabeth, b. Feb. 12, 1789	1	14
Payson Grosvenor, s. Timeus & Elizabeth, b. Sept. 10, 1781	1	14
Rizpah, d. Timeus & Elizabeth, b. July 19, 1783	1	14
Rufus, s. Timeus & Elizabeth, b. June 20, 1785	1	14
Rufus, s. Timeus & Elizabeth, d. Feb. 24, 1786	1	54
Rufus, 2d, s. Timeus & Elizabeth, b. Dec. 24, 1786	1	14
Sarah, m. Benjamin **HERRICK**, Dec. 30, 1790	1	67
Sophia, d. Timeus & Elizabeth, b. Feb. 13, 1780	1	14
Timeus, m. Elizabeth **GROSVENOR**, May 4, 1779	1	74
Timeus, d. Sept. 27, 1802, in the 52nd y. of his age	1	54
PIKE, Abigail, d. Peter & Rachel, b. Aug. 29, 1797	1	246
Abigail, m. Henry **WEBB**, 2d, Apr. 30, 1821, by Rev. Hutchins Taylor	4	3
Asa, s. Nathan & Rebeckah, b. Nov. 18, 1786	1	14
Asa, s. Peter & Rachel, b. Aug. 23, 1799	1	246
Avilda, d. Willard & Molley, b. Mar. 13, 1798	1	15
Betsey, d. Peter & Rachel, b. Oct. 23, 1804	1	246
Betsey, m. Horatio **WEBB**, b. of Brooklyn, Apr. 16, 1826, by Rev. Henry Edes, at Providence, R. I. Int. pub. in Brooklyn	4	24
Ebenezer, s. Willard & Molly, b. Aug. 6, 1788	1	14
George, s. Marsena & Betsey, b. Sept. 29, 1806	1	246
Gordon, s. Peter & Rachel, b. Feb. 19, 1808	1	246
James Dorrance, s. Peter & Rachel, b. Oct. 25, 1795	1	246
Peter, m. Rachel **DORRANCE**, Oct. 14, 1794	1	74
Peter, d. July 30, 1808, ae 63 y.	1	54
Polly, of Brooklyn, m. Samuel **DAVIS**, of Pomfret, Nov. 16, 1826, by Rev. Samuel J. May	4	26
Virgil, s. Peter & Rachel, b. Feb. 6, 1802	1	246
PLACE, Mary E., of Canterbury, m. Palmer **PELLET**, of Canterbury, July 4, 1848, by Rev. G. J. Tillotson	2	79
POND, Charles Fremont, s. Enoch & Sarah Ann, b. Oct. 26, 1856	2	43
George Enoch, s. Enoch & Sarah Ann, b. July 5, 1847	2	43
John Clark, s. Enoch & Sarah Ann, b. June 6, 1853	2	43
Lydia Maria, d. Enoch & Sarah Ann, b. Feb. 23, 1839	2	43
Mary Ann, d. Enoch & Sarah Ann, b. June 23, 1845	2	43
Theodore Dwight, s. Enoch & Sarah Ann, b. Mar. 21, 1842	2	43
POOLER, Amasa, m. Anna **PARKER**, Oct. 10, 1819	1	74
Elijah, s. Amasa & Hannah, b. Mar. 20, 1781	1	14
George Cady, s. John & Esther, b. June 29, 1815	1	247
Hannah, w. Amasa, d. June 17, 1818	1	54
John, s. Amasa & Hannah, b. May 12, 1792	1	15
John, m. Esther **NEY**, Dec. 15, 1814	1	74
Mary Ann, d. John & Esther, b. Oct. 29, 1816	1	247
Royal, s. Amasa & Hannah, b. Sept. 19, 1786	1	14
Septa, s. Amasa & Hannah, b. Sept. 23, 1784	1	14

	Vol.	Page
POTTER, Amey, b. Providence, res. Brooklyn, d. Dec. 16, 1848,		
ae 84	2	97
Edwin G., of Sterling, m. Lydia H. **JEFFERS**, of Woonsocket,		
R. I., [Feb.] 3, [1852], by Geo[rge] G. Channing	4	106
Elizabeth R., of Sterling, m. Leonard **DEAN**, of Eastford,		
Jan. 1, 1852, by Rev. George J. Tilotson	4	108
John Gallup, s. W[illia]m P., farmer, ae 29, & Esther,		
ae 30, b. May 3, 1847	2	89
Julia D., d. William P., agriculturist, & Esther, b. June 3, 1850	2	117
Lucy A., m. James **CLARKE**, b. of Hampton, Sept. 21, 1846,		
by Rev. Benjamin C. Phelps, of West Killingly	4	87
Mary, m. Joseph H. **WILLIAMS**, b. of Brooklyn, [Feb.] 28,		
1830, by John Parish, J. P.	3	11
Mary, m. Joseph H. **WILLIAMS**, b. of Brooklyn, Feb. 28,		
1830, by John Parish, J. P.	3	12
Mary, m. Joseph H. **WILLIAMS**, b. of Brooklyn, Feb. 28,		
1830, by John Parish, J. P.	4	44
William P., m. Esther **GALLUP**, b. of Brooklyn, May 19,		
1842, by Rev. G. J. Tillotson	4	76
PRATT, James A., m. Emeline **GREEN**, b. of Killingly, Dec. 11,		
1853, by Jona[than] A. Welch, J. P.	4	110
Prudy Ann, of Brooklyn, m. Henry **BROWN**, of Pomfret, Aug.		
28, 1842, by Rev. Thomas Huntington	4	77
PRENTICE, John P., of Pomfret, m. Caroline A. **DAVISON**, of		
Brooklyn, Nov. 27, 1845, by Rev. G. J. Tillotson	4	82
PRESTON, Alva, of Hampton, m. Olive **LITCHFIELD**, of		
Brooklyn, Aug. 18, 1830, by Rev. Ambrose Edson	4	42
Augustus, s. Enos Lovejoy & Wealthy, b. Nov. 17, 1851,		
at Williamsburgh, N. Y.	2	44
George Henry, s. Enos Lovejoy & We[a]lthy, b. July 6, 1839	2	44
Harriet Augusta, d. Enos Lovejoy & Wealthy, b. Dec. 19, 1844	2	44
James Albert, s. Enos Lovejoy & Wealthy, b. Feb. 25, 1843	2	44
James Hyde, s. Enos Lovejoy & Wealthy, b. Sept. 5, 1837;		
d. Sept. 24, 1839	2	44
Levi, of Mansfield, m. Maria **SAUNDERS**, of Brooklyn, Nov.		
23, [1831], by Rev. Samuel J. May	4	47
PRICHARD, Edward, of Derby, Conn., m. Martha M. **DANIELS**,		
of Brooklyn, Sept. 8, 1851, by Rev. G. J. Tillotson	4	104
PRINCE, Abel, d. Jan. 17, 1819, in the 53rd y. of his age	1	54
Catharine, d. Timothy & Julia, b. Aug. 1, 1845;		
d. [Aug.] 26, [1845]	2	43
David, m. Sophia **ELLSWORTH**, Apr. 18, 1815	1	74
David, s. David & Sophia, b. June 21, 1816	1	247
Deidama, m. Phillip **SCARBOROUGH**, Apr. 4, 1811	1	76
George Frederick, s. Uriah C. & Nancy, b. Oct. 2, 1827;		
d. Mar. 5, 1845	2	43
Helen, d. Timothy, painter, ae 28, & July, ae 25, b. Aug.		
3, 1848	2	78

	Vol.	Page
PRINCE, (cont.)		
John Allen, s. Uriah C. & Nancy, b. Nov. 30, 1822;		
d. Mar. 25, 1838	2	43
Joseph, s. Timothy, Jr. & Deidamia, b. Feb. 17, 1784	2	43
Joseph, m. Henrietta **SCARBOROUGH**, Jan. 1, 1817	1	74
Joseph, m. Henrietta **SCARBOROUGH**, Jan. 1, 1817	2	43
Joseph, d. Jan. 9, 1844	1	54
Julia, housekeeper, b. Hampton, res. Brooklyn, d. July		
6, [1849], ae 25	2	106
Lucy H., d. Timothy & Julia, b. Mar. 26, 1847	2	43
Lucy M., of Brooklyn, m. Jacob W. **DANIELSON,** of		
Killingly, Sept. 11, 1827, by Rev. Ambrose Edson	4	29
Lucy Maria, d. Abel & Lucy, b. Mar. 13, 1805	1	246
Mary Ann, d. Joseph & Henrietta, b. Apr. 4, 1819	2	43
Polly, of Brooklyn, m. William **DENISON,** of Lancaster,		
N. H., [Sept] 3, [1827], by Rev. Samuel J. May	4	30
Timothy, s. Joseph & Henrietta, b. Apr. 18, 1821	2	43
Uriah C., m. Nancy **ALLYN,** Sept. 16, 1821, by Rev. Joseph		
Chickering	4	5
Uriah C., d. Jan. 3, 1844, in the 49th y. of his age	1	54
Uriah Cady, s. Abel & Lucy, b. June 17, 1795	1	246
William, s. Abel & Lucy, b. July 23, 1791	1	246
PROFFET, Excy, m. Obadiah **ALMY,** of Canterbury, Mar. 4, 1816,		
by John Parish, J. P.	3	8
PUTNAM, Anne, m. Cha[rle]s **BACON,** Oct. 20, 1852, by Rev. R.		
Camp	4	108
Anne Coffin, d. Daniel & Katharine, b. Apr. 17, 1793	1	247
Betsey, d. Daniel & Catharine, b. Feb. 18, 1789	1	14
Caroline Mary, m. Edward **FOGG,** Jan. 6, 1834, by Rev. E.		
B. Kellogg	4	53
Catharine, d. Daniel & Catharine, b. Nov. 16, 1785	1	14
Catharine B., d. William H., farmer, & Eliza, b. Oct. 7, 1847	2	85
Daniel, s. William & Mary, b. Feb. 23, 1808	1	246
Elizabeth, d. Daniel & Katharine, b. Sept. 24, 1794	1	246
Elizabeth, m. Dr. Benjamin B. **SPALDING,** b. of Brooklyn,		
Oct. 5, 1836, by Rev. J. M. Bartlett	4	62
Emily, d. Daniel & Katharine, b. Jan. 17, 1800	1	247
Emily, m. James **BROWN,** Apr. 9, 1820	1	61
Harriet G., d. William H. & Eliza, b. Nov. 30, 1834	2	45
Harriet Wadsworth, d. Daniel & Katharine, b. Sept. 22, 1792	1	246
Israel, s. Daniel & Katharine, b. June 5, 1796;		
d. [June] 21, [1796]	1	246
Israel, s. Daniel & Katharine, d. June 21, 1796	1	54
John, s. Peter Schuyler & Lucy, b. May 9, 1786	1	14
John D., s. William H. & Eliza, b. June 19, 1837	2	45
Mary, d. William H. & Eliza, b. Oct. 28, 1835	2	45
Mehetable, m. Dan[ie]l **TYLER,** 2d, Aug. 15, 1771	1	77
Nathan, s. Peter Schuyler & Lucy, b. Aug. 23, 1788	1	14

	Vol.	Page
PUTNAM, (cont.)		
Oliver, s. Peter Schuyler & Lucy, b. Jan. 20, 1794	1	15
Oliver, s. Peter S., d. Apr. 3, 1800	1	54
Peter Schuyler, m. Lucy FRINK, July 9, 1785	1	74
Rufus, s. Reuben & Elizabeth, b. Aug. 1, 1789	1	14
Sarah, d. William H. & Eliza, b. June 29, 1839	2	45
Schuyler, s. Peter Schuyler, & Lucy, b. Jan. 26, 1790	1	14
William, s. Dan[ie]l & Catharine, b. Jan. 1, 1783	1	14
Wiiliam, m. Mary SPAULDING, Apr. 17, 1805	1	74
William, s. William H. & Eliza, b. Jan. 30, 1843	2	45
W[illia]m H., m. Eliza DAY, Mar. 12, 1834, by Rev. E. B. Kellogg	4	53
RAWSON, Geo[rge] Dennis, s. Dennis C., farmer, ae 27, & Eliza, ae 24, b. June 28, 1851	2	127
George Dennis, s. Dennis C. & Elvia* C., b. June 28, 1851 (*Eliza?)	2	50
Royal C., s. Lewis C., farmer, ae 28, & Eliza, ae 27, b. Feb. 10, 1850	2	112
Royal Copeland, s. Dennis C. & Elvia* C., b. Feb. 10, 1850 (*Eliza?)	2	50
READ, REED, Abel Spalding, s. Barzillai & Elizabeth, b. Feb. 20, 1798	1	15
Barzillai, m. Elizabeth SPAULDING, Apr. 9, 1797	1	75
Elizabeth, w. Barzillai, d. Nov. 29, 1802, in the 29th y. of her age	1	55
Loisa, d. Barzillai & Elizabeth b. Nov. 1, 1799	1	15
Loisa, d. Barzillai & Elizabeth, d. Nov. 11, 1799	1	55
Mehetable S., d. Sept. 16, 1829, ae 29 y.	1	55
Mehetable Spaulding, d. Barzillai & Elizabeth, b. May 7, 1801, at Mansfield, Conn.	1	15
Mercy A., m. Russell M. BROWN, of Jewett City, Feb. 15, 1852, by Rev. G. J. Tillotson	4	107
Sarah A., m. Abner JOHNSON, b. of Brooklyn, Mar. 13, 1845, by Rev. G. J. Tillotson	4	81
REYNOLDS, Frances, black, d. Jan. 13, 1848, ae 5 1/2 m.	2	80
Julia, housewife, black, b. Plainfield, res. Brooklyn, d. Sept. 9, 1849, ae 13	2	108
Julia, d. Peter, laborer, black, ae 28, & Jane, black, ae 23, b. Nov. 14, 1850	2	123
RICE, Charles E., s. Joseph W. & Mary, b. Feb. 6, 1811, at Brooklyn, Ct.	1	245
Frances, niece of Joseph W. & Mary Rice, b. July 16, 1803, at Tolland. "Was brought up by Joseph W. & Mary Rice"	1	245
George B., s. Joseph W. & Mary, b. June 22, 1820	1	245
John, m. Mary ALLYN, Nov. 21, 1793	1	75
Joseph W., b. Jan. 19, 1776, at Holden, Mass.	1	245
Joseph W., m. Mary ELDREDGE, Aug. 5, 1804	1	75

	Vol.	Page
RICE, (cont.)		
Joseph W., s. Joseph W. & Mary, b. July 20, 1805, at Groton	1	245
Martha, d. John & Mary, b. Apr. 5, 1794	1	15
Mary, w. John, d. Aug. 6, 1795	1	55
Mary, d. Joseph W. & Mary, b. Aug. 29, 1817	1	245
Sally, servant, of Winchester, Ct., d. June 3, 1848, ae 23	2	80
Samuel E., s. Joseph W. & Mary, b. Apr. 5, 1808, at Groton	1	245
RICH, Mary, m. Joab HALL, b. of Middletown, late residents of		
Brooklyn, Nov. 20, 1825, by David C. Bolles, J. P.	4	21
RICHARDSON, Lorenzo Dow, s. William & Elizabeth, b. May 31,		
1842	2	49
Sarah Ann, d. William & Elizabeth, b. Feb. 15, 1840	2	49
RILEY, Thomas, sailor, ae 25, of Brooklyn, m. Hannah HARRIS,		
ae 16, of Brooklyn, May 21, 1848, by Rev. Tillotson	2	79
Thomas, of Mass., m. Hannah HARRIS, of Brooklyn, May 21,		
1848, by Rev. G. J. Tillotson	4	99
ROATH, Zerviah, of Brooklyn, m. Rev. Charles FITCH, of		
Abington, May 19, [1828], by Rev. Ambrose Edson	4	32
ROBBINS, ROBINS, Adelaide Maria, d. Erastus & Lucy S., b.		
May 31, 1847	2	51
Bethiah, w. Samuel & d. of Nathan & Lydia HAILE, b. Mar.		
28, 1805, at Foster; d. Mar. 28, 1835, at Brooklyn	2	51
Charles Sheffield, s. Samuel & Sophronia, b. Apr. 11,		
1841, at Killingly	2	51
Christopher Mason, s. Theordore F., spectacle maker,		
ae 24, & Harriet L, ae 20, b. Sept. 21, 1849	2	107
Emmy L., d. Sept. 19, 1850, ae 5	2	129
George Martin, s. Samuel & Bethiah, b. Feb. 14, 1835	2	51
Hannah, of Brooklyn, m. Edmund BURNHAM, of Hampton,		
Aug. 13, 1838, by Rev. William Coe	4	66
Hannah Asenath, d. Erastus & Lucy S., b. July 18, 1841	2	51
Hannah Elizabeth, d. Elijah & Mary, b. Nov. 16, 1834	2	50
Harriet Irene, d. Erastus & Lucy S., b. Nov. 18, 1838	2	51
Hellen, d. Theodore F., silversmith, ae 24, & Harriet L.,		
ae 19, b. Aug. 31, 1848	2	95
James Henry, s. Samuel & Bethiah, b. Apr. 14, 1827	2	51
John Mason, s. Samuel & Bethiah, b. Mar. 15, 1829, at		
Hampton	2	51
Joseph Kingsbury, s. Elijah & Mary, b. Aug. 24, 1831	2	50
Lucy Jane, d. Erastus & Lucy S., b. Jan. 5, 1834	2	51
Lydia A., ae 19, b. Brooklyn, res. Plainfield, m. Perry		
G. TRIPP, farmer, ae 24, of Plainfield, Mar. 5, 1848, by		
Elder Ebenezer Loomis	2	87
Lydia A., of Brooklyn, m. Perry G. TRIPP, of Plainfield,		
Mar. 6, 1848, by Rev. E. Loomis	4	88
Lydia Ann, d. Elijah & Mary, b. Jan. 10, 1828	2	50
Mary Maria, d. Elijah & Mary, b. July 8, 1839	2	50
Maryett, d. Erastus & Lucy S., b. Apr. 9, 1836	2	51

	Vol.	Page
ROBBINS, ROBINS, (cont.)		
Nathan Haile, s. Samuel & Bethiah, b. May 15, 1831	2	51
Ruama Ann, m. George Washington **WHEATON**, [Nov.] 25,		
[1833], by Rev. Samuel J. May	4	52
Samuel, s. John & Hannah, b. Apr. 16, 1803	2	51
Samuel, m. Bethiah **HAILE**, Jan. 4, 1824	2	51
Samuel, m. Sophronia **BARD**, b. of Brooklyn, Nov. 26, 1837,		
by Rev. G. J. Tillotson	4	65
Simon A., d. July 26, [1848], ae 9 y. 26 d.	2	91
Theodore F., silversmith, ae 23, of Brooklyn, m. Harriet		
L. **BUTTS**, ae 17, of Brooklyn, Nov. 23, 1847, by Rev.		
T. Huntingon	2	79
Theodore F., m. Harriet L. **BUTTS**, b. of Brooklyn, [Nov.]		
25, [1847], by Rev. Tho[ma]s Huntington	4	99
Theodore Frances, s. Samuel & Bethiah, b. Dec. 1, 1824,		
at Foster	2	51
Timothy Dwight, s. Erastus & Lucy S., b. Oct. 6, 1844	2	51
William K., of Brooklyn, m. Elizabeth **VAN PETT**, of		
Brunswick, N. Y., Sept. 20, 1829, by Rev. Samuel J. May	4	37
ROBINSON, Alfred M., s. David, gentleman, ae 35, & Ellen, ae		
25, b. Oct. 19, 1850	2	107
Alice, d. Edwin, farmer, ae 51, & Sarah T., ae 32, b.		
May 12,. 1848	2	78
Anna, wid. Jacob, d. Dec. 8, 1851, in the 83rd y. of her age	1	55
Daniel C., m. Pamelia **KIES**, [Sept.] 22, [1828], by Rev.		
Ambrose Edson	4	33
Daniel Chapman, s. Vine & Dorcas, b. June 11, 1803	1	15
David, of Buffalo, N. Y., m. Ellen M. **WHEATON**, of		
Brooklyn, Oct. 10, 1844, by Rev. G. J. Tillotson	4	80
Edwin, s. Vine & Dorcas, b. July 22, 1797	1	15
Edwin, m. Sarah T. **WILLIAMS**, b. of Brooklyn, May 6, 1844,		
by Rev. G. J. Tillotson	4	80
Eliza, weaver in factory, b. Windham, res. Brooklyn, d.		
Sept. 22, [1850], ae 25	2	131
Erastus, Dr., m. Martha **CHANNING**, Apr. 23, 1809	1	75
Francis, s. Vine & Dorcas, b. Aug. 19, 1814	1	248
Gurdon, s. Vine & Dorcas, b. Oct. 17, 1792	1	15
Harriet, d. Vine & Dorcas, b. July 23, 1791, at Tolland	1	15
Harriet, m. Adams **WHITE**, Mar. 24, 1812	1	78
Nancy P., d. Dr. E. & Martha, b. May 6, 1811	1	15
Rufus P., b. Mobile, Ala., res. Brooklyn, d. Apr. 5,		
[1851], ae 13 y.	2	124
Sarah Ann, d. Erastus & Martha, b. Sept. 13, 1813	1	248
ROGERS, Mary M., ae 18, of Pomfret, m. Henry P. **CLEVELAND**,		
laborer, ae 19, of Brooklyn, Jan. 9, 1848, by Rev. T.		
Huntington	2	79
Mary Maria, m. Henry P. **CLEVELAND**, b. of Brooklyn,		
[Jan.] 9, [1848], by Rev. Thomas Huntington	4	88

	Vol.	Page

ROOD, G. H., of Killingly, m. Millia **HAWKINS**, of Brooklyn,
    May 16, 1849, by Rev. J. Ferris. Int. pub. May 13, 1849   4   100
    George H., carpenter, ae 29, b. N. Y. State, res. Killingly,
    m. Matilda **HAWKINS**, ae 20, b. Killingly, res. Killingly,
    May 16, 1849, by Jacob Ferris   2   100
ROSS, Arba, s. Levi & Miranda, b. Apr. 11, 1831; d. Dec. 13, 1834   2   50
    Jane, d. Levi & Miranda, b. Mar. 8, 1833   2   50
    John Gallup, s. Levi & Miranda, b. Aug. 16, 1841   2   50
    Levi, m. Miranda **ADAMS**, b. of Brooklyn, Mar. 2, 1830,
    by Rev. John O., Birdsall, at the house of Elisha Adams   4   39
    Mariah, twin with Miranda, d. Levi & Miranda, b. July 6, 1836   2   50
    Miranda, twin with Mariah, d. Levi & Miranda, b. July 6, 1836   2   50
    William, s. Levi & Miranda, b. Aug. 31, 1838   2   50
ROTHWELL, James, of Killingly, m. Emily **AYELSWORTH**, of
    Brooklyn, May 6, 1846, by Rev. Benjamin C. **PHELPS**,
    of West Killingly   4   84
    William, b. England, d. May 28, 1850, ae 17   2   120
RUDE, Elias, s. James & Hannah, b. Jan. 18, 1806   1   15
    James, m. Hannah **BUTTS**, Oct. 10, 1801   1   75
    Maria, d. James & Hannah, b. Dec. 14, 1801   1   15
RUSS, Philip F., m. Catharine **AMES**, from Williamantic, Oct.
    18, 1846, by Rev. Herman Snow   4   84
RUSSELL, Henry, of Grafton, Mass., m. Mary **BAKER**, of
    Brooklyn, Oct. 14, 1844, by Rev. Geo[rge] J. Tillotson   4   80
    Roxanna, m. William **NILES**, b. of Brooklyn, Nov. 16, 1826,
    by Rev. Samuel J. May   4   26
SABIN, Joseph Lampson, s. Charles G. & Emily, b. Aug. 24, 1841   2   54
SALISBURY, Sarah, d. David J., farmer, ae 33, & Elizabeth S.,
    ae 24, b. Oct. 14, 1848   2   103
SAMPSON, Rheuama, m. George R. **MALBONE**, June [ ], 1824,
    by John Paine   4   17
SANGER, Faith, b. in Woodstock, now of Woodstock, m. George
    M. **WILLIAMS**, b. in Foster, R. I., now of Killingly, July
    16, 1854, by Rev. Charles Morse   4   114
SAUNDERS, Maria, of Brooklyn, m. Levi **PRESTON**, of
    Mansfield, Nov. 23, [1831], by Rev. Samuel J. May   4   47
SCARBOROUGH, Albegence, s. Joseph & Deliverance, b. Apr. 1,
    1796   1   13
    Amelia, d. Luther & Nancy, b. Oct. 22, 1809   1   248
    Betsey, d. Ebenezer & Mary, b. Apr. 26, 1818   2   53
    Betsey, m. Lewis L. **WELD**, b. of Brooklyn, Jan. 5, 1842,
    by Rev. G. J. Tillotson   4   75
    Catharine, d. Phillip & Deidama, b. Sept. 6, 1823   2   53
    Catharine, of Brooklyn, m. Albert **CONANT**, of Bridgewater,
    Mass., Dec. 27, 1848, by Rev. J. Ferris. Int. pub. Dec.
    24, 1848   4   101
    Catharine, ae 25, b. Brooklyn, Ct., res. N. Y., m.
    Albert **CONANT**, "draughtsman", ae 27, b. Vermont, res.

	Vol.	Page

SCARBOROUGH, (cont.)

	Vol.	Page
N. Y., Dec. 29, 1848, by Jacob Ferris	2	97
Charles, s. Perrin & Lucy P., b. Dec. 27, 1833	2	54
Charlotte Elizabeth, d. Perrin & Hannah, b. July 4, 1844	2	54
Daniel El[l]sworth, s. Luther & Nancy, b. Nov. 15, 1811	1	248
David, s. Samuel, Jr. & Molly, b. Dec. 13, 1804	1	249
David, s. Samuel & Molly, d. Feb. 15, 1823, ae 18 y.	1	56
Deborah, m. Giles R. **ELDREDGE**, Jan. 2, 1806	1	64
Dellilah, d. Joseph & Deliverance, b. May 10, 1782	1	16
Deliverance, w. Joseph, d. Aug. 25, 1823, ae 68 y.	1	53
Eben[eze]r, s. Eben[eze]r & Hannah, b. Sept. 22, 1781	1	16
Ebenezer, m. Mary **DABNEY**, Apr. 10, 1814	2	53
Ebenezer, Jr., m. Hannah M. **LESTER**, Mar. 3, 1851, by Rev.		
Thomas O. Rice	4	103
Edwin, s. Samuel, Jr. & Molly, b. Feb. 21, 1811	1	249
Edwin, s. Ebenezer & Mary, b. May 29, 1822	2	53
Edwin, m. Nancy D. **BROWN**, Feb. 21, 1844	2	56
Edwin W., twin with Frank G., s. Perrin & Lucy P., b.		
Jan. 28, 1823	2	53
Elizabeth Brown, d. Edwin & Nancy D., b. Sept. 22, 1850	2	56
Emmille, d. Joseph & Deliverance, b. Aug. 12, 1793	1	13
Emmille, d. Joseph & Deliverance, d. Mar. 6, 1796	1	56
Emily, d. Ebenezer & Mary, b. Apr. 1, 1820	2	53
Emily, of Brooklyn, m. John D. **BIGELOW**, of Brookfield,		
Mass., Oct. 27, 1840, by Rev. G. J. Tillotson	4	73
Emily Thompson, d. Edwin & Nancy D., b. June 30, 1846	2	56
Esther D., of Brooklyn, m. Rev. Mason **GROSVENOR**, of		
Ashfield, Mass., June 19, 1833, by Rev. Geo[rge] J.		
Tillotson	4	51
Esther Delia, d. Joel & Lucretia, b. Aug. 10, 1812	1	248
Fanny Maria, d. Joseph, 2d, & Deborah, b. Oct. 23, 1802	1	16
Frances A., d. Philip & Diadamia, b. June 22, 1812	1	253
Frances A., of Brooklyn, m. Simon R. **ESTABROOK**, of		
Holden, Mass., Mar. 30, 1830, by Rev. Samuel J. May	4	42
Frances Ella, d. Perrin & Hannah, b. Nov. 19, 1842	2	54
Frank G., twin with Edwin W., s. Perrin & Lucy P., b.		
Jan. 28, 1823	2	53
Frederick, twin with George, s. Joseph, Jr. & Deborah,		
b. Apr. 5, 1805	1	13
Freeman, s. Perrin & Lucy P. b. June 24, 1830	2	54
George, twin with Frederick, s. Joseph, Jr. & Deborah,		
b. Apr. 5, 1805	1	13
George, s. Sam[ue]l, Jr. & Molly, b. July 28, 1806	1	249
Harriet D., d. Ebenezer & Mary, b. Dec. 25, 1815	2	53
Harriet D., of Brooklyn, m. George H. **SHARP**, of Pomfret,		
Nov. 9, 1842, by Rev. G. J. Tillotson	4	77
Harry, s. Perrin & Lucy P., b. May 23, 1818	2	53
Hellen Amanda, d. Edwin & Nancy D., b. Nov. 9, 1844;		

	Vol.	Page
SCARBOROUGH, (cont.)		
d. Aug. 8, 1847	2	56
Henrietta, m. Joseph **PRINCE**, Jan. 1, 1817	1	74
Henrietta, m. Joseph **PRINCE**, Jan. 1, 1817	2	43
Herbert, s. Philip & Diadamia, b. Apr. 6, 1820	1	253
Jared, s. Joseph & Deliverance, b. Jan. 26, 1781	1	16
Jeremiah, s. Joseph & Deliverance, b. Nov. 27, 1788	1	13
Jeremiah, Dea., d. Nov. 22, 1790	1	56
Jeremiah, m. Lucy **SMITH**, Nov. 25, 1813	1	76
Jeremiah, d. Apr. 3, 1830, in the 42nd y. of his age	1	53
Joel, s. Joseph & Deliverance, b. Sept. 28, 1784	1	16
Joel, m. Lucretia **SMITH**, Apr. 17, 1808	1	76
Joel, d. Sept. 27, 1824	1	53
Joel Kingsbury, s. Joel & Lucretia, b. Nov. 12, 1824	2	54
John, s. Joseph, Jr. & Deborah, d. May 4, 1813	1	13
Joseph, m. Deliverance **KINGSBURY**, Feb. 24, 1780	1	76
Joseph, 2d, m. Deborah **THAYER**, Oct. 30, 1798	1	76
Joseph, s. Joseph, 2d, & Deborah, b. Nov. 12, 1800	1	16
Joseph, s. Joseph, 2d & Deborah, d. Nov. 14, 1800	1	56
Joseph, d. Aug. 22, 1827	1	53
Joseph Abbott, s. Luther & Nancy, b. Oct. 24, 1813	1	248
Joseph Kingsbury, s. Joseph & Deliverance, b. Jan. 18, 1792	1	13
Joseph May, s. Theodore & Caroline, b. Apr. 22, 1840	2	54
Kate Louisa, d. Perrin & Hannah, b. June 3, 1847	2	54
Lizzie, d. Edwin, farmer, ae 40, & Nancy, ae 30, b. Sept. 22, 1850	2	127
Lucretia M., of Brooklyn, m. Joseph S. **WOODBRIDGE**, of Columbus, Ga., Sept. 1, 1852, by Rev. Geo[rge] J. Tillotson	4	107
Lucretia Minor, d. Joel & Lucretia, d. Aug. 25, 1813	1	56
Lucretia Minor, d. Joel & Lucretia, b. Sept. 1, 1810	1	249
Lucretia Miner, d. Jeremiah & Lucy, b. Jan. 18, 1830	2	54
Lucy, d. Perrin & Lucy P., b. Oct. 21, 1820	2	53
Lucy P., housekeeper, b. Brooklyn, Ct., res. Hingham, Mass., m. Daniel **THAXTER**, optician, b. Hingham, Mass., res. Hingham, Mass., Dec. 26, 1850, by Theodore Parker	2	125
Lucy Prince, d. Philip & Deidama, b. Apr. 16, 1816	1	253
Lucy Smith, d. Jeremiah & Lucy, b. Jan. 24, 1827; d. May 16, 1835	2	54
Luther, s. Joseph & Deliverance, b. May 12, 1787	1	16
Luther, m. Nancy **EL[L]SWORTH**, Nov. 15, 1808	1	76
Mary, w. Samuel, d. Sept. 26, 1810, in the 65th y. of her age	1	56
Mary, d. Perrin & Lucy P., b. July 1, 1827	2	54
Mary, m. Lysander **CARDER**, b. of Brooklyn, Oct. 16, 1837, by Rev. G. J. Tillotson	4	64
Mary Ann, d. Joel & Lucretia, b. Mar. 2, 1817	1	253
Molly, wid. Samuel, d. Jan. 13, 1838, ae 70 y.	1	53

	Vol.	Page
SCARBOROUGH, (cont.)		
Nelson, s. Perrin & Lucy P., b. Mar. 21, 1825; d. Jan. 20, 1826	2	54
Nelson, s. Perrin & Lucy P., d. Jan. 20, 1826	1	53
Perrin, s. Samuel & Molly, b. Feb. 10, 1786	1	16
Perrin, s. Sam[ue]l & Mary, b. Sept. 12, 1808	1	249
Perrin, m. Lucy P. **WILLIAMS**, Apr. 11, 1813	1	76
Perrin, s. Perrin & Lucy, b. Apr. 25, 1816	1	253
Phillip, s. Samuel & Molly, b. Feb. 24, 1788	1	16
Phillip, m. Deidama **PRINCE**, Apr. 4, 1811	1	76
Polly, d. Samuel & Molly, b. Jan. 3, 1775	1	16
Polly, m. Wolcot[t] Roger **WILLIAMS**, Mar. 6, 1794	1	78
Samuel, Jr., m. Molly **GILBERT**, Oct. 7, 1803	1	76
Samuel, Sr., s. Dea. Jeremiah, d. May 8, 1812, in the 72nd y. of his age	1	56
Samuel, s. Perrin & Lucy, b. Mar. 26, 1814	1	248
Samuel, s. Perrin & Lucy P., d. Sept. 3, 1818	1	53
Samuel, d. Oct. 23, 1838, in the 66th y. of his age	1	53
Samuel May, s. Philip & Diadamia, b. Mar. 13, 1822	1	253
Samuel May, s. Phillip & Didamia, d. Sept. 29, 1822	1	53
Theodore, s. Philip & Dadama, b. Mar. 19, 1814	1	248
Theodore, farmer, d. Aug. 11, [1850], ae 35	2	110
W[illia]m A., of Pomfret, m. Diadama **PIERCE**, of Brooklyn, [Feb.] 28, [1826], by Rev. A. Edson	4	23
William Amedon, s. Joseph, 2d, & Deborah, b. Sept. 21, 1799	1	16
William Smith, s. Joel & Lucretia, b. Aug. 2, 1814	1	248
----, s. Samuel, Jr. & Molly, b. Dec. 26, 1809; lived about 3 hours	1	249
----, d. Edwin, farmer, ae 39, & Nancy, ae 30, st. b. Sept. 30, 1849	2	112
----, d. Perrin, farmer, ae 41, & Hannah, ae 36, b. May 8, 1850	2	112
SCOTT, Emily, twin with Harriet, d. Joseph & Eunice, b. Apr. 11, 1805	1	13
George, s. Joseph & Eunice, b. Nov. 4, 1802	1	13
Harriet, twin with Emily, d. Joseph & Eunice, b. Apr. 11, 1805	1	13
Joseph, m. Eunice **MERRET**, Dec. 16, 1799 (Arnold Copy has "Joseph **NOTT**". Corrected by L. B. B.)	1	76
Joseph, s. Joseph & Eunice, b. Apr. 30, 180[ ]	1	16
SCRANTON, Richard, of Middletown, m. Ardelia **WHITFORD**, of Brooklyn, Aug. 14, 1838, by Rev. William Coe	4	67
SEARLES, **SEARLS**, Alice, d. John & Deborah, b. Jan. 27, 1809	2	52
Alice, m. Armin **BOLLES**, b. of Brooklyn, Apr. 8, 1839, by Rev. Thomas Huntington	4	68
Alithea, d. Phinehas & Alithea, b. Oct. 27, 1818	1	253
Alitheia, w. Phinehas, d. Feb. 15, 1825, ae 39 y.	1	53
Almary, d. Phinehas & Alithea, b. Aug. 12, 1822	2	52
Betsey, d. John & Betsey, b. Dec. 18, 1819	2	52
Betsey, m. David **GREENSLIT**, May 26, 1840, by Rev. Tho[ma]s Huntington	4	73

	Vol.	Page
SEARLES, SEARLS, (cont.)		
Charles, s. Phinehas & Alithea, b. July 5, 1815	1	248
Charles Hall, s. Richard H. & Sarah, b. Mar. 9, 1822	2	52
Charles Salter, s. Joel C. & Serviah, b. May 6, 1809	1	249
Daniel, s. Phinehas & Alithia, b. Feb. 15, 1825	2	53
Deborah, w. John, d. Sept. 19, 1814	1	53
Elijah, s. Joel C. & Zibiah, b. Mar. 25, 1816	1	248
George, s. Joel C. & Serviah, b. Oct. 4, 1807	1	249
Harriet, d. Phinehas & Martha*, b. May 28, 1805;		
d. July 8, following (*Alethea?)	1	13
Harriet, d. Phinehas & Alethea, d. July 8, 1805	1	56
Harriet, d. Joel C. & Zibah, b. Oct. 16, 1818	2	52
Joel C., m. Serviah **CLEVELAND**, Nov. 29, 1805	1	76
John, s. Salter & Alice, b. Aug. 12, 1781	1	2
John, s. Salter & Alice, b. Aug. 12, 1781	1	16
John, m. Deborah **BAKER**, Nov. 28, 1807	1	76
John, m. Betsey **TYLER**, June 2, 1816	1	76
John Salter, s. John & Deborah, b. Mar. 5, 1813	2	52
Laura, d. Joel C. & Serviah, b. June 18, 1811	1	249
Lewis, s. Phinehas & Mary, b. Sept. 2, 1828	2	54
Lewis, m. Jane F. **CLEVELAND**, b. of Brooklyn, Dec. 12,		
1853, by Rev. C. Y. DeNormandie	4	111
Maria, d. Richard H. & Sarah, b. Apr. 17, 1823	2	52
Martha Ann, d. Phinehas & Mary, b. Nov. 19, 1826	2	54
Mary Ann, d. Joel C. & Zebiah, b. Nov. 1, 1812	1	248
Mary Ann, of Brooklyn, m. Dr. Joseph Priestly **NEWLAND**,		
of Utica, N. Y., Sept. 9, 1838, by Rev. William Coe	4	67
Phinehas, m. Alathia **BROWN**, Mar. 21, 1802	1	76
Phinehas, m. Mrs. Mary **PAINE**, b. of Brooklyn, Aug. 28,		
1825, by Rev. Samuel J. May	4	22
Polly, m. Samuel **CHAPMAN**, Sept. 28, 1794	1	62
Richard H., m. Sarah **DAVISON**, Sept. 3, 1821, by Vine		
Robinson, J. P.	4	4
Richard Hall, s. Salter & Alice, b. Feb. 5, 1786	1	2
Richard Hall, s. Salter & Alice, b. Feb. 5, 1786	1	16
Sarah, d. John & Betsey, b. Aug. 23, 1822	2	52
William, s. Phinehas & Alithea, b. Jan. 26, 1811	1	248
SHARPE, SHARP, Dolly, m. Capt. Ebenezer **WITTER**, May 11,		
1806	1	78
Evan, m. Emma **TYLER**, Apr. 18, 1831, by Rev. Sam[ue]l J.		
May	4	45
George H., of Pomfret, m. Harriet D. **SCARBOROUGH**, of		
Brooklyn, Nov. 9, 1842, by Rev. G. J. Tillotson	4	77
Sophia, m. Frederick **TYLER**, Feb. 6, 1816	1	77
SHAWONE, Frederick William, s. Lucy **SHAWONE**, & gt. gd. son		
of Lucy **SHAWONE**, b. May 7, 1809	1	248
Lucy had s. Frederick William **SHAWONE**, & gt. gd. son		
of Lucy **SHAWONE**, b. May 7, 1809	1	248

	Vol.	Page
SHAWONE, (cont.)		
Lucy had gt. gd. dau. Eunice Lucinda **FRASIER**, d. of Lucy		
BERIAND, b. Mar. 28, 1813	1	238
SHELDON, Darius, m. Lydia **HATCH**, Nov. 4, 1804	1	76
Deborah Brindley, d. Darius & Lydia, b. May 19, 1806	1	13
Mary Ann, d. Darius & Lydia, b. Jan. 11, 1808	1	13
Susannah, m. John **SIMMONS**, Dec. 16, 1804	1	76
SHEPARD, Abby Moore, d. Eben & Olive, b. Oct. 25, 1813	1	253
Asa, d. Sept. 10, 1836	1	53
Betsey, d. Whitmore & Clarissa, b. Aug. 1, 1791	1	16
Chester, of Brooklyn, m. Mary **FOX**, of Hampton, [Feb.]		
18, [1827], by Rev. A. Edson	4	27
Clarissa, d. Whitmore & Clarissa, b. Nov. 23, 1787	1	16
David, s. Whitmore & Clarrissa, b. Jan. 17, 1785	1	16
David, s. Whitmore & Clarrisa, d. Aug. 2, 1788, ae 4 y.		
6 m. 16 d.	1	56
Eben, m. Olive **BACKUS**, Oct. 18, 1807	1	76
Hannah, w. Asa, d. Sept. 4, 1825	1	53
Henry Augustus, s. Eben & Olive, b. Apr. 23, 1818	1	253
Henry Hall, s. Abram, miller, ae 43, & Hannah, ae 40,		
b. Apr. 7, 1849	2	102
Horace, s. Eben & Olive, b. Apr. 2, 1812	1	249
Josiah, m. Anna **RIGHT**, Nov. 23, 1790	1	76
Julia Bethiah, d. Eben & Olive, b. June 28, 1822	2	52
Mary Clift, d. Eben & Olive, b. July 27, 1810	1	249
Mason Howard, s. Eben & Olive, b. Nov. 13, 1815	1	253
Nathan Backus, s. Eben & Olive, b. Mar. 20, 1809	1	249
Olive Maria, d. Eben & Olive, b. Mar. 19, 1825	2	54
Sterra, s. Whitmore & Clarissa, b. May 31, 1789	1	16
Whitmore, m. Clarrissa **CLEVELAND**, Mar. 10, 1784	1	76
William Leonard, s. Eben & Olive, b. July 29, 1820	1	253
SHEURMAN, Susan, of Brooklyn, m. John W. **HILL**, of Plainfield,		
Oct. 25, 1835, by Rev. Ziba Loveland, of Plainfield	4	59
SHIPPEE, SHIPPEY, Eliza P., housekeeper, b. Coventry, R. I.,		
res. Brooklyn, d. Mar. 2, [1850], ae 23	2	114
Eliza P., d. Albert, farmer, ae 28, & Eliza P., ae 23,		
b. Mar. 2, [1850]	2	114
Henry H., of Brooklyn, m. Julia A. **CORBIN**, of Brooklyn,		
Sept. 15, 1846, by Rev. Benjamin C. Phelps, of West		
Killingly	4	86
Mary G., d. Davis, wagon maker, ae 24, & Eliza, ae 22,		
b. Jan. 22, 1850	2	121
Waterman J., s. Esek, farmer, ae 39, & Catharine M., ae		
32, b. May 17, 1848	2	83
SHOALES, SHOALS, Abby Hutchins, d. Abial & Polly, b. Aug. 3,		
1824	2	53
Albert Eugene, s. Orin & Ardelia L., b. Feb. 12, 1853.		
"Physician Joseph Palmer, Canterbury"	2	55

	Vol.	Page
SHOALES, SHOALS, (cont.)		
Betsey, d. Abial & Polly, b. Jan. 15, 1808, at Preston	2	53
Betsey, m. Henry **KEMP**, b. of Brooklyn, [July] 1, [1827], by Rev. Samuel J. May	4	28
Charles Frances, s. Orrin & Ardelia, b. Sept. 30, 1838	2	55
Edward Putnam, s. Orin & Ardelia L., b. Oct. 16, 1848. "Physician J. B. Whitcomb"	2	55
Emeline, d. Orrin & Ardelia L., b. May 11, 1835, at Hampton	2	55
Emily F., d. Abial & Polly, b. Nov. 5, 1821	2	53
Georgiana, d. Orin & Ardelia L., b. Nov. 22, 1836, in Canterbury	2	55
Henry Palmer, s. Orin & Ardelia, b. [ ] 1844; d. 1863	2	55
Lucy M., of Canterbury, m. Edwin **SWEET**, of Brooklyn, May 3, 1846, by Rev. Herman Snow	4	83
Lucy Maria, d. Abial & Polly, b. Apr. 30, 1827	2	53
Mary Ann, d. Abial & Polly, b. Dec. 19, 1816	2	53
Mary Elizabeth, d. Orin & Ardelia L., b. Aug. 15, 1833	2	55
Orrin, s. Abial & Polly, b. May 14, 1813	2	53
Sally, d. Abial & Polly, b. Apr. 22, 1810	2	53
William Lewis, s. Orrin & Ardelia, b. Sept. 22, 1840	2	55
SIKES, James L., of Suffield, Mass., m. Lucy **GALLUP**, of Brooklyn, Nov. 14, [1832], by Rev. G. J. Tillotson	4	48
SIMMONS, John, m. Susannah **SHELDON**, Dec. 16, 1804	1	76
Lavinia, m. Henry D. **WILLIAMS**, b. Foster, R. I., Feb. 8, 1841, by Rev. George J. Tillotson	4	74
Mary Ann, m. Baker **TITUS**, b. of Brooklyn, [Oct.] 31, 1830, by John Parish, J. P.	3	11
Mary Ann, m. Baker **TITUS**, b. of Brooklyn, Oct. 31, 1830, by John Parish, J. P.	3	12
Mary Ann, m. Baker **TITUS**, b. of Brooklyn, Oct. 31, 1830, by John Parish, J. P.	4	43
SKINNER, Artametia, m. Joseph **BAKER**, Jr., May 18, 1801, by John Parrish, J. P.	3	1
SMALL, Lucy Maria, of Brooklyn, m. Amos T. **HUZZY**, of Townsend, Vt., persons of color, July 1, 1832, by Rev. George J. Tillotson	4	47
SMITH, David F., of Windham, m. Caroline **TYLER**, of Brooklyn, [May] 11, [1829], by Samuel J. May	4	35
Esther, housekeeper, d. Aug. 24, 1850, ae 95	2	134
Lucretia, d. Capt. William & Esther, b. Aug. 27, 1792	1	13
Lucretia, m. Joel **SCARBOROUGH**, Apr. 17, 1808	1	76
Lucy, d. Capt. W[illia]m & Esther, b. Jan. 19, 1795	1	13
Lucy, m. Jeremiah **SCARBOROUGH**, Nov. 25, 1813	1	76
Mary, m. Darius **MATHEWSON**, Dec. 2, 1800	1	71
Olive, d. Capt. William & Esther, b. Jan. 1, 1788	1	13
Olive, d. Capt. W[illia]m & Esther, d. June 1, 1789	1	56
Peter, of Brooklyn, m. Keturah **LATHROP**, of Canterbury, July 24, 1825, by Rev. Ansel Nash	4	20

	Vol.	Page
SMITH, (cont.)		
Phinehas, L[ieu]t., d. Oct. 12, 1788	1	56
William, m. Esther **YORK**, Nov. 15, 1787	1	76
William, Capt., d. Nov. 4, 1816, in the 76th y. of his age	1	56
SNOW, Amos W., of Chaplin, m. Marcia **HERRICK**, of Brooklyn,		
Nov. 30, 1837, by Rev. G. J. Tillotson	4	65
Ebenezer S., of Hampton, m. Ursula **KEMP**, of Brooklyn,		
Oct. 16, 1853, by Rev. C. Y. DeNormandie	4	110
SOLLACE, Joseph N., m. Marcia **HYDE**, b. of Brooklyn, Apr. 2,		
1833, by Rev. Geo[rge] J. Tillotson	4	50
SOULE, Susan, m. Benjamin **CHAPIN**, Oct. 7, 1815	1	62
SPAULDING, SPALDING, Abel, d. Oct. 26, 1814, in the 82nd y.		
of his age	1	56
Adeline, d. Joseph D. & Flora, b. Feb. 13, 1838;		
d. Oct. 10, 1840	2	59
Bela P., m. Betsey **BACON**, Mar. 26, 1806	1	76
Benjamin B., Dr., m. Elizabeth **PUTNAM**, b. of Brooklyn,		
Oct. 5, 1836, by Rev. J. M. Bartlett	4	62
Benjamin Bacon, s. Bela P. & Betsey, b. Oct. 6, 1811	1	249
Betsey, housekeeper, b. Canterbury, res. Brooklyn, d.		
Apr. 16, [1851], ae 66	2	134
Celia A., of Killingly, m. Richard **KING**, of Brooklyn,		
Oct. 16, 1839, by Rev. Benj[ami]n N. Harris	4	69
Charles, s. Edward & Sarah, b. Apr. 6, 1836	2	58
Ebenezer, Capt., d. June 18, 1794, ae 77 y.	1	56
Ebenezer, s. Bela P. & Betsey, b. Oct. 21, 1816	1	253
Ebenezer, of Brooklyn, m. Mrs. Patience **DENISON**, late		
of Newport, R. I., Oct. 1, 1823, by Rev. Samuel J. May	4	15
Edward, s. Bela P. & Betsey, b. May 24, 1807	1	13
Elizabeth, m. Barzillai **READ**, Apr. 9, 1797	1	75
Ellen, d. Joseph D. & Flora, b. Apr. 9, 1836	2	59
Ellison, s. Joseph D. & Flora, b. June 28, 1843;		
d. Mar. 29, 1844	2	59
Emanuel, merchant, of Eastford, m. Susan M. **BOLLES**, ae		
20, of Brooklyn, Mar. [ ], 1851, by Nicholas Branch	2	133
Emily, d. Joseph D. & Flora, b. Jan. 10, 1840	2	59
Harvey, of Plainfield, m. Christiana M. **BLAISDELL**, of		
Franklin, Me., Feb. 8, 1847, by Rev. Samuel May	4	86
James, Jr., of Brooklyn, m. Sarah Ann **THOMPSON**, of		
Hampton, [Nov.] 4, [1833], by Rev. Samuel J. May	4	52
James, d. Oct. 25, 1836	1	53
Jerusha, d. Caleb & Jerusha, b. Apr. 24, 1760;		
m. Eliakim **CADY**	1	243
Jerusha, m. Eliakim **CADY**, June 8, 1784	1	62
John, s. Dr. Luther & Maria, b. Nov. 8, 1820	1	253
Joseph, s. George & Julia Ann, b. Apr. 27, 1846	2	58
Lucretia, d. William & Amanda, b. May 15, 1795	1	253
Luther, s. Eben, Jr. & Molly, b. Oct. 24, 1789	1	16

	Vol.	Page
SPAULDING, SPALDING, (cont.)		
Lydia, of Brooklyn, m. Stephen **BROWN**, of Pomfret, Jan. 14, 1827, by Jona[than] A. Welch, J. P.	4	27
Maria, of Brooklyn, m. Dr. James B. **WHITCOMB**, of Clinton, LaPorte, Co., Ind., June 24, 1839, by Rev. William Coe	4	69
Maria Elizabeth, d. Bela P. & Betsey, b. June 4, 1809	1	249
Mary, m. Dan[ie]l **CADY**, Oct. 6, 1762	1	62
Mary, w. Capt. Eben[eze]r, d. May 22, 1790, ae 67 y.	1	56
Mary, d. William & Amanda, b. Feb. 1, 1797; d. Apr. 9, 1802	1	253
Mary, m. William **PUTNAM**, Apr. 17, 1805	1	74
Mary, of Killingly, m. Henry **YOUNG**, of Voluntown, Apr. 6, 1828, by Rev. Roswell Whitmore	4	32
Mehetable, w. Abel, d. Oct. 11, 1800, in the 50th y. of her age	1	56
Molly, w. Ebenezer, d. Oct. 23, 1821, ae 62 y.	1	56
Nancy Ann, of Brooklyn, m. John B. **MAHAN**, of New York, Sept. 27, 1835, by Daniel T. Tyler, J. P.	4	58
Susan, d. William & Amanda, b. Mar. 22, 1793	1	253
Susan, m. Benjamin E. **PALMER**, Nov. 24, 1812	1	74
William, m. Amanda **CADY**, Oct. 7, 1792	1	76
William, Tailor, d. Aug. 16, 1849, ae 81	2	108
William Elisha, s. William & Amanda, b. June 27, 1801	1	253
SPENCER, Albert, of Windham, m. Rebecca S. **KELLEY**, of Brooklyn, Oct. 1, 1845, by Rev. Benjamin C. Phelps, of West Killingly	4	81
Alice, ae 28, of Warwick, b. in East Greenwich, d. Capt. John, m. Francis **LITCHFIELD**, farmer, ae 36, of Brooklyn, s. John, Mar. 29, 1852, at Warwick, R. I., by Rev. Thomas Tillinghast	4	112
Lucius, of Pomfret, m. Caroline M. **PENNIMAN**, [Mar.] 4, [1830], by Rev. Ambrose Edson	4	40
Lucius Obadiah, s. Lucius & Caroline M., b. Feb. 16, 1832	2	56
SPRAGUE, Joseph, of Hingham, Mass., m. Martha E. **WILLIAMS**, of Brooklyn, Sept. 18, 1839, by Rev. William Coe	4	70
STANBURY, Lucy, m. Avery G. **PALMER**, b. of Brooklyn, Jan. 30, 1823, by John Parish, J. P.	3	3
Lucy, m. Avery G. Palmer, b. of Brooklyn, Jan. 30, 1823, by John Parish, J. P.	4	14
STANTON, Betsey Maria, d. Robert B. & Sarah Amanda, b. Oct. 14, 1841	2	56
Charles Robert, s. Robert B. & Sarah Amanda, b. Nov. 10, 1843	2	56
STAPLES, Bella, s. Jacob & Molly, b. Jan. 27, 1784	1	16
Zilpha, d. Jacob & Thankful, b. Apr. 10, 1778	1	16
STEDMAN, Mariaette, ae 26, b. Brooklyn, m. Edwin M. **BIGNAL**, moulder, ae 28, of E. Brooklyn, Feb. 2, 1851, by Rev. Sam[ue]l Coggeshall	2	132
Mariette, of Brooklyn, m. Edwin **BICKNELL**, of Killingly,		

	Vol.	Page

STEDMAN, (cont.)

Feb. 2, 1851, by Rev. S. W. Coggeshall — 4 — 103

STEER, Amasa S., of Brooklyn, m. Olive **TAYLOR**, of Killingly,

Feb. 28, 1830, by Rev. Sam[ue]l J. May — 4 — 40

Martha Appleby, d. Amasa S. & Olive, b. May 4, 1834 — 2 — 57

William Henry, s. Amasa S. & Olive, b. Nov. 30, 1830 — 2 — 57

STEPHENS, [see also **STEVENS**], Eunice, d. John & Thankful, b.

Jan. 4, 1782 — 1 — 16

James, s. John & Thankful, b. June 6, 1789 — 1 — 16

John, s. John & Thankful, b. Nov. 26, 1795 — 1 — 16

Joseph, s. John & Thankful, b. Feb. 10, 1780 — 1 — 16

Polly, s. John & Thankful, b. July 4, 1786 — 1 — 16

Septamus, s. John & Thankful, b. May 10, 1784 — 1 — 16

William, s. John & Thankful, b. Jan. 28, 1791 — 1 — 249

STETSON, Almira B., m. Courtland Y. **DeNORMANDIE**, b. of

Brooklyn, May 22, 1853, by Rev. I. H. Coe. Int. pub.

[May 22, 1853] — 4 — 109

Almira Backus, d. James A. & Dolly, b. May 22, 1828 — 2 — 55

James Alexander, m. Dolly **WITTER**, b. of Brooklyn, [May]

27, [1827], by Rev. Samuel J. May — 4 — 27

Joseph R., s. James A., farmer, ae 46, & Dolly W., ae 41,

b. Oct. 12, 1847 — 2 — 88

STEVENS, [see also **STEPHENS**], Abigail, m. Josiah **FASSETT***,

Apr. 16, 1789   (*Should be "**FROST**". Corrected by L.

B. B.) — 1 — 65

Eunice, m. Daniel **COPELAND**, Nov. 18, 1813 — 1 — 62

Mary, m. Daniel **COPELAND**, Feb. 5, 1807 — 1 — 62

Samuel W., m. Emeline **BROWN**, b. of Brooklyn, Sept. 5,

· 1836, by Rev. G. J. Tillotson — 4 — 62

STILLE, Alfred, M. D., of Philadelphia, Pa., m. Caroline

Christiana **BARNETT**, of Boston, Nov. 4, 1841, by Rev.

R. Camp — 4 — 75

STONE, Phebe Ann, of Thompson, m. Henry **DRESSER**, of

Pomfret, Dec. 18, 1836, by Rev. G. J. Tillotson — 4 — 63

STORRS, STORRES, Aaron H., of Prattsburgh, N. Y., m. Mary

Ann **CADY**, of Brooklyn, [Nov.] 2, [1829], by Rev.

Ambrose Edson — 4 — 37

Abby Ward, d. Aaron H. & Mary Ann, b. Apr. 16, 1843 — 2 — 59

Ann E., of Brooklyn, m. George E. **WHEATON**, of

Burlington, Vt., Nov. 27, 1851, by Rev. G. J. Tillotson — 4 — 105

Ann Elizabeth, d. Aaron H. & Mary Ann, b. Apr. 23, 1833 — 2 — 59

Ardelia Cady, d. Aaron H. & Mary Ann, b. Feb. 24, 1850 — 2 — 59

Betsey, m. John **WEAVER**, July 25, 1802 — 1 — 78

Edward Hovey, s. Aaron H. & Mary Ann, b. Apr. 26, 1852 — 2 — 59

Harriet Maria, d. Aaron H. & Mary Ann, b. Mar. 5, 1840 — 2 — 59

Martha Waldo, d. Aaron H. & Mary Ann, b. July 24, 1846 — 2 — 59

STOWELL, Asa Tyler, s. John & Talitha, b. Sept. 6, 1813 — 2 — 52

Bishop, s. John & Talitha, b. May 23, 1808 — 2 — 52

	Vol.	Page
STOWELL, (cont.)		
Horace, s. John & Talitha, b. Mar. 9, 1805, at Abington		
in Pomfret	2	52
Jamin, s. John & Talitha, b. Dec. 27, 1811	2	52
John, m. Talitha **TYLER**, Feb. 4, 1801	2	52
John Cutler, s. John & Talitha, b. Oct. 19, 1806	2	52
Lora, d. John & Talitha, b. Sept. 23, 1801, at Abington	2	52
Maria, d. George M., blacksmith, ae 25, & Eliza Jane,		
ae 26, b. Mar. 5, 1850	2	107
Maria J., d. Sept. 5, 1849, ae 1 1/2 y.	2	108
Maria Jane, d. George M., Blacksmith, ae 23, & Eliza		
Jane, ae 23, b. Feb. 28, 1848	2	78
Mary Ann, d. John & Talitha, b. June 5, 1815	2	52
Oran, s. John & Talitha, b. Jan. 30, 1810	2	52
Sophia, d. John & Talitha, b. Mar. 30, 1803, at Abington	2	52
Sophia, of Brooklyn, m. Ebson **ARNOLD**, of Thompson, Mar.		
17, 1822, by Rev. John Paine, of Hampton	4	9
Talathy, farmer's widow, d. Mar. 25, [1851], ae 75	2	130
STOWS, Adella Cady, d. Aaron H., silversmith, ae 44, & Mary		
Ann, ae 40, b. Feb. 24, 1850	2	121
STRAIT, John D., of Canterbury, m. Sarah M. **GREEN**, of		
Brooklyn, Dec. 31, 1843, by Sam Webb, J. P.	4	79
SUMNER, Chauncey, of Spencer, Mass., m. Deborah **GILBERT**, of		
Brooklyn, June 1, 1854, by Rev. G. J. Tillotson	4	113
Eliza, m. Thomas Cotton **HAYWARD**, Apr. 30, 1801	1	67
SWEET, Edwin, of Brooklyn, m. Lucy M. **SHOALS**, of Canterbury,		
May 3, 1846, by Rev. Herman Snow	4	83
Frederick Dawly, s. Andrew J., blacksmith, ae 22, & Susan,		
ae 21, b. Feb. 20, 1851	2	129
Polly, m. Reuben **GRAVES**, Nov. 6, 1804	1	66
SYMONDS, Amelia M. W., m. Samuel G. **NYE**, b. of		
Danielsonville, Dec. 25, 1854, by Rev. C. Y.		
DeNormandie	4	115
TANNER, Adelia Parkhurst, d. Olney, farmer, ae 47, & Martha,		
ae 42, b. Aug. 2, 1848	2	78
Benjamin, m. Sally **ADAMS**, Jan. 23, 1807	1	77
George, s. Olney & Martha, b. Mar. 22, 1831	2	61
John Weaver, s. Olney & Martha, b. Nov. 4, 1834	2	61
Olney, m. Martha **KEMP**, Jan. 18, 1830, by Rev. Sam[uel]		
J. May	4	39
TARBOX, Anna, d. Daniel & Lucelia, b. Sept. 8, 1847	2	60
Anna, d. Daniel, farmer, ae 43, & Lucretia, ae 30, b.		
Sept. 8, 1847	2	78
Anthony, m. Eunice **LUMMIS**, b. of Coventry, R. I., Jan. 1,		
1844, by Rev. Geo[rge] J. Tillotson	4	79
Colonel, m. Sally **ADAMS**, Feb. 3, 1799	1	77
Daniel, s. Daniel & Lucelia, b. May 19, 1844	2	60
Eliphal Day, s. Colonel & Sally, b. Sept. 9, 1803	1	17

	Vol.	Page
TARBOX, (cont.)		
Eliphal Waterman, s. Eliphal D. & Louisa Ann, b. Jan. 30, 1834	2	60
Eliphal Whipple, s. Eliphal D. & Louisa Ann, b. Nov. 3, 1829	2	60
Hiram, s. Colonel & Sally, b. Mar. 14, 1808	1	17
Joseph Curnel, s. Daniel & Sarah Maria, b. July 12, 1835, in New York, N. Y.	2	60
Louis Perret, s. Daniel & Sarah Maria, b. May 20, 1839	2	60
Lucelia, d. Daniel & Lucelia, b. Oct. 16, 1845	2	60
Sally Maria, d. Curnel & Sally, b. Aug. 23, 1808	1	250
Sally Maria, w. Daniel, d. Mar. 25, 1841, in Brooklyn, Conn., ae 32 y. 6 m. 20 d.	1	57
Sarah Avis, d. Curnel & Sally, b. Dec. 18, 1819	2	60
Sarah Esther, d. Daniel & Sarah Maria, b. Aug. 20, 1837; d. Aug. 10, 1844	2	60
Sarah Esther, d. Daniel & Sally Maria, d. Aug. 10, 1844, ae 7 y. less 10 d.	1	57
Welthy, d. Curnal & Sally, b. Apr. 9, 1813	1	250
Wealthy Maria, d. Daniel & Sarah Maria, b. Mar. 14, 1841	2	60
TAYLOR, Caroline, m. Jehiel **JUSTIN**, Dec. 27, 1828, by John Parish, J. P.	3	10
Caroline, m. Jehiel **JUSTIN**, Dec. 27, 1828, by John Parish, J. P.	4	34
Daniel Allen, of Providence, m. Delia Scarborough **KIES**, of Brooklyn, Mar. 2, [1834], by Samuel J. May	4	54
Elizabeth, d. Rev. Hutchins & Eliza, b. Mar. 27, 1821	1	250
Emeline S., m. Jasper **MARTIN**, b. of Brooklyn, Nov. 19, 1838, by Rev. William Coe	4	68
Emily, d. Havilah & Calista, b. June 5, 1817	1	250
Emily Louisa, d. Havilah & Calista, b. Mar. 30, 1822	2	60
Hannah, m. William H. **CARVER**, b. of Brooklyn, [Jan.] 18, [1835], by Rev. Samuel J. May	4	57
Havilah, m. Calista **CADY**, Dec. 22, 1816	1	77
Jane M., m. Andrew **JOHNSON**, b. of Brooklyn, Jan. 25, 1852, by Rev. Geo[rge] J. Tillotson	4	108
Lydia, m. Lemuel **CADY**, Apr. 27, 1819, by John Parish, J. P.	3	2
Lydia, m. Lemuel **CADY**, Apr. 29, 1819	2	12
Lydia had d. Sally, d. Nov. 8, 1824	1	57
Olive, of Killingly, m. Amasa S. **STEER**, of Brooklyn, Feb. 28, 1830, by Rev. Sam[ue]l J. May	4	40
Rachel, farmer's wife, b. Griswold, res. Canterbury, d. Dec. 24, 1849, ae 68	2	113
Sally, d. Lydia, d. Nov. 8, 1824	1	57
Sophronia Emeline, d. Havilah & Calista, b. Feb. 15, 1820	1	250
William, s. Havilah & Calista, b. Jan. 22, 1824	2	60
William, trader, d. July 27, [1849], ae 25	2	106
THAXTER, Daniel, optician, b. Hingham, Mass., res. Hingham, Mass., m. 2d w. Lucy P. **SCARBOROUGH**,		

	Vol.	Page
THAXTER, (cont.)		
housekeeper, b. Brooklyn, Ct., res. Hingham, Mass., Dec.		
26, 1850, by Theodore Parker	2	125
THAYER, Ann, dressmaker, d. Dec. 14, [1850], ae 98	2	124
Betsey, d. Elijah & Anne, b. Oct. 13, 1774	1	17
Deborah, d. Elijah & Anna, b. Apr. 6, 1776	1	17
Deborah, m. Joseph **SCARBOROUGH**, 2d, Oct. 30, 1798	1	76
Elijah, m. Anna **CADY**, Dec. 30, 1773	1	77
Fanny Maria, d. Elijah & Anna, d. May 16, 1801	1	57
Fanny Maria, d. Elijah & Anna, b. Oct. 16, 1794	1	17
John, s. Elijah & Anne, b. May 23, 1779	1	17
Joseph, s. Elijah & Anne, b. Sept. 20, 1790	1	17
Joseph, m. Elizabeth C. **WEBB**, Aug. 20, 1837, by Rev.		
R. Camp	4	64
Polly, d. Elijah & Anne, b. Nov. 6, 1785	1	17
William, s. Elijah & Anne, b. Sept. 24, 1782	1	17
THOMPSON, Randal, of North Stonington, m. Lucy **FAULKNER**,		
of Brooklyn, July [27], 1823, by John Parish, J. P.	3	3
Sarah Ann, of Hampton, m. James **SPALDING**, Jr., of		
Brooklyn, [Nov.] 4, [1833], by Rev. Samuel J. May	4	52
THORNTON, Susan, m. W[illia]m **WHEELER**, Oct. 18, 1835, by		
W[illia]m Hutchins, J. P.	4	59
Susan, m. James **LITCHFIELD**, b. of Brooklyn, Sept. 4,		
1836, by Rev. G. J. Tillotson	4	62
THURSTON, Sarah, b. Brooklyn, N. Y., res. Brooklyn, d. Feb.		
28, [1851], ae 29	2	134
TIFFANY, Harriet A., of Brooklyn, Conn., m. Daniel **TREMBLY**,		
of Brooklyn, N. Y., Sept. 11, 1838, by Roswell Whitmore	4	67
TILLINGHAST, Isaac, of Killingly, Conn., m. Sarah A. **LOVE**,		
of Coventry, R. I., Mar. 21, 1853, by Rev. Courtland Y.		
DeNormandie	4	109
TILLOTSON, Elizabeth L., d. Geo[rge] J., clergyman, ae 44,		
& Elizabeth K., ae 31, b. Sept. 13, 1839	2	107
TILTON, Catharine Jane, d. Leonard & Catharine, b. Aug. 6, 1833	2	61
Charles Henry, s. Leonard & Catharine, b. Nov. 30, 1829	2	61
Eliza Ann, d. Leonard & Catharine, b. Nov. 25, 1835	2	61
Horatio Willard, s. Leonard & Catharine, b. Sept. 17, 1831;		
d. Nov. 5, 1832	2	61
TINKER (?), Cynthia E., b. Brooklyn, res. East Brooklyn, d.		
Oct. 23, 1848, ae 3 d. (Perhaps "**FOSTER**,"?)	2	104
TITUS, Baker, m. Mary Ann **SIMMONS**, b. of Brooklyn, [Oct.] 31,		
1830, by John Parish, J. P.	3	11
Baker, m. Mary Ann **SIMMONS**, b. of Brooklyn, Oct. 31,		
1830, by John Parish, J. P.	3	12
Baker, m. Mary Ann **SIMMONS**, b. of Brooklyn, Oct. 31,		
1830, by John Parish, J. P.	4	43
Samuel L., of Brooklyn, m. Jane **CUMMINGS**, of Killingly,		
Dec. 12, 1837, by Rev. G. J. Tillotson	4	65

	Vol.	Page

TITUS, (cont.)

Sarah, of Killingly, m. Archibald **WILLIAMS,** of Brooklyn,
Apr. 12, 1829, by John Parish, J. P. · 3 · 10

Sarah, of Killingly, m. Archibald **WILLIAMS,** of Brooklyn,
Apr. 12, 1829, by John Parish, J. P. · 4 · 35

Sophronia, m. Evolin **PENFIELD,** b. of Brooklyn, Nov. 28,
[1839], by Rev. William Coe · 4 · 70

TOWN, Dwight, s. Asa & Mary Ann, b. Dec. 23, 1842 · 2 · 61

Edgar, s. Asa & Mary Ann, b. Nov. 3, 1841 · 2 · 61

Frances L., d. Asa, farmer, & Mary L., b. July 9, [1850] · 2 · 115

Theresa E., d. Asa & Mary Ann, b. Feb. 13, 1846 · 2 · 61

TOWNSEND, George, of Exeter, R. I., m. Abby Mary **PIERCE,** of
Brooklyn, Aug. 5, 1827, by Uriel Fuller, J. P. · 4 · 29

TRACY, Andrew A., d. Aug. 7, 1849, ae 1 · 2 · 122

TREMBLY, Daniel, of Brooklyn, N. Y., m. Harriet A. **TIFFANY,**
of Brooklyn, Conn., Sept. 11, 1838, by Roswell Whitmore · 4 · 67

TRIPP, TRIP, Charles Henry, s. Stephen H. & Abby L., b. Sept.
23, 1852 · 2 · 61

Emily Ann, d. Stephen H., farmer, ae 24, & Abby L., ae
25, b. Sept. 3, 1850 · 2 · 130

Mary Eliza, d. Stephen, farmer, ae 25, & Abby, ae 21,
b. Oct. 15, 1848 · 2 · 99

Perry G., farmer, ae 24, of Plainfield, m. Lydia A.
ROBBINS, ae 19, b. Brooklyn, res. Plainfield, Mar. 5,
1848, by Elder Ebenezer Loomis · 2 · 87

Perry G., of Plainfield, m. Lydia A. **ROBBINS,** of Brooklyn,
Mar. 6, 1848, by Rev. E. Loomis · 4 · 88

Perry G., s. Perry G., farmer, ae 25, of Plainfield,
& Lydia A. ae 20, of Plainfield, b. Feb. 25, [1849] · 2 · 100

Samuel, m. Betsey **KEACH,** [b. of Brooklyn], June 24, 1849,
by Rev. S. W. Coggeshall · 4 · 100

Samuel, shoemaker, ae 29, b. Canterbury, res. Brooklyn,
m. Betsey **KEACH,** weaver on looms, ae 26, of
Brooklyn, July 8, 1849, by Rev. Coggeshall · 2 · 104

Sarah L., d. Samuel, shoemaker, ae 30, & Betsey, ae 25,
b. Mar. 29, 1850 · 2 · 119

Stephen H., farmer, of Brooklyn, m. Abby L. **PIDGE,** ae
20, of Brooklyn, Jan. 11, 1848, by Rev. Ebenezer Loomis · 2 · 79

Stephen H., m. Abby L. **PIDGE,** b. of Brooklyn, Jan. 11,
184[8], by Rev. E. Loomis · 4 · 88

TUCKER, Hannah, m. Almond **BAKER,** May 19, 1807 · 1 · 61

Jasper, of West Brookfield, Mass., m. Lucinda **DABNEY,**
of Brooklyn, Sept. 5, 1837, by Rev. G. J. Tillotson · 4 · 64

W[illia]m C., s. W[illia]m K., farmer, ae 25, & Mary
Ann, ae 26, b. Feb. 14, 1850 · 2 · 107

TURNER, Sarah Ann, m. Charles **WOOD,** b. of Gloucester, R. I.,
May 17, 1846, by Rev. Herman Snow · 4 · 83

TYLER, Alemeran, s. Asa & Anstress, b. Mar. 12, 1767 · 1 · 250

	Vol.	Page
TYLER, (cont.)		
Alemeran, s. Asa & Anstress, d. Dec. 26, 1768	1	57
Alemeran, 2d, s. Asa & Anstress, b. Feb. 6, 1769	1	250
Alemeran, 2d, s. Asa & Anstress, d. Jan. [ ], 1772	1	57
Alemon, s. Asa & Anstress, b. Oct. 16, 1784	1	250
Alvan, s. Asa & Anstress, b. Jan. 26, 1773	1	250
Asenath, d. Asa & Anstress, b. Dec. 10, 1779	1	250
Bernice, d. Asa & Anstress, b. Jan. 20, 1775	1	250
Betsey, d. Dan[ie]l & Mehetable, b. Apr. 16, 1784	1	17
Betsey, m. John **SEARLES**, June 2, 1816	1	76
Caroline, of Brooklyn, m. David F. **SMITH**, of Windham, [May] 11, [1829], by Samuel J. May	4	35
Caroline Elizabeth, d. Paschal P. & Elizabeth, b. Apr. 24, 1802	1	17
Caroline Elizabeth, m. Hulings **COWPERTHWA[ITE]**, of Philadelphia, [Nov.] 24, 1824, by A. Edson	4	18
Cornelia J., m. Thomas **BRAMAN**, b. of Brooklyn, Apr. 7, 1836, by Rev. G. J. Tillotson	4	60
Dan[ie]l, 2d, m. Mehetable **PUTNAM**, Aug. 15, 1771	1	77
Daniel, 2d, m. Sally **CHAPLIN**, June 10, 1790	1	77
Daniel, s. Daniel & Sally, b. Jan. 7, 1799	1	17
Daniel, 2d, m. Olive **CADY**, Apr. 13, 1806	1	77
Daniel, 2d, m. Olive **CADY**, b. of Brooklyn, Apr. 13, 1806, by John Parrish, J. P.	3	7
Daniel P., m. Emily C. **TYLER**, b. of Brooklyn, June 9, 1834, by Rev. Geo[rge] J. Tillotson	4	54
Daniel Putnam, s. Dan[ie]l, 2d, & Mehetable, b. Nov. 21, 1776	1	17
Edwin, s. Dan[ie]l & Mehetable, b. Nov. 24, 1793	1	17
Edwin, s. Frederick & Sophia, b. Nov. 1, 1816	1	250
Edwin, s. Frederick & Sophia, d. Feb. 10, 1818	1	57
Edwin, m. Alla Mary **EDWARDS**, Sept. 4, 1821, by Rev. Joseph Chickering	4	5
Eliza, d. Dr. James & Eliza, b. Apr. 25, 1798	1	17
Elizabeth, d. William & Waty, b. Oct. 19, 1809	1	250
Elizabeth, d. Stephen & Betsey, d. Mar. 18, 1819	1	57
Emily, m. Andrew F. **LEE**, Dec. 30, [1832], by Rev. Samuel J. May	4	49
Emily C., m. Daniel P. **TYLER**, b. of Brooklyn, June 9, 1834, by Rev. Geo[rge] J. Tillotson	4	54
Emma, m. Evan **SHARPE** Apr. 18, 1831, by Rev. Sam[ue]l J. May	4	45
Frederick, s. Dan[ie]l & Mehetable, b. May 7, 1795	1	17
Frederick, s. Alemon & Hannah, b. June 22, 1806	1	250
Frederick, m. Sophia **SHARP**, Feb. 6, 1816	1	77
Gardiner, s. Alamon & Hannah, b. May 20, 1804, at Pomfret, Ct.	1	17
George Frederick, s. Frederick & Sophia, b. Aug. 4, 1822	2	60
Hannah P., of Brooklyn, m. David **GILLMUR**, of Munson, Mass., [July] 14, [1840], by Rev. Thomas Huntington	4	73

	Vol.	Page
TYLER, (cont.)		
Hannah Putnam, d. William & Waty, b. Mar. 15, 1819	2	60
Henrietta Mariah, d. Asa & Anstress, b. Nov. 6, 1771	1	250
Hitty, m. Richard **GOODELL**, Jr., Dec. 26, 1803	1	66
Jabez, s. Asa & Anstress, b. June 6, 1786	1	250
James, s. James & Sarah, b. Sept. 16, 1774	1	17
James, s. Dr. James & Eliza, b. Sept. 28, 1800	1	17
Jamin, s. Asa & Anstress, b. Dec. 20, 1781	1	250
Jane, d. James & Sarah, b. Jan. 26, 1779	1	17
Joseph, s. James & Sarah, b. June 12, 1776	1	17
Joseph, m. Annis **KENDAL**, b. of Brooklyn, [Sept] 17, [1827], by Rev. Sam[uel] J. May	4	29
Lyman, s. Alemon & Hannah, b. May 18, 1805	1	250
Maria C., m. John **GALLUP**, 3rd, b. of Brooklyn, [Sept.] 11, [1832], by Rev. George J. Tillotson	4	48
Mary Ann, d. Daniel, 2d, & Olive, b. May 19, 1808	1	250
Mary Baker, d. Pascal P. & Elizabeth, b. Aug. 17, 1812	1	250
Mary Baker, m. James **HOLBROOK**, b. of Brooklyn, June 9, 1833, by Rev. Geo[rge] J. Tillotson	4	51
Mehetable, w. Capt. Daniel, d. Nov. 28, 1789	1	57
Milly, d. James & Mehitable, b. Feb. 5, 1783	1	17
Molly, d. Dan[ie]l, 2d, & Mehetable, b. Aug. 1, 1772	1	17
Pascal, farmer, d. Aug. 31, 1847, ae 73	2	80
Paschal Paoli, s. Dan[ie]l, 2d, & Mehetable, b. May 15, 1774	1	17
Pascal Paoli, m. Elizabeth **BAKER**, Sept. 17, 1797	1	77
Patty, d. James & Mehitable, b. June 18, 1784	1	17
Putnam Daniel, s. Daniel & Mehetable, d. Jan. 18, 1798 (Probably "Daniel Putnam **TYLER**")	1	57
Putnam Daniel, s. Paschal P. & Elizabeth, b. July 17, 1798	1	17
Sally Edward, d. Edwin & Alla Mary, b. Sept. 18, 1822	2	60
Sally Pierpoint, d. Daniel, 2d, & Mehetable, b. Apr. 25, 1791	1	17
Sarah, d. James & Sarah, b. July 16, 1772	1	17
Sarah, w. James, d. Mar. 11, 1781, in the 32nd y. of her age	1	57
Sarah Sophia, d. Frederick, & Sophia, b. June 29, 1820	1	250
Septimus, s. Dan[ie]l, 2d, & Mehetable, b. Sept. 12, 1779	1	17
Septimus, s. Daniel, 2d, d. May 26, 1782	1	57
Septimus, s. Dan[ie]l & Mehetable, b. June 7, 1788	1	17
Stevens, m. Betsey **ALLYN**, b. of Brooklyn, Aug. 6, 1809, by John Parrish, J. P.	3	5
Talithammi, d. Asa & Anstress, b. Dec. 26, 1776	1	250
Talitha, m. John **STOWELL**, Feb. 4, 1801	2	52
Waty W., of Brooklyn, m. Benjamin **HOWE**, of Topsfield, Mass., May 31, 1842, by Rev. G. J. Tillotson	4	76
William, s. Dan[ie]l, 2d, & Mehetable, b. Oct. 4, 1781	1	17
William, m. Waty **WILLIAMS**, Jan. 1, 1809	1	77
UNDERWOOD, Mary H., d. Jerome, carpenter, ae 31, & Amanda W., ae 30, b. Jan. 26, 1849	2	105
UPHAM, Louisa, of Leicester, Mass., m. John R. **WILLIAMS**, of		

	Vol.	Page

UPHAM, (cont.)

Brooklyn, Sept. 20, 1826, by John Nelson, V. D. M.,
Leicester, [Mass.} — 4 — 25

UTLEY, Lavina M., of Brooklyn, m. Samuel W. **BUTLER**, of
Ashford, May 28, 1823, by Rev. James Porter, of Pomfret — 4 — 13

Mary, m. Beriah **DAVISON**, Apr. 2, 1807 — 1 — 63

Sarah, of Douglass, m. Charles **JOSSELYN**, of Burrelville,
[Jan.] 11, [1835], by Rev. Samuel J. May — 4 — 57

VAN PETT, Elizabeth, of Brunswick, N. Y., m. William K.
ROBBINS, of Brooklyn, Sept. 20, 1829, by Rev. Samuel
J. May — 4 — 37

WADE, Mary, m. Curtis **CARTER**, b. of Brooklyn, Nov. 24, 1836,
by Rev. G. J. Tillotson — 4 — 63

WALDO, Francis, of Brooklyn, m. Eliza **WENWOOD**, of
[Newport, R. I.], Feb. 5, 1828, by Rev. John Overton
Choules, Newport, R. I. — 4 — 44

Godfrey Wenwood, s. Francis & Eliza F., b. Nov. 12, 1830;
d. Dec. 20, 1830 — 2 — 62

Obadiah T., of Westminster Soc., Canterbury, m. Eliza
GALLUP, of Brooklyn, [Mar.] 31, [1826], by Rev. A.
Edson — 4 — 24

WALKER, Arnold, Col., of Scituate, R. I., m. Mrs. Hannah C.
WEBB, of Windham, Oct. 10, 1824, by W[illia]m D.
Foster, J. P. — 4 — 18

WALLS, Louisa, m. Robert **KINNE**, b. of Plainfield, Aug. 19, 1832,
by Uriel Fuller, J. P. — 4 — 48

WARNER, Adeline Elizabeth, d. Earl & Adeline Elizabeth, b. May
2, 1836 — 2 — 68

Earl, m. Harriet S. **GILBERT**, b. of Brooklyn, June 5,
1833, by Rev. G. J. Tillotson — 4 — 50

Earl, s. Earl & Adeline Elizabeth, b. Feb. 8, 1838 — 2 — 68

Frances Lester, d. Earl & Adeline Elizabeth, b. May 16, 1840 — 2 — 68

Harriet S., w. Earl, d. Oct. 18, 1834, ae 26 — 1 — 58

Harriet S., w. Earl, d. Oct. 18, 1834, ae 26 — 2 — 68

Juliaette Augusta, d. Earl & Harriet S., b. Mar. 20, 1834 — 2 — 68

Sarah Belton, d. Earl & Adeline Elizabeth, b. Apr. 23, 1842;
d. Dec. 14, 1843 — 2 — 68

W[illia]m L., of New London, m. Roxa Ann **DABNEY**, of
Brooklyn, Sept. 30, 1839, by G. J. Tillotson — 4 — 69

Winslow, s. Eddy & Azuba, b. Sept. 26, 1797 — 1 — 9

WARREN, Edmund L., of Killingly, m. Lucretia **PARKHURST**, of
Brooklyn, [Mar.] 13, [1844], by Rev. Thomas Huntington — 4 — 79

Harriet, Mrs., of Brooklyn, m. George W. **ELLISON**, of
Uxbridge, Mass., Sept. 3, 1851, by Rev. George J.
Tillotson — 4 — 104

Jacob C., of Killingly, m. Harriet **PARKHURST**, of Brooklyn,
Mar. 29, 1842, by Rev. Thomas Huntington — 4 — 75

WASHBURN, Henry, Jr., of Taunton, Mass., m. Lucretia Maria

	Vol.	Page
WASHBURN, (cont.)		
PALMER, Nov. 20, [1833], by E. B. Kellogg	4	52
WEAVER, Anna, m. Ephraim DAVISON, Mar. 12, 1795	1	63
Benjamin, s. Remington & Molly, b. Sept. 20, 1776	1	18
Benj[amin], m. Betsey BUTTS, Dec. 8, 1797	1	78
Benjamin, s. Benjamin & Betsey, b. Jan. 28, 1803	1	9
Benjamin, m. Hannah HUMES, May 28, 1806	1	78
Betsey, d. Benj[ami]n & Susannah, b. Sept. 5, 1783	1	18
Betsey, d. Remington & Molly, b. Aug. 24, 1790	1	18
Betsey, w. Benjamin, d. Nov. 10, 1805, in the 28th y.		
of her age	1	58
Betsey, w. John, d. Mar. 20, 1852, ae 73 y.	1	59
Betsey H., of Brooklyn, m. Edwin ELY, of Killingly,		
Nov. 13, 1836, by Rev. G. J. Tillotson	4	63
Caleb, b. May 23, 1779	1	252
Firella, d. Benjamin & Betsey, b. Feb. 26, 1801	1	9
John, s. Remington & Molly, b. Dec. [ ], 1786	1	18
John, d. Apr. 5, 1787	1	58
John, m. Betsey STORRS, July 25, 1802	1	78
Luara S., of Brooklyn, m. Hezekiah L. DANIELSON, of		
Killingly, Jan. 18, 1826, by Rev. Roswell Whitmore	4	23
Laura Storrs, d. John & Betsey, b. Feb. 6, 1806	1	5
Liny, d. Benj[amin] & Betsey, b. Feb. 13, 1799	1	9
Maria, d. Remington & Molly, b. May 18, 1780	1	18
Molly, d. Remington & Molly, b. June 1, 1778	1	18
Phebe, domestic, d. Oct. 6, 1848, ae 7	2	104
Phebe A., d. Apr. 7, 1850	2	118
Polly, d. Remington & Molly, b. Oct. [ ], 1782	1	18
Polly, m. Luther BUTTS, Apr. 15, 1798	1	61
Remington, s. Remington & Molly, b. July 12, 1788	1	18
Remington, m. Esther LITCHFIELD, Feb. 16, 1812, by John		
Parish, J. P.	3	8
Sally, d. Benjamin & Susannah, b. Mar. 31, 1781	1	18
Sally, m. John CHAMBERLAIN, Dec. 11, 1796	1	62
Shub[a]el, s. Remington & Molly, b. Dec. 5, 1784	1	18
Susannah, m. Peter DAVISON, Nov. 6, 1781	1	63
WEBB, Caroline, d. Henry & Abigail, b. June 17, 1828	2	68
Elizabeth C., m. Joseph THAYER, Aug. 20, 1837, by Rev.		
R. Camp	4	64
Frances, d. Horatio & Betsey, b. Oct. 31, 1828	2	68
Hannah C., of Windham, m. Col. Arnold WALKER, of		
Scituate, R. I., Oct. 10, 1824, by W[illia]m D. Foster, J. P.	4	18
Henry, 2d, m. Abigail PIKE, Apr. 30, 1821, by Rev.		
Hutchins Taylor	4	3
Horatio, m. Betsey PIKE, b. of Brooklyn, Apr. 16, 1826,		
by Rev. Henry Edes, at Providence, R. I. Int. pub. in		
Brooklyn	4	24
Horatio, of Windham, m. Elizabeth DORRANCE, of Brooklyn,		

	Vol.	Page
WEBB, (cont.)		
June 15, 1834, by Rev. G. J. Tillotson	4	54
Jeremiah S., s. Joshua & Elizabeth, b. July 15, 1838	2	68
John E., s. Joshua & Elizabeth, b. Nov. 1, 1835	2	68
Joshua, m. Elizabeth **MAIN**, May 4, 1830, by E. B. Kellogg	4	41
Mary Elizabeth, d. Ralph & Almira Elizabeth, b. July 28, 1835	2	76
Ralph, m. Almira Elizabeth **BAILEY**, [Jan.] 4, [1835], by		
Rev. Samuel J. May	4	57
Sarah, of Brooklyn, m. John G. **GILBERT**, of Mendon, Mass.,		
May 29, 1844, by Rev. G. J. Tillotson	4	80
Sibel, b. Windham, res. Brooklyn, d. Mar. 30, 1848, ae 67	2	87
Zippera A., ae 26, b. Windham, res. Woodstock, m. Serel		
S. **CHAF[F]EY**, farmer, ae 32, of Woodstock, May 4,		
1848, by Rev. Geo[rge] J. Tillotson	2	87
Zipporah A., of Brooklyn, m. Cyriel S. **CHAF[F]EE**, of		
Woodstock, May 4, 1848, by Rev. G. J. Tillotson	4	99
WEBBER, Abiah, m. Gideon **CADY**, Mar. 28, 1777	1	62
WEEKS, Abel, of Canterbury, m. Abbey E. **BATTEY**, Nov. 3,		
1850, by Rev. G. J. Tillotson	4	103
Lemuel(?), m. Sybbel **PARISH**, b. of Pomfret, Mar. 6, 1809,		
by John Parrish, J. P.	3	5
WELCH, Charles Augustus, s. Jonathan A., & Mary D., b. June		
9, 1828	2	64
Ebenezer Baker, s. Jonathan A. & Mary D., b. Feb. 20, 1821	2	64
James Edward, s. Jonathan A. & Mary D., b. July 28, 1833	2	64
Joseph Ashley, s. Jonathan A. & Mary D., b. Aug. 13, 1830	2	64
Louis B., b. Boston, Mass., res. [Boston?], d. Aug. 31,		
1848, ae 2 y. 8 m.	2	96
Louis Dwight, s. Jonathan A. & Mary D., b. Oct. 22, 1825	2	64
Mary Clarrissa, d. Jonathan A. & Mary D., b. May 30, 1823	2	64
Palmer, of Windham, m. Betsey **DEAN**, of Chaplin, Oct. 29,		
1843, by Daniel Bennett, J. P.	4	78
WELD, George Henry, s. Lewis L. & Betsey, b. Feb. 9, 1843	2	77
Lewis L., m. Betsey **SCARBOROUGH**, b. of Brooklyn, Jan.		
5, 1842, by Rev. G. J. Tillotson	4	75
WENWOOD, Eliza, of Brooklyn, m. Francis **WALDO**, of Newport,		
Feb. 5, 1828, by Rev. John Overton Choules, of Newport,		
R. I.	4	44
WESCOTT, Phebe M., of Coventry, R. I., m. Elliot **BROWN**, of		
Brooklyn, Aug. 26, 1849, by Rev. J. Ferris. Int. pub.		
Aug. 26, 1849	4	102
WESTON, Stephen C., of Willington, m. Mary W. **FRANKLIN**, of		
Brooklyn, [Dec.] 25, [1828], by Rev. Ambrose Edson	4	34
WHEAT, Elizabeth, m. Nathan **MERIT**, Dec. 24, 1795	1	71
WHEATON, Ellen M., of Brooklyn, m. David **ROBINSON**, of		
Buffalo, N. Y., Oct. 10, 1844, by Rev. G. J. Tillotson	4	80
George E., of Burlington, Vt., m. Ann E. **STORRS**, of		
Brooklyn, Nov. 27, 1851, by Rev. G. J. Tillotson	4	105

	Vol.	Page

WHEATON, (cont.)

George Washington, m. Ruama Ann **ROBBINS**, [Nov.] 25,
   [1833], by Rev. Samuel J. May   4   52

WHEELER, Fanny, d. John & Almira, b. Aug. 23, 1801   1   5

Ira, s. John & Elmira, b. Mar. 30, 17[ ]   1   18

Ira, m. Phebe **BICKFORD**, Apr. 2, 1815   1   78

Ira, m. Hannah **MAIN**, b. of Brooklyn, Apr. 10, 1845, by
   Rev. Herman Snow   4   81

James, s. John & Almira, b. Feb. 12, 1795   1   5

Jesse, s. John & Elmira, b. Aug. 31, 1789   1   18

John, d. Nov. 16, 1832, in the 76th y. of his age   1   59

Mira, d. John & Almira, b. Aug. 19, 1798   1   5

Mira, m. Josiah **PIDGE**, Nov. 27, 1823, by Rev. Samuel J.
   May. Int. pub.   4   15

Phebe, d. John & Almira, b. Mar. 14, 1785, at Pomfret   1   5

Phebe, w. Ira, d. Oct. 27, 1843, ae 55   1   58

Rebe, m. Timothy **HERRICK**, Sept. 19, 1805   1   67

Stephen, s. John & Almira, b. Feb. 10, 1792, at Killingly   1   5

Stephen, of Brooklyn, m. Lydia **NILES**, of Pomfret, Mar.
   11, 1821, by John Parish, J. P.   3   3

Stephen, of Brooklyn, m. Lydia **NILES**, of Pomfret, Mar.
   11, 1821, by John Parish, J. P.   4   14

Stephen, m. Lucy Ann **HUNTINGTON**, Aug. 4, [1833], by
   Rev. Samuel J. May   4   52

William, s. John & Almira, b. Oct. 3, 1806   1   5

W[illia]m, m. Susan **THORNTON**, Oct. 18, 1835, by
   W[illia]m Hutchins, J. P.   4   59

W[illia]m, of Canterbury, m. Betsey **DARBY**, of Brooklyn,
   [Sept.] 11, [1836], by Rev. Thomas Huntington   4   61

WHITAKER, Lemuel, s. Sam[ue]l & Mary, b. June 17, 1783   1   5

Polly, d. Sam[ue]l & Mary, b. Sept. 18, 1780   1   5

WHITCOMB, Edwin Augustus, s. James Bedingfield & Mary
   Louisa, b. Feb. [ ], 1837   2   74

James B., Dr., of Clinton, LaPorte Co., Ind., m. Maria
   SPALDING, of Brooklyn, June 24, 1839, by Rev.
   William Coe   4   69

James Holman, s. James Bedingfield & Mary Louisa, b.
   Nov. 16, 1834   2   74

WHITE, Adams, b. Feb. 13, 1784, at Windham   1   252

Adams, m. Harriet **ROBINSON**, Mar. 24, 1812   1   78

Betsey, b. Pomfret, res. Brooklyn, d. Nov. 17, 1848, ae 83   2   97

Catharin[e], d. Adams, Jr. & Harriet, b. May 3, 1831   1   252

Charles, s. Adams & Harriet, b. Aug. 16, [ ]   1   251

Edwin, s. Adams & Harriet, b. Apr. 5, 1818   1   252

Eugenia Robinson, d. Adams, Jr. & Harriet, b. Apr. 29,
   1829; d. Aug. 25, 1830   1   252

Eugenia Robinson, d. Adams, Jr. & Harriet, d. Aug. 25, 1830   1   59

Giles, s. Adams, Jr. & Harriet, b. Nov. 22, 1821   1   252

	Vol.	Page
WHITE, (cont.)		
Harriet, d. Adams, Jr. & Harriet, b. Mar. 8, 1829	1	252
Henry, s. Adams & Harriet, b. Jan. 3, 1815	1	252
Henry, s. Adams, Jr. & Harriet, d. Mar. 1, 1816	1	59
Henry Kirke, s. Adams & Harriet, b. Oct. 2, 1811	1	252
Henry Kirk, s. Adams, Jr. & Harriet, d. Sept. 27, 1822	1	59
Martha, d. Adams & Harriet, b. Sept. 5, 1823	1	252
Martha, m. Henry A. **DYER**, b. of Brooklyn, Oct. 26, 1846, by Rev. Riverius Camp	4	86
Nancy, m. Lodowick **GALLUP**, b. of Pomfret, Sept. 22, 1834, by Rev. G. J. Tillotson	4	56
Robert, s. Adams, Jr. & Harriet, b. Dec. 4, 1833	1	252
Sarah Elizabeth, d. Adams, Jr. & Harriet, b. Oct. 28, 1835	1	252
Sidney Adams, s. Adams, Jr. & Harriet, b. Sept. 15, 1825	1	252
WHITFORD, Abby Ardelia, d. William & Abigail, b. Dec. 9, 1817	2	64
Ardelia, of Brooklyn, m. Richard **SCRANTON**, of Middletown, Aug. 14, 1838, by Rev. William Coe	4	67
Loren Rawson, s. William & Abigail, b. Sept. 28, 1823	2	64
Nancy Amelia, d. William & Abigail, b. Oct. 11, 1825	2	64
William, m. Abigail **WHITTEMORE**, Feb. 5, 1815	2	64
William Sidney, s. William & Abigail, b. July 24, 1821	2	64
WHITNEY, Abigail, m. Benjamin **WOOD**, Apr. 5, 1792	1	78
Elizabeth, m. John **PARRISH**, May 30, 1790	1	74
Eunice, m. Stephen **BACKUS**, Sept. 2, 1798	1	61
Sophia, m. Elisha **LORD**, Nov, 28, 1799	1	70
WHITTEMORE, Abigail, m. William **WHITFORD**, Feb. 5, 1815	2	64
Hannah, w. Daniel, d. Apr. 2, 1821, ae 62 y. 1 w.	1	59
WILBUR, Augustus E., s. Clark & Orrilla, b. Dec. 11, 1836	2	65
Augustus Western, s. Clark & Orrilla, b. Aug. 10, 1825; d. Mar. 12, 1833	2	65
Henry Clark, s. Clark & Orrilla, b. June 22, 1829	2	65
Maria E., d. Clark & Orrilla, b. Sept. 16, 1834	2	65
WILLARD, Harry Bradford, s. Emery & Vienna, b. June 3, 1802	1	251
Harry Bradford, s. Emory & Vienda, d. Nov. 1, 1805	1	58
John, s. Emery & Vienna, b. Sept. 16, 1805	1	251
Waty Vaughan, d. Emery & Vienna, b. July 6, 1803	1	251
WILLIAMS, Abigail, d. William & Martha, b. Sept. 2, 1758	1	5
Abigail, m. Joseph **DOWNING**, Sept. 14, 1778	1	63
Amelia Sumner, d. Herbert & Lucy, b. June 29, 1829	2	65
Andrew, s. Joseph & Betsey, b. Dec. 4, 1828	2	66
Archibald, of Brooklyn, m. Sarah **TITUS**, of Killingly, Apr. 12, 1829, by John Parish, J. P.	3	10
Archibald, of Brooklyn, m. Sarah **TITUS**, of Killingly, Apr. 12, 1829, by John Parish, J. P.	4	35
Barnard Upham, s. John R. & Louisa, b. May 9, 1833	2	72
Betsey, d. Asa & Hannah b. Jan. 4, 1787	1	18
Betsey, m. Dr. Ebenezer **BAKER**, Feb. 17, 1805	1	61
Betsey, w. Joseph, d. Dec. 9, 1828, in the 35th y. of her age	1	59

	Vol.	Page
WILLIAMS, (cont.)		
Caleb Davis, s. John, 2d, & Sukey, b. Oct. 18, 1802	1	9
Cecelia, d. Capt. Roger W. & Polly, b. Oct. 4, 1801	1	9
Cecilia, of Brooklyn, m. Rev. Charles **BROOKS**, of Hingham,		
Mass., [June] 27, [1827], by Rev. Samuel J. May	4	28
Charles Archibald, s. Archibald & Sarah, b. July 12, 1831	2	69
Charles Elmer, s. Elmer & Lodicea A., b. Aug. 28, 1836	2	62
Charles Gardiner, s. Nathaniel & Hannah, b. Apr. 12, 1820	2	63
Clarrissa, w. Samuel, d. Oct. 21, 1822, in the 54th y. of her age	1	59
Daniel, s. Asa & Hannah, b. Apr. 14, 1784	1	18
Daniel, s. John & Sukey, b. Mar. 3, 1809	1	251
Daniel, s. John R. & Louisa, b. Mar. 31, 1835	2	72
Dolly Amanda, d. Elmer & Lodicea A., b. July 20, 1838;		
d. Sept. 16, 1839	2	62
Edward, s. Roger W. & Polly, b. June 14, 1799	1	9
Edward, s. Roger W. & Polly, d. Jan. 16, 1805	1	58
Edward, s. Joshua P. & Mary, b. Feb. 1, 1822; d. Aug. 2, 1823	2	63
Edward D., s. Caleb D. & Florinda, b. Nov. 1, 1835	2	70
Elisha, s. Sam[ue]l & Hannah, b. Apr. 5, 1788	1	18
Eliza Sumner, d. John, 2d, & Sukey, b. Feb. 7, 1797	1	9
Eliza Sumner, d. of John, d. Jan. 28, 1812	1	59
Elizabeth Hubbard, d. John R. & Louisa, b. July 18, 1831	2	72
Ellen, d. Joshua P. & Mary, b. Jan. 9, 1824	2	63
Elmer, s. Elmer & Sarah, b. May 11, 1804	1	5
Elmer, m. Lodicea Ann **FISK**, Mar. 29, 1829, by Rev. Orrin		
Catlin, at Sanywait Village, N. Y.	2	62
Emily Lucretia, d. Elmer & Lodicea A., b. Aug. 20, 1835	2	62
Fanny, m. Eleazer **MATHER**, Oct. 24, 1802	1	71
Flavel, s. Stephen, d. Mar. 19, 1799	1	58
Flavel M., m. Lodema **DOWNING**, Apr. 9, 1826, by Rev.		
Samuel J. May	4	23
Frances, d. Roger W. & Polly, b. June 6, 1797	1	9
Frances, d. Roger W. & Polly, d. Apr. 19, 1816, in the		
19th y. of her age	1	59
Frances Gardiner, s. Joseph & Rizpah, b. July 9, 1833	2	66
Franklin, s. John R. & Louisa, b. Aug. 7, 1827	2	72
Franklin, of Buffalo, N. Y., m. Olive **WILLIAMS**, of		
Brooklyn, Dec. 2, 1852, by Rev. George G. Channing	4	106
Frederick A., s. Elmon, shoemaker, ae 46, & Lodera Ann,		
ae 44, b. Sept. 27, 1849	2	121
Frederick Alden, s. Elmer & Lodicea A., b. Sept. 27, 1849	2	62
Frederick Stanley, s. Elmer & Sarah, b. Dec. 23, 1806	1	251
Freelove, m. Capt. Nathaniel **COGSWELL**, May 12, 1791	1	62
George M., b. in Foster, R. I., now of Killingly, m. 2d		
w. Faith **SANGER**, b. in Woodstock, July 16, 1854, by		
Rev. Charles Morse	4	114
George Martin, s. Martin H. & Dolly A., b. Jan. 16, 1840	2	73
Godfrey, s. Capt. Roger W. & Polly, b. Mar. 23, 170[ ]	1	9

	Vol.	Page
WILLIAMS, (cont.)		
Godfrey, s. Roger W. & Polly, d. Apr. 5, 1812	1	59
Hannah, w. Samuel, Jr., d. Feb. 25, 1800	1	58
Hannah, farmer, d. Feb. 12, 1848, ae 60	2	81
Harriet Ward, d. Joseph & Betsey, b. Feb. 15, 1827	2	66
Henry, s. Joshua P. & Mary, b. Feb. 8, 1826	2	63
Henry D., m. Lavinia **SIMMONS**, b. of Foster, R. I., Feb.		
8, 1841, by Rev. George J. Tillotson	4	74
Herbert, s. Roger W. & Polly, b. May 27, 1795	1	9
Herbert, m. Lucy **BIGELOW**, of Leicester, Mass., Aug. 19,		
1822	1	78
Herbert, m. Lucy **BIGELOW**, of Leicester, Mass., Aug. 19,		
1822	2	65
James, illeg. child of Lydia **HARRIS**, b. Dec. 2, 1795	1	9
James Alexander, s. Elmer & Lodicea A., b. Aug. 2, 1840;		
d. Aug. 18, 1841	2	62
Jane Eliza, d. Caleb D. & Florinda, b. Aug. 8, 1844	2	70
Job, s. Samuel, 2d, d. Oct. 1, 1793, in the 36th y. of his age	1	58
John, 2d, m. Sukey **FARRINGTON**, Dec. 25, 1793	1	78
John, 3rd, m. Polly **CADY**, Mar. 7, 1799	1	78
John, d. Mar. 5, 1832	1	59
John Gardiner, s. Samuel & Hannah, b. Apr. 22, 1782	1	18
John R., of Brooklyn, m. Louisa **UPHAM**, of Leicester, Mass.,		
Sept. 20, 1826, by John Nelson, V. D. M., of Leicester,		
[Mass.]	4	25
John Ruggles, s. John, 2d, & Sukey, b. July 20, 1800	1	9
Joseph, s. Samuel, 2d, & Hannah, b. Dec. 31, 1793	1	9
Joseph H., m. Mary **POTTER**, b. of Brooklyn, [Feb.] 28, 1830,		
by John Parish, J. P.	3	11
Joseph H., m. Mary **POTTER**, b. of Brooklyn, Feb. 28, 1830,		
by John Parish, J. P.	3	12
Joseph H., m. Mary **POTTER**, b. of Brooklyn, Feb. 28, 1830,		
by John Parish, J. P.	4	44
Joseph Prescott, s. Joseph & Betsey, b. Apr. 28, 1825	2	66
Joshua P., m. Mary **WILLIAMS**, of Killingly, Apr. 28, 1818	2	63
Joshua P., d. Nov. 3, 1828, in the 33rd y. of his age	1	59
Joshua Phipps, s. John & Sukey, b. Dec. 6, 1794	1	9
Louisa Augustus, d. Caleb D. & Florinda, b. May 5, 1840	2	70
Lucy, d. Elmer & Sally, b. Mar. 22, 179[ ]	1	9
Lucy Bigelow, d. John R. & Louisa, b. May 12, 1836	2	72
Lucy P., m. Perrin **SCARBOROUGH**, Apr. 11, 1813	1	76
Lucy Phipps, d. Sam[ue]l & Hannah, b. Jan. 18, 1791	1	18
Lydia, d. Asa & Hannah, b. Nov. 3, 1781	1	18
Maria, d. Sept. 4, 1850, ae 50	1	134
Marian, wid. Tho[ma]s. d. July 1, 1798	2	58
Marian Noyes, d. Roger W. & Polly, b. Feb. 28, 1806	1	251
Martha, w. Capt. Samuel, d. Dec. 28, 1804, in the 69th		
y. of her age	1	58

	Vol.	Page
WILLIAMS, (cont.)		
Martha E., of Brooklyn, m. Joseph **SPRAGUE**, of Hingham,		
Mass., Sept. 18, 1839, by Rev. William Coe	4	70
Martha M., m. William **COLWELL**, b. of Brooklyn, Jan. 5,		
1839, by Rev. William Coe	4	68
Martin, s. Elmer & Sally, b. June 20, 1803	1	9
Martin Herrick, m. Dolly Amanda **FARNAM**, Mar. 2, [1834],		
by Samuel J. May	4	54
Mary, d. Sam[ue]l, 2d, d, Jan. 15, 1794, in the 31st y.		
of his age	1	58
Mary, m. Rufus **BROWN**, May 16, 1797	1	61
Mary, d. Samuel, 2d, & Clarrissa, b. July 7, 1801	1	9
Mary, of Killingly, m. Joshua P. **WILLIAMS**, Apr. 28, 1818	2	63
Mary, d. Nathaniel & Hannah, b. Apr. 27, 1822	2	63
Mary Ann, d. John, 2d, & Sukey, b. Oct. 25, 1805	1	5
Mary E., ae 23, b. Newburyport, Mass., *m. Richard C.		
EDWARDS, merchant, ae 30, b. Hunter, N. Y., res. N. Y.		
City, June 6, 1849, by Prof. Edwards A. Parke (*Miss.?)	2	105
Mary E., of Brooklyn, m. Richard Cunningham **EDWARDS**, of		
New York, June 6, 1849, by Rev. Edward A. Park, of		
Andover Theological Seminary	4	101
Mary M., d. Charles G. ae 28, & Lucy E., ae 26, b. July		
30, 1848	2	81
Nancy Maria, d. Nathaniel & Hannah, b. Oct. 4, 1816	2	63
Nathan, farmer, of Canterbury, d. Mar. 14, 1848, ae 87	2	80
Nathaniel, s. Sam[ue]l & Hannah, b. Oct. 29, 1783	1	18
Nathaniel, m. Hannah **WITTER**, Apr. 22, 1811	2	63
Nathaniel, m. Mary A. **GILBERT**, b. of Brooklyn,		
[1852], by Rev. Sylvester Barrows	4	108
Nathaniel Gallup, s. Charles G., farmer, ae 30, & Lucy		
E., ae 29, b. May 21, 1850	2	109
Nelson, s. Joshua P. & Mary, b. Jan. 7, 1828	2	63
Olive, of Brooklyn, m. Franklin **WILLIAMS**, of Buffalo,		
N. Y., Dec. 2, 1852, by Rev. George G. Channing	4	106
Palmer, m. Sally **HERRICK**, May 31, 1795	1	78
Patty Maria, d. Elmer & Sally, b. May 22, 1800	1	9
Philley, d. Asa & Hannah, b. May 18, 1788	1	18
Polly, w. Roger W., d. Dec. 6, 1820, in the 46th y. of her age	1	59
Robert, s. John R. & Louisa, b. Dec. 20, 1829	2	72
Robert Brick*, s. Stephen & Sarah, b. Mar. 26, 1789 *(Bush?)	1	9
Robert Rush*, s. Stephen & Sarah, d. Sept. 1, 1791 *(Bush?)	1	58
Roger W., s. Tho[ma]s & Marian, b. Aug. 25, 1764	1	9
Roger W., d. Oct. 1, 1821, in the 58th y. of his age	1	59
Sally, d. Elmer & Sally, b. Aug. 26, 179[ ]	1	9
Samuel,, 3rd, m. Hannah **GARDINER**, June 12, 1781	1	78
Samuel, Capt., d. Feb. 4, 1805, in the 84th y. of his age	1	58
Samuel, d. Dec. 17, 1828, in the 72nd y. of his age	1	59
Samuel Cephas, s. Sam[ue]l & Hannah, b. Mar. 18, 1789	1	18

	Vol.	Page
WILLIAMS, (cont.)		
Samuel Walter, s. Nathaniel & Hannah, b. Aug. 11, 1818;		
d. Feb. 20, 1826	2	63
Sarah [ ], m. Asa D. **BENNETT**, Nov. 6, 1853, by Rev. R.		
Camp	4	110
Sarah Baker, d. Archibald & Sarah, b. Jan. 24, 1830	2	69
Sarah Eliza, d. Elmer & Lodicea A., b. Sept. 21, 1833	2	62
Sarah T., m. Edwin **ROBINSON**, b. of Brooklyn, May 6, 1844,		
by Rev. G. J. Tillotson	4	80
Serepta, d. Stephen & Sarah, b. Apr. 1, 1791	1	9
Sarepta, m. Nathaniel **MARTIN**, Feb. 4, 1810	1	71
Sarepta, d. Stephen & Sarah, b. Apr. 1, 1791; m. Nathaniel		
MARTIN, Feb. 4, 1810	2	35
Stephen Paine, s. Stephen & Sarah, b. Mar. 14, 1789 (sic)	1	9
Susan F., d. Caleb D. & Florinda, b. Feb. 13, 1838	2	70
Susan Farrington, d. Joshua P. & Mary, b. Jan. 14, 1820	2	63
Thomas Albert, s. Martin H. & Dolly A., b. May 2, 1834	2	73
Ursula, d. Roger W. & Polly, b. Sept. 10, 1813	1	252
Ursula, d. Roger W. & Polly, d. Mar. 29, 1814	1	59
Warren, s. Nathaniel & Hannah, b. Feb. 25, 1824	2	63
Warren, farmer, d. May 31, [1850], ae 26	2	110
Waty, m. William **TYLER**, Jan. 1, 1809	1	77
William, s. Sam[ue]l & Hannah, b. Nov. 17, 1786	1	18
William P., s. Caleb D. & Florinda, b. Jan. 13, 1834	2	70
Wolcott Bigelow, s. Herbert & Lucy, b. Aug. 13, 1823	2	65
Wolcot[t] Roger, m. Polly **SCARBOROUGH**, Mar. 6, 1794	1	78
WILSON, WILLSON, Betsey, d. Ignatius & Anna, b. Mar. 5, 1789	1	18
Daniel Allyn, s. Ignatius & Anna, b. May 31, 1782	1	18
Esther, d. Ignatius & Anna, b. Feb. 8, 1786	1	18
Esther, d. Ignatius & Anna, d. Nov. 3, 1787	1	58
Ignatius, m. Anne **ALLYN**, Nov. 30, 1780	1	78
Mary Ann, of Brooklyn, m. Ebenezer S. **BENNETT**, of		
Canterbury, May 5, 1850, by Cha[rle]s Adams, J. P.	4	102
Orinda, d. Ignatius & Anna, b. Mar. 5, 1784	1	18
Orinda, d. Ignatius & Anne, d. Oct. [ ], 1787	1	58
[WINDSOR], WINSOR, Albert G., d. Nov. 6, 1849, ae 4	2	120
Harriet C., d. Stephen, manufacturer, ae 37, & Ardelia,		
ae 36, b. Oct. 26, 1849	2	119
WINSLOW, Eddy, m. Azuba **ALLYN**, July 5, 1795	1	78
WINTER, Henry A., b. Brooklyn, res. E. Brooklyn, d. July 25,		
[1851] ae 8	2	132
WITHEY, Erastus, s. Hazail & Abigail, b. Sept. [ ], 1801	1	9
Fanny Maria, twin with Mary Stems, d. Hazael & Abigail,		
b. July 16, 1811	1	252
Hazel, m. Abigail **BOYDEN**, Nov. 24, 1799	1	78
Hazel, d. Mar. 1, 1820	1	59
Henry Boiden, s. Hazel & Abigail, b. Sept. 29, 1803	1	9
Lois, m. Erastus **BAKER**, Nov. 4, 1787	1	61

	Vol.	Page
WITHEY, (cont.)		
Mary Sterns, twin with Fanny Maria, d. Hazael & Abigail,		
b. July 16, 1811	1	252
Sibbel, w. Hazel, d. July 2, 1798	1	58
WITTER, Asa, s. Nathan, Jr. & Mary, b. July 20, 1795	1	9
Cynthia, d. Nathan & Kezia, b. Mar. 27, 1768	1	18
Cynthia, m. Roswell **MORGAN,** Nov. 22, 1786	1	71
Dolly, d. Capt. Ebenezer & Dolly, b. July 8, 1807	1	251
Dolly, m. James Alexander **STETSON,** b. of Brooklyn, [May]		
27, [1827], by Rev. Samuel J. May	4	27
Eben, m. Sophia **CLARK,** Sept. 21, 1848, by Daniel P.		
Tyler, J. P.	4	100
Ebenezer, Capt., m. Dolly **SHARPE,** May 11, 1806	1	78
Elizabeth, d. Nathan & Kezia, b. Jan. 28, 1765	1	18
Elizabeth, d. Nathan, d. Oct. 7, 1776, ae 10 y. 8 m. 10 d.	1	58
Ellen Maria, d. John & Mary Ann, b. Sept. 3, 1838	2	75
Emily E., d, Nathan, Jr. & Abigail, b. Aug. 25, 1823	2	67
Emily E., m. Addison **MASCRAFT,** Feb. 12, 1854, by Rev.		
C. Y. DeNormandie	4	113
Hannah, d. Nathan, 2d, & Mary, b. Apr. 17, 1788	1	9
Hannah, m. Nathaniel **WILLIAMS,** Apr. 22, 1811	2	63
Jacob, s. Nathan & Kezia, b. Mar. 25, 1772	1	18
Jacob B., m. Olive **BROWN,** Nov. 23, 1794	1	78
Jacob B., d. Mar. 13, 1839, ae 67 y. lacking 12 d.	1	59
James Henry, s. Nathan, Jr. & Abigail, b. Feb. 6, 1834	2	67
John, s. Nathan & Kezia, b. May 16, 1770	1	18
John, s. Nathan, d. Oct. 14, 1776, ae 6 y. 4 m. 29 d.	1	58
John, s. Jacob B. & Olive, b. Feb. 4, 1796	1	9
John Jacob, s. John & Mary Ann, b. Dec. 6, 1841	2	75
Kezia, d. Nathan & Kezia, b. July 5, 1763	1	18
Keziah, w. Dea. Nathan, d. Oct. 25, 1806, in the 71st y.		
of her age	1	58
Lucy, d. Nathan & Kezia, b. Feb. 2, 1757	1	18
Mary, d. Nathan & Kezia, b. Nov. 2, 1754	1	18
Mary, of Brooklyn, m. Nathan **PAINE,** of Pomfret, Feb. 26,		
1807, by John Parish, J. P.	3	4
Nancy, d. Nathan, 2d, & Mary, b. Nov. 11, 1786	1	9
Nathan, m. Kezia **BRANCH,** Dec. 15, 1753	1	78
Nathan, s. Nathan & Kezia, b. Feb. 20, 1761	1	18
Nathan, 2d, m. Mary **FULLER,** Mar. 18, 1784	1	78
Nathan, s. Nathan, 2d, & Mary, b. Oct. 19, 1790	1	9
Nathan, Dea., d. Oct. 30, 1822, in the 91st y. of his age	1	59
Nathan P., m. Harriet **HAWKINS,** b. of Brooklyn, Mar. 8,		
1846, by Rev. Herman Snow	4	82
Nathan Pierce, s. Nathan, Jr. & Abigail, b. July 18, 1819	2	67
Noah, s. Nathan & Kezia, b. Apr. 20, 1759	1	18
Olive Elizabeth, d. John & Mary Ann, b. Oct. 22, 1836	2	75
Orrin, s. Jacob B. & Olive, b. July 15, 1797	1	9

	Vol.	Page
WITTER, (cont.)		
Pashal, s. Nathan & Kezia, b. Dec. 6, 1778	1	18
Polly, d. Nathan & Mary, b. Jan. 30, 1785	1	18
Ruamah, d. Nathan, d. Dec. 13, 1778, ae 1 y. 7 d.	1	58
Sarah, d. Nathan & Kezia, b. Nov. 23, 1779	1	18
Sarah, m. Uriah **LITCHFIELD,** Nov. 27, 1788	1	70
-----, s. Nathan & Kezia, b. Apr. 10, 1775	1	18
WOOD, Benjamin, m. Ruhamah **BENNET,** Nov. 23, 1786	1	78
Benjamin, m. Abigail **WHITNEY,** Apr. 5, 1792	1	78
Charles, m. Sarah Ann **TURNER,** b. of Gloucester, R. I.,		
May 17, 1846, by Rev. Herman Snow	4	83
Emily, d. Benja[min] & Abigail, b. Feb. 13, 1791	1	9
Gurdon, s. Benjamin & Abigail, b. Jan. 3, 1793	1	9
Robert Brick Whitney, s. Benjamin & Abigail, b. May 15, 1795	1	9
Ruhamah, w. Benjamin, d. Mar. 8, 1791	1	43
WOODARD, [see under **WOODWARD**]'		
WOODBRIDGE, Joseph S., of Columbus, Ga., m. Lucretia M.		
SCARBOROUGH, of Brooklyn, Sept. 1, 1852, by Rev.		
Geo[rge] J. Tillotson	4	107
William, s. William, physician, ae 29, & Mary Ann, ae 24,		
b. July 23, 1848	2	78
WOODWARD, WOODARD, Aaron, s. Ward & Rebeckah, b. Sept.		
20, 1781	1	251
Abigail, d. Capt. Ward & Rebeckah, b. Jan. 11, 17[ ]	1	251
Abigail, m. Joseph **AUSTIN,** Jan. 5, 1815	1	60
Artemus, s. Capt. Ward & Rebeckah, d. Nov. 13, 1810	1	58
Artemus, s. Capt. Ward & Rebeckah, b. Feb. 19, [ ]	1	251
Augustus, s. Capt. Ward & Rebeckah, b. [ ]	1	251
Calvin Hamilton, s. Augustus & Caroline, b. Jan. 14, 1838	2	71
David, s. Capt. Ward & Rebeckah, b. Nov. 12, 17[ ]	1	251
David, m. Mrs. Nancy W. **LITTLEHALE,** of Northbridge,		
Mass., Jan. 14, 1849, by Rev. J. Ferris. Int. pub. Jan. 14,		
1849	4	101
David, mason, ae 49, of Brooklyn, m. 2d w. Nancy		
LITTLEHALE, weaver, b. Mass., res. Mass., ae 35, Jan.		
28, 1849, by Rev. Ferris	2	104
Deidama, d. Capt. Ward & Rebeckah, b. Oct. 8, 1790	1	251
Eleazer, s. Capt. Ward & Rebeckah, b. July 11, 1792	1	251
Ephraim P., s. Capt. Ward & Rebeckah, b. June 2, 1787	1	251
Huldah, wid. Ephraim, d. Aug. 21, 1810, in the 96th y.		
of her age	1	58
James Brown, s. Augustus & Caroline, b. Dec. 30, 1843	2	71
John Putnam, s. Augustus & Caroline, b. June 7, 1841	2	71
Nancy Seymour, d. Augustus & Caroline, b. Mar. 11, 1846	2	71
Rebecca, housekeeper, b. Lyndeborough, N. Y., res. Brooklyn,		
d. Oct. 18, 1848, ae 87	2	99
Sarah, d. Capt. Ward & Rebeckah, b. Apr. 1, 17[ ]	1	251
Sewell, s. Capt. Ward & Rebeckah, b. Feb. 8, 1783	1	251

	Vol.	Page
WOODWARD, WOODARD, (cont.)		
Ward, Jr., s. Capt. Ward & Rebeckah, b. Sept. 12, 1785	1	251
Ward, Capt., d. Apr. 12, 1810, in the 59th y. of his age	1	58
Warren Wheeler, s. Augustus & Caroline, b. June 27, 1834	2	71
WOODWORTH, Clarence D., b. W. Killingly, res. E. Brooklyn,		
d. Oct. 13, 1850, ae 16 m.	2	132
Emily, of Brooklyn, m. Nathaniel **FRY**, of Griswold, Mar. 1,		
1835, by Rev. Thomas Huntington	4	60
Giles, of Killingly, m. Philury **HYDE**, of Brooklyn, Nov.		
27, 1823, by Rev. Roswell Whitmore	4	16
WORDEN, Hannah R., of Brooklyn, m. Albert H. **COLE**, of		
Killingly, June 21, 1846, by Rev. Herman Snow	4	83
Lewis, m. Sarah **DARBY**, b. of Brooklyn, Sept. 17, 1844,		
by Rev. G. J. Tillotson	4	80
[W]RIGHT, Anna, m. Josiah **SHEPARD**, Nov. 23, 1790	1	76
YORK, Esther, m. William **SMITH**, Nov. 15, 1787	1	76
YOUNG, Benjan, of Killingly, m. Lucina **HYDE**, of Brooklyn,		
Mar. 9, 1834, by Daniel Williams, Clerk, at Killingly	4	53
Benjamin, farmer, d. Mar. 5, 1849, ae 39	2	104
Fre[e]born, of Killingly, m. Mary **HUBBARD**, of Brooklyn,		
Oct. 21, 1804, by John Parrish, J. P.	3	6
Hannah, m. Alfred **ASHCRAFT**, Dec. 29, 1803	1	60
Henry, of Voluntown, m. Mary **SPALDING**, of Killingly,		
Apr. 6, 1828, by Rev. Roswell Whitmore	4	32
Luther, m. Matilda **BENNETT**, b. of Brooklyn, Mar. 31,		
[1831], by Rev. Roswell Whitmore	4	44
Susannah, m. Bela **DARBE**, Feb. 26, 1807	2	14
ZEBEDEE, Eunice, m. Abijah **NORTON**, Nov. 14, 1820, by John		
Parish, J. P.	4	13
Eunice, m. Abijah **NORTON**, Dec. 15, 1820, by John Parish,		
J. P.	3	2

BROOKLYN ADMISSIONS OF ELECTORS
Volume 1, Pages 21 - 27

Page

CADY, (cont.)

John C., adm. fr. Apr. 13, 1801	21
Jonathan adm. fr. Apr. 8, 1805	23
Lemuel, adm. fr. Apr. 11, 1803	22
Lovel, adm. fr. Apr. 11, 1808	23
Lyman, adm. fr. July 4, 1818	27
Pascal, adm. fr. July 4, 1818	27
Samuel, adm. fr. Apr. 7, 1816	26
William, adm. fr. Sept. 21, 1818	27
Wyllys, adm. fr. Apr. 13, 1807	23
CARPENTER, Job, adm. fr. Sept. 19, 1814, Brooklyn	25
CARTER, Adin, adm. fr. July 4, 1818	27
CASHMAN, Lathrop, adm. fr. Sept. 17, 1804	22
CHAMBERLAIN, John, adm. fr. Sept. 17, 1804	22
CHAPMAN, Samuel, adm. fr. Sept. 17, 1792	21
CLARKE, CLARK, Caleb, Jr., adm. fr. Sept. 17, 1804	22
James, adm. fr. Apr. 11, 1803	22
Moses, adm. fr. Apr. 12, 1790	21
CLEVELAND, Davis, adm. fr. Apr. 11, 1791	21
Isaac, adm. fr. Sept. 17, 1804	22
COGSWELL, Daniel, adm. fr. Apr. 8, 1805	23
William, adm. fr. Apr. 8, 1816	26
COLLAR, Henry, adm. fr. Sept. 19, 1808	23
COLWELL, Arnold, adm. fr. Sept. 16, 1811	24
Harris, adm. fr. Sept. 15, 1817	27
COOPER, Nathaniel, adm. fr. Apr. 10, 1809	23
COPELAND, Daniel, adm. fr. Apr. 7, 1806	23
Jonathan, adm. fr. Sept. 15, 1794	21
Royal, adm. fr. July 4, 1818	27
Wyllis, adm. fr. Apr. 11, 1803	22
CURTIS, Chauncey, adm. fr. July 4, 1818	27
DABNEY, John G., adm. fr. Sept. 21, 1818	27
William, adm. fr. July 4, 1818	27
DAINS, Daniel, adm. fr. July 4, 1818	27
DARBY, DARBE, Alpheas, adm. fr. Sept. 12, 1786	21
Alpheas, adm. fr. Sept. 15, 1805	23
Asahel, adm. fr. "several years ago". Recorded Sept. 18, 1815	26
Daniel, adm. fr. July 4, 1818	27
David, adm. fr. Sept. 21, 1818	27
Nathan, adm. fr. Sept. 21, 1818	27
W[illia]m, adm. fr. Sept. 15, 1800	21
DAVIS, Bela, adm. fr. Sept. 15, 1806	23
DAVISON, Aaron, adm. fr. Apr. 11, 1803	22
Benjamin, adm. fr. Apr. 5, 1819	27
Beriah, adm. fr. Sept. 19, 1808	23
Daniel Jr., adm. fr. Sept. 21, 1812	25
Joel, adm. fr. Apr. 11, 1814	25
Joseph, adm. fr. Apr. 9, 1787	21

Page

DAVISON, (cont.)
    Nathan, adm. fr. July 4, 1818   27
    Peter, adm. fr. Apr. 11, 1803   22
    Septimus, adm. fr. Apr. 7, 1816   26
DAY, John, adm. fr. Sept. 18, 1815   26
DEAOLPH, Amasa, adm. fr. Sept. 15, 1805   23
    Giles M., adm. fr. Sept. 17, 1804   22
    Wyllys, adm. fr. Sept. 19, 1803   22
DORRANCE, John G., adm. fr. Sept. 16, 1816 26
    Samuel, adm. fr. Apr. 12, 1802   22
DOUGLASS, Ann William made affidavit that William DOUGLASS, was
    adm. fr. Sept. 19, 1796, at Plainfield   23
    William, adm. fr. Sept. 19, 1796 at Plainfield according to
    affidavit made by Ann William DOUGLASS 23
DOWNIING, Abner, adm. fr. Sept. 21, 1818   27
    Dyer, adm. fr. Sept. 21, 1818   27
    Ichabod, adm. fr. Sept. 19, 1803   22
ELDRED, James, adm. fr. Sept. 12, 1786   21
ELDRIDGE, Giles, adm. fr. Sept. 19, 1803 22
    Joseph, adm. fr. Sept. 19, 1803   22
EVANS, Elijah, adm. fr. Sept. 21, 1818   27
FAULKNER, Samuel, adm. fr. Apr. 8, 1805 23
FOGG, Edward, adm. fr. July 4, 1818   27
FOSSSETT, FOSSET, Joab, adm. fr. Apr. 11, 1791 21
    Joseph, adm. fr. Apr. 11, 1791   21
FOSTER, Samuel P., adm. fr. July 4, 1818 27
    William, adm. fr. July 4, 1818   27
FRANKLIN, Ezra, adm. fr. Apr. 11, 1803 22
    Henry T., adm. fr. July 4, 1818   27
    James, adm. fr. July 4, 1818   27
FROST, Stephen, adm. fr. Sept. 12, 1786 21
FULLER, Josiah, adm. fr. Apr. 7, 1788   21
GILBERT, Benj[ami]n, adm. fr. Apr. 11, 1791 21
    Calvin, adm. fr. Sept. 21, 1801   21
    John W., adm. fr. "several years ago". Recorded Apr. 8, 1805 22
    Joseph, adm. fr. Apr. 11, 1791   21
    Joseph C., adm. fr. Apr. 13, 1818   27
    Wyllys, adm. fr. Apr. 12, 1813   25
GOODELL, Richard, adm. fr. Sept. 15, 1805 23
    Wyllys, adm. fr. Sept. 17, 1804   22
GRAY, John, Jr., adm. Sept. 16, 1816, North Stonington 26
HARRIS, Heber, adm. fr. Apr. 11, 1803   22
    Hosea, adm. fr. Apr. 11, 1803   22
    Martin, adm. fr. Apr. 5, 1819   27
HEBBARD, Jeptha, adm. fr. Apr. 11, 1814 25
    William, adm. fr. Apr. 13, 1818   27
HERRICK, James P., adm. fr. Apr. 8, 1805 23
    Timothy, adm. fr. Apr. 7, 1816   26

BURLINGTON VITAL RECORDS
1806 - 1852

	Vol.	Page
ADAMS, Ezra S., of Canton, m. Lydia **POND**, of Burlington, May 19, 1825, by Erastus Clapp, V. D. M.	7	12
James, of New Hartford, m. Salley **MOODEY**, of Burlington, Nov. 27, [1831?], by Alden Handury	7	24
Thomas, of Canton, m. Lucy **LEE**, of Burlington, June 12, 1837, by Rev. Richard Hayton	7	36
Thomas, of Burlington, m. Rhoda Jane **LEE**, of Plymouth, Apr. 19, 1840, by Rev. Aaron S. Hill	7	41
ADDIS, Thomas, of Litchfield, m. Polly **BECKWITH**, of Burlington, Oct. 17, 1830, by Erastus Scranton, V. D. M.	7	22
ALCOTT, [see also **ALCOX**], Charles W., m. Jane **GRIGGS**, b. of Plymouth, Apr. 4, 1852, by Rev. Cephas Brainard	7	67
ALCOX, [see also **ALCOTT**], Lucius, of Wolcott, m. Emily **ROBERTS**, of Burlington, Nov. 5, 1823, by Erastus Clapp, V. D. M.	7	11
ALDERMAN, Chestine, of Burlington, m. Theodore **LEVENWORTH**, of Goshen, Jan. 26, 1842, by Rev. David Miller	7	45
Eli, m. Harriet A. **BELDEN**, Mar. 10, 1841, by Rev. Philip L. Hoyt	7	42
Emely, m. Alonzo **ELTON**, b. of Burlington, May 31, 1847, by J. Henson	7	56
Esther Loiza, m. Henry **ELTON**, b. of Burlington, Apr. 30, 1848, by Peter Tatro, Jr.	7	57
Julia, Mrs., m. Lathrop **RICHARDSON**, b. of Burlington, June 7, 1848, by Peter Tatro, Jr.	7	58
Marilla, of Burlington, m,. Nathaniel **WEBSTER**, of Farmington, Jan. 11, 1835, by Rev. John B. Beach	7	33
Nancy, of Burlington, m. Amos **CASE**, of Canton, Apr. 9, 1838, by Rev. Richard Haytee	7	38
ALDRICH, Warren, of Collinsville, m. Lois A. **HITCHCOCK**, of Burlington, June 16, 1844, by Rev. James Noyes	7	50
ALFORD, William, of Harwinton, m. Mary **HITCHCOCK**, of Burlington, Oct. 17, 1841, by Rev. Ezra Jagger	7	44
ALLEN, Edwin P., of Avon, m. Charlotte **ROBERTS**, of Burlington, Mar. 15, 1832, by Erastus Scranton, V. D. M.	7	24
John, of Collinsville, m. Eunice **MUNSEL**, of Windsor, Feb. 22, 1849, by Rev. Charles B. McLean	7	61
Sally, of Plymouth, b. Dec. 20, 1781, m. David **NORTON**, of Bristol, [ ]	1	16

	Vol.	Page
BACON, (cont.)		
Rosanna, [d. Moses & Rosanna], b. Oct. 11, 1779	1	3
Rosanna, w. Moses, d. Jan. 15, 1812	1	3
BAILEY, Rachel, of New Hartford, m. Samuel **GOODSELL**, of		
Burlington, Aug. 5, 1827, by Erastus Clapp, V. D. M.	7	17
BALDWIN, Joseph M., of Harwinton, m. Eliza M. **SMITH**, of		
Burlington, Jan. 1, 1851, by James L. Wright	7	65
William S., of Harwinton, m. Susan S. **SMITH**, of Burlington,		
Nov. 27, 1845, by Rev. James Noyes	7	52
BALL, Edward C., m. Cynthia M. **BRONSON**, May 7, 1848, by		
Luther Hart	7	19
Elizabeth, of Burlington, m. Samuel **CRANE**, of East Windsor,		
Oct. 24, 1826, by Erastus Clapp, V. D. M.	7	15
William, m. Marella **STONE**, June 3, 1828, by Erastus Clapp,		
V. D. M.	7	19
BANNET, Sybel, m. Challenge **WHEELER**, Feb. 27, 1822, by		
Jonathan Miller, V. D. M.	1	21
BANNING, Laura L., m. Charles F. **HILL**, b. of Hartford, May 2,		
1852, by Cephas Brainard	7	67
Mary Ann, m. Manley **PALMETER**, b. of Burlington, Oct. 6,		
1841, by Rev. David Miller	7	43
BARBER, Orville, m. Emeline **BROOKS**, July 11, 1833, by Rev.		
David L. Parmelee	7	30
BARNES, BARNS, Albert, m. Sarah Eliza **ANDREWS**, b. of New		
Hartford, Oct. 28, 1835, by Erastus Scranton, V. D. M.	7	35
Almira, of Burlington, m. Eli **HULL**, of Farmington, Aug.		
4, 1824, by Datus Ensign, Elder	7	12
Andrew, of New Hartofrd, m. Celia **BARNS**, of Burlington,		
Dec. 8, 1840, by P. L. Hoyt	7	42
Belinda, m. Samuel J. **JOHNSON**, July 16, 1835, by John B.		
Beach	7	34
Celia, of Burlington, m. Andrew **BARNS**, of New Hartford,		
Dec. 8, 1840, by P. L. Hoyt	7	42
Eunice, of Burlington, m. Levi **BRONSON**, of Winchester,		
Oct. 5, 1828, by William Marsh, J. P.	7	19
Jeremiah, m. Susanna **RICHARDS**, Sept. 19, 1832, by Erastus		
Scranton, V. D. M.	7	28
Leenora, of Burlington, m. Calvest H. **COTTON**, of Otis,		
Mass., July 8, 1838, by Rev. Aaron S. Hill	7	38
Lois, of Burlington, m. Mynor **ANDRUSS**, of Berlin, Oct.		
15, 1823, by Erastus Clapp, V. D. M.	7	11
Pamelia, m. Franklin **NORTON**, b. of Burlington, Dec. 25,		
1833, by Erastus Scranton, V. D. M.	7	32
Polly, m. Nathan **CULVER**, Mar. 13, 1828, by William Marks,		
J. P.	7	18
Rowenah, m. Fayette **BUTLER**, b. of Burlington, Mar. 21,		
1848, by Peter Tatro, Jr.	7	57
Timothy A., farmer, ae 25, of New Hartford, m. Lydia A.		

	Vol.	Page

	Vol.	Page
BECKWITH, (cont.)		
Parnel, of Burlington, m. Israel **DIBBLE**, of Granby, Aug.		
4, 1831, by Erastus Scranton, V. D. M.	7	23
Polly, of Burlington, m. Thomas **ADDIS**, of Litchfield,		
Oct. 17, 1830, by Erastus Scranton, V. D. M.	7	22
Vashti, of Burlington, m. Homer **WOODING**, of Farmington,		
Mar. 10,. 1829, by Willard Hitchcock, J. P.	7	20
BELDEN, Ai, m. Sylvia **BROOKS**, Nov. 7, 1826, by Rev. Joseph		
McCreerey	7	15
Emeline, m. Romeo **ELTON**, Mar. 13, 1842, by Rev. David		
Miller	1	25
Emeline, m. Romeo **ELTON**, Mar. 13, 1842, by Rev. David		
Miller	7	45
Harriet A., m. Eli **ALDERMAN**, Mar. 10, 1841, by Rev. Philip		
L. Hoyt	7	42
Isaac, Jr., m. Cynthia **POND**, b. of Burlington, Apr. 29,		
1840, by Rev. Aaron S. Hill	7	41
Larey, m. Catharine **SESSIONS**, b. of Burlington, Nov. 17,		
1842, by Erastus Scranton, V. D. M.	7	49
Lorena, m. Orrin **UPSON**, b. of Burlington, Dec. 24, 1823,		
by Datus Ensign, Elder	7	11
Mary P., of Burlington, m. Asaph **FULLER**, of Bristol,		
Apr. 27, 1848, by Peter Tatro, Jr.	7	57
Samuel, m. Mrs. Amanda M. **CLARK**, b. of Burlington, Nov.		
22, 1840, by Rev. Philip L. Hoyt	7	42
BENHAM, Abigal, [d. Elias & Sally], b. Nov. 23, 1829	1	17
Abigail, of Burlington, m. John G. **HART**, of Bristol,		
Nov. 12, 1848, by Rev. James L. Wright	7	60
Adelia, [d. Elias & Sally], b. Apr. 17, 1816	1	17
Delia, of Burlington, m. George **GRIDLEY**, of Waterbury,		
Apr. 24, 1834, by Erastus Scranton, V. D. M.	7	33
Ebenezer, 2nd, [s. Elias & Sally], b. May 30, 1812	1	17
Edward, [s. Elias & Sally], b. May 31, 1835	1	17
Elias, m. Sally **WOODIN**, May 1, 1811	1	17
Elizabeth, 2nd, [d. Elias & Sally], b. June 19 , 1814	1	17
Louis, of Burlington, m. Hezekiah **ROGERS**, of Camden,		
N. Y., Oct. 12, 1825, by William Marks, J. P.	7	13
Lucy, [d. Elias & Sally], b. June 1, 1819	1	17
Samuel, of Burlington, m. Anna **CARRINGTON**, of		
Farmington, Sept. 4, 1831, by William Marks, J. P.	7	23
Sarah, [d. Elias & Sally], b. Feb. 20, 1828	1	17
BICKFORD, Mary Ann, of Burlington, m. Horace **WEAVER**, of		
Salsbury, Sept. 1, 1840, by Rev. George B. Atwell, of		
Canton	7	41
BLACKMAN, Lemuel, m. Lucy **ELTON**, b. of Burlington, Oct. 9,		
1831, by Erastus Scranton, V. D. M.	7	24
[BOARDMAN], **BORDMAN**, Jason, Jr., of Wethersfield, m. Maria		
BRADLEY, of Burlington, Jan. 12, 1831, by Erastus		

	Vol.	Page

[BOARDMAN], BORDMAN, (cont.)
Scranton, V. D. M.   7   22
BOND, Nancy, of Plymouth, m. David **ROBERTS**, of Burlington,
   Jan. 25, 1829, by William Marks, J. P.   7   19
BOTSFORD, BOTCHSFORD, Shorlotte*, Abigail, [d. Daniel &
   Polly Betsey], b. June 28, 1807   *(Charlotte")   1   15
Daniel, of Bristol, b. Aug. 21, 1782; m. Polly Betsey
   FOOT, Oct. 5, 1800   1   15
Lucius Daniel, [s. Daniel & Polly Betsey], b. Aug. 14, 1804   1   15
Lugeane(?), m. Mary **BECKWITH**, Sept. 10, 1822, by
   Jonathan Miller, V. D. M.   1   24
Luzon Marsena, [child of Daniel & Polly Betsey], b.
   June 4, 1802   1   15
Polly Elmina, [d. Daniel & Polly Betsey], b. June 19, 1809   1   15
Urana Ursula, [d. Daniel & Polly Betsey], b. Nov. 5, 1813   1   15
BRADLEY, Abigail, of Burlington, m. Thomas **LAMSON**, of Mt.
   Washington, May 28, 1850, by James L. Wright   7   64
Albert A., m. Harriet **MOLTHROPT**, b. of Burlington, Oct.
   21, 1841, by Rev. David Miller   7   44
Maria, of Burlington, m. Jason **BORDMAN**, Jr., of
   Wethersfield, Jan. 12, 1831, by Erastus Scranton, V. D.
   M.   7   22
Orilla C., of Burlington, m. George R. **HOLBROOK**, of
   Oxford, Nov. 25, 1847, by Rev. William Goodwin, Jr.   7   56
Rosena, m. Sylvester **POND**, b. of Burlington, Oct. 23,
   1842, by Erastus Scranton, V. D. M.   7   48
Susannah, of Burlington, m. Andrew G. **GRAHAM**, of Berlin,
   Apr. 15, 1838, by Erastus Scranton, V. D. M.   7   38
Uriel, of Mereden, m. Phebe **PHELPS**, of Burlington, Aug.
   22, 1827, by Erastus Clapp. V. D. M   7   17
BREWER, Joshua B., m. Harriet **PAYNE**, Oct. 5, 1840, by Calvin
   Butler   7   41
BRISTOL, Betsey, m. Joseph **FINN**, b. of Harwinton, July 15,
   1845, by Rev. J. B. Beach   7   51
BROADRICK, Stephen A., of Farmington, m. Louisa G. **BROOKS**,
   of Burlington, Apr. 9, 1851, by Rev. Cephas Brainard   7   66
BRONSON, Cynthia M., m. Edwin C. **BALL**, May 7, 1848, by
   Luther Hart   7   19
Ira, m. Laura **FRISBIE**, Aug. 28, 1814   1   12
Levi, of Winchester, m. Eunice **BARNS**, of Burlington,
   Oct. 5, 1828, by William Marsh, J. P.   7   19
Samuel Humphrey, [s. Dr. Samuel S. & Ursula], b. July 12,
   1815; d. Dec. 23, 1815   1   11
Samuel S., Dr., m. Ursula **HUMPHREY**, Apr. 28, 1814   1   11
Sarah Ann, m. Sylvester N. **TAYLOR**, b. of Burlington,
   Apr. 8, 1843, by Erastus Scranton, V. D. M.   7   48
BROOKS, Austin, m. Nancy **POND**, b. of Burlington, July 20,
   1837, by Rev. Harvey Husted   7   36

	Vol.	Page

BROOKS, (cont.)

Caroline, of Burlington, m. Lewis **WILCOX**, of Hartford,
  Sept. 5, 1832, by Rev. Henry Stanwood, of Bristol | 7 | 29

Celestia, of Burlington, m. Joseph D. **IVES**, of Middletown,
  Sept. 28, 1830, by Rev. Luther Mead | 7 | 22

Emeline, m. Orville **BARBER**, July 11, 1833, by Rev. David
  L. Parmelee | 7 | 30

Fanny M., m. Rush F. **MASON**, b. of Burlington, Nov. 5,
  1844, by Rev. James Noyes | 7 | 50

Henry A., m. Mary Ann **WRIGHT**, b. of Burlington, Nov. 10,
  1846, by Joseph Hinson | 7 | 55

Louisa G., of Burlington, m. Stephen A. **BROADRICK**, of
  Farmington, Apr. 9, 1851, by Rev. Cephas Brainard | 7 | 66

Martha, m. Seth **UPSON**, Jr., Feb. 14, 1828, by Gershom
  Pierce, Elder | 7 | 18

Ransby, of Burlington, m. Louisa **POND**, of Plymouth, Aug.
  27, 1829, by Rev. Henry Stanwood, of Bristol | 7 | 20

Sylvester, m. Prudence **PECK**, Apr. 17, 1822, by Jonathan
  Miller, V. D. M. | 1 | 23

Sylvia, m. Ai **BELDEN**, Nov. 7, 1826, by Rev. Joseph
  McCreerey | 7 | 15

BROWN, BROWNE, Edwin, Jr., m. Nancy B. **JOHNSON**, May 5,
  1844, by Rev. Henry Lounsbury | 7 | 50

Fanny, ae 18, b. Burlington, m. John **SAUNDERS**, moulder,
  ae 34, b. England, res. Unionville, Nov. 30, 1848, by Rev.
  Peter Tatro, Jr. | 7 | 60

Gardner Shepherd, Rev., of Hinsdale, N. H., m. Mary E.
  P. **SCRANTON**, of Burlington, Sept. 30, 1838, by
  Erastus Scranton, V. D. M. | 7 | 38

James, of Burlington, m. Mrs. Sophia **RUST**, of Harwinton,
  May 31, 1830, by Erastus Scranton, V. D. M. | 7 | 21

James F., of Ware, Mass., m. Eunice **WOODFORD**, of
  Burlington, June 13, 1841, by George B. Atwell | 7 | 43

Maria, m. Jerome B. **THOMPSON**, b. of Burlington, Feb. 23,
  1840, by Rev. Aaron S. Hill | 7 | 40

Rosanna, m. Samuel **GILLET**, May 15, 1846, by J. B. Beach | 7 | 53

Sophia, m. Seth **UPSON**, b. of Burlington, Dec. 16, 1838,
  by Erastus Scranton, V. D. M. | 7 | 38

BRUCE, Philamelia, m. Hart H. **WELDEN**, June 12, 1832, by
  William Marks, J. P. | 7 | 28

BUCK, Ruth C., m. Luther B. **ROPER**, [Aug. 7, 1842], by Rev.
  David Miller | 7 | 46

BUGBEE, William A., of Collinsville, m. Zada A. **WOODFORD**,
  of Burlington, Aug. 30, 1835, by Rev. Stephen Mason, of
  Collinsville | 7 | 34

BULL, Eliza Ann, of Burlington, m. Luther P. **DARROW**, of
  Bristol, Oct. 15, 1846, by Rev. James Noyes | 7 | 54

Frederick, m. Mary A. **MASON**, b. of Burlington, May 8,

	Vol.	Page

BULL, (cont.)

1830, by Erastus Scranton, V. D. M.   7   22

Frederick, m. Mary A. **MASON**, b. of Burlington, May 8,
1831, by Erastus Scranton, V. D. M.   7   23

Julia, of Burlington, m. Augustus T. **MERRELL**, of Litchfield,
May 12, 1833, by Erastus Scranton, V. D. M.   7   30

Maria, of Burlington, m. Enos **HAMLIN**, of Granby, Sept.
23, 1838, by Erastus Scranton, V. D. M.   7   38

Mary, of Burlington, m. Amos **HAMBLIN**, of Farmington,
May 2, 1825, by Erastus Clapp, V. D. M.   7   12

Samuel, m. Emily **CLEVELAND**, b. of Burlington, May 11,
1825, by Erastus Clapp, V. D. M.   7   12

BUNNELL, BUNNEL, Chester, m. Sylvia E. **GRISWOLD**, Jan. 20,
1828, by William Marks, J. P.   7   18

Daniel, m. Dolly **HILL**, b. of Burlington, Apr. 19, 1841,
P. L. Hoyt   7   43

Edwin, of Bristol, m. Jennet **LOWREY**, of Burlington,
Feb. 21, 1836, by Rev. Orsamus Allen, of Bristol   7   35

Edwin, m. Mrs. Caroline **VOSE**, Dec. [ ], 1840, by P. L. Hoyt   7   42

Eliza Ann, of Burlington, m. Carlo **HOWE**, of Blackersfield,
Vt., Nov. 18, 1838, by Rev. Aaron S. Hill   7   39

Enos, of Harwinton, m. Matilda **MOSES**, May 24, 1837, by
Erastus Scranton, V. D. M.   7   36

Hezekiah, m. Amanda **SHEPHARD**, b. of Burlington, Sept.
8, 1829, by Willard Hitchcock, J. P.   7   20

Sidney P., of Bristol, m. Polly E. **MARKS**, of Burlington,
Apr. 13, 1831, by Rev. Luther Mead   7   22

BURWELL, Jerry, m. Helen A. **PLUMB**, Feb. 26, 1845, by Rev.
James Noyes   7   51

BUTLER, Fayette, m. Rowenah **BARNS**, b. of Burlington, Mar. 21,
1848, by Peter Tatro, Jr.   7   57

Harriet, m. James **FORD**, b. of Burlington, Apr. 3, 1822,
by Dotis Ensign, Elder   1   23

Helen M., of Burlington, m. William **BEACH**, of Granby,
Feb. 6, 1845, by Rev. J. B. Beach   7   51

Miron, m. Sarah Ann **MORRIS**, b. of Burlington, May 3,
1848, by Peter Tatro, Jr.   7   58

William E., of Wethersfield, m. Martha A. **GRIDLEY**, of
Burlington, May 6, 1841, by Charles Bentley   7   44

BYINGTON, Joseph W., of Bristol, m. Susan **PALMETER**, of
Burlington, May 26, 1850, by James L. Wright   7   64

CALLENDER, CALENDER, Ira, of Wethersfield, m. Mary M.
GRIDLEY, of Burlington, Nov. 27, 1834, by Erastus
Scranton, V. D. M.   7   33

Maria, m. John **LARKIN**, Apr. 14, 1843, by Rev. David Miller   7   48

CARRINGTON, Anna, of Farmington, m. Samuel **BENHAM**, of
Burlington, Sept. 4, 1831, by William Marks, J. P.   7   23

Emily F., of Penn., m. Jairus N. **FOOT**, of Burlington,

	Vol.	Page
CARRINGTON, (cont.)		
Dec. 31, 1848, by Rev. John L. Wright	7	60
Monson, of Bristol, m. Maria **HUMPHREY**, of Farmington,		
Apr. 6, 1830, by Erastus Scranton, V. D. M.	7	21
CARTER, Asahel, of Southington, m. Eunice A. **POND**, of		
Burlington, Oct. 27, 1833, by Erastus Scranton, V. D. M.	7	32
George, of Wethersfield, m. Elizabeth T. **WILLIAMS**, of		
Burlington, Apr. 30, 1832, by Erastus Scranton, V. D. M.	7	24
CARUSTES (?), Henry, of Burlington, m. Elizabeth **DOUD**, of		
Harwinton, Jan. 2, 1833, by Erastus Scranton, V. D. M.	7	29
CASE, Almond, m. Lucinda W. **SISSION**, Nov. 29, 1827, by		
Erastus Clapp, V. D. M.	7	18
Amos, of Canton, m. Nancy **ALDERMAN**, of Burlington, Apr.		
9, 1838, by Rev. Richard Haytee	7	38
Betsey, m. S. **MILLS**, of Canton, Sept. 20, 1837, by Erastus		
Scranton, V. D. M.	7	36
Everett C., m. Harriet **BECKWITH**, b. of Burlington, Dec.		
1. 1834, by Erastus Scranton, V. D. M.	7	33
CATLIN, George O., of Harwinton, m. Mary E. **SMITH**, of		
Burlington, Mar. 24, 1834, by Rev. John Nixon	7	33
Stanley, of Harwinton, m. Mary **RICHARDSON**, of		
Farmington, July 24, 1838, by Erastus Scranton, V. D. M.	7	38
CHURCHILL, Abigail, Mrs., m. Ezra **WAY**, Apr. [ ], 1792	1	4
Lewis, of Wolcott, m. Mrs. Amy **HUMPHREYS**, of		
Burlington, [ ], 1847, by Joseph Hinson	7	55
CLAPP, Bela S., of Southampton, Mass., m. Rosanna **TAYLOR**, of		
Burlington, June 3, 1824, by William Marks, J. P.	7	11
CLARK, Amanda M., Mrs., m. Samuel **BELDEN**, b. of Burlington,		
Nov. 22, 1840, by Rev. Philip L. Hoyt	7	42
Amanda Maria, m. Albert Hatsell **POND**, b. of Burlington,		
May 9, 1839, by William Marks, J. P.	7	39
Anna Ame, [d. Asa & Rhoda], b. Dec. 23, 1790	1	18
Asa, b. May 2, 1746	1	18
Asa, of Richmond, s. Amos, of Westly, decd., m. Rhoda		
POTTER, Mar. 28, 1784, by Simeon Clark, Jr., J. P.	1	18
Asa, Jr., [s. Asa & Rhoda], b. Feb. 4, 1795	1	18
Asa, m. Experience **WEST**, Apr. 28, 1810, by Laban Clark.		
Witnesses: Elisha West & Elioner West	LR1	558
Caroline, of Burlington, m. Hezekiah **BEACH**, of Winchester,		
Apr. 23, 1833, by Erastus Scranton, V. D. M.	7	28
Charlotte, m. Justin **FULLER**, b. of Burlington, Jan. 17,		
1838, by Erastus Scranton, V. D. M.	7	38
Corydon B., m. Charlotte **BEACH**, b. of Burlington, Nov.		
28, 1839, by Rev. Aaron S. Hill	7	40
Elizabeth, [d. Asa & Rhoda], b. June 27, 1784	1	18
Elmina, [d. Asa & Rhoda], b. July 7, 1800	1	18
Florilla M., m. Sylvester **HULL**, Apr. 9, 1843, by Rev.		
David Miller	7	48

	Vol.	Page
CLARK, (cont.)		
Harriet, [d. Asa & Rhoda], b. Jan. 31, 1798	1	18
Harriet, m. William **TAYLOR**, July 23, 1832, by Erastus		
Scranton, V. D. M.	7	14
Jonathan, [s. Asa & Rhoda], b. Jan. 17, 1789	1	18
Jude, of Burlington, m. Anna **CUMMINGS**, of Goshen, July		
16, 1848, by Rev. Peter Tatro, Jr.	7	59
Maria L., of Burlington, m. John **DeWOLF**, of Farmington,		
Apr. 14, 1851, by Rev. Cephas Brainard	7	66
Mary, of Harwinton, m. Henry G. **HOTCHKISS**, Apr. 16,		
1823, by [ ]	7	62
Rhoda, [d. Asa & Rhoda], b. Feb. 16, 1793	1	18
Rhoda, w. Capt. Asa, d. Feb. 15, 1809	1	18
Rhoda, Jr., [d. Asa & Rhoda], d. Feb. 13, 1813	1	18
Sarah J., of Burlington, m. Elam H. **GAYLORD**, of Cannistota,		
N. Y., Jan. 6, 1852, by Cephas Brainard	7	67
Sophrona, m. Allen **ROBINSON**, Aug. 4, 1824, by E. Clapp,		
V. D. M.	7	11
Susanna, [d. Asa & Rhoda], b. Dec. 13, 1786	1	18
Sybil Ann, of Burlington, m. John D. **HILLS**, of Farmington,		
Nov. 19, 1851, by Cephas Brainard	7	66
Worster N., of Burlington, m. Harriet A. **GAYLORD**, of		
Canastota, N. Y., Nov. 28, 1850, by James L. Wright	7	65
CLEVELAND, Charlotte, of Burlington, m. Russell **WININS**, of		
Westford, N. Y., Dec. 30, 1835, by Rev. Seth Higley	7	34
Emily, m. Samuel **BULL**, b. of Burlington, May 11, 1825,		
by Erastus Clapp, V. D. M.	7	12
[E]unice, Mrs., m. Mark **HADSELL**, b. of Burlington, May		
26, 1842, by Erastus Scranton, V. D. M.	7	46
Ezra, of Burlington, m. Eunice **DOOLITTLE**, of Waterbury,		
Jan. 21, 1827, by Rev. Ebenezer Hall	7	16
John, m. Candace **ROBERTS**, of Burlington, Nov. 5, 1832,		
by Rev. Henry Stanwood, of Bristol	7	29
COE, Caroline m. William **CURRIE**, b. of Winsted, Apr. 15, 1833,		
by Rev. Charles Sherman	7	30
COLLIER, Caroline, m. George **PATTISON**, b. of Burlington,		
Nov. 16, 1825, by Erastus Clapp, V. D. M.	7	13
CORNWALL, Ervin Spencer, s. Chauncey & Polly, b. June 23,		
1808	7	27
COTTON, Calvest H., of Otis, Mass., m. Leenora **BARNES**, of		
Burlington, July 8, 1838, by Rev. Aaron S. Hill	7	38
CRAFTS, Major, of Hamilton, Ga., m. Lydia E. **WEBSTER**, of		
Burlington, June 18, 1846, by Rev. James Noyes	7	53
CRANDALL, CRANDAL, Hannah, m. Benedict **TYLER**, Nov. 11,		
1827, by Elias Wooding, J. P.	7	17
Philander, m. Eliza L. **RICHARDSON**, Dec. 7, 1841, by Rev.		
David Miller	7	44
Philena, m. Aurelius H. **POND**, b. of Burlington, Dec. 28,		

	Vol.	Page

CRANDALL, CRANDAL, (cont.)

1834, by Erastus Scranton, V. D. M. 7 33

CRANE, Charlotte Elizabeth, of Burlington, m. William
  GOODWIN, Jr., of New Hartford, Jan. 1, 1848, by Rev.
  Harley Goodwin, of South Canaan 7 57

John, m. Nancy **CURTIS,** Mar. 17, 1843, by Rev. David Miller 7 47

Samuel, of East Windosr, m. Elizabeth **BALL,** of Burlington,
  Oct. 24, 1826, by Erastus Clapp, V. D. M. 7 15

Warren S., of Hartford, m. Julia **MERRELLS,** of Burlington,
  Feb. 20, 1837, by Erastus Scranton, V. D. M. 7 35

William, m. Sarah Ann **PERKINS,** b. of Burlington, Jan.
  16, 1845, by Rev. J. B. Beach 7 51

CROOK, Sophia, of Burlington, m. Jared **HOLT,** of East Haven,
  Dec. 4, 1826, by Erastus Clapp, V. D. M. 7 15

CROW, Austra, of Burlington, m. Wareham **FILLEY,** of
  Bloomfield, Apr. 27, 1845, by Rev. J. Burton Beach 7 51

CULVER, Electa, b. July 3, 1787; m. James **ELTON,** Apr. 25,
  1804; d. Feb. 9, 1842, ae 54 y. 7 m. 6 d. 1 25

Mary Ann, of Burlington, m. Albert S. **FROST,** of Waterbury,
  Nov. 21, 1841, by Erastus Scranton, V. D. M. 7 44

Nathan, m. Polly **BARNES,** Mar. 13, 1828, by William Marks,
  J. P. 7 18

CUMMINGS, Anna, of Goshen, m. Jude **CLARK,** of Burlington,
  July 16, 1848, by Rev. Peter Tatro, Jr. 7 59

CURRIE, William, m. Caroline **COE,** b. of Winsted, Apr. 15,
  1833, by Rev. Charles Sherman 7 30

CURTIS, CURTISS, Amy, of Burlington, m. Trumbull **BEACH,** of
  Harwinton, Oct. 6, 1832, by Erastus Scranton, V. D. M. 7 29

Charlotte, m. Philo **CURTIS,** b. of Burlington, Sept. 3,
  1829, by William Marks, J. P. 7 20

Eli, of Camden, N. Y., m. Julia **FEN[N],** of Burlington,
  Apr. 2, 1834, by Erastus Scranton, V. D. M. 7 32

Elizabeth, of Burlington, m. Andrew O. **NORTON,** of New
  Hartford, May 9, 1852, by Rev. Cephas Brainard 7 68

Miles Henry, m. Mary P. **GILLETT,** b. of Burlington, Oct.
  23, 1839, by Erastus Scranton, V. D. M. 7 40

Nancy, of Burlington, m. Luzene **TUTTLE,** of Middletown,
  Dec. 27, 1842, by Rev. Samuel W. Smith 7 45

Nancy, m. John **CRANE,** Mar. 17, 1843, by Rev. David Miller 7 47

Patrick, of Waterbury, m. Louisa A. **BACON,** of Burlington,
  Nov. 3, 1839, by Rev. Aaron S. Hill 7 38

Philo, m. Charlotte **CURTIS,** b. of Burlington, Sept. 3,
  1829, by William Marks, J. P. 7 20

Samuel L., m. Elizabeth **GILLET,** b. of Burlington, May
  15, 1846, by J. B. Beach 7 53

William, m. Charlotte **STONE,** b. of Burlington, Apr. 11,
  1826, by Jonathan Cone, V. D. M. 7 13

DAILEY, Charles G., m. Amelia **FOOT,** Aug. 18, 1824, by Erastus

	Vol.	Page
DAILEY, (cont.)		
Clapp, V. D. M.	7	12
DANIELS, Eveline P., of N. Granby, m. Elizur D. **PHELPS**, of		
Windsor, Nov. 27, 1851, by Cephas Brainard	7	67
DARREMUS, Titus H., of Plymouth, m. Celia **HILLS**, Apr. 3,		
1837, by Erastus Scranton, V. D. M.	7	36
DARROW, Luther P., of Bristol, m. Eliza Ann **BULL**, of		
Burlington, Oct. 15, 1846, by Rev. James Noyes	7	54
DEWEY, Wilson, of Granby, m. Mary M. **SPENCER**, of New		
Hartford, Sept. 28, 1841, by Rev. Cyrus Yale	7	45
DeWOLF, Edward R., of Farmington, m. Emily M. **SLATER**, of		
New Britain, Apr. 14, 1851, by Rev. Cephas Brainard	7	66
John, of Farmington, m. Maria L. **CLARK**, of Burlington,		
Apr. 14, 1851, by Rev. Cephas Brainard	7	66
DIBBLE, Israel, of Granby, m. Parnel **BECKWITH**, of Burlington,		
Aug. 4, 1831, by Erastus Cranton, V. D. M.	7	23
DOOLITTLE, Eunice, of Waterbury, m. Ezra **CLEVELAND**, of		
Burlington, Jan. 21, 1827, by Rev. Ebenezer Hall	7	16
DORMAN, James, of Burlington, m. Mary **TOWEVILLE***, of		
Granby, Apr. 12, 1827, by Erastus Clapp, V. D. M.		
*(" **LOWEVILLE**"?)	7	16
Maria A., of Burlington, m. Justin S. **HARRINGTON**, of New		
Brittain, Sept. 7, 1847, by Erastus Scranton, V. D. M.	7	56
DOUD, Elizabeth, of Harwinton, m. Henry **CARUSTES(?)**, of		
Burlington, Jan. 2, 1833, by Erastus Scranton, V. D. M	7	29
DRIGGS, Prudence, m. Christopher **STONE**, Oct. 27, 1785	LR1	557
ELTON, Alonzo, [s. James & Electa]., b. Sept. 10, 1807	1	25
Alonzo, m. Emely **ALDERMAN**, b. of Burlington, May 31,		
1847, by J. Henson	7	56
Alva, [s. James & Electa], b. Aug. 7, 1815	1	25
Anna, [d. James & Electa], b. July 26, 1805	1	25
Anna, m. Caleb T. **SCOVEL**, b. of Burlington, June 21,		
1825, by Erastus Clapp, V. D. M.	7	12
Betsey, m. David B. **SCRIBNER**, b. of Burlington, Nov. 26,		
1829, by Rev. David Bennet	7	20
Electa, w. James, d. Feb. 9, 1842, ae 54 y. 7 m. 6 d.	1	25
Harriet, [twin with Henry, d. James & Electa], b. Feb. 3, 1827	1	25
Helen Evaline, [d. Romeo & Emeline], b. May 1, 1851	1	25
Henry, [twin with Harriet, s. James & Electa], b. Feb. 3, 1827	1	25
Henry, m. Esther Loiza **ALDERMAN**, b. of Burlington, Apr.		
30, 1848, by Peter Tatro, Jr.	7	57
James, b. Mar. 24, 1778; m. Electa **CULVER**, Apr. 25, 1804;		
d. Aug. 17, 1871, ae 93 y. 4 m. 23 d.	1	25
James, of Burlington, m. Mrs. Caroline **HALE**, of Hartford,		
July 4, 1845, by Erastus Scranton, V. D. M.	7	52
Lucy, [d. James & Electa], b. June 24, 1809	1	25
Lucy, m. Lemuel **BLACKMAN**, b. of Burlington, Oct. 9,		
1831, by Erastus Scranton, V. D. M.	7	24

	Vol.	Page
ELTON, (cont.)		
Romeo, [s. James & Electa], b. Feb. 2, 1817	1	25
Romeo, m. Emeline **BELDEN,** Mar. 13, 1842, by Rev. David Miller	1	25
Romeo, m. Emeline **BELDEN,** Mar. 13, 1842, by Rev. David Miller	7	45
Samuel, [s. Romeo & Emeline], b. July 27, 1849	1	25
Samuel, [s. Romeo & Emeline], d. June 8, 1850, ae 10 m. 11 d.	1	25
William, [s. James & Electa], b. Nov. 5, 1811	1	25
William, Jr., m. wid. Mary **HOTCHKISS,** July 22, 1812	1	10
William, m. Marilla **HOPKINS,** of Harwinton, Dec. 29, 1839, by Erastus Scranton, V. D. M.	7	40
William Calvin, [s. Romeo & Emeline], b. Oct. 10, 1843	1	25
William Calvin, [s. Romeo & Emeline], enlisted in 25th Reg. Conn. Vol. Co. J., Sept. 8, 1862. Killed May 27, 1863, at the seize of Port Hudson, La., ae 19 y. 7 m. 17 d.	1	25
FARNSWORTH, Sarah A., of Burlington, m. Charles **RECOR,** of New Britain, Dec. 19, 1849, by James L. Wright	7	61
[FENN], FEN, FINN, Joseph, m. Betsey **BRISTOL,** b. of Harwinton, July 15, 1845, by Rev. J. B. Beach	7	51
Julia, of Burlington, m. Eli **CURTIS,** of Camden, N. Y., Apr. 2, 1834, by Erastus Scranton, V. D. M.	7	32
FIELDS, Edward E., m. Lodenia **HOTCHKISS,** b. of Burlington, July 10, 1833, by Rev. Charles Sherman	7	30
FILLEY, Wareham, of Bloomfield, m. Austra **CROW,** of Burlington, Apr. 27, 1845, by Rev. J. Burton Beach	7	51
FINN, [see under **FENN**]		
FOOT, Amelia, m. Charles G. **DAILEY,** Aug. 18, 1824, by Erastus Clapp, V. D. M.	7	12
Ariel, m. Julian **WEBSTER,** b. of Burlington, Sept. 3, 1833, by Erastus Scranton, V. D. M.	7	32
Asahel, m. Caroline **BECKWITH,** b. of Burlington, Aug. 28, 1827, by Erastus Clapp, V. D. M.	7	17
Jairus N., of Burlington, m. Emily F. **CARRINGTON,** of Penn., Dec. 31, 1848, by Rev. John L. Wright	7	60
Lucy, of Burlington, m. John **THOMPSON,** of New Haven, Mar. 23, 1834, by Erastus Scranton, V. D. M.	7	31
Lucy, of Burlington, m. John **THOMPSON,** of New Haven, Mar. 23, 1834, by Erastus Scranton, V. D. M.	7	32
Polly Betsey, b. Sept. 25, 1782; m. Daniel **BOTSFORD,** Oct. 5, 1800	1	15
FORD, James, m. Harriet **BUTLER,** b. of Burlington, Apr. 3, 1822, by Dotis Ensign, Elder	1	23
FREEMAN, Jane, of Burlington, m. Peter **FREEMAN,** of Farmington, Aug. 4, 1822, by Jonathan Miller, V. D. M.	1	24
Peter, of Farmington, m. Jane **FREEMAN,** of Burlington, Aug. 4, 1822, by Jonathan Miller, V. D. M.	1	24
FRISBIE, Amos Rosseter, of Washington, Pa., m. Mary		

<table>
<tr><td></td><td>Vol.</td><td>Page</td></tr>
</table>

FRISBIE , (cont.)

WEBSTER, of Burlington, June 18, 1850, by Rev.
Jonathan Coe, of Winsted — 7 — 65

Earl, m. Emeline JOHNSON, b. of Burlington, Jan. 26,
1826, by Erastus Clapp, V. D. M. — 7 — 13

Earl Theodore, [s. Major Gad & Eliza], b. June 21, 1804 — 1 — 4

Elizabeth E., of Burlington, m. Julius NORTON, of
Montgomery, Ala., Sept. 17, 1834, by Erastus Scranton,
V. D. M. — 7 — 33

Elizabeth Eleanor, [d. Major Gad & Eliza], b. Apr. 24, 1808 — 1 — 4

Gad, Major, m. Mrs. Eliza PETTIBONE, [   ] — 1 — 4

James, m. Henrietta PETTIBONE, Apr. 27, 1843, by David
Miller — 7 — 48

John, m. Jane Rosanna LEWIS, b. of Burlington, Sept. 23,
1845, by Rev. John Burton Beach — 7 — 52

Laura, m. Ira BRONSON, Aug. 28, 1814 — 1 — 12

Mary Ann, [d. Major Gad & Eliza], b. Feb. 16, 1812 — 1 — 4

Sarah, [d. Major Gad & Elisza], b. Sept. 24, 1813 — 1 — 4

Sarah, of Burlington, m. Walter G. SIMPSON, of Auburn,
N. Y., July 15, 1840, by Rev. M. P. L. Hoyt — 7 — 41

Susan Maria, [d. Major Gad & Eliza], b. Nov. 27, 1805 — 1 — 4

Zebulon Gates, [s. Major Gad & Eliza], b. Nov. 26, 1809 — 1 — 4

-----, m. Elizabeth HOPKINS, b. of Harwinton, May 3, 1839,
by Erastus Scoranton, V. D. M. — 7 — 40

FROST, Albert S., of Waterbury, m. Mary Ann CULVER, of
Burlington, Nov. 21, 1841, by Erastus Scranton, V. D. M. — 7 — 44

FULLER, Alonzo, of Canton, m. Genitt PAYNE, of Burlington,
[   ], 1847, by Joseph Hinson — 7 — 55

Asaph, of Bristol, m. Mary P. BELDEN, of Burlington,
Apr. 27, 1848, by Peter Tatro, Jr. — 7 — 57

A[u]gusta, m. Aron SMITH, Sept. 8, 1825, by Erastus
Clapp, V. D. M. — 7 — 12

Augustus, m. Eunice PERKINS, July 24, 1827, by Gershom
Pierce, Elder — 7 — 17

Julia, m. John MILLS, Dec. 13, 1827, by Gershom Pierce,
Elder — 7 — 19

Justin, m. Charlotte CLARK, b. of Burlington, Jan. 17,
1838, by Erastus Scranton, V. D. M. — 7 — 38

Rebecca, Mrs., m. James ANDREWS, Nov. 24, 1808 — 1 — 2

Riley H., saw grinder, ae 27, b. Farmington, res. Unionville, m.
Mary A. UPSON, ae 18, b. Burlington, res. same, Nov. 1,
1848, by Rev. Peter Tatro, Jr. — 7 — 59

GARRET, Bigelow C., m. Ann E. HADSELL, May 17, 1846, by
Rev. James Noyes — 7 — 53

GAYLORD, Elam H., of Cannistota, N. Y., m. Sarah J. CLARK,
of Burlington, Jan. 6, 1852, by Cephas Brainard — 7 — 67

Harriet A., of Canastota, N. Y., m. Worster N. CLARK, of
Burlington, Nov. 28, 1850, by James L. Wright — 7 — 65

	Vol.	Page
GAYLORD, (cont.)		
Philip, m. Helen **HITCHCOCK,** b. of Burlington, Apr. 14, 1847, by Joseph Hinson	7	55
Ruth, b. Mar. 12, 1792; m. Abraham **PETTIBONE,** 3rd, May 9, 1821	7	26
GILBERT, Joseph F., of Plymouth, m. Jerusha **PETTIBONE,** of Burlington, Feb. 23, 1832, by Erastus Scranton, V. D. M.	7	24
GILLET, GELLET, GILLITT, Caroline, [twin with Catharine, d. John, Jr. & Philathesia], b. Aug. 1, 1809	1	8
Catharine, [twin with Caroline, d. John, Jr. & Philathesia], b. Aug. 1, 1809	1	8
Delia, [d. John, Jr. & Philathesia], b. Nov. 7, 1707* *(Written over "1807")	1	8
Elizabeth, m. Samuel L. **CURTIS,** b. of Burlington, May 15, 1846, by J. B. Beach	7	53
John, Jr., b. Dec. 16, 1783; m. Philathesia **ANDREWS,** Dec. 21, [ ]	1	8
John, m. Mary **JOHNSON,** b. of Burlington, May 15, 1826, by Erastus Clapp, V. D. M.	7	13
Mariah S., m. Rev. David L. **MARKS,** of Burlington, Oct. 2, 1839, by Rev. Philip L. Hoyt	7	39
Mary, of Burlington, m. Timothy **WADSWORTH,** of Farmington, Mar. 3, 1824, by Jonathan Miller, V. D. M.	7	11
Mary P., m. Miles Henry **CURTIS,** b. of Burlington, Oct. 23, 1839, by Erastus Scranton, V. D. M.	7	40
Samuel, m. Rosanna **BROWN,** May 15, 1846, by J. B. Beach	7	53
Susanna, [d. John, Jr. & Philathesia], b. Oct. 28, 1811	1	8
GOODENOUGH, Viola, of Burlington, m. Renselier **RAINSFORD,** · of Mass., Dec. 22, 1840, by P. L. Hoyt	7	42
GOODSELL, GOODSEL, Alnora, of New Hartford, m. Alfred **LOWRY,** of Burlington, Oct. 1, 1846, by Rev. James Noyes	7	54
Samuel, of Burlington, m. Rachel **BAILEY,** of New Hartford, Aug. 5, 1827, by Erastus Clapp, V. D. M.	7	17
GOODWIN, Mary Ann, ae 18, m. John W. **STODARD,** husbandman, ae 23, b. of Burlington, Dec. 23, 1848, by Rev. Peter Tatro	7	60
William, Jr., of New Hartford, m. Charlotte Elizabeth **CRANE,** of Burlington, Jan. 1, 1848, by Rev. Harley Goodwin, of South Canaan	7	57
GRAHAM, Andrew G., of Berlin, m. Susannah **BRADLEY,** of Burlington, Apr. 15, 1838, by Erastus Scranton, V. D. M.	7	38
Isaac, of Bristol, m. Lucy M. **HOTCHKISS,** of Burlington, Nov. 27, 1851, by Cephas Brainard	7	67
William L., of Haddam, m. Elmira **WILLMOT,** of Burlington, [ ], [1834?], by Rev. Daniel Coe	7	32
GRIDLEY, Cynthia C., of Burlington, m. Joshua R. **KING,** of Berlin, Sept. 7, 1842, by Charles Bentley	7	47

	Vol.	Page

GRIDLEY, (cont.)

George, of Waterbury, m. Delia **BENHAM**, of Burlington,
Apr. 24, 1834, by Erastus Scranton, V. D. M. — 7 — 33

Martha A., of Burlington, m. William E. **BUTLER,** of
Wethersfield, May 6, 1841, by Charles Bentley — 7 — 44

Mary M., of Burlington, m. Ira **CALENDER,** of Wethersfield,
Nov. 27, 1834, by Erastus Scranton, V. D. M. — 7 — 33

Salmon, of Harwinton, m. Mary W. **PETTIBONE,** of
Burlington, Dec. 24, 1826, by Erastus Clapp, V. D. M. — 7 — 15

GRIFFIS, Elizabeth, m. Whittey **ANDRUS,** Oct. 30, 1824, by
William Marks, J. P. — 7 — 12

GRIGGS, Jane, m. Charles W. **ALCOTT,** b. of Plymouth, Apr. 4,
1852, by Rev. Cephas Brainard — 7 — 67

GRISWOLD, Sylvia E., m. Chester **BUNNEL,** Jan. 20, 1828, by
William Marks, J. P. — 7 — 18

GROVER, Royal, m. Diana **WARNER,** b. of Middletown, May 24,
1830, by Erastus Scranton, V. D. M. — 7 — 21

HADSELL, Ann E., m. Bigelow C. **GARRET,** May 17, 1846, by
Rev. James Noyes — 7 — 53

Ira, m. Elvira **HART,** b. of Burlington, Dec. 9, 1829, by
Erastus Scranton, V. D. M. — 7 — 21

Major, m. Mrs. Caroline **TALBERT,** b. of Burlington, Mar.
17, 1839, by Rev. Aaron S. Hill — 7 — 39

Mark, m. Mrs. [E]unice **CLEVELAND,** b. of Burlington, May
26, 1842, by Erastus Scranton, V. D. M. — 7 — 46

HALE, [see also HALL], Caroline, Mrs. of Hartford, m. James
ELTON, of Burlington, July 4, 1845, by Erastus
Scranton, V. D. M. — 7 — 53

Lucy Emily, m. Sherman **SMITH,** b. of Burlington, Feb. 23,
1836, by Erastus Scranton, V. D. M. — 7 — 35

HALL, [see also HALE & HULL], Edward, of Bristol, m. Hannah
G. **PECK,** of Burlington, May 29, 1851, by Rev. William
H. Goodwin, of Bristol — 7 — 66

Keziah M., m. George E. **JOHNSON,** b. of Burlington, Apr.
23, 1826, by Erastus Clapp, V. D. M. — 7 — 13

HAMLIN, HAMBLIN, Amos, of Farmington, m. Mary **BULL,** of
Burlington, May 2, 1825, by Erastus Clapp, V. D. M. — 7 — 12

Enos, of Granby, m. Maria **BULL,** of Burlington, Sept. 23,
1838, by Erastus Scranton, V. D. M. — 7 — 38

Herman, of Canton, m. Celesta **WOODFORD,** of Burlington,
June 8, 1826, by Rev. Isaac Kimball. Int. Pub. — 7 — 14

HARRINGTON, Justin S., of New Brittain, m. Maria A.
DORMAN, of Burlington, Sept. 7, 1847, by Erastus
Scranton, V. D. M. — 7 — 56

HARRISON, Deborah, of Burlington, m. Nathaniel **WALLING,** of
New Hartford, June 14, 1841, by Rev. David Miller — 7 — 43

HART, Amos, [s. Lemuel], b. July 23, 1800 — 1 — 18

Anna, [d. Simeon & Mary], b. July 6, 1786 — 1 — 5

	Vol.	Page
HART, (cont.)		
Anna Charlotte, m. William **MORSE**, Mar. 29, 1835, by Rev.		
David L. Parmalee	7	34
Ara, [s. Lemuel], b. Jan. 22, 1803	1	18
Ard, Capt., m. Amelia *****ROBERTS**, Mar. 10, 1788		
*****("Millicent **ROBERTS**" in **HART** Genealogy)	1	13
Asa, m. Lucy **HOTCHKISS**, b. of Burlington, Jan. 22, 1827,		
by Erastus Clapp. V. D. M.	7	16
Belinda, [d. Capt. Ard & Millicent], b. Apr. 24, 1793	1	13
Charlotte, [d. John C. & Ann], b. Jan. 4, 1820	1	22
Chauncey, [s. Capt. Ard & Millicent], b. June 9, 1802	1	13
Chester, [s. Simeon & Mary], b. Jan. 2, 1789; d. Jan. 26, 1789	1	5
Clarinda, [d. Lemuel], b. July 9, 1795; d. Mar. 14, 1806	1	18
Delia, [d. Capt. Ard & Millicent], b. May 19, 1795	1	13
Delia, m. Billings **HILLS**, Dec. 1, 1814	1	6
Elvira, [d. Capt. Ard & Millicent], b. Oct. 20, 1811	1	13
Elvira, m. Ira **HADSELL**, b. of Burlington, Dec. 9, 1829,		
by Erastus Scranton, V. D. M.	7	21
Fanny, [d. Simeon & Mary], b. Dec. 29, 1800	1	5
James Monroe, [s. Lemuel], b. Aug. 2, 1805	1	18
Jehiel Chester, [s. Simeon & Mary], b. Feb. 3, 1792	1	5
Joel, [s. Lemuel], b. Jan. 22, 1788	1	18
John, m. Millecent **HART**, b. of Burlington, Feb. 15, 1827,		
by Erastus Clapp, V. D. M.	7	16
John C., m. Ann **LAWREY**, Sept. 2, 1817	1	22
John G., of Bristol, m. Abigail **BENHAM**, of Burlington,		
Nov. 12, 1848, by Rev. James L. Wright	7	60
Julianna Belinda, [d. Lemuel], b. Sept. 6, 1807	1	18
Lemuel, b. Aug. 24, 1759	1	18
Lewas, [s. Simeon & Mary], b. June 5, 1784; d. Oct. 16, 1813	1	5
Mellicent, [d. Capt. Ard & Millicent], b. June 14, 1799	1	13
Millecent, m. John **HART**, b. of Burlington, Feb. 15, 1827,		
by Erastus Clapp. V. D. M.	7	16
Nancy, [d. Capt. Ard & Millicent], b. Feb. 22, 1789	1	13
Narissa, [d. Simeon & Mary], b. Apr. 26, 1790;		
d. Apr. 27, 1790	1	5
Newton, [s. Lemuel], b. May 23, 1793	1	18
Orra, [s. Lemuel], b. Nov. 3, 1785	1	18
Polly, [d. Lemuel], b. Nov. 22, 1783	1	18
Polly, [d. Simeon & Mary], b. Apr. 18, 1798	1	5
Sally, [d. Capt. Ard & Millicent], b. Jan. 26, 1807	1	13
Simeon, m. Mary **WARNER**, Oct. 27, 1783	1	5
Simeon, 3rd, [s. Simeon & Mary], b. Feb. 5, 1794;		
d. Feb. 6, 1794	1	5
Simeon, 4th, [s. Simeon & Mary], b. Nov. 4, 1795	1	5
Simeon, of Burlington, m. Mrs. Parmelia **PETTIBONE**, of		
New Hartford, Jan. 30, 1822, by Cyrus Yale	1	21
Urainia, [d. Lemuel], b. Oct. 27, 1797	1	18

	Vol.	Page
HART, (cont.)		
Walter, [s. John C. & Ann], b. Aug. 23, 1818	1	22
William, [s. Capt. Ard & Millicent], b. Sept. 2, 1804	1	13
HENDRICK, Norman B., of New Hartford, m. Lucy **HILLS**, of		
Burlington, [Nov. 27, 1823], by Erastus Clapp, V. D. M.	7	11
HILLS, HILL, Billings, m. Delia **HART**, Dec. 1, 1814	1	6
Celia, [d. Billings & Delia], b. Jan. 25, 1816	1	6
Celia, m. Titus H. **DARREMUS**, of Plymouth, Apr. 3, 1837,		
by Erastus Scranton, V. D. M.	7	36
Charles F., m. Laura L. **BANNING**, b. of Hartford, May 2,		
1852, by Cephas Brainard	7	67
Dolly, m. Daniel **BUNNEL**, b. of Burlington, Apr. 19, 1841,		
by P. L. Hoyt	7	43
Hariet, [d. Billings & Delia], b. Nov. 5, 1817	1	6
John D., of Farmington, m. Sybil Ann **CLARK**, of Burlington,		
Nov. 19, 1851, by Cephas Brainard	7	66
Lewis Hart, [s. Billings & Delia], b. May 13, 1820	1	6
Lucy, of Burlington, m. Norman B. **HENDRICK**, of New		
Hartford, [Nov. 27, 1823], by Erastus Clapp, V. D. M.	7	11
Morris, of Reading, m. Rhoda Ann **SMITH**, of Burlington,		
May 15, 1837, by Rev. John B. Beach	7	36
Noble, of Bristol, m. Susannah **MARKS**, of Burlington,		
Nov. 15, 1829, by William Marks, J. P.	7	21
Seldon, of Bristol, m. Elisa **BEACH**, of Burlington, July		
11, 1830, by Erastus Scranton, V. D. M.	7	21
HITCHCOCK, Aaron, Dr., m. Militia **MANN**, July 6, 1808	1	5
Almon, [s. Oliver], b. July 10, 1804	LR1	557
Annah Phylora, [d. Willard & Adaline], b. Feb. 2, 1824	7	26
Helen, m. Philip **GAYLORD**, b. of Burlington, Apr. 14,		
1847, by Joseph Hinson	7	55
Janett, [d. Dr. Aaron & Militia], b. Mar. 7, 1809	1	5
Lois A., of Burlington, m. Warren **ALDRICH**, of Collinsville,		
June 16, 1844, by Rev. James Noyes	7	50
Mary, of Burlington, m. William **ALFORD**, of Harwinton,		
Oct. 17, 1841, by Rev. Ezra Jagger	7	44
Meriam, [d. Oliver], b. May 8, 1799; d. June 27, 1825	LR1	557
Oliver Franklin, [s. Oliver], b. Jan. 24, 1802	LR1	557
Peres, [child of Dr. Aaron & Militia], b. Apr. 18, 1811	1	5
Willard, b. July 22, 1796; m. Adaline **WELTON**, Apr. 3, 1822	7	26
Willard, [s. Oliver], b. July 22, 1796	LR1	557
HOBART, Adin P., of Oak Creek, Wis., m. Clarissa A.		
BECKWITH, of Burlington, June 11, 1850, by James L.		
Wright	7	65
HOLBROOK, George R., of Oxford, m. Orilla C. **BRADLEY**, of		
Burlington, Nov. 25, 1847, by Rev. William Goodwin, Jr.	7	56
HOLT, Jared, of East Haven, m. Sophia **CROOK**, of Burlington,		
Dec. 4, 1826, by Erastus Clapp, V. D. M.	7	15
HOPKINS, Elizabeth, m. [ ] **FRISBIE**, b. of Harwinton, May 3,		

	Vol.	Page
HOPKINS, (cont.)		
1839, by Erastus Scranton, V. D. M.	7	40
Emily, m. John **HOTCHKISS**, b. of Burlington, Aug. 6, 1838,		
by Rev. Aaron S. Hill	7	38
Marilla, of Harwinton, m. William **ELTON**, Dec. 29, 1839,		
by Erastus Scranton, V. D. M.	7	40
Sarah M., m. Justice **WEBSTER**, Dec. 21, 1842, by Rev.		
David Miller	7	47
HORTON, Samuel L., of Collinsville, m. Delia **NEARING**, of		
Burlington, June 11, 1835, by Erastus Scranton, V. D. M.	7	35
HOTCHKISS, HITCHKISS, Amon, [s. Samuel & Rachel], b. June		
10, 1792	1	19
Andrew S., m. Adelia C. **POND**, Jan. 11, 1846, by Rev.		
John B. Beach	7	52
Ann Eliza, [d. Henry G. & Mary], b. Mar. 20, 1836	7	62
Carlos, [s. Samuel & Rachel], b. Sept. 5, 1797	1	19
Caroline, m. Coleman **TOWNSAND**, of N. Y., Nov. 5, 1840,		
by Philip L. Hoyt	7	42
Hannah, of Burlington, m. Dr. G. **POTTER**, of Bristol,		
Mar. 31, 1844, by Rev. James Noyes	7	50
Harriet, [d. Lieut. Stephen & Mary], b. Oct. 7, 1801	1	10
Harriet, m. Oliver **PETTIBONE**, Apr. 25, 1822, by Jonathan		
Miller, V. D. M.	1	23
Harriet M., of Burlington, m. John C. **NORTON**, of Plainville,		
Sept. 17, 1849, by James L. Wright	7	64
Henry G., b. Sept. 16, 1799; m. Mary **CLARK**, of Harwinton,		
Apr. 16, 1823, by [ ]	7	62
Henry Grove, [s. Lieut. Stephen & Mary], b. Sept. 16, 1799	1	10
Hiram, m. Mamra Ann **LOWREY**, b. of Burlington, Feb. 18,		
1847, by Irenus Adkins	7	55
Isaac, [s. Samuel & Rachel], b. May 18, 1781	1	19
John, m. Emily **HOPKINS**, b. of Burlington, Aug. 6, 1838,		
by Rev. Aaron S. Hill	7	38
John Phelps. [s. Zenas & Lydia], b. May 1, 1815	1	13
Josephus, m. Lowley **STONE**, b. of Burlington, Jan. 25,		
1827, by Erastus Clapp, V. D. M.	7	16
Julius C., [s. Lieut. Stephen & Mary], b. May 10, 1792	1	10
Laura, [d. Samuel & Rachel], b. Aug. 29, 1794	1	19
Lodenia, m. Edward E. **FIELDS**, b. of Burlington, July		
10, 1833, by Rev. Charles Sherman	7	30
Lucretia, [d. Samuel & Rachel], b. Dec. 10, 1787	1	19
Lucy, [d. Lieut. Stephen & Mary], b. Sept. 7, 1797	1	10
Lucy, m. Asa **HART**, b. of Burlington, Jan. 22, 1827, by		
Erastus Clapp, V. D. M.	7	16
Lucy M., [d. Henry G. & Mary], b. Dec. 7, 1829	7	62
Lucy M., of Burlington, m. Isaac **GRAHAM**, of Bristol, Nov.		
27, 1851, by Cephas Brainard	7	67
Mabel, [d. Lieut. Stephen & Mary], b. June 13, 1784	1	10

	Vol.	Page

HOTCHKISS, HITCHKISS, (cont.)

Martha, of Burlington, m. Luman S. **JUDD**, of Berlin,
    Feb. 17, 1847, by Erastus Scranton, V. D. M. — 7 — 55
Mary, [d. Lieut. Stephen & Mary], b. Apr. 1, 1788 — 1 — 10
Mary, wid., m. William **ELTON**, Jr., July 22, 1812 — 1 — 10
Mary, of Burlington, m. Julius W. **PEASE**, of Winsted,
    Jan. 1, 1844, by Rev. James Noyce — 7 — 49
Mary, w. Henry G., d. Mar. 10, 1860, ae 59 — 7 — 62
Mary C., [d. Henry G. & Mary], b. Nov. 4, 1844 — 7 — 62
Mary Newell, [d. Samuel & Rachel], b. Aug. 22, 1779 — 1 — 19
Mary Newell, m. Daniel **ANDREWS**, Jan. 22, 1800 — 1 — 3
Rachel, [d. Samuel & Rachel], b. Mar. 20, 1783 — 1 — 19
Sally Victory, [d. Zenas & Lydia], b. July 14, 1810 — 1 — 13
Samuel, m. Mrs. Rachel **UPON**, Jan. 26, 1778 — 1 — 19
Samuel, [s. Samuel & Rachel], b. Oct. 5, 1789 — 1 — 19
Samuel, m. Ruth **SMITH**, b. of Burlington, Apr. 30, 1834,
    by Erastus Scranton, V. D. M. — 7 — 33
Stephen, [s. Lieut. Stephen & Mary], b. Feb. 9, 1790 — 1 — 10
Stephen, Lieut., d. Feb. 13, 1802 — 1 — 10
Stephen, Lieut., m. Mary **UPSON**, [　] — 1 — 10
Silvia, [d. Lieut. Stephen & Mary], b. Aug. 1, 1794 — 1 — 10
Thankfull C., [d. Lieut. Stephen & Mary], b. May 9, 1786 — 1 — 10
Thankfull C., [d. Henry G. & Mary], b. Dec. 22, 1841 — 7 — 62
Theodore B., [s. Henry G. & Mary], b. Mar. 1, 1828 — 7 — 62
Theodore B., [s. Henry G. & Mary], d. Aug. 21, 1831 — 7 — 62
Theodore B., [s. Henry G. & Mary], b. May 21, 1832 — 7 — 62
William G., [s. Henry G. & Mary], d. Mar. 10, 1825 — 7 — 62
W[illia]m J., [s. Henry G. & Mary], b. Jan. 28, 1826 — 7 — 62
Zenas, [s. Samuel & Rachel], b. Dec. 12, 1785 — 1 — 19
Zenas, m. Lydia **PHELPS**, Nov. 26, 1808 — 1 — 13

HOWE, Carlo, of Blackersfield, Vt., m. Eliza Ann **BUNNEL**, of
    Burlington, Nov. 18, 1838, by Rev. Aaron S. Hill — 7 — 39
HUGHS, Robert, Jr., of Canton, m. Selina **MOSES**, of Burlington,
    May 18, 1848, by Peter Tatro, Jr. — 7 — 58
HULL, [see also **HALL**], Eli, of Farmington, m. Almira **BARNES**,
    of Burlington, Aug. 4, 1824, by Datus Ensign, Elder — 7 — 12
Sarah Adelia, of Burlington, m. William Burnham **WEBSTER**,
    of Harwinton, Oct. 19, 1837, by Rev. Joseph S. Covill, of
    Bristol — 7 — 36
Sylvanus, of Burlington, m. Eveline **POND**, Sept. 19, 1839,
    by F. B. Woodard — 7 — 40
Sylvester, m. Florilla M. **CLARK**, Apr. 9, 1843, by Rev.
    David Miller — 7 — 48
HUMPHREY, HUMPHREYS, Amy, Mrs. of Burlington, m. Lewis
    CHURCHILL, of Wolcott, [　], 1847, by Joseph Hinson — 7 — 55
Maria, of Farmington, m. Monson **CARRINGTON**, of Bristol,
    Apr. 6, 1830, by Erastus Scranton, V. D. M. — 7 — 21
Orrin, of Canton, m. Mary Ann **PALMITER**, of Burlington,

	Vol.	Page
KING, Joshua R., of Berlin, m. Cynthia C. GRIDLEY, of		
Burlington, Sept. 7, 1842, by Charles Bentley	7	47
KINNEY, Sheldon, of Vernon, m. Lucy NEARING, of Burlington,		
Aug. 9, 1831, by Erastus Scranton, V. D. M.	7	14
LAMPSON, LAMSON, Samuel M., of Mt. Washington, Mass., m.		
Lydia B. SESSIONS, of Burlington, May 4, 1852, by		
James L. Wright	7	68
Thomas, of Mt. Washington, Mass., m. Abigail BRADLEY, of		
Burlington, May 28, 1850, by James L. Wright	7	64
LANGDON, LANKTON, Arba, b. May 12, 1786; m. Thankfull		
NEWTON, Nov. 1, 1805	1	20
Augustus Smith, m. Mary Ann SEGAR, of New Hartford,		
[July 23, 1832], by Erastus Scranton, V. D. M.	7	14
Betsey, [d. Arba & Thankfull], b. Mar. 19, 1808	1	20
Dwight, of Southington, m. Manerva UPSON, of Burlington,		
May 9, 1849, by James L. Wright	7	63
Eli, [s. Arba & Thankfull], b. May 20, 1813	1	20
George H., m. Mary LOWREY, b. of Burlington, Oct. 7, 1832,		
by Rev. Henry Stanwood, of Bristol	7	29
Orpha, [d. Arba & Thankfull], b. Oct. 2, 1806	1	20
Thomas, [s. Arba & Thankfull], b. Aug. 30, 1810	1	20
LARKIN, John, m. Maria CALLENDER, Apr. 14, 1843, by Rev.		
David Miller	7	48
[LEAVENWORTH], LEVENWORTH, Theodore, of Goshen, m.		
Chestine ALDERMAN, of Burlington, Jan. 26, 1842, by		
Rev. David Miller	7	45
LEE, Henry, of Barkhamsted, m. Mary AUSTIN, of New Hartford,		
Sept. 17, 1835, by Erastus Scranton, V. D. M.	7	35
Lucy, of Burlington, m. Thomas ADAMS, of Canton, June 12,		
1837, by Rev. Richard Hayton	7	36
Rhoda Jane, of Plymouth, m. Thomas ADAMS, of Burlington,		
Apr. 19, 1840, by Rev. Aaron S. Hill	7	41
LEWIS, Celestia Chappell, d. James & Achsah, b. Jan. 20, 1830,		
in Wethersfield, Rock Hill	7	27
Frederick, m. Polly BEACH, Aug. 18, 1834, by Erastus		
Scranton, V. D. M.	7	33
James Edward, [s. James & Achsah], b. Dec. 3, 1836	7	27
Jane Rosanna, m. John FRISBIE, b. of Burlington, Sept.		
23, 1845, by Rev. John Burton Beach	7	52
LOOMIS, Betsey, of Winchester, m. Benjamin PLACE, of		
Burlington, Dec. 3, 1827, by Erastus Clapp. V. D. M.	7	18
LOWEVILLE (?), Mary, see under TOWEVILLE		
LOWRY, LOWREY, LAWREY, Alfred, of Burlington, m. Alnora		
GOODSEL, of New Hartford, Oct. 1, 1846, by Rev.		
James Noyes	7	54
Almira, [d. Wait & Amira], b. Feb. 18, 1814	1	23
Almira Peck, [d. Waite & Almira], b. Feb. 18, 1814	7	27
Ann, m. John C. HART, Sept. 2, 1817	7	23

	Vol.	Page
LOWRY, LOWREY, LAWREY, (cont.)		
Charles John, [s. Wait & Amira], b. Oct. 21, 1820	1	23
Charles John, [s. Waite & Almira], b. Oct. 21, 1820	7	27
David, m. Mary S. **PETTIBONE**, b. of Burlington, May 16,		
1849, by James L. Wright	7	63
Hannah Jane, [d. Waite & Almira], b. Jan. 30, 1826	7	27
James Norton, [s. Waite & Almira],. b. Dec. 16, 1823	7	27
Jennet, of Burlington, m. Edwin **BUNNEL**, of Bristol, Feb.		
21, 1836, by Rev. Orsamus Allen, of Bristol	7	35
Juliette, [d. Wait & Amira], b. May 15, 1812	1	23
Juliette Elenor, [d. Waite & Almira], b. May 15, 1812	7	27
Mamra Ann, m. Hiram **HOTCHKISS**, b. of Burlington, Feb.		
18, 1847, by Irenus Adkins	7	55
Mary, m. George H. **LANGDON**, b. of Burlington, Oct. 7,		
1832, by Rev. Henry Stanwood, of Bristol	7	29
Samuel Waite, [s. Wait & Amira], b. Oct. 17, 1818	1	23
Samuel Waite, [s. Waite & Almira], b. Oct. 17, 1818	7	27
Sarah Ann, [d. Wait & Amira], b. Mar. 14, 1816	1	23
Sarah Ann, [d. Waite & Almira], b. Mar. 14, 1816	7	27
Wait, b. Aug. 27, 1781, in Farmington; m. Mrs. Amira **PECK**,		
May 2, 1811	1	23
Waite, b. Aug. 27, 1781, in Farmington; m. Almira **PECK**,		
May 2, 1811	7	27
MACKEY, McKEY, Clarissa*, m. Amasa **STONE**, Oct. 15, 1807		
*(Written "Clarissa M. **KEY**)	LR1	558
Phebe, m. David **MARKS**, Nov. 14, 1802	1	16
MANN, MAN, Frances, [d. Dr. Peres & Frances], b. Jan. 4, 1793	1	6
Frances, b. Jan. 4, 1793; m. Carril **PETTIBONE**, July 13, 1815	7	46
Frances, Jr., m. Carril **PETTIBONE**, July 13, 1815	1	7
Melitia, [d. Dr. Peres & Militia], b. Aug. 23, 1787	1	6
Melitia, w. Dr. Peres, d. Nov. 19, 1789	1	6
Militia, m. Dr. Aaron **HITCHCOCK**, July 6, 1808	1	5
Peres, Dr., m. Mrs. Militia **WHITE**, Oct. 25, 1786	1	6
Peres, Dr., m. Frances **TREAT**, Feb. 8, 1792	1	6
MARKS, Almoron, of Durham, N. Y., m. Mary **PHELPS**, of		
Burlington, Sept. 18, 1834, by Erastus Scranton, V. D. M.	7	33
Anna, of Burlington, m. Ebenezer W. **TWING**, of Springfield,		
Mass., Apr. 16, 1846, by J. B. Beach	7	53
Chloe, m. Ramon **PETTIBONE**, b. of Burlington, Dec. 7,		
1826, by Erastus Clapp. V. D. M.	7	15
David, b. May 18, 1754, at Milford; m. Susannah [ ],		
Sept. 7, 1775, at Milford	1	16
David, Jr., [s. David & Susannah], b. Mar. 17, 1778	1	16
David, m. 2nd w. Phebe **MACKEY**, Nov. 14, 1802	1	16
David L., Rev. of Burlington, m. Mariah S. **GILLET**, of [ ],		
Oct. 2, 1839, by Rev. Philip L. Hoyt	7	39
Enoch, [s. David & Phebe], b. Oct. 11, 1803	1	16
Jeremiah, [s. David & Susannah], b. Mar. 20, 1786	1	16

	Vol.	Page
MARKS, (cont.)		
Malvina, of Burlington, m. Lewis F. **SPERRY**, of Alford,		
Mass., Feb. 14, 1839, by Rev. Aaron S. Hill	7	39
Mary, [d. David & Susannah], b. Jan. 20, 1780	1	16
Polly E., of Burlington, m. Sidney P. **BUNNELL**, of Bristol,		
Apr. 13, 1831, by Rev. Luther Mead	7	22
Susannah, [d. David & Susannah], b. Aug. 18, 1776	1	16
Susannah, w. David, d. June 30, 1802	1	16
Susannah, of Burlington, m. Noble **HILL**, of Bristol,		
Nov. 15, 1829, by William Marks, J. P.	7	21
Urane, [d. David & Susannah], b. Feb. 28, 1782	1	16
Urane, [d. David & Susannah], d. May 17, 1787	1	16
William, [s. David & Susannah], b. Nov. 20, 1783	1	16
MARSH, Lewis, of Northfield, m. Emeline **STONE**, of Burlington,		
Sept. 21, 1848, by Rev. James L. Wright	7	59
MASON, Mary A., m. Frederick **BULL**, b. of Burlington, May 8,		
1830, by Erastus Scranton, V. D. M.	7	22
Mary A., m. Frederick **BULL**, b. of Burlington, May 8, 1831,		
by Erastus Scranton, V. D. M.	7	23
Rush F., m. Fanny M. **BROOKS**, b. of Burlington, Nov. 5,		
1844, by Rev. James Noyes	7	50
MATHEWS, Harpey L., m. Charlotte R. **RICHARDSON**, Aug. 8,		
1848, by Rev. James L. Wright	7	59
Newell, of Burlington, m. Lavina **ROOT**, of Farmington,		
Mar. 31, 1825, by Erastus Clapp, V. D. M.	7	12
MAY, William, m. Margaret **TAYLOR**, b. of Burlington (late of		
Reading, Pa.), Nov. 22, 1846, by William Marks, J. P.	7	54
MERRELL, MERRELLS, Augustus T., of Litchfield, m. Julia		
BULL, of Burlington, May 12, 1833, by Erastus Scranton,		
V. D. M.	7	30
Catharine, d. Miles, of New Hartford, m. Samuel **RUSSELL**,		
of Burlington, s. Samuel, of Derby, Apr. 27, 1842, by		
Rev. R. Woodruff, at Farmington	7	46
Julia, of Burlington, m. Warren S. **CRANE**, of Hartford,		
Feb. 20, 1837, by Erastus Scranton, V. D. M.	7	35
MILLER, Elizabeth, m. Thomas **YOUNGS**, of Farmington, Feb. 13,		
1822, by Jonathan Miller, V. D. M.	1	21
MILLS, John, m. Julia **FULLER**, Dec. 13, 1827, by Gershom		
Pierce, Elder	7	19
Mary, of Burlington, m. Russel L. **PERKINS**, of Wolcottsville,		
Sept. 6, 1849, by Rev. James L. Wright	7	63
S., of Canton, m. Betsey **CASE**, Sept. 20, 1837, by Erastus		
Scranton, V. D. M.	7	36
MOODEY, Salley, of Burlington, m. James **ADAMS**, of New		
Hartford, Nov. 27, [1831?], by Alden Handury	7	24
MORE, William, Jr., m. Amelia **PETTIBONE**, b. of Burlington,		
Mar. 31, 1839, by Erastus Scranton, V. D. M.	7	40
MORRIS, Harvin, m. Lovica **WIARD**, b. of Burlington, Oct. 2,		

	Vol.	Page
MORRIS, (cont.)		
1846, by Rev. James Noyes	7	54
Sarah Ann, m. Miron **BUTLER**, b. of Burlington, May 3,		
1848, by Peter Tatro, Jr.	7	58
MORSE, MOSS, Elihu, m. Miranda **NEAL**, b. of Burlington, May		
3, 1835, by William Marks, J. P.	7	34
Mary M., ae 24, of Burlington, m. Mansfield **STACY**,		
mechanic, ae 27, b. Springfield, res. New Britain, Jan. 3,		
1849, by Rev. Peter Tatro, Jr.	7	61
Orson, m. Amanda **KELLOGG**, Apr. 26, 1824, by William		
Marks, J. P.	7	11
Polly, m. Homer **NORTON**, b. of Burlington, Nov. 9, 1831,		
by Rev. Qurtis Stenert	7	23
William, m. Anna Charlotte **HART**, Mar. 29, 1835, by Rev.		
David L. Parmalee	7	34
MOSES, Mary, m. Lucius D. **POND**, b. of Burlington, Oct. 25,		
1843, by Rev. James Noyes	7	49
Matilda, m. Enos **BUNNEL**, of Harwinton, May 24, 1837, by		
Erastus Scranton, V. D. M.	7	36
Orrin, of Burlington, m. Mary **TUTTLE**, of Bristol, Mar.		
22, 1826, by Erastus Clapp, V. D. M.	7	13
Rhoda, m. Ruel **PALMETER**, b. of Burlington, Nov. 27, 1823,		
by Erastus Clapp, V. D. M.	7	11
Selina, of Burlington, m. Robert **HUGHS**, Jr., of Canton,		
May 18, 1848, by Peter Tatro, Jr.	7	58
Solomon, of Skenaatelas, N. Y., m. Fidelia S. **PETTIBONE**,		
of Burlington, Oct. 7, 1852	7	68
[**MOULTHROP**], MOLTHROPT, Harriet, m. Albert A.		
BRADLEY, b. of Burlington, Oct. 21, 1841, by Rev.		
David Miller	7	44
MUNSEL, Eunice, of Windsor, m. John **ALLEN**, of Collinsville,		
Feb. 22, 1849, by Rev. Charles B. McLean	7	61
NEAL, Miranda, m. Elihu **MORSE**, b. of Burlington, May 3, 1835,		
by William Marks, J. P.	7	34
NEARING, Delia, of Burlington, m. Samuel L. **HORTON**, of		
Collinsville, June 11, 1835, by Erastus Scranton, V. D. M.	7	35
Lucy, of Burlington, m. Sheldon **KINNEY**, of Vernon, Aug.		
9, 1831, by Erastus Scranton, V. D. M.	7	14
NEGUEST, Benjamin H., of Litchfield, m. Diantha **PALMETER**,		
of Burlington, Apr. 27, 1834, by Erastus Scranton,		
V. D. M.	7	33
NEWELL, David A., m. Eliza **PECK**, Apr. 10, 1839, by Rev.		
David L. Parmelee	7	39
NEWTON, Betsey, w. Hezekiah, d. Oct. 13, 1806, ae 26	LR1	558
Chauncey Johnson, [s. Hezekiah & Betsey], b. July 11, 1803	LR1	558
Emma Betsey, [d. Hezekiah & Betsey], b. Mar. 20, 1802	LR1	558
Hezekiah m. Betsey **JOHNSON**, May 14, 1801	LR1	558
Thankfull, b. Dec. 29, 1787; m. Arba **LANKTON**, Nov. 1,		

	Vol.	Page
NEWTON, (cont.)		
1805	1	20
William Washington, [s. Hezekiah & Betsey], b. Mar. 11, 1805	LR1	558
NORTON, Ammi, of Bristol, m. Martha **SMITH,** Dec. 14, 1837, by Erastus Scranton, V. D. M.	7	36
Andrew O., of New Hartford, m. Elizabeth **CURTIS,** of Burlington, May 9, 1852, by Rev. Cephas Brainard	7	68
David, of Bristol, b. Mar. 16, 1779; m. Sally **ALLEN,** of Plymouth, [ ]	1	16
Franklin, [s. David & Sally], b. June 9, 1810	1	16
Franklin, m. Pamelia **BARNES,** b. of Burlington, Dec. 25, 1833, by Erastus Scranton, V. D. M.	7	32
Homer, m. Polly **MORSE,** b. of Burlington, Nov. 9, 1831, by Rev. Qurtus Stenert	7	23
Honor Josephine, [d. David & Sally], b. June 22, 1807	1	16
John C., of Plainville, m. Harriet M. **HOTCHKISS,** of Burlington, Sept. 17, 1849, by James L. Wright	7	64
Julius, of Montgomery, Ala., m. Elizabeth E. **FRISBIE,** of Burlington, Sept. 17, 1834, by Erastus Scranton, V. D. M.	7	33
Mary Wolcott, [d. David & Sally], b. Sept. 19, 1805	1	16
Sarah Ann, [d. David & Sally], b. Mar. 20, 1814	1	16
Sarah Ann, of Burlington, m. Philamon **WOOLWORTH,** of Bristol, Jan. 20, 1847, by Irenus Adkins	7	55
OLCOTT, Feom (?), m. Susan E. **TAYLOR,** b. of Wolcott, Feb. 8, 1835, by Erastus Scranton, V. D. M.	7	35
OLMSTEAD, Eliza, of Canton, m. Ebenezer **SEXTON,** of Torrington, Feb. 17, 1846, by J. B. Beach	7	52
PALMITER, PALMETER, Antonett E., ae 22, of Burlington, m. Ira T. **SMITH,** mechanic, ae 24, of Prospect, Dec. 26, 1848, by Rev. Peter Tatro, Jr.	7	61
Diantha, of Burlington, m. Benjamin H. **NEGUEST,** of Litchfield, Apr. 27, 1834, by Erastus Scranton, V. D. M.	7	33
Eunice, of Burlington, m. Sheffield C. **WRIGHT,** of Southington, Aug. 20, 1826, by William Marks, J. P.	7	14
Manley, m. Mary Ann **BANNING,** b. of Burlington, Oct. 6, 1841, by Rev. David Miller	7	43
Mary Ann, of Burlington, m. Orrin **HUMPHREY,** of Canton, Sept. 14, 1825, by James Humphreys, J. P.	7	13
Orrey, m. King **PARKES,** Sept. 2, 1832, by Erastus Scranton, V. D. M.	7	28
Ruel, m. Rhoda **MOSES,** b. of Burlington, Nov. 27, 1823, by Erastus Clapp, V. D. M.	7	11
Susan, of Burlington, m. Joseph W. **BYINGTON,** of Bristol, May 26, 1850, by James L. Wright	7	64
PARKES, King, m. Orrey **PALMITER,** Sept. 2, 1832, by Erastus Scranton, V. D. M.	7	28
PATTISON, George, m. Caroline **COLLIER,** b. of Burlington, Nov. 16, 1825, by Erastus Clapp, V. D. M.	7	13

	Vol.	Page
PAYNE, Genitt, of Burlington, m. Alonzo **FULLER**, of Canton,		
[ ], 1847, by Joseph Hinson	7	55
Harriet, m. Joshua B. **BREWER**, Oct. 5, 1840, by Calvin		
Butler	7	41
PEASE, Julius W., of Winsted, m. Mary **HOTCHKISS**, of		
Burlington, Jan. 1, 1844, by Rev. James Noyce	7	49
PECK, Amira, Mrs., b. Apr. 5, 1791; m. Wait **LOWRY**, of		
Farmington, May 2, 1811	1	23
Almira, b. Apr. 5, 1791; m. Waite **LAWREY**, of Farmington,		
May 2, 1811	7	27
Eliza, m. David A. **NEWELL**, Apr. 10, 1839, by Rev. David		
L. Parmelee	7	39
Hannah G., of Burlington, m. Edward **HALL**, of Bristol,		
May 29, 1851, by Rev. William H. Goodwin, of Bristol	7	66
Perintha, of Burlington, m. Lyman **SPENCER**, of New		
Hartford, Dec. 12, 1832, by Erastus Scranton, V. D. M.	7	29
Prudence, m. Sylvester **BROOKS**, Apr. 17, 1822, by Jonathan		
Miller, V. D. M.	1	23
PERKINS, Eunice, m. Augustus **FULLER**, July 24, 1827, by		
Gershom Pierce, Elder	7	17
Mariah, m. Frederick G. **PHELPS**, Sept. 30, 1823, by Elias		
Wooding, J. P.	7	11
Russel L., of Wolcottsville, m. Mary **MILLS**, of Burlington,		
Sept. 6, 1849, by Rev. James L. Wright	7	63
Sarah Ann, m. William **CRANE**, b. of Burlington, Jan. 16,		
1845, by Rev. J. B. Beach	7	51
PERRY Philamon, of Barkhamsted, m. Amret **BECKWITH**, of		
Burlington, June 26, 1825, by Erastus Clapp, V. D. M.	7	12
PETTIBONE, Abraham, Col., b. Nov. 12, 1751; d. Nov. 27, 1834,		
ae 83 y. 15 d.	7	25
Abraham, m. Amelia **SMITH**, May 20, 1778	7	25
Abraham, s. Abraham & Amelia, b. Apr. 24, 1781	7	25
Abraham, 3rd, b. Apr. 24, 1781; m. Ruth **GAYLORD**, May 9,		
1821	7	26
Abraham, of New Hartford, d. Jan. 19, 1797, in the 70th		
y. of his age	7	25
Abraham, m. Huldah **PRINDLE**, of Harwington, Mar. 23, 1797	7	25
Abraham **GAYLORD**, 4th, [s. Abraham, 3rd & Ruth], b. Mar.		
6, 1824	7	26
Amelia, d. Abraham & Amelia, b. Nov. 7, 1791	7	25
Amelia, d. Abraham & Amelia, d. Mar. 8, 1794	7	25
Amelia, w. Abraham, d. May 19, 1796, in the 38th y.		
of her age	7	25
Amelia, [d. Carril & Frances], b. July 22, 1817	7	46
Amelia, m. William **MORE**, Jr., b. of Burlington, Mar. 31,		
1839, by Erastus Scranton, V. D. M.	7	40
Carrel, s. Abraham & Amelia, b. Apr. 19, 1793	7	25
Carril, b. Apr. 19, 1793; m. Frances **MANN**, July 13, 1815	7	46

	Vol.	Page
PETTIBONE, (cont.)		
Carril, m. Frances **MANN**, Jr., July 13, 1815	1	7
Carrel, [s. Abraham & Amelia], d. Jan. 17, 1834, ae 40 y.		
9 m., lacking 2 d.	7	25
Carril, d. Jan. 17, 1834, ae 40 y. 9 m., except 2 d.	7	46
Catharine Elizabeth, [d. Abraham 3rd & Ruth], b. Mar.		
17, 1833	7	26
Deforest, s. Abraham & Amelia, b. May 13, 1796	7	25
Eliza, Mrs., m. Major Gad **FRISBIE**, [ ]	1	4
Erastus, [s. Theophilus & Esther], b. Dec. 1, 1795	1	7
Esther, m. Josiah **POND**, of Harwinton, Dec. 13, 1837, by		
Erastus Scranton, V. D. M.	7	36
Esther M., [d. Theophilus & Esther], b. May 19, 1803	1	7
Fidelia S., of Burlington, m. Solomon **MOSES**, of Skenaatelas,		
N. Y., Oct. 7, 1852, by James L. Wright	7	68
Fidelia Smith, [d. Abraham, 3rd & Ruth], b. Feb. 5, 1822	7	26
Frances, [d. Carril & Frances], b. Sept. 13, 1819	7	46
George, m. Huldah **WEARD**, July 31, 1822, by Jonathan		
Miller, V. D. M.	1	24
Henrietta, m. James **FRISBIE**, Apr. 27, 1843, by Rev.		
David Miller	7	48
Hiram, [s. Theophilus & Esther], b. June 19, 1815	1	7
Huldah, 2nd w. Abraham, d. Nov. 9, 1822, ae 63 y. 7 m.	7	25
Jerusha, [d. Theophilus & Esther], b. Feb. 13, 1813	1	7
Jerusha, of Burlington, m. Joseph F. **GILBERT**, of Plymouth,		
Feb. 23, 1832, by Erastus Scranton, V. D. M.	7	24
Lucy Prindle, [d. Carril & Frances], b. Feb. 26, 1828	7	46
Mary S., m. David **LOWREY**, b. of Burlington, May 16, 1849,		
by James L. Wright	7	63
Mary Susannah, [d. Abrahan, 3rd & Ruth], b. Apr. 2, 1825	7	26
Mary W., of Burlington, m. Salmon **GRIDLEY**, of Harwinton,		
Dec. 24, 1826, by Erastus Clapp, V. D. M.	7	15
Oliver, [s. Theophilus & Esther], b. May 6, 1801	1	7
Oliver, m. Harriet **HOTCHKISS**, Apr. 25, 1822, by Jonathan		
Miller, V. D. M.	1	23
Parmelia, Mrs. of New Hartford, m. Simeon **HART**, of		
Burlington, Jan. 30, 1822, by Cyrus Yale	1	21
Polly M., [d. Theophilus & Esther], b. Apr. 2, 1807	1	7
Ramon, [s. Theophilus & Esther], b. Sept. 24, 1799	1	7
Ramon, m. Chloe **MARKS**, b. of Burlington, Dec. 7, 1826,		
by Erastus Clapp, V. D. M.	7	15
Ruth Ann, [d. Abraham, 3rd & Ruth], b. Jan. 4, 1831	7	26
Samuel T., [s. Carril & Frances], b. Nov. 29, 1824	7	46
Samuel Treat, [s. Carril & Frances], d. Jan. 17, 1825, ae 7 w.	7	46
Solomon, [s. Theophilus & Esther], b. Nov. 12, 1809	1	7
Sylvester Norton, [s. Abrahan, 3rd & Ruth], b. Sept. 15, 1828	7	26
Theophilus, [s. Theophilus & Esther], b. Sept. 30, 1797	1	7
Theophilus, m. Esther **WELMORE**, [ ]	1	7

	Vol.	Page
PHELPS, Elizur D., of Windsor, m. Eveline P. DANIELS, of N.		
Granby, Nov. 27, 1851, by Cephas Brainard	7	67
Frederick G., m. Mariah PERKINS, Sept. 30, 1823, by Elias		
Wooding, J. P.	7	11
Hannah B., of Burlington, m. Truman HUMPHREY, of		
Canton, Apr. 24, 1834, by Erastus Scranton, V. D. M.	7	33
Laura, of Burlington, m. Isaac STEEL, of New Hartford,		
Sept. 28, 1823, by Erastus Clapp, V. D. M.	7	11
Lorena, m. Luman SPENCER, b. of Burlington, July 19,		
1846, by Rev. James Noyes	7	53
Lydia, m. Zenas HITCHKISS, Nov. 26, 1808	1	13
Mary, of Burlington, m. Almoron MARKS, of Durhan, N. Y.,		
Sept. 18, 1834, by Erastus Scranton, V. D. M.	7	33
Phebe, of Burlington, m. Uriel BRADLEY, of Mereden, Aug.		
22, 1827, by Erastus Clapp, V. D. M.	7	17
PITKIN, Edward, of New Hartford, m. Nancy SMITH, of		
Burlington, Nov. 14, 1821, by Cyrus Yale	1	19
Nancy, wid., m. Major TYLER, b. of Burlington, Mar. 28,		
1833, by Erastus Scranton, V. D. M.	7	14
PLACE, Benjamin, of Burlington, m. Betsey LOOMIS, of		
Winchester, Dec. 3, 1827, by Erastus Clapp, V. D. M.	7	18
PLUMB, Helen A., m. Jerry BURWELL, Feb. 26, 1845, by Rev.		
James Noyes	7	51
POND, Adelia C., m. Andrew S. HOTCHKISS, Jan. 11, 1846, by		
Rev. John B. Beach	7	52
Albert Hatsell, m. Amanda Maria CLARK, b. of Burlington,		
May 9, 1839, by William Marks, J. P.	7	39
Aurelius H., m. Philena CRANDALL, b. of Burlington, Dec.		
28, 1834, by Erastus Scranton, V. D. M.	7	33
Cynthia, m. Isaac BELDEN, Jr., b. of Burlington, Apr. 29,		
1840, by Rev. Aaron S. Hill	7	41
Eunice, of Plymouth, m. Edward K. JONES, of Southington,		
May 4, 1831, by Rev. Henry Stanwood, of Bristol	7	23
Eunice A., of Burlington, m. Asahel CARTER, of Southington,		
Oct. 27, 1833, by Erastus Scranton, V. D. M.	7	32
Eveline, m. Sylvanus HULL, Sept. 19, 1839, by F. B. Woodard	7	40
Josiah, of Harwinton, m. Esther PETTIBONE, Dec. 13, 1837,		
by Erastus Scranton, V. D. M.	7	36
Louisa, of Plymouth, m. Ransby BROOKS, of Burlington,		
Aug. 27, 1829, by Rev. Henry Stanwood, of Bristol	7	20
Lucius D., m. Mary MOSES, b. of Burlington, Oct. 25, 1843,		
by Rev. James Noyes	7	49
Lydia, of Burlington, m. Ezra S. ADAMS, of Canton, May		
19, 1825, by Erastus Clapp, V. D. M.	7	12
Nancy, m. Austin BROOKS, b. of Burlington, July 20, 1837,		
by Rev. Harvey Husted	7	36
Susan, of Burlington, m. Edmund A. WOODING, of		
Woodbridge, Dec. 18, 1825, by Erastus Clapp, V. D. M.	7	13

Vol.   Page

POND, (cont.)

Sylvester, m. Rosena **BRADLEY**, b. of Burlington, Oct. 23,
1842, by Erastus Scranton, V. D. M.   7   48

POST, Peter B., m. Elizabeth **SMITH**, Nov. 15, 1842, by Rev.
David Miller   7   47

POTTER, G., Dr. of Bristol, m. Hannah **HOTCHKISS**, of
Burlington, Mar. 31, 1844, by Rev. James Noyes   7   50

Rhoda, b. June 20, 1756   1   18

Rhoda, m. Asa **CLARK**, of Richmond, s. Amos, of Westly,
decd., Mar. 28, 1784, by Simeon Clark, Jr., J. P.   1   18

PRIEST, Rosanna, m. Moses **BACON**, Dec. 25, 1777   1   3

PRINDLE, Huldah, of Harwington, m. Abraham **PETTIBONE**,
Mar. 23, 1797   7   25

RAYMOND, Frederick A., m. Lydia M. **BEACH**, b. of Burlington,
May 28, 1839, by Erastus Scranton, V. D. M.   7   40

[RAYNSFORD], RAINSFORD, Renselier, of Mass., m. Viola
GOODENOUGH, of Burlington, Dec. 22, 1840, by P. L.
Hoyt   7   42

RECOR, Charles, of New Britain, m. Sarah A. **FARNSWORTH**, of
Burlington, Dec. 19, 1849, by James L. Wright   7   61

REYNOLDS, Samuel, of Warren, m. Phebe **WIARD**, of Burlington,
Dec. 17, 1835, by Erastus Scranton, V. D. M.   7   35

RICHARDS, Susanna, m. Jeremiah **BARNES**, Sept. 19, 1832, by
Erastus Scranton, V. D. M.   7   28

RICHARDSON, Charlotte R., m. Harpey L. **MATHEWS**, Aug. 8,
1848, by Rev. James L. Wright   7   59

Cordelia S., of Burlington, m. Jared B. **WALKER**, of
Southington, Nov. 30, 1843, by [   ]   7   50

Eliza L., m. Philander **CRANDAL**, Dec. 7, 1841, by Rev.
David Miller   7   44

Lathrop, m. Mrs. Julia **ALDERMAN**, b. of Burlington, June
7, 1848, by Peter Tatro, Jr.   7   58

Mary, of Farmington, m. Stanley **CATLIN**, of Harwinton,
July 24, 1838, by Erastus Scranton, V. D. M.   7   38

ROBERTS, Amelia*, m. Capt. Ard **HART**, Mar. 10, 1788
*("Millicent **ROBERTS**," in Hart Genealogy)   1   13

Augusta Ann, m. Oliver **WELDEN**, June 12, 1832, by William
Marks, J. P.   7   28

Candace, m. John **CLEVELAND**, b. of Burlington, Nov. 5,
1832, by Rev. Henry Stanwood, of Bristol   7   29

Caroline, m. John **WOODING**, b. of Burlington, June 26,
1832, by Rev. Henry Stanwood, of Bristol   7   28

Charlotte, of Burlington, m. Edwin P. **ALLEN**, of Avon,
Mar. 15, 1832, by Erastus Scranton, V. D. M.   7   24

David, of Burlington, m. Nancy **BOND**, of Plymouth, Jan.
25, 1829, by William Marks, J. P.   7   19

Eliza, of Burlington, m. H. **WARNER**, of New Hartford,
May 27, 1835, by Erastus Scranton, V. D. M.   7   35

	Vol.	Page

ROBERTS, (cont.)

Emily, of Burlington, m. Lucius **ALCOX**, of Wolcott, Nov.
5, 1823, by Erastus Clapp, V. D. M.   7   11

Henry Hart, m. Marilla **THOMPSON**, b. of Burlington, Nov.
10, 1828, by Rev. Aaron Perrin   7   19

Millicent, see Amelia **ROBERTS**   1   13

ROBINSON, Allen, m. Sophrona **CLARK**, Aug. 4, 1824, by E.
Clapp, V. D. M.   7   11

Emeline F., [d. Erastus & Ada], b. Nov. 3, 1829   7   27

Erastus L., [s. Erastus & Ada], b. Feb. 11, 1824   7   27

Eunice E., [d. Erastus & Ada], b. June 1, 1817   7   27

Jane M., [d. Erastus & Ada], b. Aug. 25, 1827   7   27

John G., [s. Erastus & Ada], b. Sept. 8, 1819   7   27

Sarah E., [d. Erastus & Ada], b. Oct. 3, 1821   7   27

Surfrena An[n], [d. Erastus & Ada], b. Sept. 7, 1825   7   27

William L., [s. Erastus & Ada], b. Aug. 27, 1815   7   27

ROGERS, Hezekiah, of Camden, N. Y., m. Louis **BENHAM**, of
Burlington, Oct. 12, 1825, by William Marks, J. P.   7   13

ROOT, Harvey, of Plymouth, m. Lovisa **THOMSON**, of Burlington,
July 25, 1833, by Rev. Charles Sherman   7   30

Lavina, of Farmington, m. Newell **MATHEWS**, of Burlington,
Mar. 31, 1825, by Erastus Clapp, V. D. M.   7   12

ROPER, Luther B., m. Ruth C. **BUCK**, [Aug. 7, 1842], by Rev.
David Miller   7   46

RUSSELL, Samuel, of Burlington, s. Samuel, of Derby, m.
Catharine **MERRELL**, d. Miles, of New Hartford, Apr.
27, 1842, by Rev. R. Woodruff, at Farmington   7   46

RUST, Sophia, Mrs. of Harwinton, m. James **BROWN**, of
Burlington, May 31, 1830, by Erastus Scranton, V. D. M.   7   21

SAUNDERS, John, moulder, ae 34, b. England, res. Unionville,
m. Fanny **BROWN**, ae 18, b. Burlington, Nov. 30, 1848,
by Rev. Peter Tatro, Jr.   7   60

SCOVEL, Caleb T., m. Anna **ELTON**, b. of Burlington, June 21,
1825, by Erastus Clapp, V. D. M.   7   12

SCRANTON, Mary E. P., of Burlington, m. Rev. Gardner Shepherd
BROWNE, of Hinsdale, N. H., Sept. 30, 1838, by Erastus
Scranton, V. D. M.   7   38

SCRIBNER, David B., m. Betsey **ELTON**, b. of Burlington, Nov.
26, 1829, by Rev. David Bennet   7   20

SEGAR, Mary Ann, of New Hartford, m. Augustus Smith
LANGDON, [July 23, 1832], by Erastus Scranton,
V. D. M.   7   14

SELDEN, Henry P., of West Hartford, m. Fidelia **SMITH**, of
Burlington, June 14, 1842, by Rev. David Miller   7   45

SESSIONS, SISSIONS, SISSONS, Calvin, m. Lydia **BECKWITH**,
Jan. 1, 1822, by Rev. Noah Porter, of Farmington   1   19

Catharine, m. Larey **BELDEN**, b. of Burlington, Nov. 17,
1842, by Erastus Scranton, V. D. M.   7   49

	Vol.	Page

SESSIONS, SISSIONS. SISSONS, (cont.)

Lucinda W., m. Almond **CASE,** Nov. 29, 1827, by Erastus
Clapp, V. D. M.   7   18

Lydia B., of Burlington, m. Samuel M. **LAMPSON,** of Mt.
Washington, Mass., May 4, 1852, by James L. Wright   7   68

SEXTON, Ebenezer, of Torrington, m. Eliza **OLMSTEAD,** of
Canton, Feb. 17, 1846, by J. B. Beach   7   52

SHARP, Nancy, of Burlington, m. John **SMITH,** of New York City,
Dec. 17, 1827, by Erastus Clapp, V. D. M.   7   18

SHELTON, Caroline m. William **SPERRY,** b. of Burlington, Feb.
18, 1824, by Datus Ensign, Elder   7   11

SHEPHARD, Amanda, m. Hezekiah **BUNNEL,** b. of Burlington,
Sept. 8, 1829, by Willard Hitchcock, J. P.   7   20

SIMPSON, Walter G., of Auburn, N. Y., m. Sarah **FRISBIE,** of
Burlington, July 15, 1840, by Rev. M. P. L. Hoyt   7   41

SISSONS, [see under **SESSIONS**]

SLATER, Emily M., of New Britain, m. Edward R. **DeWOLF,** of
Farmington, Apr. 14, 1851, by Rev. Cephas Brainard   7   66

SMITH, Aron, m. Agusta **FULLER,** Sept. 8, 1825, by Erastus
Clapp, V. D. M.   7   12

Amelia, m. Abraham **PETTIBONE,** May 20, 1778   7   25

Anna, m. Ralph P. **HUMPHREY,** b. of Burlington, Nov. 22,
1821, by Jonathan Miller, V. D. M.   1   19

Eliza M., of Burlington, m. Joseph M. **BALDWIN,** of
Harwinton, Jan. 1, 1851, by James L. Wright   7   65

Elizabeth, m. Peter B. **POST,** Nov. 15, 1842, by Rev.
David Miller   7   47

Fidelia, of Burlington, m. Henry P. **SELDEN,** of West
Hartford, June 14, 1842, by Rev. David Miller   7   45

Hector, of Granville, m. Elizabeth **WEARD,** of Burlington,
Apr. 7, 1833, by Erastus Scranton, V. D. M.   7   30

Ira T., mechanic, ae 24, of Prospect, m. Antonett E.
PALMETER, ae 22, of Burlington, Dec. 26, 1848, by
Rev. Peter Tatro, Jr.   7   61

John, of New York City, m. Nancy **SHA[R]P,** of Burlington,
Dec. 17, 1827, by Erastus Clapp, V. D. M.   7   18

Martha, m. Ammi **NORTON,** of Bristol, Dec. 14, 1837, by
Erastus Scranton, V. D. M.   7   36

Mary E., of Burlington, m. George O. **CATLIN,** of Harwinton,
Mar. 24, 1834, by Rev. John Nixon   7   33

Nancy, of Burlington, m. Edward **PITKIN,** of New Hartford,
Nov. 14, 1821, by Cyrus Yale   1   19

Rachel, m. Martin **BACON,** Nov. 16, 1815   1   8

Rhoda Ann, of Burlington, m. Morris **HILLS,** of Reading,
May 15, 1837, by Rev. John B. Beach   7   36

Ruth, m. Samuel **HOTCHKISS,** b. of Burlington, Apr. 30,
1834, by Erastus Scranton, V. D. M.   7   33

Sherman, m. Lucy Emily **HALE,** b. of Burlington, Feb. 23,

	Vol.	Page

SMITH, (cont.)

1836, by Erastus Scranton, V. D. M. 7 35

Susan S., of Burlington, m. William S. **BALDWIN**, of
Harwinton, Nov. 27, 1845, by Rev. James Noyes 7 52

SPENCER, Fanny, m. Elias M. **WOODEN**, b. of Burlington, June
10, 1832, by Erastus Scranton 7 29

Luman, m. Lorena **PHELPS**, b. of Burlington, July 19, 1846,
by Rev. James Noyes 7 53

Lyman, of New Hartford, m. Perintha **PECK**, of Burlington,
Dec. 12, 1832, by Erastus Scranton, V. D. M. 7 29

Mary M., of New Hartford, m. Wilson **DEWEY**, of Granby,
Sept. 28, 1841, by Rev. Cyrus Yale 7 45

SPERRY, Desdemonia, Mrs. of Burlington, m. Smith M.
WHEELER, of Penn., July 1, 1838, by Rev. Orsamus
Allen 7 38

Lewis F., of Olford, Mass., m. Malvina **MARKS**, of
Burlington, Feb. 14, 1839, by Rev. Aaron S. Hill 7 39

William, m. Caroline **SHELTON**, b. of Burlington, Feb.
18, 1824, by Datus Ensign, Elder 7 11

STACY, Mansfield, mechanic, ae 27, b. Springfield, res. New
Britain, m. 2nd w. Mary M. **MORSE**, ae 24, of
Burlington, Jan. 3, 1849, by Rev. Peter Tatro, Jr. 7 61

STANARD, Morgan, of Winsted, m. Jane S. **TYLER**, of Burlington,
Apr. 7, 1850, by Erastus Scranton, V. D. M. 7 64

STARKS, Luther, of Mt. Pleasant, Pa., m. Eleanor **WEST**, of
Burlington, [   ] 9, 1834, by Rev. John Nixon 7 33

STEEL, Isaac, of New Hartford, m. Laura **PHELPS**, of Burlington,
Sept. 28, 1823, by Erastus Clapp, V. D. M. 7 11

Sarah B., m. Selah **WOODRUFF**, b. of New Hartford, Feb.
19, 1837, by Erastus Scranton, V. D. M. 7 35

STILLMAN, Eleanor, m. Elisha **WEST**, Oct. 13, 1803, at
Farmington, by Daniel Welman LR1 558

Eleanor, m. Elisha **WEST**, Oct. 13, 1803, by Daniel Weldman 1 15

STODARD, John W., husbandman, ae 23, m. Mary Ann
GOODWIN, ae 18, b. of Burlington, Dec. 23, 1848, by
Rev. Peter Tatro 7 60

STONE, Abarilla, [d. Christopher & Prudence], b. [   ] LR1 557

Alfred, [s. Christopher & Prudence], b. July 10, 1788 LR1 557

Amasa, [s. Christopher & Prudence], b. Oct. 24, 1786 LR1 557

Amasa, m. Clarissa M. **KEY***, Oct. 15, 1807   *("**McKEY**"?) LR1 558

Charlotte, m. William **CURTISS**, b. of Burlington, Apr.
11, 1826, by Jonathan Cone, V. D. M. 7 13

Christopher, m. Prudence **DRIGGS**, Oct. 27, 1785 LR1 557

Cyrenus, [s. Christopher & Prudence], b. Aug. 29, 1790 LR1 557

Elizabeth, m. William **STONE**, Sept. 13, 1829, by William
Marks, J. P. 7 20

Elmina, [d. Christopher & Prudence], b. Nov. 26, 1800 LR1 557

Emeline, of Burlington, m. Lewis **MARSH**, of Northfield,

	Vol.	Page
STONE, (cont.)		
Sept. 21, 1848, by Rev. James L. Wright	7	59
Emeline L., m. Lawson J. **WOODEN**, b. of Burlington, Nov.		
25, 1847, by Rev. Lester Lewis	7	56
Erastus, [s. Christopher & Prudence], b. June 17, 1795	LR1	557
Esther, [d. Christopher & Prudence], b. Feb. 26, 1793	LR1	557
Liverus, [s. Christopher & Prudence], b. Apr. 9, 1798	LR1	557
Lowley, m. Josephus **HOTCHKISS**, b. of Burlington, Jan.		
25, 1827, by Erastus Clapp, V. D. M.	7	16
Marella, m. William **BALL**, June 3, 1828, by Erastus		
Clapp, V. D. M.	7	19
Mary Anne, m. Orvil **BECKWITH**, b. of Burlington, Sept.		
8, 1830, by Willard Hitchcock, J. P.	7	22
Prudence, [d. Christopher & Prudence], b. Sept. 15, 1803	LR1	557
Sterling Graves, [s. Amasa & Clarissa M.], b. Feb. 19, 1808	LR1	558
William, m. Elizabeth **STONE**, Sept. 13, 1829, by William		
Marks, J. P.	7	20
STRICTLAND, George W., m. Jane B. **WILLMOT**, b. of		
Burlington, Dec. 2, 1842, by Rev. David Miller	7	47
SUTLEY, Lydia, m. Miles **BEACH**, Sept. 21, 1806	1	24
TALBERT, Caroline, Mrs., m. Major **HADSELL**, b. of Burlington,		
Mar. 17, 1839, by Rev. Aaron S. Hill	7	39
TAYLOR, Florilla, m. Stephen **WITTIER**, Mar. 6, 1822, by		
Simeon Hart, J. P.	1	21
Margaret, m. William **MAY**, b. of Burlington (late of		
Reading, Pa.), Nov. 22, 1846, by William Marks, J. P.	7	54
Rosanna, of Burlington, m. Bela S. **CLAPP**, of Southampton,		
Mass., June 3, 1824, by William Marks, J. P.	7	11
Susan E., m. Feom (?) **OLCOTT**, b. of Wolcott, Feb. 8, 1835,		
by Erastus Scranton, V. D. M.	7	35
Sylvester N., m. Sarah Ann **BRONSON**, b. of Burlington,		
Apr. 8, 1843, by Erastus Scranton, V. D. M.	7	48
William, m. Harriet **CLARK**, July 23, 1832, by Erastus		
Scranton, V. D. M.	7	14
TERRY, Erastus, m. Mary **TREADWELL**, Aug. 30, 1814	1	9
John Strong, [s. Erastus & Mary], b. Dec. 17, 1815	1	9
THOMAS, Elijah T., of N. Y., m. Mrs. Hannah **WHEELER**, Oct.		
13, 1840, by Philip L. Hoyt	7	42
THOMPSON, THOMSON, Jerome B., m. Maria **BROWN**, b. of		
Burlington, Feb. 23, 1840, by Rev. Aaron S. Hill	7	40
Jerusha E., of Burlington, m. Harvey W. **BASSETT**, of		
Plymouth, Oct. 3, 1847, by Erastus Scranton, V. D. M.	7	56
John, of New Haven, m. Lucy **FOOT**, of Burlington, Mar.		
23, 1834, by Erastus Scranton, V. D. M.	7	31
John, of New Haven, m. Lucy **FOOT**, of Burlington, Mar.		
23, 1834, by Erastus Scranton, V. D. M.	7	32
Lovisa, of Burlington, m. Harvey **ROOT**, of Plymouth,		
July 25, 1833, by Rev. Charles Sherman	7	30

	Vol.	Page
THOMPSON, THOMSON, (cont.)		
Marilla, m. Henry Hart **ROBERTS**, b. of Burlington, Nov.		
10, 1828, by Rev. Aaron Perrin	7	19
TOWEVILLE*, Mary, of Granby, m. James **DORMAN**, of		
Burlington, Apr. 12, 1827, by Erastus Clapp, V. D. M.		
*(Perhaps "LOWEVILLE")	7	16
TOWNSAND, Coleman, of N. Y., m. Caroline **HOTCHKISS**, of		
[ ], Nov. 5, 1840, by Philip L. Hoyt	7	42
TREADWELL, Mary, m. Erastus **TERRY**, Aug. 30, 1814	1	9
TREAT, Frances, m. Dr. Peres **MANN**, Feb. 8, 1792	1	6
TREMBLE, George, of Albany, N. Y., m. Elnora **WOODRUFF**, of		
Burlington, Sept. 1, 1839, by Aaron S. Hill	7	39
TUTTLE, Luzene, of Middletown, m. Nancy **CURTIS**, of		
Burlington, Dec. 27, 1842, by Rev. Samuel W. Smith	7	45
Mary, of Bristol, m. Orrin **MOSES**, of Burlington, Mar.		
22, 1826, by Erastus Clapp, V. D. M.	7	13
TWING, Ebenezer W., of Springfield, Mass., m. Anna **MARKS**, of		
Burlington, Apr. 16, 1846, by J. B. Beach	7	53
TYLER, Asaph, m. Alma **BACON**, Dec. 11, 1827, by Elias		
Wooding, J. P.	7	17
Benedict, m. Hannah **CRANDALL**, Nov. 11, 1827, by Elias		
Wooding, J. P.	7	17
Jane S., of Burlington, m. Morgan **STANARD**, of Winsted,		
Apr. 7, 1850, by Erastus Scranton, V. D. M.	7	64
Major, m. wid. Nancy **PITKIN**, b. of Burlington, Mar. 28,		
1833, by Erastus Scranton, V. D. M.	7	14
UPSON, UPON, Amanda, [d. Timothy], b. Nov. 10, 1794	LR1	557
Joel Johnson, [s. Timothy], b. Jan. 23, 1797	LR1	557
Martin, [s. Timothy], b. Jan. 8, 1793	LR1	557
Mary, [d. Timothy], b. July 19, 1801	LR1	557
Mary, m. Lieut. Stephen **HOTCHKISS**, [ ]	1	10
Mary A., ae 18, b. Burlington, res. same, m. Riley H.		
FULLER, saw grinder, ae 27, b. Farmington, res.		
Unionville, Nov. 1, 1848, by Rev. Peter Tatro, Jr.	7	59
Manerva*, of Burlington, m. Dwight **LANGDON**, of		
Southington, May 9, 1849, by James L. Wright		
*("Minerva")	7	63
Orrin, m. Lorena **BELDIN**, b. of Burlington, Dec. 24,		
1823, by Datus Ensign, Elder	7	11
Rachel, Mrs., m. Samuel **HOTCHKISS**, Jan. 26, 1778	1	19
Salome, [d. Timothy], b. Sept. 16, 1804	LR1	557
Seth, Jr., m. Martha **BROOKS**, Feb. 14, 1828, by Gershom		
Pierce, Elder	7	18
Seth, m. Sophia **BROWN**, b. of Burlington, Dec. 16, 1838,		
by Erastus Scranton, V. D. M.	7	38
Timothy Norton, [s. Timothy], b. May 18, 1808	LR1	557
William Robinson, [s. Timothy], b. Apr. 3, 1799	LR1	557
VOSE, Caroline, Mrs., m. Edwin **BUNNEL**, Dec. [ ], 1840,		

	Vol.	Page
VOSE, (cont.)		
by P. L. Hoyt	7	42
WADSWORTH, Timothy, of Farmington, m. Mary **GILLET,** of		
Burlington, Mar. 3, 1824, by Jonathan Miller, V. D. M.	7	11
WALKER, Jared B., of Southington, m. Cordelia S.		
RICHARDSON, of Burlington, Nov. 30, 1843, by [ ]	7	50
WALLING, Nathaniel, of New Hartford, m. Deborah **HARRISON,**		
of Burlington, June 14, 1841, by Rev. David Miller	7	43
WARNER, Diana, m. Royal **GROVER,** b. of Middletown, May 24,		
1830, by Erastus Scranton, V. D. M.	7	21
H., of New Hartford, m. Eliza **ROBERTS,** of Burlington,		
May 27, 1835, by Erastus Scranton, V. D. M.	7	35
Mary, m. Simeon **HART,** Oct. 27, 1783	1	5
WAY, Abigail, [d. Ezra & Abigail], b. Feb. 20, 1800	1	4
Anna, [d. Ezra & Abigail], b. Sept. 29, 1806	1	4
Benjamin, [twin with Franklin, s. Ezra & Abigail], b.		
Feb. 27, 1814	1	4
Ezra, m. Mrs. Abigail **CHURCHILL,** Apr. [ ], 1792	1	4
Ezra, [s. Ezra & Abigail], b. Jan. 2, 1812; d. Sept. 1, 1814	1	4
Fanny, [d. Ezra & Abigail], b. June 10, 1795	1	4
Franklin, [twin with Benjamin, s. Ezra & Abigail], b.		
Feb. 27, 1814	1	4
Joseph, [s. Ezra & Abigail], b. Jan. 11, 1802	1	4
Lydia, [d. Ezra & Abigail], b. July 24, 1797	1	4
Lydia, [d. Ezra & Abigail], b. May 8, 1804	1	4
Phila, [d. Ezra & Abigail], b. Nov. 17, 1792	1	4
WEARD, [see under **WIARD**]		
WEAVER, Horace, of Salsbury, m. Mary Ann **BICKFORD,** of		
Burlington, Sept. 1, 1840, by Rev. George B. Atwell, of		
Canton	7	41
WEBSTER, Clarissa J., of Burlington, m. Riley **WHITING,** of		
Winsted, Aug. 28, 1843, by Rev. Davis W. Clark, of		
Winsted	7	49
George, of Windsor, m. Calesta **JOHNSON,** of Harwington,		
Jan. 24, 1830, by Erastus Scranton, V. D. M.	7	21
Julian, m. Ariel **FOOT,** b. of Burlington, Sept. 3, 1833,		
by Erastus Scranton, V. D. M.	7	32
Justice, m. Sarah M. **HOPKINS,** Dec. 21, 1842, by Rev.		
David Miller	7	47
Lydia E., of Burlington, m. Major **CRAFTS,** of Hamilton,		
Ga., June 18, 1846, by Rev. James Noyes	7	53
Mary, of Burlington, m. Amos Rosseter **FRISBIE,** of		
Washington, Pa., June 18, 1850, by Rev. Jonathan Coe, of		
Winsted	7	65
Nathaniel, of Farmington, m. Marilla **ALDERMAN,** of		
Burlington, Jan. 11, 1835, by Rev. John B. Beach	7	33
William Burnham, of Harwinton, m. Sarah Adelia **HULL,** of		
Burlington, Oct. 19, 1837, by Rev. Joseph S. Covill, of		

	Vol.	Page
WEAVER, (cont.)		
Bristol	7	36
WELDEN, Hart H., m. Philamelia **BRUCE**, June 12, 1832, by		
William Marks, J. P.	7	28
Oliver, m. Augusta Ann **ROBERTS**, June 12, 1832, by		
William Marks, J. P.	7	28
WELMORE, Esther, m. Theophilus **PETTIBONE**, [ ]	1	7
WELTON, Adaline, b. June 15, 1803; m. Willard **HITCHCOCK**,		
Apr. 3, 1822	7	26
WEST, Amos Stillman, [s. Elisha & Eleanor], b. Mar. 4, 1808	LR1	558
Amos Stillman, [s. Elisha & Eleanor], b. Mar. 4, 1808	1	15
Ansel, [s. Elisha & Eleanor], b. Sept. 25, 1810	LR1	558
Asahel, [s. Elisha & Eleanor], b. Sept. 25, 1810	1	15
Eleanor, of Burlington, m. Luther **STARKS**, of Mt. Pleasant,		
Pa., [ ] 9, 1834, by Rev. John Nixon	7	33
Elisha, m. Eleanor **STILLMAN**, Oct. 13, 1803, at Farmington,		
by Daniel Welman	LR1	558
Elisha, m. Eleanor **STILLMAN**, Oct. 13, 1803, by Daniel		
Weldman	1	15
Experience, m. Asa **CLARK**, Apr. 28, 1810, by Laban Clark.		
Witnesses: Elisha West & Elioner West	LR1	558
Romantha Stillman, [child of Elisha & Eleanor], b. Jan.		
28, 1805	LR1	558
Romanta Stillman, [d. Elisha & Eleanor], b. Jan. 18, 1805	1	15
WHEELER, Challenge, m. Sybel **BANNET**, Feb. 27, 1822, by		
Jonathan Miller, V. D. M.	1	21
Hannah, Mrs., m. Elijah T. **THOMAS**, of N. Y., Oct. 13,		
1840, by Philip L. Hoyt	7	42
Smith M., of Penn., m. Mrs. Desdemonia **SPERRY**, of		
Burlington, July 1, 1838, by Rev. Orsamus Allen	7	38
WHITE, Militia, Mrs., m. Dr. Peres **MAN**, Oct. 25, 1786	1	6
WHITING, Riley, of Winsted, m. Clarissa J. **WEBSTER**, of		
Burlington, Aug. 28, 1843, by Rev. Davis W. Clark, of		
Winsted	7	49
WIARD, WEARD, Elizabeth, of Burlington, m. Hector **SMITH**, of		
Granville, Apr. 7, 1833, by Erastus Scranton, V. D. M.	7	30
Huldah, m. George **PETTIBONE**, July 31, 1822, by Jonathan		
Miller, V. D. M.	1	24
Lovica, m. Harvin **MORRIS**, b. of Burlington, Oct. 2, 1846,		
by Rev. James Noyes	7	54
Nancy, of Burlington, m. Allen **WOODRUFF**, of Farmington,		
May 8, 1825, by Erastus Clapp, V. D. M.	7	12
Phebe, of Burlington, m. Samuel **REYNOLDS**, of Warren,		
Dec. 17, 1835, by Erastus Scranton, V. D. M.	7	35
WILCOX, Lewis, of Hartford, m. Caroline **BROOKS**, of		
Burlington, Sept. 5, 1832, by Rev. Henry Stanwood, of		
Bristol	7	29
WILLIAMS, Elizabeth T., of Burlington, m. George **CARTER**, of		

	Vol.	Page
WILLIAMS, (cont.)		
Wethersfield, Apr. 30, 1832, by Erastus Scranton,		
V. D. M.	7	24
WILLMOT, Elmira, of Burlington, m. William L. **GRAHAM**, of		
Haddam, [, 1834?], by Rev. Daniel Coe	7	32
Jane B., m. George W. **STRICTLAND**, b. of Burlington,		
Dec. 2, 1842, by Rev. David Miller	7	47
WILSON, Mary, m. John P. **BEACH**, June 13, 1794	LR1	558
WININS, Russell, of Westford, N. Y., m. Charlotte **CLEVELAND**,		
of Burlington, Dec. 30, 1835, by Rev. Seth Higley	7	34
WITTIER, Stephen, m. Florilla **TAYLOR**, Mar. 6, 1822, by		
Simeon Hart, J. P.	1	21
WOODFORD, Celesta, of Burlington, m. Herman **HAMLIN**, of		
Canton, June 8, 1826, by Rev. Isaac Kimball. Int. Pub.	7	14
Eunice, of Burlington, m. James F. **BROWN**, of Ware, Mass.,		
June 13, 1841, by George B. Atwell	7	43
Zada A., of Burlington, m. William A. **BUGBEE**, of		
Collinsville, Aug. 30, 1835, by Rev. Stephen Mason, of		
Collinsville	7	34
WOODING, WOODEN, Edmund A., of Woodbridge, m. Susan		
POND, of Burlington, Dec. 18, 1825, by Erastus Clapp,		
V. D. M.	7	13
Elias M., m. Fanny **SPENCER**, b. of Burlington, June 10,		
1832, by Erastus Scranton	7	29
Homer, of Farmington, m. Vashti **BECKWITH**, of Burlington,		
Mar. 10, 1829, by Willard Hitchcock, J. P.	7	20
John, m. Caroline **ROBERTS**, b. of Burlington, June 26,		
1832, by Rev. Henry Stanwood, of Bristol	7	28
Lawson J., m. Emeline L. **STONE**, b. of Burlington, Nov.		
25, 1847, by Rev. Lester Lewis	7	56
Sally, m. Elias **BENHAM**, May 1, 1811	1	17
WOODRUFF, Allen, of Farmington, m. Nancy **WEARD**, of		
Burlington, May 8, 1825, by Erastus Clapp, V. D. M.	7	12
Elnora, of Burlington, m. George **TREMBLE**, of Albany,		
N. Y., Sept. 1, 1839,. by Aaron S. Hill	7	39
Selah, m. Sarah B. **STEEL**, b. of New Hartford, Feb. 19,		
1837, by Erastus Scranton, V. D. M.	7	35
WOOLWORTH, Philamon, of Bristol, m. Sarah Ann **NORTON**, of		
Burlington, Jan. 20, 1847, by Irenus Adkins	7	55
WRIGHT, Mary Ann, m. Henry A. **BROOKS**, b. of Burlington,		
Nov. 10, 1846, by Joseph Hinson	7	55
Sheffield C., of Southington, m. Eunice **PALMITER**, of		
Burlington, Aug. 20, 1826, by William Marks, J. P.	7	14
YOUNGS, Thomas, of Farmington, m. Elizabeth **MILLER**, Feb. 13,		
1822, by Jonathan Miller, V. D. M.	7	21
NO SURNAME, Susannah, m. David Marks, Sept. 7, 1775,		
at Milford	7	16